SAGE was founded in 1965 by Sara Miller McCune to support the dissemination of usable knowledge by publishing innovative and high-quality research and teaching content. Today, we publish more than 750 journals, including those of more than 300 learned societies, more than 800 new books per year, and a growing range of library products including archives, data, case studies, reports, conference highlights, and video. SAGE remains majority-owned by our founder, and on her passing will become owned by a charitable trust that secures our continued independence.

Los Angeles | London | Washington DC | New Delhi | Singapore

Saving Capitalism
from the Capitalists

Saving Capitalism from the Capitalists

WORLD CAPITALISM AND
GLOBAL HISTORY

Hartmut Elsenhans

Copyright © Hartmut Elsenhans, 2015

All rights reserved. No part of this book may be reproduced or utilized in any form or by any means, electronic or mechanical, including photocopying, recording or by any information storage or retrieval system, without permission in writing from the publisher.

First published in 2015 by

SAGE Publications India Pvt Ltd
B1/I-1 Mohan Cooperative Industrial Area
Mathura Road, New Delhi 110 044, India
www.sagepub.in

SAGE Publications Inc
2455 Teller Road
Thousand Oaks, California 91320, USA

SAGE Publications Ltd
1 Oliver's Yard, 55 City Road
London EC1Y 1SP, United Kingdom

SAGE Publications Asia-Pacific Pte Ltd
3 Church Street
#10-04 Samsung Hub
Singapore 049483

Published by Vivek Mehra for SAGE Publications India Pvt Ltd, typeset in 10/12 Adobe Garamond Pro by RECTO Graphics, Delhi and printed at Saurabh Printers Pvt Ltd., New Delhi.

Library of Congress Cataloging-in-Publication Data

Elsenhans, Hartmut, 1941–
  Saving capitalism from the capitalists : world capitalism and global history / Hartmut Elsenhans.
    pages cm
  Includes bibliographical references and index.
  1. Capitalism. 2. Capitalism—History. 3. Economics. 4. Economic history. I. Title.
  HB501.E4174   330.12'2—dc23   2015   2014035044

ISBN: 978-93-515-0056-8 (HB)

The SAGE Team: N. Unni Nair, Sandhya Gola, Nand Kumar Jha and
                    Rajinder Kaur

For my daughters, Cynthia and Julia

Thank you for choosing a SAGE product! If you have any comment, observation or feedback, I would like to personally hear from you. Please write to me at contactceo@sagepub.in

—Vivek Mehra, Managing Director and CEO,
SAGE Publications India Pvt Ltd, New Delhi

Bulk Sales

SAGE India offers special discounts for purchase of books in bulk. We also make available special imprints and excerpts from our books on demand.

For orders and enquiries, write to us at

Marketing Department
SAGE Publications India Pvt Ltd
B1/I-1, Mohan Cooperative Industrial Area
Mathura Road, Post Bag 7
New Delhi 110044, India
E-mail us at marketing@sagepub.in

Get to know more about SAGE, be invited to SAGE events, get on our mailing list. Write today to marketing@sagepub.in

This book is also available as an e-book.

Contents

Introduction: Defending Capitalism Against the Privileged   ix

1. Profitable Capitalism and Rising Mass Incomes   1
2. Stratification Without Transition to Capitalism and the European Distinctiveness   28
3. Pre-capitalist Origins of Culture: The A-cultural Character of Capitalism and the Cultural Turn   59
4. The Nature of Capitalism   73
5. Globalisation and Its Contradictions   114
6. Alliances for Imposing Capitalism: The Globalisation of Profit Against the Globalisation of Rent   159
7. An International Community of Rentier Governments: Noble Intentions or a Return to the Past   194

Bibliography   203
Index   315
About the Author   326

Introduction: Defending Capitalism Against the Privileged

Globalisation and capitalism are considered as twin brothers. This is dangerous as it may lead to the loss of the achievements of capitalism: competition and equality and the removal of politically acquired privilege. Capitalism has many aspects which are dealt with in this contribution. One characteristic often highlighted in the critique and the praise of capitalism does not belong to capitalism. This is the tendency towards 'unlimited accumulation'. Capital accumulation, and especially unlimited capital accumulation, is only superficially a goal in capitalism. It is only an instrument. Capitalists have to compete for the accumulation of capital. But they can accumulate only in so far as they, involuntarily, increase consumption. Although a non-capitalist landowner and a capitalist owner of a factory both expect to earn income from their property, there are important differences: the landowner can expect income even if he lives autarchically, as he can consume his own agricultural surplus or use it to feed his workers, whereas the capitalist will earn money only if there is a market for the products he manufactures in his factory. In contrast to the non-capitalist landholder he depends on demand or rather, as will be shown, on rising demand.

The distinction between the functional requirements of capitalism and the rules set for different social groups within capitalism is a permanent endeavour in this contribution. Socio-economic systems are not necessarily created by conscious action. They result from the interplay between very diffuse interests in which nobody among the protagonists has a master design. There has to be no isomorphy between the rules within a system, but only compatibility.

Certainly, consumption can increase also if some privileged ones consume more. But in this case, these privileged ones have to be protected from competition. The mechanism which is decisive for the efficiency and the superiority of capitalism in comparison to other socio-economic arrangements is weakened, decisively weakened, if privileges become politically institutionalised. Competition and rising consumption can be maintained only in case of rising mass consumption, ultimately by the empowerment of labour, at best directly in their position on the labour market.

The basic link between accumulation and consumption is due to the fact that capital is limited in the real economy, limited, that is, by demand and not by supply. Capital can be owned as property and, on the basis of which, capitalists make money through that asset by organising the production process—which yields products which can be sold. Only those 'means of production', equipment, buildings, infrastructures, which are required for production are 'valuable' as capital, because they are contributing to value formation. The higher the growth of the volume of production, the more capital is required. But under capitalism, the opposite does not hold: the higher the financial resources theoretically available for investment, the higher the output does not hold—these additional resources may just not be invested. Financial resources put aside as 'savings' are in principle without value and may only become valuable, if they are scarce and required for processes in the real economy. In the real economy, the only savings which are possible are investments. 'Overinvestment', that is, spending on investment for which there is no use in production for a demand articulated on the market, is waste. The build up of financial assets beyond the requirements of the real economy is at best waste, at worst a limit to the expansion of the real economy.

The link between accumulation and consumption has always been threatened since capitalism emerged against the 'pre-capitalist' forms of enrichment of the politically powerful. There are three mechanisms which threaten this link today in a particularly dangerous way.

Capitalism is expansionary but not contagious. Capitalism 'penetrates' other modes of production but does not necessarily transform them into the capitalist form, although it may well 'deform' them. It is superior in efficiency in comparison to others socio-economic arrangements, a fact which may be demonstrated by a comparison of labour productivity and the productivity of funds invested as 'capital'. Because of this superiority, non-capitalist societies are drawn into its orbit. They become suppliers of goods. They attract capitalist enterprises and provide their resources, labour, raw materials and 'factors of production' to them. In doing so, they may, however, not be transformed into capitalist ones. Market relations may emerge without a scarcity of labour, and hence also without the empowerment of labour. Similarly, if the capitalist impact is too weak to create high levels of employment, then labour will also not become empowered. All depends on the impact this opening to the capitalist 'world system' exercises on them, ultimately whether the capitalist mechanism of increasing consumption is transferred via scarcity of labour. This mechanism consists in the empowerment of the mass of potential consumers through the labour market and ultimately through final demand.

Capitalism has certainly benefited from the political struggles of the mass of consumers, especially the struggle of labour and the emergence of the labour movement for the improvement of the standard of living of the masses. But the decisive form of empowerment of labour in capitalism consists in the necessity for entrepreneurs to hand over the fruits of their innovation under competition, increasing productivity, to labour in the form of higher wages they have to pay because labour is scarce. This means higher wages for all labour, not just for highly skilled labour, but also for labour which they do not directly employ because labour overall becomes scarce due to overall demand. If the increase in demand is sufficient to drive and increase in the scarcity of labour, then all employers, even those who assume to have political rights over labour on the basis of pre-capitalist arrangements, must increase the remuneration of labour in order to keep their workers. Otherwise, these workers would migrate to the new employment opportunities. When there exists a scarcity of labour and higher wages in more dynamic sectors, the labour employed under poor working conditions will simply leave such pre-capitalist labour arrangements. All over the world, migration and colonisation have shown this to be the rational behaviour of labour. Finally, if labour becomes scarce, then capitalist relations of production penetrate and emerge in new areas.

Today capitalism expands into societies where labour cannot become scarce because of underdevelopment and specific structural blockages connected to it. Capitalism does not create capitalist structures of power when it penetrates not yet capitalist societies.

The second threat is the result of the success of capitalism: The success of capitalism has raised the standard of living of the mass of the population in capitalist countries. This results in new needs. The mass of this population no longer wants only to consume more or better products. Other 'post-materialist' needs emerge. One of these needs is security in the future. It implies provisions for the future. Just as for capitalists, so too are there limits to accumulation under capitalism for non-entrepreneurial households: individual households can save because other households accept higher indebtedness. Collectively, 'savings' done today cannot be stored for the future. Such savings are just a limit on demand, hence on accumulation and employment, and therefore disempower labour. Public debts are not the result of overconsumption, but of oversaving. Without the public sector incurring greater debt, higher levels of unemployment would emerge much more quickly.

In addition, the need for distinction further disempowers labour. One fine thing about capitalism is that it was imposed if mass consumption grew, whatever people thought about it. Capitalism could thrive quite nicely with the illusion that more money for the capitalists drove the system if only mass consumption expanded fast enough. There were no problems in everybody hoping to be better off than the Joneses, provided that even the workers with the lowest level of skills were required for meeting overall demand.

This integrative capacity of capitalism gets weaker when the level of material well-being makes new needs more important which do not trigger off additional production of goods and services. Needs such as these may be non-materialistic, like security in the future.

This third threat is constituted by the rise of needs which cannot be supplied in the form of goods to individual consumers who purchase them in isolation. Collective needs become more important: The success of capitalism in exploiting nature for the material needs of humans brings humankind to the limits of sustainability of the ecological system. Collective needs can only be satisfied by collective decision-making. Whether this leads to the provision of these needs by market-oriented enterprises or by politically managed entities is of secondary importance for the political and social implications of the collective character of this consumption. In the first case, there may be competition between enterprises about how to provide the service most efficiently. In both cases, the decision about how much of the collective good has to be provided is achieved by non-market coordination, hence politically.

There are many divergences in interests between the participants. In contrast to a market system, participants cannot solve these divergences simply in the process of coming to decisions about collective goods, that is, by just choosing to purchase the amount of the collective goods they deem suitable. There are free rider effects. Free riders can reap benefits without providing efforts. They use strategic positions for rent-seeking which deny equal chances for all. The disadvantaged ones may create countercoalitions. The struggle over collective goods is typically politicised. The world system may not be capitalist in large domains but characterised by political struggles over resources.

Will capitalism be able to rely on structures and values in the non-economic realm in order to maintain the principles of fairness and equality in the economic realm which characterised the emergence of capitalism? Will capitalism be maintained by competition and rising mass consumption? I will not fully exploit this point in this contribution. The contribution will, however, focus on the problems of the capacity of capitalism to dissolve political privilege and politically instituted inequality: Privilege and politically instituted inequality have spin-offs in other social spheres. To what extent a 'bourgeois' culture of equal participation and distribution based on the basis of equal effort has to be stabilised for capitalism in order to counteract these tendencies to inequality? How much can capitalism contribute to that effort?

There are serious doubts about capitalism's capacity to have achieved a fundamental transformation in the direction of economic and social equality in non-economic spheres. The success story of capitalism cannot be explained without taking into consideration that it was made possible precisely because it did not really need and further on also does not really need to provoke a 'political' or 'cultural' revolution. I will show that capitalism was adopted by the most varied elites because they could hope to maintain their privileges by adapting to the rules of market competition and that this adaptation was imposed by the strength of labour at first on the labour market, and only afterwards and only perhaps as a collectively organised force. Capitalism tolerated inequality as long as it was confirmed by the market. Capitalism did not require a principled objection against pre- or non-capitalist forms of inequality. The values of equality implied in competition had never been imposed otherwise than by maintaining competition, and this implied at least temporarily market imperfections.

Furthermore, the fundamental principles of capitalism are not the objective of those who benefit most obviously from capitalism and who appear as such to be powerful. On the contrary, capitalism depends in its daily reproduction on the pursuit of happiness and the enrichment of the many. Those in control of financial resources have to invest them in those areas where the best yields are available. Their objective has to be to maintain and increase their relative income position in order to maintain their capacity to invest. Investment of surplus in the best yielding opportunities improves production and hence the possibilities for consumption in relation to the amount of investment. However, the improvement of their relative income position is only their own individual objective. It allows them to reproduce the financial assets under their control to maintain or improve their position in relation to other holders of financial resources. Such is not an objective of the macroeconomic regulation of the system. Permanent competition reduces advances in relative income.

As capitalism has such an imperfect impact on the non-economic spheres, the only way to maintain it when competition weakens consists in the deliberate extension of its principles to the non-economic spheres. Competition, rising mass consumption and equality of incomes due to the equal accessibility for all to skills will translate into the slogan of the French Revolution '*guerre aux châteaux, paix aux chaumières*'. It would have to establish the unity of the values of the bourgeois and the socialist revolutions which Marx to my view incorrectly has considered as historically opposed to each other (Marx 1843: 356, 366; Marx & Engels 1848: 472). Where markets function, market regulation should be defended and the more markets are possible, the better, because other modes of regulation like political coordination imply delegation and ultimately the danger of the 'iron law of oligarchy' (Michels 1925: esp. 182 f.). The more which can be left to the markets, the easier the struggle to check the tendencies to oligarchy in the non-economic spheres.

Such an approach to the analysis of capitalism fundamentally diverges from mainstream interpretations which can be summarised in the following way: The pursuit of capitalism and market fundamentalism has brought about numerous problematic tendencies. Even as incomes have increased, there has been acute increase in economic inequalities within countries and across the globe. Capitalism has brought about alienation and periodic cyclical booms and busts, with mass insecurity and poverty for large numbers of people despite the enrichment of even many.

These phenomena undoubtedly exist, but they are not the core tendency of capitalism. Rather, they demonstrate the breakdown of capitalism presaging its demise. They are not constitutive of its basic arrangement for giving rise to economic advantage, they do not necessarily follow from profit-making or from anonymous markets and they are dependent on political power. So the difference is made clear when it can be shown that profit depends on expanding demand and that expanding demand under conditions of competition depends on expanding mass markets and mass incomes, and this only becomes possible in cases of consistently high levels of employment which market relations per se do not produce. Jean-Baptiste Say's global equilibria were conceived on the basis of an economy with gold money so that increases in saving triggered off gold production which created employment and incomes. In a fiat money economy, additional savings do not trigger additional employment by fact of increases in demand for it. This issue is dealt by the equilibria on money markets where interest rates cannot fall below zero but where the supply of liquidity can be extremely high. Monetary Keynesianism has attempted to deal with this problem in a purely economic manner without significant results. In contrast, the approach of real economy Keynesianism, presented here, identifies mass consumption and hence empowerment of labour as the basic mechanism of socially embedding capitalism and making profit safe and sustainable.

Therefore, in the following, socialism will be opposed to capitalism in a polarised way. The bureaucratic management of economies of the Soviet type has nothing to do with the aspirations of the political movements which took socialism as their goal. The Communist variant of the working-class movement was already in a minority position before 1914 and survived the Russian October Revolution in the industrialised countries only because of the committed struggle of the Communists against fascism in the 1930s and 1940s.

Socialism is the appropriation of society by society, the management of each of the different realms of social existence by democratic governance. Such democratic governance implies the subordination of all other modes of regulation in the society to the overarching objectives democratically defined the society. It implies modes of regulation of different types (including capitalism): the market, centrally coordinated administrative orders, locally imposed administrative rules. In contrast to capitalism, it is not the modes of regulation but the 'roles' of the modes of regulation which are important. Under capitalism, overall equilibria are supposed to be achieved by decentralised decision-making and agents coordinated only through the market. Under socialism, the market regulation is relativised and consciously embedded. Capitalism is characterised by the unconscious embedding or regulation and a simple and unintentionally favourable social environment. Under contemporary capitalism, the development of the productive forces of the economy no longer allows such simplistic embeddedness of the regulating structure and therefore requires a politically active environment.

Socialism as the democratic management of society would then be the political complement to capitalism in the non-economic spheres of collective goods. My argument would, therefore, be that such a democratic socialism as the transparent, egalitarian and as much as sensible decentralised decision-making on the basis of equal access to participation is the necessary complement of capitalism, with as much markets as possible in order to make democratic control in those spheres workable in which markets cannot work.

1

Profitable Capitalism and Rising Mass Incomes

Capitalism differs from other class societies by the predominance of profit over rent as the form of surplus. Profit is appropriated on the basis of the sale of commodities on in principle perfectly competitive markets. The capitalist enterprise earns profit without being supported by any political or organised social group which assists it with non-economic means and intervention in markets. In contrast to profit, other forms of surplus as tax or rent are appropriated on the basis of market imperfections created by political measures through the limited capacity of access to resources or technologies which all create privileged conditions. Profit as income earned on the basis of perfect competition requires equal access of all existing and potential entrepreneurs to all factors of production. Factors of production have to be traded on factor markets. This implies commodification of all relevant factors of production.

Wage labour is such a commodification of labour. Slave labour and other forms of unfree labour can also be traded. Capitalists can employ such unfree labour, even if there is a labour management problem. Unfree labour may be disinterested in the results of production and difficult to be motivated for the goals of the enterprise, although the practice of manumission has introduced such elements into the deal between the employer and the unfree labourer.

Such appropriation of surplus on perfect markets depends ultimately on the rise of mass consumption. This requires that the incomes of all workers with average skills and not only of highly skilled workers increase. Otherwise rising productivity as expected from competition will increase the available surplus beyond any absorptive capacity of the capitalist entrepreneurs who then can get access to this surplus or even produce this potentially available surplus only if they restrict competition. There is no agency in the capitalist class or in the state which capitalists decisively influence, which has as its purpose of existence the promotion of the rise of mass incomes. Under perfect competition, entrepreneurs cannot individually increase the consumption of the labour they employ, even if they are motivated by benign feelings. They have to face labour as a factor of production which negotiates the terms of its employment on the labour market. It will be shown that from the side of consumptive capacity of the system, this requires labour being bought as free wage labour. Slave labour on plantation economies or 'feudal' economies can achieve their transition to capitalism on the basis of intensified market relations. Such market relations may exist between their various constituent units, but are steps in the direction of capitalism only in the context of their being linked to capitalist economies based on wage labour, as was the case with the American plantation economies in the 16th century.

Market relations existed long before capitalism and where all this restricted when full competition made surplus appropriation on perfect markets impossible. The defining criteria for capitalism is not markets, but perfect markets where the participants will not introduce market imperfections because the overall development of demand allows for profits without market restrictions.

For labour to accept to be free of bondage, to emerge as the doubly free proletarian (free of any property in its means of production and also free of any bonds, cf. Marx 1867: 742), labour has to have a reasonable perspective of a chance to sell its labour power. If this condition is not met, labour will prefer to accept bonds, even to really engage in bonded labour as the various forms of debt peonage demonstrate which can be observed in 19th century Latin America or India.[1]

Capitalists employ wage labour if this labour adds more to production than it costs. The marginal product of labour has to be at least as high as the cost of labour. The productivity of labour has to be high enough for marginal labour to yield at least as much its cost. If the marginal product of labour is lower than the cost of reproduction, which labour has inevitably to earn in order to survive, labour cannot be fully employed and some labour can be reproduced only on the basis of its activity in a non-capitalist sector.[2] This leads to the observation that the transition to capitalism is based on the appropriation of surplus from non-capitalist sectors. Female household production is the example which is most often quoted in gender-studies-oriented critiques of capitalism. Obviously, the rule of behaviour of maximising profit will induce capitalists to exploit any sector which allows them to appropriate resources. This will not, however, lead to the transition to capitalism, as the long history of the coexistence of politically dominant non-capitalist structures demonstrates. Long-distance trade and local markets over millennia did not lead to capitalism in the ancient empires of Asia. However, in some cases the support of the non-capitalist sector will go to labour which becomes employable despite a low marginal product. If employment is the result this may greatly accelerate the transition to capitalism.

There may be possibilities of covering the cost of reproduction of labour on the basis of access to resources produced in a non-capitalist sector. Export-oriented manufacturing production based on cheap family labour is a case about which I will discuss later. We will see such possibilities especially in the case of catching up economies which are following export-led growth where sufficient demand is provided by a leading capitalist centre. Such arrangements are, however, either dependent or unstable. One configuration may be characterised by the non-capitalist sector being poor; in this case, it cannot provide demand for the capitalist one—which applies to the remark, above, about the blockage to capitalist appropriation of the surplus as profit because of a lack of demand. Another configuration may be characterised by the non-capitalist sector being rich, and in that case more efficient management of its factors of production will allow capitalist entrepreneurs to enter it. The old non-capitalist monopolists are disempowered. They lose their old instruments of defending their incomes. They may turn into capitalists and provide demand to the capitalist sector as much as they are as capitalists. This was often the case for the owners of natural monopolies. These monopoly rights even capitalists had to respect.

In both cases the non-capitalist sectors cannot perform the role of supplying sufficient additional demand.

If there are no capitalist economies which have already experienced the transition to capitalism on the basis of their own rising mass incomes, the transition to capitalism depends on empowerment of labour. Where labour is not empowered, rising productivity can be appropriated by the privileged strata only if they are not exposed to perfect competition. Access to free labour is a condition for efficient management of factors of production; empowered wage labour is a condition for unrestricted competition between capitalist entrepreneurs. The empowerment of wage labour ultimately depends on wage labour yielding a surplus, hence being productive enough to produce more that it costs. Wage labour and perfect competition between the privileged both imply a level of productivity where not only surplus production is possible but where even marginally productive labour produces at least as much as necessary for its reproduction. Capitalism depends on a certain level of marginal productivity which goes with a higher level of average productivity, but the degree to which average productivity has to be higher than marginal productivity is not determined. There may be economies with very high average productivity (for example, the very rich pre-capitalist economies of Asia) where marginal productivity is low so that they appear to be rich without developing capitalism. As well, the transition to capitalism should be possible also for economies with low average productivity, provided that marginal productivity is high. The reference to Europe having been poor in relation to Asia, but well irrigated by rain on large agricultural areas in opposition to the dependence of Asia on rich irrigated valleys, is obvious.

The problem of too low marginal productivity is basically a problem of what has been called the dialectics between man and nature, that is, the embeddedness of production in the natural conditions in which a society lives. Where natural conditions do not matter, technologies can be reproduced at will without a declining productivity. In agriculture, natural conditions of production matter; with rising labour input, production rises but with a declining rate of increase in relation to the increase of labour input. At some point in time, additional labourers produce less than they have to consume, and therefore, cannot be employed. In an economy which has diversified because of productivity increases, the share of sectors with declining marginal product decreases. Any increase in labour input in agriculture with declining marginal product may be compensated by productivity increases in other sectors of the economy provided that the share of agriculture in total consumption rests moderate. In such a case, prices of agricultural products rise. Because workers in agriculture already have access to other than food products, the relative decline in the prices of the non-food products may compensate the rise of the price in food products so that the total consumption of these workers is still lower than their declining marginal product. This requires, however, an already relatively high average productivity of the economy. In case of an increase in the importance of nature in production at higher levels of economic development as modelled in the resource crisis and the environmental limits to growth, such limits to marginal productivity being higher than minimum or average per capita consumption may re-emerge.

The condition of marginal productivity being higher than the cost of reproduction has been assumed as always fulfilled by classical and Marxist economists. Their experience was based on European economies with their relatively homogeneous and universally rain-fed soils, a condition completely absent from the semi-arid regions of the south where some soils are highly fertile because of irrigation while many others are not. The absence of this condition as demonstrated in the form of the existence of marginalised people, the poor, was considered as a problem of charity even if organised through an administration, or a problem of wrong incentives (Malthus 1958: Vol. 2, 57 f.) or a problem of overexploitation (Marx 1867: 703), but not an issue which will foreclose the stable reproduction of capitalist relations of production.

The generalisation of commodity relations, including the commodification of labour, depends, hence, on conditions, wage labour based on a sufficient level of marginal productivity. Polanyi's capitalist 'aberration'[3] becomes possible because of the level of marginal productivity which empowers even marginal labour. Hence, market relations may exist where capitalism does not exist. This has been dealt in the discussions about ancient capitalism or capitalism in China or India before the 16th century. Obviously, profit-making requires markets, but markets do not constitute a characteristic which distinguishes capitalism from other structures. For at least three millennia markets, regional and supra-regional networks of trade existed without capitalism.[4] To differing degrees, there are market relations within communitarian structures and between such communities (Coquery-Vidrovitch 1969: 65; Moore & Lewis 2000). Ancient China[5] and ancient India had markets for agricultural and non-agricultural products, just as most other pre-capitalist tributary modes of production (Ray 1987: 88; Sharma 1974: 5). The Arab world constituted itself along the trade routes of the ancient world[6] and traders were an important social class, as in ancient India (Beaujard 2005: 431; Varshney 2002: 228) or ancient China.[7]

Hammurabi's law-making concerned also markets (Neumann 2009: 199 f.). The development of writing is linked to markets, as shown by the cuneiform script and other of phonetic scripts.[8] Religious knowledge or socially related praising of the deeds of the powerful may have been worth of being documented and have provoked the development of scripts: The value of their contents created incentives for developing non-universally accessible symbols such as hieroglyphs or the Chinese characters[9] but sometimes such texts have been so valuable that they had been transmitted only orally such as the holy texts of ancient India which only later on were written down (Kroll 2007; Majumdar et al. 1978: 47).

Pre-capitalist markets are linked to rules of moral economy. In addition, the tendencies of capitalists to enrich themselves endangers capitalism itself, in pre-capitalist societies where there are no economic checks on the powerful from the side of labour, there are other checks, in the form of social checks, but also often imposed by political agencies. These are normally summarised as 'moral economy' and consist of politically imposed rulings such as fair prices, etc. It is only in capitalism that economies are not subordinated to such a moral order. Capitalism can undermine these checks because it does not need a 'moral economy'. This has an important implication. The cultural opposition between capitalism and non-capitalism is not on content and norms, as the Weberians think, but on the very relation between culture and the economy. As will be shown, capitalism can be 'a-cultural'. Previously, markets were perfect only to a limited extent with the permanent possibility of intervention from the authorities to implement the rules of moral economy.

Markets are universal as exchange tends to be universal, but markets are not necessarily perfect. Perfect markets are in principle characterised by perfect competition: Products necessary for production can be purchased with money by anybody with everybody having access to alternative suppliers so that in principle everybody has a fair chance to find the cheapest supplier and the most interesting consumer. In non-capitalist settings, markets will never be perfect, but there will always be intervention or the possibility of intervention from the authorities which implement the rules of moral economy. Capitalist profit-making occurs in perfect markets. Capitalists do not need any support for making profit. Profits are earned in perfect markets under conditions of perfect competition. Such capitalist profit is different from other forms of surplus appropriation, also called profit which are made on markets with restrictions—established and maintained politically—on access to the cheapest seller and barriers to entry to markets for new suppliers.

Under perfect competition, every seller will lower the price of his products possibly until he earns only a very small margin over his costs and the question is why this margin is acceptable if everybody lowers his prise and nobody withdraws from this trade. Who will produce for a market and engage resources in risky and lengthy production processes if one can no longer rely on politically established restrictions against other suppliers who are still ready to lower their prices and to accept smaller margins?

If there are no trade restrictions as on non-capitalist imperfect markets, then how can the 'profit' rate be maintained on an attractive level?

The 'Inverse' Link Between Investment and Profit

A popular view links the increase of productivity and production, technical progress and growth to investment, basically new machinery which is financed from profit and accumulated as capital. I do not deny this perception. However, I will argue that enterprises do not have access to profit if they do not create incomes for their products. The required income is created in production, but in order to reach levels to enable enterprises to make profits there has to be spending on investment goods independently of the growth of production which is triggered off by the use of these new investment goods.

In the usual modelling of a capitalist mode of production, there are two 'departments' of the private sector of the economy. One department sells products to households. These are consumed by the households as households are not expected to earn a profit in using these products but to enjoy other advantages, such as survival or pleasure, the utilities of households. The other goods are sold to enterprises which hope to make money with better or cheaper products on the basis of the use of these new goods. Those products which are used during the period of production are considered as not having been capitalised, that is, added to the stock of equipment, machinery and buildings which house the equipment. Among the non-capitalised goods, those inputs which become part of consumption goods are considered as consumption goods, that is, the flour and salt used to make the bread or the fibres used to make textiles which are transformed into garments. Those which are used for investment goods, that is, steel for machines, form part of the value of these investment goods. Investment goods are those products which enterprises buy in order to use them for a longer time than one production period and, hence, which do not entirely enter the value formation neither of the investment goods nor the consumption goods sold during this period. Part of the investment goods are used up during the period of production. The value of this part of the investment needed is called amortisation.

In addition to the assumption of two departments of production, we assume that there are two classes, wage earners and entrepreneurs, as well as two types of income, wages and profits. Part of the income of the entrepreneurs which those consume is considered as a wage for management duties they perform independently of property relations. All wages, but only wages, are spent on consumption goods. Profits are not spent on consumption goods, as we assume that competition forces entrepreneurs to live frugally and not to spend income on consumption goods beyond their wage for management duties.

For simplicity, we assume that foreign trade is balanced: imports equal exports. As well, we assume the government sector as balanced. The government takes as much from the private sector as it spends.

The costs of the producers of consumption goods are the sum of their labour costs, the cost of their inputs (and, hence, also the cost of labour in the production of these inputs) and their amortisations. As only wage earners buy consumption goods, the total proceeds from sales equal the total of the wages paid by all enterprises. The producers of the consumption goods can sell their goods at prices where the total sum of their sales is higher than the total sum of their costs; hence, they make a profit only because there are wages which are not paid by the producers of consumption goods. All wages in the production of consumption goods and in the production of inputs—the replacement of worn out machinery and buildings—are costs of production for the producers of the consumption goods.

There is the usual mathematical proof with Y = national income, P = profit, W = wages, I = net investment goods production and C = consumption. Total earnings in consumption goods equal total wages, as only wages, but all wages are used for the purchase of consumption goods.

The total earnings of the consumption goods department is

$$C = W_I + W_C. \tag{1}$$

The total incomes paid in the consumption goods department is

$$C = P_C + W_C. \tag{2}$$

Integrating equation (1) and equation (2) we obtain

$$P_C = W_I. \tag{3}$$

The amount of profit of the consumption goods department is, hence, the function on the level of activity in the investment goods department. A positive value of W_I implies a positive rate of profit in the consumption goods department.

Nobody will commit investible funds into the investment goods department if there is no perspective of achieving the same profit rate as in consumption goods production. Those active in investment goods production can shift to consumption goods production, as any technical innovation

Profitable Capitalism and Rising Mass Incomes

in consumption goods production requires new or adapted investment goods. Any new product or any better production process for an old product requires new machinery. The design of new machinery is possible only on the basis of a comprehensive understanding of the innovative aspects of the product to be manufactured. The investment goods producer has, therefore, the possibility to produce consumption goods under conditions which are comparable to the ones which are enjoyed by those already active in the consumption goods department. He cannot be kept from entering this department under conditions of perfect competition. The investment goods producers will either shift their investments to consumption goods production or be able to impose prices for their investment goods which provide them with the same profit rate which is achieved in consumption goods production. The receipts for investment goods are therefore

$$I = W_I + P_I \tag{4}$$

From equation (3) we obtain

$$I = P_C + P_I \tag{5}$$

Hence, the total profit equals the value of net investment goods production at the profit rate determined by the sum of decisions about the net investment.

Hence, net profit (gross profit minus amortisations) should become negative during economic crises. This has been observed during the great depression of the 1930s (Kreps 1935: 594; Levadoux 1980: 968). Subsequently, it was often hidden statistically by accounting practices with respect to amortisations and provisions for losses, as well as by 'financial' profits in case of a delinking of the growth of financial markets from the growth of the real economy.

The profit rate depends on the decisions of all entrepreneurs about new investment. This decision then depends on cost calculations based on expectations.

Investment is not constrained by the availability of financial means earned in previous periods. Capitalist economies are based on fiat money and not on commodity monies such as gold, even if such universal commodities may initially have played an important role, as long as trust in contracts was limited. The bill of exchange is the simplest form of creation of purchasing power for an entrepreneur before the corresponding value of commodities has been produced. The creation of credit money by banks is nowadays the predominant form. The money multiplier (p. 145) describes the mechanism by which banking systems create credit money in excess of savings previously done either by the banks themselves or the holders of bank accounts.

The real limit to investment goods production is on the supply-side the capacity of the economy to supply subsistence goods for workers in investment goods production, because these workers consume consumption goods, but do not produce consumption goods. The real limit for investment goods production on the demand side is the readiness of entrepreneurs to commit resources to the risky introduction of new goods and new production processes. Besides the production of a surplus of wage goods, investment requires a demand for new equipment. This demand is created by demand for new consumption goods which are produced by equipment. The configuration of social forces which trigger off this demand is the essence of the explanation of the transition to capitalism, as surpluses of wage goods are found in many pre-capitalist societies.

Obviously, capitalism requires the availability of surplus. Surplus creates incentives to appropriate it by any means. Capitalism only emerges if the access to surplus depends on the use of surplus for investment. There are other avenues to surplus, especially if unfavourable demand conditions keep decentralised capitalists from perceiving profitability of investment. In that case they refrain from committing resources to capacity creating plants and equipment. As surplus is available, those in command of power and even capitalists who want to have access to safe surplus may turn to appropriate surplus for nurturing the bases of power from which they can draw rent as an income different from profit. They may be able to do so by creating a climate of insecurity in which protection becomes important (Gilman 1981: 7). They become increasingly capable of doing so, if they are able to eliminate the means of self-defence of agricultural producers by disarming the peasantries.[10] They are favoured by the fact that the costs of production of harvests are high for peasants in relation to the costs of robbing them, so that peasants may be ready to pay high prices in order to be protected: The robber has to concentrate his military forces on a limited space and in a limited time; peasants have to protect large areas permanently. Robbers can get their food from many walks of agriculture; peasants who have lost their harvest cannot hope to get subsistence elsewhere.

There is no natural tendency for adopting appropriation of a surplus on the basis of competition markets where demand is high because of the presence of investment goods producers.

Impasse of Accumulation: Accumulation and the Non-centrality of Capital in Capitalism

Classical and Marxist economists normally have deduced economic growth from the use of more and more expensive equipment in the production process, so that the purchase of more and more expensive investment goods constitutes the driving force of capitalist growth. Both Ricardo and Marx, in particular, formalised this growth of investment with a rate of growth of net capital (capital stock employed in production and not yet amortised) higher than the rate of growth of net production (Y). They derived from these differences in growth rates of capital stock and net production the notion that capitalism might be exposed to a decline in the total sum of profits in relation to the net value of the capital. This has been discussed by Marx as the tendential fall of the rate of profit (1894: 223 ff.). In criticising Marx's law, Bortkiewicz (1907: 456 f.) and later on Okishio (1961) have argued that in capitalism, a new technology is considered as productive only if it allows to increase the total output more rapidly than the increase in the total costs for labour, inputs and equipment it implies. An entrepreneur who automatises the production of an item with huge outlays for machinery in order to save labour can compete with a less modern production process only if he achieves lower unit costs. If he fails, he loses his capital, because he has invested it inefficiently (Samuelson 1972).

Any new technology is only chosen because it lowers unit costs and, therefore, it is characterised by the fact that it increases the availability of goods in relation to the factors of production employed. As this applies to all technologies, the acceleration of investment by raising the share of investment goods in total production without expanding the other forms of demand, wages, can, therefore, lead only temporarily to employment of all available factors of production. Productive capacity increases more rapidly than purchasing power, so that either there is overproduction in relation to purchasing power or lower capacity utilisation. Lenin's (1899: 42) vision of the development of capitalism exclusively through increasing the demand for investment goods is not applicable in capitalism in the longer term.[11] Luxemburg (1912: 88–92) has insisted on this in her criticism of Marx's so-called schemes of enlarged reproduction of capital. She has insisted on the fact that there is no interest among capitalists to accumulate if there is no expansion of demand.

Defenders of Marx's law of the tendential fall of the rate of profit have insisted on a variety of mechanisms, among them joint production.

Their arguments are contradictory and do not take into account the necessary long term.[12] The only relevant criticism of Bortkiewicz and Okishio consist in showing that their terms of comparison do not cover the introduction of new products. Obviously, the criterion of declining unit costs can apply only to identical products or substitutes. The unit costs between artisan-like produced bread and automated bread production, and also between carriages and cars can be compared, but not between computers and paper sheets used for taking notes for memory. But new products can only be introduced if the households can satisfy their old needs: No computers if the demands for food or for clothes are not satisfied. Therefore, the introduction of new products equally requires the rise of real incomes. Investors in the computer industry will start production only if they expect that they can achieve the same profit rate as in old industries and they can hope so if households are ready to buy these initially expensive products. This depends on the development of the purchasing power of the households, hence on their real wages. So the profit rate may fall, but only if real wages increase and give rise to the production of new goods.

There is no tendential fall of the rate of profit due to capital deepening and no growth of capitalism without increasing mass incomes (Elsenhans 1983a, b).

Empirically, the observation of more and more costly equipment in relation to production is not confirmed under capitalism. The relation between capital and net product is called the capital-output ratio (COR). Economic history has now produced a large amount of research which concludes on the relative stability of the COR,[13] a lower COR today than in the early phases of the industrial revolution,[14] declining incremental capital-output ratio (ICOR) at least in the last decades of the 19th century (Bicanic 1962; Mayor 1968), a lower COR in capitalism in comparison to centrally planned economies (a reason for their downfall)[15] and also in comparison to capital-starved underdeveloped economies in case of their state-led efforts for industrialisation.[16] We might be impressed in looking at huge factories which are said to be so expensive. This impression is misleading. The costs of the equipment reflect the increasing real and nominal wages. The cost of the labour embodied in new equipment increases with rising real incomes. Price stability is guaranteed if nominal wages do not rise more rapidly than productivity in consumer goods production. Higher prices for new capital goods embody, therefore, more costly labour. In consumption goods production we measure price stability by comparing identical goods in different times. Productivity increases here are often observed as cheaper goods: more goods are produced with the same input of labour.

But productivity increases consist also of better goods. This is especially the case with machines. Enterprises, normally, do not simply look for more machines but better machines which perform more efficiently.

When measuring the cost of capital stock, we measure the sum of plant and equipment, not isolated single items. We see the total amount of capital goods, whereas in the consumption goods sector we see the price of a single item in comparison to its previous price. If my argument is correct that the value of capital does not increase during capitalist accumulation, this value should not increase if we deflate the actual cost of capital by the index of real wage increase. This demonstration is conclusive for both Germany and the United States. We do not have more costly equipment in terms of labour expended on its production but only more and better performing equipment (Elsenhans 1976: 101 ff., 1979b: 145 ff.).

Capitalism is capital saving. Technical progress does not depend on a higher share of labour engaged in investment goods production. Endogenous growth theory has integrated the Keynesian observation of a constant or even declining COR by introducing technical progress which is not financed by higher outlays (Nelson 1998: 505). Disembodied technical progress or human capital is the notions employed.[17] Neoclassical economists have tried to measure human capital by outlays for education.[18] The economic results were not conclusive.[19] The political results were disastrous: underdeveloped countries, explicitly India, were presenting a bill for their costs of accepting the brain drain, the emigration of educated labour (doctors and engineers) to developed capitalist countries, especially the United States. They called this reverse technical assistance of the Third World to the developed capitalist world.[20] The measurement of human capital shifted to the calculation of income streams caused by higher skills of some labour in relation to labour with average skills (Collins & Bosworth 1996: 151 ff.; Sahota 1978: 14). This differential was considered as an interest paid on the unknown amount of the capital of the more skilled labour. At an assumed interest rate, the amount of capital could be calculated just as the stock exchange value of a financial title. In an economy with higher wages, the amount of human capital was higher if compared to an economy with lower wages.[21] If the human capital was calculated by comparing wage differentials inside a particular economy where human capital was abundant because of universally highly skilled labour and, hence, low wage differentials, such an economy had less human capital than an inegalitarian economy with scarcity of skilled labour. As developed economies are normally characterised by high average levels of skills of their labour force (and low differences of wages) whereas skilled workers are scarce in underdeveloped economies, developed economies or the East Asian tigers with efficient educational and training systems have low levels of human capital in comparison to economies with less success in training and education (Krugman 1994: 71 ff.).

The questions to be answered are therefore: Why do skills and knowledge increase in a capitalist economy without this being reflected in the outlays for capital formation? Why does labour become more productive?

Mass Consumption and the Technical Progress

The most important source of technical progress is economies of scale.[22] Any innovation depends on a discovery, done by a skilled worker who devotes brain for discovery of a better product or production process. He does so in order to save on labour for an operation as the discovery can be applied to any subsequent similar operation. If you have to drill one hole, you will use a simple device, but if there are many you will eventually buy a drilling machine from a super market. If you have billions of holes, you will invent a drilling machine, if you know that you cannot avoid making these holes.

The use of economies of scale is not specific to capitalism. The pottery desk or the spinning wheel reflects the attempt of the lazy man to reduce tedious work by employing his brains in order to work more intelligently.

Until the microelectronics revolution, machines were mechanical devices which could execute repetitive relatively uniform operations. Machines can, therefore, be used more frequently the more uniform the products are. As well, machine-made products are at least in the initial stages of industrial development of standard quality (Nef 1940: 137; Rezneck 1931: 801). These products can serve the essential requirements for which they are designed. Additional characteristics such as design or the capacity to perform additional operations are costly and avoided. Henry Ford argued: 'You can have a car in any colour, provided it is black' (Grübler 2003: 31). The gadget distinguishes the owner only if it appears rarely. Adding it to a standard model by machine production would be costly because of the small number of products to which it is added.

American clocks could be produced in the 19th century because the distinguishing decorations were not sculpted into the frame but only painted on the frame.[23]

Machines are designed to replace repetitive and tedious labour and are produced by rather innovative workers whom we can assume to be opposed to tedious labour, although the employment of these machines may lead to more boring labour for other workers (assembly line). We do not have to assume that all labour prefers innovative labour. Because innovative labour leads to innovations which increase tedious labour, we can assume that there is no shortage of innovators. Innovators will not disappear if they cannot cream off the benefits their invention allows in the form of higher individual incomes. As machines increase the employability of -non-innovative labour, the innovators permanently reduce the need for their type of work. We can, therefore, assume that human society tends to a permanent oversupply of potential innovators.

Economies of scale are possible if demand is relatively uniform. They are based on the replacement of some repetitive and relatively low-skilled labour by some innovative relatively highly skilled labour. This highly skilled labour is not more expensive in relation to tedious labour to the degree of its higher productivity because remuneration follows scarcity and work effort, but not productivity. By benefiting from economies of scale, the use of more intelligent labour can become more widespread and can increase. We are more or less born as animals into a world where we are adapted to standard operations in order to survive. We need, however, reserve capacity for critical situations. Early on we had to use it because we are a relatively unspecified animal with mediocre capacities in running, swimming, climbing, hearing, etc. (Gehlen 1962: 35). We compensate this mediocrity by understanding and cooperation. Knowledge, once discovered, opens up new possibilities to all of us. All of us have imagination and innovativeness. Pooling tedious work does not provide savings in effort. Pooling innovativeness does. The increasing productivity becomes possible because there are many more human beings who are capable of imagination and innovation than the ones directly necessary for innovation in the daily struggle for survival at the early levels of development of productive forces. This mine of productivity increasing contributions can be tapped if we succeed in mechanising the tedious tasks. This shift from non-innovative to innovative labour for a larger number is made possible by equality of distribution (Allen 2009: 903). In addition, productivity increases through the introduction of special purpose machinery are made possible if the series are so large that there exist among similar steps in production subgroups with still more common characteristics which can be more extensively mechanised. This gives rise to special purpose machines (Siemens 1972: 151).

The cheapening of a product allows the shifting of factors of production to new goods. The solution of technical problems for the cheapening of a product allows technical solutions to be applied to other known products and to other technical challenges. Innovation spreads to other products. Rising mass incomes allow the democratisation of the consumption of new goods on the basis of the development of solutions towards their better standardisation. These provide insights into new technical possibilities which contribute to solve challenges for the invention of new products. The sewing machine and the bicycle provided the technical solutions which made car production thinkable.[24] Without cars there would have been no aeroplanes.

Technical progress is, therefore, a discovery process which is driven by the availability of new insights. Although this process has aspects of self-generated development of scientific discovery, most major innovations have been triggered off by economic challenges: mechanical engineering by windmills and pumping problems (Woude 2003: 65), watch-making by navigation problems (Derry & Williams 1960: 348 f.), steam engines by lack of water power and mining problems (Goldstone 2000: 186). There was a permanent pressure of tedious labour becoming expensive in European industrialisation, because innovative labour increased the productivity of tedious labour. At the same time innovative labour remained relatively cheap due to the preferences of much of the labour force for innovative work. This created permanent incentives to reduce tedious work by technical innovation.

Nevertheless, technical progress is not infinitely fast in producing innovation, also because learning depends on applying innovations in production processes which take time. If we suppose that technical progress is dependent on the application of innovation and, hence, on consumption which increases the production of items where learning takes place, the following contradiction can emerge. The accumulation of financial resources and physical investment in plant and equipment may exceed the rate of technical progress especially if mass consumption does not expand at an appropriate speed. If parsimonious entrepreneurs on the model of the Weberian ideal world would engage all available resources for accumulation, the configuration of fall of the rate of profit would occur.

There are two countervailing tendencies. Increasing labour incomes reduce the surplus available for investment. The democratisation of the consumption of new products increases the possibilities of technical change and learning by introducing new products and their manufacture in increasing quantities through mechanisation and standardisation. New production processes become outlets for new investment. New opportunities to achieve economies of scale emerge.

Classical economists will not disagree. They consider rising real wages as the natural outcome of higher productivity. As long as an entrepreneur increases his production more than his costs by hiring an additional worker, hence if the marginal product is higher than the wage of an additional worker, entrepreneurs will continue to hire, as they make a profit (Gerfin 1977: 144; Pagenstecher 1964: 720). Keynesians disagree: For Say (1972: 139 ff.) and his followers, capitalists have to use their incomes and, hence, the profits which accrue to them for purchases of produced goods or services. Even if they want to acquire liquidity, they purchase products in species form, that is, commodity money.

As capitalists are under competition, however most of these purchases are investment goods. For Keynes, the function of money to allow the storage of income implies that holders of financial assets may refrain from investment even if cheap labour is available (Keynes 1936: 131). If capitalists do not expect to be able to sell additional products they can produce on the basis of additional investment, they prefer to hold money as liquidity (hence, there is liquidity preference). Committing their money to the purchase of investment goods, ultimately machinery which subsequently can no longer be sold, but only be converted into income by the selling of products manufactured with their help, implies that they lose money. In preferring liquidity, they do not lose money, but forego only uncertain possibilities of earning additional money. With liquidity preference, employment decreases due to a lack of investment goods production.

So only the perspective of further expanding markets provides capitalists with the necessary confidence for committing their money to the purchase of investment goods.

Rising Real Wages: A Non-intended Result of Power Relations

Rising mass incomes are, hence, a condition for continued and stable reproduction of capitalist relations of production. This is not the argument that capitalists as competing entrepreneurs may have an interest in rising wages at least of their competitors and other branches. It is true that they cannot influence the wage bargain in other enterprises and are opposed to higher wages for their own workers. By arguing that rising wages are a condition of capitalist growth, I do not maintain that rising wages are a political objective consciously pursued by the entrepreneurs in their quality as the ruling class. Instead, I argue that capitalism is viable only if the ruling class is not able to impose its preferences, as rising wages are the result of constraints on capitalists, which they cannot change or remove themselves.

From my theory of profit, I deduce, however, that the 'rich' can continue to exist as capitalist entrepreneurs only if the equilibrium of power between capital and labour is maintained. Capitalists themselves are neither interested in profit nor in capitalism. They want to make money, whether as rent or as profit. They even prefer rent over profit, as rent is safer because it is based on market imperfections. Market imperfections are supported at the political level by Braudel's treason of the bourgeoisies (Braudel 1966, t. 2: 67–74) as exemplified also by the permanent tendencies of 'refeudalisation' of such bourgeoisies (Mörke 1983: 152 f.). Capitalists continuously try to create market imperfections. As capitalists do not support capitalism, the argument that they are not interested in higher wages is not conclusive. They are not in favour of capitalism nor are they in favour of high wages, but they cannot escape them as long as they cannot remove capitalism. Capitalists are neither interested in maintaining the neoclassical basics of capitalism, competition, nor the basics suggested by me, that is, higher wages.

In the neoclassical description of capitalism, equilibrium between productive and consumptive capacity of the economy is maintained by competition between the entrepreneurs. Enterprises which discover a new product or a new technology will initially reap extra profits. They try to expand production by hiring additional labour. Under conditions of tight labour markets and high employment, they offer higher wages. With expanding production, they have to accept declining prices and will feel less inclined to offer above average wage rates. Branches with less favourable demand conditions will lose labour and have to reduce production. At lower levels of their production, absolutely or in relation to other branches, they can sell their products at higher prices. They, therefore, can keep a possibly lower amount of labour by paying also higher wages.

In this process, average wages emerge which do not depend on branch-wise or enterprise-dependent productivity growth but on average productivity growth (Salter 1960: 161). Branches with above average growth of productivity face saturated markets when they expand production. In cases of full employment in the economy, those branches with below average rate of growth of productivity lose workers to other branches. At a lower level of production, they can defend their employment by raising their wages and by increasing the prices of their products. Productivity measured in monetary terms converges. Labour conditions in different branches tend to become similar. This is the basis of the flexibility of a capitalist economy and the constitution of the working class, and the basis of the political and social empowerment of labour. Productivity as measured in prices converges within economic areas where labour is mobile and this is because price relations between products change. With homogeneous productivities, small changes in technical productivity or demand lead to rapid adaptation of supply, as factors of production flow easily between different branches and enterprises. This flexibility-creating process depends on high levels of employment which are the basis of rising wages.

The so-called homogeneity of capitalism in the centres of the world system has nothing to do with a particular level of technical development. Processes of adaptation of relative prices based on the scarcity of factors of production, especially labour, create this flexibility.

The Agricultural Barrier to the Transition to Capitalism

This process of the flexibility-creating convergence in productivities depends on the scarcity of labour. It depends on the fact that there is no labour which is cut off from producing a surplus. Therefore, a certain type of agricultural progress is decisive for the emergence of capitalism. In a closed economy which cannot import large amounts of food, low levels of agricultural labour productivity constitute a barrier to the emergence of capitalism. If agriculture is not capable of producing a surplus of food over consumption of agricultural producers, the excess population is condemned to disappear in the wake of famines. Suppose that there are , however, some rich regions, where huge surpluses can be produced, for example by using irrigation, whereas the majority of peasants in some more marginal lands produce less than they need for survival. In such a case, these poor peasants may survive in being supported from the rich harvests in the fertile regions.

The existence of labour which does not produce as much as it has to consume makes classical and Marxist economy irrelevant for a large group of economies. Marxist, classical and neoclassical theories of capitalism do not deal with this condition. Those theories assume that all labour available on the market is producing a surplus provided that wages are low enough. All labour, therefore, is always scarce if wage rates go down sufficiently. If, however, the marginal product of labour is less than the cost of subsistence, there is always a surplus of labour. In classical theory, at low enough wages, all labour is employed. If there is, however, marginal labour, even labour employed in productive activities will not be able to raise its income above subsistence income. Increasing average productivity will not lead to increasing average wages. This absence of possible scarcity of labour also withdraws the basis for the tendency of the market to achieve full employment and equilibrium of the classical theory.

In order to keep marginal labour from starving, redistribution in favour of such workers and their families has to take place. This is possible if those in control of agricultural surplus maintain the less productive workers because they need their services. They may use them for 'non-productive' services (military, domestic services; in this case, their existence depends on the readiness of those who employ them to use their services) or for the production of industrial goods for themselves. In both the cases, the subsistence of these marginal workers is independent of their productivity in agricultural activities. Their incomes depend on the prices of the food they need for their survival. The size of the section of labour which can survive outside agriculture depends on the amount of surplus production of food. They add nothing to the availability of food.

If in such structures, with high levels of labour which produces in agriculture less than its subsistence, market relations are introduced and dissolve such mechanisms of redistribution, the marginal workers are shed as unproductive.

These observations explain two sources of increasing joblessness in case of capitalist penetration into pre-capitalist economies: The surplus appropriating class shifts from the consumption of locally produced services and industrial goods to imported ones. This shedding of labour has often occurred when pre-capitalist economies were opened up to trade with more advanced capitalist ones during the 19th-century European colonial expansion. As well, 'traditional' agriculture may release labour if capitalist considerations of surplus maximisation are adopted in order to maximise the agricultural surplus available for exports (often in the case of plantation economies).

To the difference of the large variety of non-agricultural products, food is an essential input of food production, with high shares (50%–70%) in household consumption of producers in agriculture at still low levels of economic development. The relation between the input of food and the output of food is not changed if prices change, as in the case of the relation between industrial output and agricultural output. If there are labourers who produce less in agriculture than they have to consume for their survival with the implication that they have to be subsidised from the surplus produced by more productive workers in agriculture, the following dilemma emerges: Should they produce non-agricultural products or contribute at least a little to the rise in agricultural output, although this activity leads to a decrease in the surplus of the food available. Those who produce less additional food than they have to consume even at subsistence level are economically unable to stand in the market as agricultural labour (hence, my qualification as 'marginal'). In case of non-market regulation of the economy, they can survive in agriculture if there are politically (by the landlord, by the state) or socially (solidarity relations within primary groups, like tribe or large family) established mechanisms of redistribution or if the economy is already developed as much as to create employment in non-agricultural production, for example, industrial production for mass markets, which implies that the problem of sufficient food production is resolved.

If the economy opts for producing more food but less surplus, hence if the economy is steered against the principle of producing the highest possible surplus, it is possible that the higher level of employment goes with a greater orientation of the possibly smaller industrial sector to mass needs.

If surplus is maximised and marginal workers are employed only outside agriculture, total employment will be less and total surplus higher with a higher share of industrial production than if the marginal labour is kept in agriculture.[25] If there are no other bases of the empowerment of labour than employment, it is improbable that a large marginal population can be employed for ordinary industrial consumption of the agriculturally active population. The demand of an increased share of non-agricultural products so that marginal population can be shifted to the industrial sector is likely to take its origin in the consumption of a privileged stratum of lords. Here, capitalist competition tends to be excluded as the lords can engage in higher consumption only if there is no price competition on perfect markets for their own products. As there is an agricultural surplus available, marginal labour which is shed in agriculture can be fed from a surplus of agriculture. Many lords will be successful in breaking perfect market competition by political power on the basis of employing this surplus labour and feeding it from this surplus product.

There is a fundamental difference between the production of industrial goods for the needs of the lord and industrial goods for a market with many customers. In the first case, the lord selects the artist for his personal qualities and the artist has very little opportunity to find somebody else who has the same preferences and tastes. In the second case, the craftsman produces standard goods which the lord may commercialise and, therefore, command from him on the basis of what they earn on an anonymous market so that the craftsman has some negotiating power. He could produce the same type of goods under the control of another lord who would commercialise them.

The alternative consists in increasing demand for non-agricultural products by the mass of the population. Here, agricultural producers have to be able to massively increase their incomes. This implies massive increases in agricultural labour productivity at least on a considerable part of the available agriculturally useful land. This implies a technical revolution in agriculture: Higher levels of agricultural productivity, especially marginal productivity, are a condition for higher mass consumption.

Higher levels of agricultural productivity will invariably create incentives for 'lords' or would-be 'lords' to get control of the land and its surplus either through 'conquest' of rich agricultural societies, by raising taxes in order to avoid such conquests by others, or by purchasing estates in order to become a rich class of private landlords.

The agrarian barrier to the emergence of capitalism is removed if population massively decreases despite high degrees of labour productivity (for example, the great plague in Europe during the 14th and 15th centuries), marginal productivity of labour increases[26] through technical innovation (for example, the increase of yields in English food producing agriculture during 16th–18th centuries);[27] this within a framework of power relations where lords were unable to curtail the economic freedom of the agricultural producers' (counterexample: slavery in sub-Saharan Africa) redistributive mechanisms are strong enough to reduce surplus appropriation by the lords to levels where the social reproduction of lords depends on their becoming efficient in the production of mass consumption goods (the English poor laws worked in this direction);[28] another economy provides cheap food and then nevertheless has enough comparative disadvantages in a sufficiently large gamut of industrial products it is ready to import (a mechanism which operates in favour of some export-oriented industrialising economies of today and which was at the basis of regional specialisation in Europe in favour of proto-industrialisation in the agriculturally less favoured regions).

The Centrality of the Empowerment of Labour

The crucial element for expanding markets is rising mass incomes. Capitalism depends on rising mass incomes because the extension of mass markets is the economic foundation for the specific behaviour of the holders of financial resources which makes them capitalists and keeps them from using their money for the creation of political structures which allow surplus appropriation on the basis of market imperfections, ultimately power. This counterweight of labour is always unstable, as there are many dangers that labour is disempowered, especially if the economic or political perspectives of capitalists worsen.

Capitalism depends on the reciprocal empowerment of labour and capital although both pursue their own selfish interests: capital the increase of money; labour the increase of its consumption. Only capital but not labour can wreck the system, so that the empowerment of labour is more important than the empowerment of capital. Capitalists have to pursue their interest in lower wages by improving technology and maintaining discipline of labour. In improving technology, they provide jobs in investment goods production. By cutting wages, they reduce consumption. Because of the characteristics of profitable investment, capitalists cannot contribute to an overall lasting rising consumption.

If labour increases its consumption, it cannot reduce the production of investment goods. The limit to consumption is the capacity of the consumption goods industry to produce consumption goods. Money incomes in excess of the capacity of the consumption goods industry to supply products lead to inflation, Keynes's (1930: 154) forced savings. The central bank can raise interest rates, make credit more expensive, and crowd out investment and reduce expected profit rates. Employment in investment goods industries and consumption goods industries declines. Labour may be able to trigger off inflation but not reduce profits beyond spending on investment goods production. In case of high increases in nominal wages, entrepreneurs may even decide to accelerate the creation of new plant and equipment, and finance the additional investments by credit so that real wages may even decline. Entrepreneurs contribute with such investment to accelerate inflation and to reduce real consumption of households by bringing more labour into employment in the investment goods production. Labour cannot defend itself on the labour market against such consequences. With a reasonably efficient central bank in charge of monetary supply, labour cannot trigger off inflation and wreck the system. The share of labour is ultimately determined by the investment spending of capital and not by the wage bargain. Labour can influence the system only through its wage demand by keeping its wage demand high enough in order to keep the system near full employment. As long as labour does not engage in saving, labour cannot redistribute the income shares of capital as long as this income is used for investment.

Business often asks for lower wages with the argument of the necessity of financing investment spending. There are, however, no examples of profitable investment not been undertaken because of a lack of financial resources in capitalist societies with a local industrial sector capable of investment goods production, reasonably efficient local bank systems and local capacities for wage goods production.

There are, however, many examples of the failure of injecting more financial resources into the economy for triggering off investment which does not come up. The discussion of managing the business cycle through monetary policies agrees on the observation that the central bank is capable of avoiding an overheating of the economy by increasing the cost of credit, but less capable of launching the economy by easing the supply of credit. The 'horses may be brought to the drinking trough but refuse to drink' is a common description of this difficulty. During the 1930s (Germany; cf. Abelshauser 1999: 504; Spoerer 2004: 236) and the early 1940 (USA; cf. Bateman & Taylor 2003: 252 f.), it was government deficit spending on armaments, but not better money supply through more credits to industry which led to full employment. Taking sides with business for more financial resources may even block recovery and wreck the system because this limits consumption and final demand.

As a result labour-oriented Keynesian strategies become inapplicable when labour is weak during crises whereas monetarist policies which business advocates do rarely work, so that only military Keynesianism can easily command political majorities. Examples, here, include the overcoming of the great depression of the 1930s and the boom of the American economy under Reagan.

The issue, hence, is whether the empowerment of labour can be maintained within a socio-economic system where a minority of business owners commands the means of production, when the following new conditions emerge: large-scale satisfaction of the material needs of labour in those economies which have achieved capitalism or/and integration of socio-economic systems into the world economy where the empowerment of labour has not yet taken place.

Capitalism: An Accident in History and the Permanent Dangers It Faces

In case of doubts, the question could be raised whether the experience of capitalism in the centre and its demonstration effect on the non-capitalist world have created a civilisational impact where 'culture' and, hence, attitudes have emerged and been solidly implanted, which support the maintenance of these unstable equilibria capitalist growth requires. Neither the emergence of capitalism nor its expansion to other societies, not even today under the conditions of economic and cultural globalisation, provide evidence for such a possible role of culture despite the widespread attempt of various social groups to promote economic growth by adopting capitalism or by complementing it through additional arrangements considered as favourable to growth.

The 'invention' of capitalism was a collective process of creating institutions without any master plan and did not depend on a comprehensive guidebook which supported it. Capitalism was an accident of human history. Capitalism is not the result of a process of civilisation. The process of accumulation of cultural refinement and philosophical insights at best led to an elitist structure, even if this did not exclude the assertion of a fundamental equality of all human beings in their dignity and also freedom in the most diverse cultural settings.

As well, capitalism has not been the result of the accumulation of technical knowledge. Such a process conceived as increasing 'mastery over nature' and increasing surplus production and investment is implied in theories of economic evolution (historical materialism,[29] the German historical school from household economy via estate economy to market economy; cf. Sombart 1921a: 40–66) or theories of the succession of states of consciousness (Comte 1963: 32). Increased availability of surplus led to more stratified socio-economic systems which developed technical progress of a specific kind: They were not oriented to increasing the availability of standard goods for mass consumption which would have required the use of machinery but to the improvement of goods for minorities which aimed at excellence and artistic performance.

Capitalism, therefore, required a re-orientation of the 'civilisational' process. This does not exclude that in this re-orientation new attitudes and institutional set-ups and obviously new technologies were developed. Such developments may have had three effects: They may have stabilised a specific orientation of the European social, cultural and political systems. They may have created advantages of Europe in this type of evolution which allowed Europe to benefit from the circumstances favourable to capitalism all over the world, for example, through the specialisation of Europe on mass consumption products so that Europe benefited from the capture of these markets in other countries for European exports. They may have created a demonstration effect which allowed social classes outside Europe to learn from Europe and to become more efficient in imposing orientations on their own societies which could favour the emergence of capitalism.

Such linkages may allow to play down the idea of the European superiority based on some specific cultural or economic inheritance, the idea that the development of capitalism in Europe did play the role of revolutionising an otherwise stationary rest of the world and the idea that the unique pattern of development of Europe did benefit from drawing on resources from the rest of the world.

Indeed, the necessarily regionally limited emergence of capitalism, as it was an accident of history, made the European experience expansionary with the result of contributing to the growth of this model in, however, contradictory ways with the result of challenging other socio-economic structures, which in their attempts to adapt had consequences as well for the further growth of capitalism and for its further expansion.

If capitalism was an accident which consisted in the re-orientation of a normal evolution of human kind, this normal evolution is first to be described. This normal evolution consists in population increases triggering off attempts to improve mastery over nature and the emergence of highly stratified inegalitarian structures.

Notes and References

1. Ahuja 2002: 798 f.; Heipel 1986: 209; Kadam 1991: 81; Nickel 1976. Similar on Egypt: Brown 1994: 119.
2. Benería 1981: 24; Bennholdt-Thomsen 1979: 57; Chen et al. 1999; Collectif rémois 1977: 109; Deere 1976; Schiel & Stauth 1981: 137.
3. Polanyi argues that labour and land become commodities in capitalism and that this constitutes a process of disembodying the economy from its social setting, cf. Polanyi 1944: esp. 231.
4. Bentley 1996: 755 ff.; Caspers 1978: 124; Davis 1996: 48 f; Ward 1964.
5. Beaujard 2005: 424; Coquery-Vidrovitch 1969: 65; Dale 2009: 85.
6. Breuer 1987: 195; Poncet 1967: 31; Laroui 1970: 136.
7. Liu 1988: 5; Moll-Murata 2008: 217. On the Muslim world: Baer 1970: 145; Zubaida 1972: 324. On Precolombian America: Sanders & Webster 1988: 536.
8. Alden 1982: 613; Geiss 1980: 571; Gurukkat 2007: 16; Haude 1999: 6; Huot 2005: 964; Kohl 1978; Morenz 2002: 179; Shendge 1982: 873.
9. Glassner 2005: 487; Islam 2011: 4; Tuchscherer 1999: 55.
10. Gohain 2010: 42; Mukhia 1997: 130 f.; Richards 2004: 398; reports on armed peasantries.
11. For a critique of Lenin, Hoffmann 1967: 206; and also Elsenhans 1986: 274.
12. Bowles 1981; Hunt 1983; Parijs 1980: 1–16; Roemer 1979. Critics insisted on the possibility of a falling profit rate in the case of joint-production of

goods: Bidard 1988: 355–360; Funke 1984; Renten 1991: 87 Salvadori 1981, neglects devalorisation. Schutz 1987 insists on declining productivity due to natural resources, but then the process is not caused by capital accumulation. Armstrong & Andrew 1980: 67, and Scott 1992 introduce imperfect competition and lack of correct technology assessment. Kliman 1997: 46, introduces false expectations without mentioning that this would lead to devalorisation of capital.

13. Domar 1961: 101–114; Helmstädter 1969: 48–91; Hesse & Gahlen 1965: 472; Hoffmann 1969: 23; Kendrick 1961: 166; Kocoglu 2001; Patel 1963: 301; Robinson 1977: 1331.
14. Brito & Williamson 1973; DuBoff 1966: 431; Field 1983: 413.
15. With further references: Andreff 1990: 17; Ark 1995: 89; Bergson 1971: 602; Bergson et al. 1966: 237; Brubaker 1968: 309; Elsenhans 2000c.
16. Abdel-Fadil 1971: 621; Baer & Maneschi 1971: 180; Balassa 1970: 43; Benelli 1979: 55 ff.; Chakravarty 1984: 845; Hashim 1991: 3; O'Donnell 1978: bases his theory of the emergence of bureaucratic-authoritarian structures on this increase.
17. Denison 1967a, b; 1980; Griliches 1996.
18. Blaug 1976: 839; Psacharopoulos & Layard 1979: 492; Schultz 1961.
19. Bayraktar 2006; Lindsay 1971; Rosés 1997: 41.
20. Gupta 1973: 191; Logan 1987: 603; Toh 1977: 37.
21. In reaction to the Leontiev-paradoxe Balassa 1979: 265, 1981: 265; Baldwin 1971: 127; Fareed 1972: 638.
22. Rosenberg 1976: 158–161. I refer also to the early introduction of the interchangeable parts system in America: Behagg 1998: 3.
23. Bolino 1988; Brady 1964: 175; Church 1975: 627.
24. Hounshell 1984: 189 f; Thomson 1984: 249; Tolliday & Zeitlin 1988: 154;.
25. The alternative is relevant for the problems of agrarian reform. If surplus can be used for investment goods for agriculture which allow us to increase agricultural production, then an egalitarian redistribution of land may be inferior to landlord agriculture. If this possibility does not exist, a radical redistribution of land following the argument of the size/yield inverse is superior. For an extensive discussion, cf. Schaller 2006: 160 f.
26. Clark 2007: 98, describes the increase of the marginal product of farm labour since 1600.
27. Allen 1989: 80; Allen 1999: 230; Braudel 1966: 9; Slicher van Bath 1963: 28, 35, 45.
28. Block & Somers 2003; Broad 2000; Coats 1976; Elsenhans 1980, English translation Elsenhans 1992; Geremek 1987: 18, 132; Hufton 1974: 17; Oxley 1974; Solar 1995.
29. The Marxian enumeration of stages is purely descriptive and does not develop the idea of a necessary sequence of these stages, cf. Marx 1858: 258.

2

Stratification Without Transition to Capitalism and the European Distinctiveness

There are two barriers to capitalism, the absence of empowerment of the poor, the marginals, which blocks mass consumption and the empowerment of the rich which leads to rent. It is not surplus which makes capitalism because resources for financing investment are generated by investment itself in case of capitalist inventions. Surplus is, however, the basis of rent which blocks capitalism.

The process of cumulative technical development has an importance for capitalism as an enabling condition not because it increases the availability of surplus but because it increases the marginal product of labour which may go in many cases with an increase in the availability of surplus. But this increase in availability of surplus which may be associated with an increase in the marginal product of labour at the same time greatly favours the emergence of political power structures which allow the appropriation of surplus as rent.

In the race between empowerment of the many and empowerment of the few, the empowerment of the few prevails in history until the emergence of capitalism. The inverse relation between empowerment of the many and empowerment of the few depends on accidentally occurring events. Therefore, many of those special characteristics of Europe which are used to explain why Europe was first can be found also in many non-European societies. Some may have supported the transition to capitalism, some may have been irrelevant, some may be useful for a process of imitating the transition to capitalism in not yet capitalist areas, but can have had a positive effect only in case of their contribution to the empowerment labour.

The Dissolution of Communitarian Modes of Production

With the neolithical revolution the emergence of surplus becomes inevitable. Surplus implies organisation with delegation of competencies and power. Power is no longer based on the mere capacity to exercise naked violence but on structure. We do not need to make more than the simplest assumptions about human behaviour to explain this process: Humans are lazy and work averse. They try to minimise effort in relation to results. They have a preference for their own interests and the interests of their closer relatives (especially their parents and their children—blood is stronger than water) and are capable of foresight out of fear so that they try to conjure the fate by whatever means they deem appropriate on the basis of imagination which is linked to language.

With the desire to limit the relation between effort and result, the agricultural revolution becomes inevitable whenever humans understand simple biological mechanisms. The problem of how this shift from hunting and gathering to agriculture and cattle raising was realised, whether types of activity coexisted for longer times, how gradual this shift was, etc. is of secondary importance (Kabo 1985: 609). For the evolution of social organisation one point is decisive: Whenever agriculture (more than cattle raising) becomes the basis of access to food, the production of a surplus becomes more likely. The agriculturalist has to determine a level of sown area in function of a planned harvest. The size of the fields to be sown has to be estimated on the basis of a non-average year, hence, on the basis of a worst case scenario of weather conditions. This will normally lead to harvests in excess of consumption needs. As nobody will just forgo production which can be achieved in the later phase of the maturing process with little additional effort, in years with average or good weather conditions the cultivator will reap a 'windfall'. As the next year might be bad he will keep this windfall at least for a time.

In order to keep it, this surplus has to be protected. Protection implies cooperation and division of labour as there are economies of scale in this activity. Patrolling day and night is practically beyond the capacity of a single family. Not all members of a group are equally efficient in providing protection. The young men are better in fighting than the children and the elderly. The group has, therefore, to manage the distribution of varieties of labour supplied in the cooperation.

Already at the level of communitarian socio-economic structures a highly complicated economic problem has to be resolved: the 'reduction' of concrete labour to abstract equally valuable labour. This requires institutions. Disagreeing members of the community have the option of exit and voice, as we may assume that fertile land is still largely available. But given the existence of economies of scale in the activity of protection, the option of exit is costly. The production of surplus makes voice important. In order to give voice an impact, and this to the difference of the option of exit, coalitions are useful. Reiterated patterns of coalitions lead to routines which reduce transaction costs of coalition building. Once achieved, compromises lead to arrangements which we may call institutions. Those who feel disadvantaged in such negotiations will try to maintain at least some exit options. We may assume that anybody looks for a balance between cooperation and exit options. Property rights especially in land but also in other means of production such as access to water are an important exit option. The division of labour and property rights are both mechanisms of social differentiation which are directly associated with surplus production.

As institutionalisation reduces transaction costs, an office structure emerges which has been early on described by Africanist anthropologists: the lord of the land, the lord of the water, etc.[1] Surplus production implies a political structure where competencies are delegated and property rights recognised. The recognition of property rights limits the domain where only voice counts. The owner can reject majority votes with respect to his property without having to simultaneously admit his exit from the community within which he cooperates with others. Institutionally, limited powers are a sort of combination of exit and voice.

Because of the principle of delegation such structures imply hierarchy even if these hierarchies are shallow because otherwise the benefits of lower transaction costs cannot be achieved. Surplus implies hierarchy.

Surplus may be perceived as a danger for the equality of the members of the group. It is, therefore, periodically destroyed, hence, when it exceeds the amount necessary for providing security.[2]

My argument does not imply that the emergence of surplus is the only mechanism through which communitarian social structures get differentiated. Anthropologists have shown that the possibility of storing leads to hierarchies even before the advent of settled agriculture (Keen 2006: 19). But here exit remains as a solution which at maximum costs the loss of the stock which can easily be replaced by new gatherings. My argument only implies that the emergence of a surplus makes differentiation inevitable. Differentiation becomes difficult to reverse, as the result of doing so would be either retreat into hunting and gathering or new arrangements for cooperation which once more constitute new bases of differentiation.

In such negotiations under uncertainty and incomplete information about the intentions of others, all players in the game will try to take refuge for their claims by sticking to easily recognisable principles, using arguments for the justification of their positions. In order to prevail, they use distinction. Anthropologists have discovered a multitude of criteria on which distinction can be based (Biller 1986: 11): age,[3] leadership of an extended family,[4] early establishment in the place of settlement (against newcomers)[5] but also late arrival as the right of conquest,[6] command of deviant behaviour interpreted as contact to spirits (Mandelbaum 1965: 283; Silverman 1967). Because of the importance of family, leadership roles in a family provide distinction, hence the lineage mode of production (Meillassoux 1978: 327). Magic is important because of the low level of technical mastery of nature. Contact with the other world is sought after as in this other world are the souls of the ancestors who are thought to be able to mediate between the world of spirits and to influence more powerful invisible spirits.[7] Because of the preference for one's own family, there is the attempt to make distinction and the rights attached to it hereditary. The only oral transmission of secret knowledge is just a manifestation of this goal (Haude 1999: 6; Lewis 1977: 176).

The Stabilisation of Hierarchy in Tributary Modes of Production

Suppose that in such a socio-economic structure demographic growth occurs, as parents depend on their children in their old age and do not know how many of their born children will survive. The availability of nearby favourable natural conditions of production decreases. A growing population can counteract this deterioration of the natural environment for production either by efforts to improve the land or the water supply (hence, investment through labour) or by greater mobility. With demographic growth migrations intensify.[8] The groups which interact multiply. Better means of transportation are looked for. They may be costly like horses.[9] As a result, the means of efficient access to production and surplus get concentrated either on the basis of naked power or on the basis of distinction.

If neither migrations nor investment into the improvement of the nearby factors of production can compensate demographic growth, the availability of highly productive factors of production in relation to the population will decrease at some (variable) level of population. The returns in relation to efforts devoted to production will decrease following the law of diminishing returns. Even in case that every household is still economically independent, bad harvests may render an increasing proportion of households dependent on the surplus of the community which has gone into the stock. These surpluses may be increasingly produced on land held by the distinguished families who may even have access to labour services of poorer households or migrants.

In such a situation, the deficit households will consider the periodical destruction of the surplus as an inefficient form of winning the support of the otherworldly world. They will propose permanent worship of the gods, often the ancestors of those who are better off in exchange for material support. This will be embedded in an overarching worldview of the group's solidarity and its linkage to the trans-natural world which implies a readiness to accept dependence within the framework of communitarian structures (Jansen 2008: 256). An alliance between the poorer strata and the apex of the socio-economic structure, the very rich who produce and perhaps also control a larger amount of surplus, will develop. This alliance will check the anti-hierarchical leanings of the larger middle strata. Such alliances will provide the apex of the structure first with ritual power[10] then with social power. Such alliances will reinforce the position of those ruling at the apex of the structure, for example, by imposing the recognition of the claims of the better off to distinction and furthermore to the right to decision-making and even material rewards attached to distinction. Functionally, necessary hierarchies become the basis of social power.[11]

Since Leach's (1954: esp. 223 ff.) studies on the Kachin we know that such processes of social differentiation are opposed in the communitarian modes of production. The periodic destruction of the surplus in religious festivities in honour of the gods or the ancestors removes the basis of such an emerging political centre. It keeps the privileged ones from becoming an increasingly autonomous ruling class by institutionalised mechanisms of destitution of privileged strata. A distant remnant can be seen in the practice of ostracism in the Greek cities.

Differentiation, however, may succeed: The ruling class becomes closed and identifies itself through common characteristics to which the other, even the middle strata, has no access (descent, religion, distinction). Then there are no more serious checks on attempts by the ruling class to increase surplus production and to centralise the surplus. A socio-economic structure emerges which is usually called a tributary mode of production where surplus is appropriated by political power, the 'legitimate' use of violence. The state emerges on the basis of surplus appropriation and the legitimisation of this violent exploitation by overarching ideologies of justification.

A class opposition neatly emerges between a more or less centralised class of lords and the direct producers, mostly peasants. The direct producers especially in agriculture will survive at higher or lower levels of misery and pay taxes to the power centre and rents to lower lords according to contextual parameters, at worst the whims of the powerful.

As long as the powerful cannot increase the productivity of labour through more collective working methods they have no interest in intervening in the production process. Peasant families will still organise themselves in their work process. Slavery or other forms of unfree labour are less productive than peasant labour and yield only higher surpluses in case this labour can be employed without paying for the cost of its reproduction. Slavery is either the joint product of warfare (slaves as prisoners of war)[12] or based on unequal exchange between a technically more advanced economy and a technically less advanced economy. For the more advanced economy the products with which slaves are bought from the slave-hunting society are cheaper than raising labour. For the slave-hunting society these products are valuable and difficult to produce locally. The amount of labour would be higher than the slave-hunting required to buy them for which slave-hunting is economically interesting for the technically less advanced society as it can buy products from the more advanced economy which would otherwise be inaccessible. The Atlantic slavery in the 16th–18th centuries with the triangular trade is a good example (Elsenhans 2007b: 248).

In a tributary structure there may be taxes and rents in kind or labour but also money payments. But the transition to money rents and taxes in specie does not indicate a transition to capitalism but only more centralisation of the ruling class (Claessen 1984: 370). Rewards in kind imply a relation between the beneficiary and the dutiable producers where both have to negotiate the amount of different products to be supplied. The beneficiary is advised by his own superiors to look for the delivery of the goods he is entitled to. So it is the lower rank who himself defines his due in the interaction with the subaltern surplus providing class. Lower segments of the ruling class become here independent agents of tax administration with the right of determining themselves how to deal with the taxpayers. Their tendencies to autonomy increase. The opposite tendency of an extension of monetary forms of exchange even in the form of the shift to money rents is, therefore, not per se a step into the direction of the transition to capitalism.

The stability of such a structure is guaranteed by a political organisation of the centralisation and allocation of the surplus. The lords are always a minority capable of using organisation of their repressive forces against the majority. The overall relation in numbers is always unfavourable to the exploiters because at low levels of productivity many have to be exploited in order to provide substantial benefits to few. An individual lord can maintain himself against a majority he exploits if he is able to command the support of his fellow lords in case of crises or revolts. The larger his own repressive apparatus he maintains from the surplus he extracts, the higher his own value as an ally for other lords. If he succeeds in becoming an overlord he can limit the surplus appropriated by lower lords in exchange for granting them protection. By increasing the number of his followers he becomes a still more valuable ally for other powerful lords. He can, thus, prevent other lords from becoming his overlords. A tributary structure is, therefore, characterised by the permanent struggle between lords whatever be the degree of formal institutional centralisation. More powerful ones try to increase centralisation and to enlarge the territory under their direct control administered by the staff totally dependent on them. The less powerful ones permanently plot against the overlords. But they also permanently court the overlords in order to win their favour. Their ultimate goal is to achieve independent status, especially if the geographical location of their fief makes their control by the centre difficult.[13] In this struggle, naked power is complemented not only by all the sorts of power such as finance but also by prestige, where prestige is considered as depending on beliefs and perceptions of others. Ritual confirmation contributes and transforms prestige into legitimacy. So the struggle over ritual power is important. The natural religions of the communitarian structures are complemented by trans-regional gods.[14] The more central lords claim to have specifically strong links with those central gods. A most varied world of hierarchically interacting gods projects this—worldly hierarchies into an imagined other world. Central lords draw on the role of the shaman in the natural religions as mediators with the supernatural world. The Japanese institution of the emperor maintains still some of these attributes (Ohnuki-Tierney 1991: 199 ff.).

These claims do not go unopposed. It is noteworthy that the axial revolution with its insistence on the fundamental equality of all humans in their relation with the transcendental has not only taken place in the most diverse settings of tributary modes of production but also in tributary modes of production with established structures of social inequality.[15] Where the socio-economic structures were not yet very diversified as in the deserts of the Middle East, Judaism with its heirs Christianity and Islam but also Zaroastraism (Messelken 1977: 271) and the Mithras cult[16] were the manifestations of a radical form of ritual equality. In monotheism all were equal children of God and equally powerless in relation to the supernatural. In the already more stratified societies like India with its city republics and urban citizens of much higher cultural level than the surrounding peasantries, Jainism[17] and Buddhism[18] established ritual equality with less radical simplifications in the emerging transcendental world. Buddhism could accommodate with mild forms of hierarchisation of the transcendental world which characterises the Chinese[19] world with its strong remnants of ancestral and, hence, shamanic religious practices inherited from the communitarian socio-economic structures.[20]

At the higher end of the social hierarchy, legitimacy was acquired by the lords through justice and ritual power. Both implied some respect for essential human needs. The respect for such needs was described as the characteristics of the good emperor. The good emperor could expect that the transaction costs for uniting the subalterns against this structure were high enough to prevent general rebellion. Non-respect as evidenced by general immiserisation leads to general revolt. General revolt could always draw on some unsubdued elements living at the verge of society. Hobsbawm's (1962) social rebels are so common in Chinese history that they today form the basis of a very successful Chinese movie production.[21]

The respect for such essential needs of the subalterns is the basis of a major element of tributary socio-economic structures. This respect implies at least the responsibility of the lords to work against famine and, therefore, to respect redistributive mechanisms at the level of the subalterns. Tributary socio-economic structures tolerate some level of self-organisation of the subalterns which very often continue the self-organisation of communitarian modes of production. Tributary modes of production appear regularly as a superimposition of a centralised ruling class over a (in reality, a multitude of even disparately organised with different degrees of tightness; Mizuno 1976: 13 f.) communitarian mode(s) of production (Aydin & Özel 2006: 51 ff.). The Chinese family system is such a form of an in principle communitarian self-organisation but has been generalised and extended only under the auspices of the Imperial State (Chun 1996: 432 f.; David 2006: 1294). The caste system in India is another form of self-organisation, in modern words 'civil society', which transcended the extended family (Bairy 2007: 152; Mukherjee 2010: 62). Invariably, the extended family even in socio-economic structures with less visible organisations of solidarity among the subalterns provided support for those who had difficulties to survive physically.

Such self-organisation by necessity stabilises the existence of a population which at the given endowment with land cannot produce as much as it needs for subsistence. If the normal path of evolution is characterised by population growth in excess of the growth of the availability of fertile land, the implied emergence of a population threatened by starvation is counteracted by the capacity of the society for self-organisation. Deficit households survive provided there is a surplus of agriculture produced by other households in command of better land. Households will have a high number of children as long as these children support them in the old age directly or indirectly. Households with more children will have more voice within the organisational structures of the subalterns these households can address for their claims to subsistence. It can be fairly assumed that the lords will hesitate to raise a large-scale revolt by interfering with this mechanism in order to raise the surplus they can cream off.

In a setting where there are no uniform wage rates but where incomes depend on special arrangements for access to complementary productive factors (land, water, labour contracts for services), there are in each small group at the subaltern level (extended family, caste, member of temple association: in reality, we observe a great innovativeness of the subalterns inventing the most diversified bases for such associations[22]) some individuals with better contracts than others. They cannot avoid their obligations of solidarity on which they may become dependent, if their own access to better contracts disappears. They will not free themselves from these obligations if they are not sure to be free from need definitively. Their capacity to fulfil these obligations depends on their above average incomes which they achieve only on the basis of these special contracts and, hence, on the basis of the benevolence of the lords. Their privileges confer on them better living conditions than those of the households who openly suffer from insufficient endowment with such assets, including (social) relations. The privileged subalterns, therefore, are capable to link the fulfilment of the obligations to the behaviour of the recipients of their support: Recipients cannot claim assistance if they endanger the access of the better off to their better endowment. The better off are interested in the existing arrangements and capable of imposing the respect of these arrangements on the worse off and, thus, preventing revolt as long as the basic needs of subsistence are provided also to the worse off. By accepting to fuel the mechanisms of redistribution with an acceptable share in the surplus in the hands of these privileged subalterns, the lords create the social basis for the maintenance of the overall system at very low levels of mass consumption.

It is clear that also at the lower levels social relations of hierarchy are maintained by an appropriate pattern of interaction where moral order is internalised and prestige and legitimacy are held up. The need for face-saving is universally accepted in social relations based on power. Face-saving provides prestige as a result of power without entailing other than the direct costs of merely showing it. This behaviour is, therefore, replicated also on the level of the subalterns. No privileged subaltern can be forced to give to a destitute member of his group who is considered to be lazy or seditious.

No Technical Progress Through Luxury Orientation

The apex of a tributary class permanently strives to increase its control over all other elements of this ruling class. The concentration of purchasing power in the hands of such a ruling class implies a demand for non-food products for distinction. The objective of excellence discourages capitalist development: palaces, the military, luxuries, but no standard quality mass produced consumption goods. Ibn Khaldûn has nicely described this tendency to increasing luxuries (1967: 570–579). There is technical progress as demonstrated by the achievements in many fields of excellence, especially excellent luxuries. The historians of art describe these improvements and the succession of ever more splendid and larger palaces. Each Mughal emperor built a larger mausoleum, until Aurangzeb could no longer outpace his forebears and decided to have a tomb only as large as could be paid from his income for copying the Qur'an, his obligation as a simple pious Muslim. There is technical progress, even innovations in the form of new machinery, especially in the military field, but also in the production of intermediate products. But there is no systematic search for designing machinery for cheaper production of standard goods.[23]

In addition, there is no competition between the producers of such equipment on markets because there are a few customers, mainly the courts, which are able to keep prices low and to control their suppliers by other means than markets. Even branches less close to the courts are soliciting government protection. Without expanding markets, the only possibility to improve their incomes for the traders and craftsmen consists in erecting barriers to entry. Guilds, associations of producers which limit access and production are universal characteristics of industrial production in tributary socio-economic structures.[24] This leads to the often described three-tiered structure of pre-capitalist industrial production,[25] a government-protected 'high technology' sector, a non-dynamic sector producing some mass consumption goods often closely connected to villages and a natural-resource-based sector which governments capture as a tollgate for taxes[26] (salt, precious metals; government royalties are a remnant of these arrangements).

The recent discussion started by Frank (1998: 172), Pomeranz (2000: 44) and Parthasarathi (1998: 103), about the superiority of Asia in technical development before the English breakthrough at the end of the 18th century is perhaps relevant for gauging the position of both continents with respect to a civilisational process (whatever this might be, a category which does not belong to my model of explanation), but relatively far away from the issue of the transition to capitalism. Capitalist development is linked to a special pattern of development which may go at least initially with low levels of development of refinement and quality. Asia was superior as shown by the fact that Europe imported so many luxuries, including life styles of Asia. Luxuries were called in France 'chinoiseries' (Honour 1961). Vasco da Gama had diplomatic difficulties when he arrived in Calicut as his presents of courtesy to the sultan were interpreted as deliberate insult because of their clumsiness (Parry 1975: 209).

Goldstone tried to capture the difference between Asia and Europe introducing a 'state of efflorescence'. This term should describe a relatively rich urban economy within a well-ordered society and some market relations where the peasantry had reasonable levels of subsistence but where industrial breakthrough was only contingent (Goldstone 2002: 332 ff.).

Such interpretations, including the California School, are inspired by pre-Keynesian models of growth where growth is considered as dependent on 'richness' and the availability of 'capital' defined as financial resources in a basically path-dependent evolutionary way. They, therefore, neglect that the industrial breakthroughs and the transition to capitalism were not linked to high-quality industries even if those may have been oriented to markets. Venice and Italy blocked their textile industry development because they were oriented towards high-income markets.[27] Flanders[28] and later on France,[29] however highly advanced in industrial techniques, lost to Britain which specialised on low-quality products.[30] The manufactories which appeared in Colbertist[31] France were, therefore, interpreted by the historical school as a success and the basis of the Industrial Revolution (Sombart 1921b: 738 f.). The success of Britain had to appear as abnormal (Elsenhans 2007a: 140; Klaveren 1964: 157): Britain had relied on land industry outside the established industrial cities and succeeded in the Industrial Revolution.[32] Later on these industries moved back to some old cities but into the previously old guild dominated ones only if this dominance had already been shaken (Mantoux 1905: 180 f.; Pohl 1999: 167). Goldstone's areas of efflorescence may have attracted industries which had grown up outside the old tributary system, but even if they could find their place in such areas, they lost dynamism. Mantoux's observation of ever rising new strata of entrepreneurs, obviously with new industries, outside such regulated areas remains pertinent (Mantoux 1905: 34 f.).

In the last three decades the debate on proto-industrialisation (Linde 1980: 105; Mager 1988: 302) has shown that new regions were the champions of the industrial revolution and less the urban craftsmanship or the manufactories, although those may have contributed to skill formation. Broadberry's (Broadberry & Gupta 2006: 4) observation of an advance of Europe in silver wages but not in grain wages describes an essential fact: European industrial products were relatively cheap in relation to Asia and to food (so that at the same amount of surplus the purchasing power of the surplus peasant was higher). Berg's studies about the cheapening of products of Asian origin through import-substituting industrialisation in England during the late 17th and 18th centuries by 'simplifying' them complement this observation (Berg 2002: 3). Within or besides the technologically most advanced regions of efflorescence within the old tributary socio-economic structures, in some regions of Europe a pole of production for popular needs had become increasingly dynamic which supplied rising middle classes and rural and urban lower income strata with relatively cheap industrial products (Berg 1993; Thirsk 1978: 65).

The Frank–Pomeranz debate was able to show high levels of industrial skills as well as high nutritional standards (Xue 2007) in China but not important industrial sectors which resemble the English rural industry or the European proto-industry.

Nobody ever denied that there were important achievements in agricultural production in tributary modes of production. But Frank implicitly admits the point in comparing Europe and Asia by insisting on the early specialisation of Europe on cheap products (Frank 1998: 286). The English meaning of industry veils this important difference by calling non-agricultural manufacturing products industrial whether produced by machines or skilled craftsmen. Admiring the achievements of English industry, the German latecomer realises already the decisive difference between both types of production and distinguishes between 'Gewerbe' (all non-agricultural production) and industry (standardised and realised in factories).

The production of items for the use of a distinguished customer who aims at distinction in consuming this product, in engaging in conspicuous consumption, aims at excellence. An industrial product in the German meaning of the word 'industrial' designates a product manufactured not only for an anonymous market (which can be the case also of a craft product) but manufactured for a customer who cares only for some standard characteristics of the product. This limitation on the requirements associated with a product allows its simplification so that it can be produced by mechanical devices like machines (Broadberry & Gupta 2009: 281).

Machines are the physical counterpart of investment spending. Machines can execute at least initially only repetitive operations programmed into them by the arrangement of mechanical parts on which non-human energy is applied (for example, size of the tool).

Capitalist Progress and the Failure of the Ruling Strata

I suggest to call a pole of popular industry an industry which produces goods with limited prestige value and, therefore, limited characteristics which confer distinction to its customers beyond their direct use value. The market for these products is constituted by people who do not care for distinction in relation to others and who, therefore, are interested only or in priority in the use value of the product. It is this type of products which the European land and proto-industry produced in priority (as does today but only today the Chinese industry). And this distinguishes Europe from other tributary modes of production.

This orientation of some and increasing part of Europe's industrial production has its roots in the weakness of the European exploiting classes: the European cities tried of course to supply better paying customers but German cities like Nuremberg (Rader 1971: 82; Swanson 1989: 152) had early on a high share of such mass-consumption-oriented industries. In Germany, peasants were found to be important customers of such industries already since the 13th century (Becker & Gehrisch 1977: 1372).

The emergence of such markets in Europe has probably gone with the rate of exploitation of the peasantry which allowed the peasants to buy them. There is convergent information that peasantries in Western Europe were well-off to the extent they could buy the products of urban craftsmen

(Kellenbenz 1962; Warde 2006: 289). Medieval peasants were highly integrated into local markets (Biddick 1985: 831; Dyer 1989: 321). There were close ties of exchange between the countryside and the cities in Central and Northwestern Europe (Emigh 2003; Hopcroft & Emigh 2000: 23). In being less exploited, the peasantries could either eat more or increase the amount of products they bought from the market, hence from industry as 'amenities' (Allen 2009: 549; Ogilvie 2010: 290 f.). This may have contributed to the growth of urban mass-oriented industries as we observe in the central and northwestern European cities. The dependence of urban industrial production on the purchasing power of the peasantry in Europe is proverbial (Becker & Gehrisch 1977: 1378).

Political structures may have been connected to this. Well-established ruling classes with well-centralised means of repression can be considered as powerful instruments for increasing the rate of surplus extraction from powerless rural populations. I do not maintain that such a pole of popular industry did not exist in other tributary modes of production. The Indian jajmani system of rural artisans is, however, found to be very undynamic.[33] Chinese studies on pre-capitalist industrial production concentrated on an industrial production which was oriented towards the demand of the better off. It was, therefore, early on under government protection (Lewin 1974: 190 f.). Also, Asia had its periods of the decline of luxury consumption in the periods of dynastic decline and subsequent political disorder. In a period of decline as described in the theory of the dynastic cycle in a more centralised tributary mode of production the amount of resources taken from the peasantries can be expected to have declined (Habib 1985a: 48; Pearson 1976). Peasants here also may have become richer and, hence, possible customers for industrial products. At least they could afford more food and supply additional craftsmen living in the countryside. On the other hand, the decline of state centralisation may have created security problems. The services provided by the state, even if only by its local ramifications, for agriculture in the form of irrigation may or may not have been affected. This may have led to an overall decline of production. The outmigration of peasants from the area of state control raises doubts about the importance of services. There are many examples of such migrations. The eastern parts of Bengal were colonised because tributary structures were weak. In Bengal, tributary structures had their bases on the western banks of the Ganga/Brahmaputra delta (Eaton 1993: 221; Rostovtzeff 1929: 351 ff.). Peasants around Angkor left the irrigated economy around that city during the 13th century. They withdrew from the irrigated areas near the city to rain-fed agriculture distant from the centre of power and, thus, stopped this brilliant civilisation.[34] Vietnamese peasants migrated to the South where state control was weak. When land resources for further colonisation were exhausted, private 'condottieri' could usurp property in land and become landlords (Cooke 1998: 143 ff.; Tchechkov 1969: 40), because of the weakness of the state, a fact not so dissimilar from East Central Europe in the 13th century. The Han people migrated for similar reasons to Southern China (Hostetler 2000: 643 ff.).

There are very few differences worldwide in the permanence of the struggles of direct producers in agriculture, the peasants, against those who command tribute in its various forms of a surplus appropriated of the basis of power (for the state or for 'private' lords, a nearly meaningless distinction where property rights do not lead to market competition). There are, however, no dynamic poles of popular industry capable of seizing markets in those areas. Goldstone's areas of efflorescence existed worldwide but outside the centre of the transition to capitalism in Northwestern Europe there was no transition to dynamic poles of popular industry, even if peasants were able to reduce exploitation elsewhere.

The difference between the European tributary modes of production and the non-European ones seems, therefore, to lie in the fact that in some parts of Europe the pole of popular industry could achieve and maintain some dynamism in periods of improving productivity in agriculture and/or decreasing exploitation, whereas in Asia increases in productivity and/or decreasing exploitation were used for other purposes. Such purposes could be increased consumption for the ruling class including its privileged dependents in cities or rural population growth.

An explanation of the different outcomes has to deal, therefore, with the following questions: the reproductive behaviour of the rural population, power relations in the countryside concerning the rate of exploitation and the relations within the ruling class which affect its capacity to extract surplus.

In the discussion about the transition to capitalism in Europe, changes in the reproductive behaviour of the peasantries are mentioned.[35] It is shown that since the 17th century, English peasants practiced not only contraception but tended to limit the growth of their families. Similar and even more pronounced demographic controls by French peasants did not,[36] however, increase the dynamic of the pole of popular industry in the late 18th and 19th centuries in France. The absence of such practices especially in the proto-industrial regions but also in the western part of Germany did not block the development of the pole of popular industry there.[37]

Agricultural history of Europe has a focus on the relations between the lords and the peasants. Especially the discussion on the second serfdom in Eastern Europe and the differences between 'Gutsherrschaft' and 'Grundherrschaft' show that scarcity of labour may lead either to less freedom or to more freedom of the peasants. The outcome depended on the political power relations at the ground level in the villages (Schöffer 1959: 56). This implies that the outcome cannot be satisfactorily explained by economic determinism. English peasants became free in the 14th century because they were able to transform their scarcity to better labour conditions and incomes.[38] East German and Polish peasants were not able to achieve this goal, despite similar political institutions, similar cultural settings and an initially even higher degree of freedom.[39] East German peasants had been better off than West German peasants as better conditions for their lives and production were a condition for attracting them to the eastern territories.[40] This outmigration even entailed better conditions for the remaining peasants in the West (Malowist 1966: 19; Mottek 1964: 13 f.). Enserfment was tried also in Western Germany in the 15th and 16th centuries but succeeded only in the East (Schultz 1972: 164; Sreenivasan 2001: 45).

Natural conditions, the independence of European agriculture from large irrigation projects, the richly available natural resources on the 'commons', grass in meadows which did not need special attention by a property owner, as well as forests were available all over the northern plains of Europe, to the difference of the semi-arid areas of Africa and Asia in which most of the other tributary modes of production were located.

Detailed local studies on particular regions show that peasants may have been more powerful where their special effort was required, for example, in land improvement[41] or where cities were close where they could migrate to and establish themselves.[42] This may have led, however, in some places to less favourable deals because lords were ready to use more power. The Hungarian struggle between lords and peasants over the right to sell the (high income) product wine is an example.[43]

Limited possibility to draw on external resources for repression available to the lords is often quoted in order to explain greater reliance of the lords on agreements with the peasantries on rates of exploitation.[44] In a well-established tributary mode of production, the state gets most of the surplus of agriculture and land tax and pays the members of the (relatively centralised) ruling class on the basis of office. The local representative of the ruling class has no individual interest in the long-term development of agricultural productivity. Such offices were scarce in Europe until the advent of absolutism.[45] European research on feudalism had, therefore, underlined the interest of feudal lords in improving the productivity of their territories by associating their peasants in investment-related work through sharing the benefits.[46] There are many examples, but the relevance of the argument is limited: Research on Asian hydraulic societies can show that it was much less Wittfogel's[47] despotic state but the locally powerful and locally entrenched landholding families who realised these improvements.[48] The argument of a 'localisation' of the European feudal nobility which distinguishes it from other tributary modes of production had been proposed by Engels. Marx's co-author insisted on the fact that the European nobles adopted the language of their peasantries to the difference of the Asian ruling classes, because they were more dependent on them (Engels 1884: 395).

A Special Political Process? Fragmentation Versus Centralisation

Political scientists and historians without politico-economic leanings have drawn on European constitutional struggles in order to explain the singularity of the European tributary mode of production.[49] These are authors who argue on the basis of a certain reading of the work of Max Weber. Anglo-Saxon political science refers to Max Weber often without understanding that he presented a politico-economic and not just a political or sociological denial of the link between economics and politics as he tried to reject Marx.[50] They have taken for granted the view of the European nobility that Europe lacked a despotic state because of its cultural traditions, an argument which has become the scapegoat of the anti-Orientalists.[51] It certainly cannot be denied that the nobilities in Europe, often allying with other opponents to the royal power such as the cities, have struggled in order to limit the royal prerogative (Osiander 2007: 366). It is, however, not clear whether a ruling class composed of feuding gangs is more favourable to peasants than a centralised one. Also in Europe, the peasants identified good government with the maintenance of royal authority and misery with the periods of troubles,[52] just as in China.[53] In any case, neither in Europe[54] nor in Asia (Wright 1951: 257) peasants lacked the possibility of getting leaders from the ranks of the privileged strata. They could have their Robin Hoods if they rose in rebellion whether the ruling class was centralised or decentralised. Sects and secret societies in China were a powerful form of institutionalised opposition which compares favourably with highly temporary movements launched by the peasantries in Europe often in alliance with religious movements.[55]

Nevertheless in most cases these struggles led to power diffusion and increasing autonomy of other powers, like the estates and also the cities. The diffusion of power was facilitated by the fact that there were competing hierarchies with at least two apexes, the Emperor and the Pope[56] and, later, with the weakening of the Emperor's claim to universal monarchy, the rivalling kings which claimed to be sovereign.[57] There is, however, no evidence of an empowerment of the peasantry through the achievements in the struggle for political representation and limitation of the absolute power on the crowns. Peasant preservation had been a policy of Tudor absolutism (Hill 1967: 52; Tawney 1912: 289). The role of parliament in the enclosure movement of the 18th century seems not to have been clearly pro-peasant (Bogart & Richardson 2009; Shaw-Taylor 2001: 124).

However, these struggles within the ruling classes further increased the autonomy of local bodies and city governments which initially did not differ between Europe[58] and Asia[59] in the association between the representatives of the trades (craftsmen) and the representative of the central power who had the last say. But if there was no central power, cities could become independent, elect their own leaders, in Italy the podestà, even form alliances against their overlords (in Italy and in Germany; Berthold 1982: 204; Blok 1972: 118) and defend their claims (rights in their views). In Germany and Italy, two major areas of old Europe, they could exploit rivalries between the Pope and the Emperor as well as between other more powerful lords.[60] Conflicts were, however, intense in Europe and in Asia. In Italy there were strong internal conflicts within the increasingly autonomous cities which were often manageable only by leaders from outside (Italian podestà; Kudrna 1990: 99), similar to the 'stranger' king (Henley 2004: 112) in early African and Asian state formation (Büttner 1964: 470). Despite the temporary disappearance of a secular central power in the western part of the (Old) Roman Empire, the Catholic church, despite having stepped into the power vacuum, had not been able to check the rise of new secular powers (Osiander 2007: 215). Western Europe did not become a Tibet.

With the exception of England, Italy and Germany,[61] regionally restricted central powers, that is, the kings of the different monarchies (Marx 1854: 440 f.), were able to reduce the claims of the intermediate powers' autonomy. They co-opted their leaders into a newly created homogenous block as in the East which collectively abolished further autonomy of the non-noble sector. The ideal of the most powerful part of the ruling class of

Europe were the more centralised tributary modes of production: Frederic II. (1212–1250) created a more centralised class in his kingdom of Sicily which depended on him in order to administer the central and richest part of his empire. He followed Arab rules of governance which he knew fairly well.[62]

One of the most intensive conflicts between the ruling classes of the Middle Ages, the conflict between the Emperor and the Pope on the nomination of the bishops with secular powers in the Empire was just the result of a miscalculated attempt to progress in the direction of more centralised and more bureaucratised tributary mode productions in Europe.[63] In order to curb the increasing powers of lower nobles, the German emperors handed over the richest part of the German kingdom to bureaucrats who could not have legitimate heirs, the bishops who had to practice celibacy. These were the archbishoprics of Cologne, Mayence and Trier, on the Rhine, but also at the most important strategic positions on the eastern boundary, Magdeburg and Meissen. The German kings could not imagine that by disempowering the local grandees such as dukes (tribal leaders), they would create a much more dangerous challenger to their central power, the ecclesiastical hierarchy headed by the Pope.

The secular lords got disempowered by the construction and development of the European monarchies and the gradual uniformisation of the territories the dynasties had grabbed and assembled in their composite monarchies (Elliot 1992: 58). The French kings indeed were disempowering their estates not only at the national level but also in the major part of their provinces as described in the standard narrative on the origins of the French Revolution (Egret 1962: 306). For the most modern thinkers of economic development in 18th-century Europe, the physiocrats, China and its well-ordered government was the example to follow (Demel 2001: 36 ff.). Because of the preference of the European monarchies for centralised bureaucracies, the aristocratic reaction denounced Asia as despotic (Craeybeckx 1970: 55 f.; Jonas 1982: 153).

On the other side of the claimed radical difference between Europe and Asia, the centralised character of the Asian tributary modes of production as transmitted in the writings inspired by the aristocratic reaction in Europe was just a fiction. The Mughal Empire was composed by units directed by local lords with differing degrees of autonomy. Some considered themselves as independent with obligations to pay tribute; others had to hand over parts of their tax incomes in order to be granted some shares of it by the Mughal emperor.[64] In China, regions also coexisted with direct administration by 'bureaucrats' appointed by the centre and others administered by local lords. These differences in status caused conflicts quite similar to conflicts in Europe over the respect of hereditary rights of the local lords in their fiefs (Bello 2005; Huang 2008). The Islamic distinction between the directly administered *bilad al-sultan* and the indirectly 'administered', in reality often only influenced *bilad al-sibah* is just an illustration of the fragmented centralisation of the non-European tributary modes of production from another cultural area (Lacoste 1973: 49; Nouschi 2005: 421).

The opposition between 'Asian' centralisation and 'European' feudalisation is an issue of degree of centralisation but not an issue of essence. Any ruling class which is not permanently revocable or constrained in its privileges by property rights in well-defined assets will permanently be characterised by the struggle of its centre to monopolise its resources against its 'periphery' which is, however, powerful because the centre cannot do without it. The centre can exercise its power only by relying on a periphery which by the very process of governance acquires some veto power. The literature on state formation in India confirms this perspective of some lords becoming powerful enough to impose their will on others, to complement local gods by their own ones and to integrate local gods and their temples into overarching areopagusses which support the legitimacy of their claims to overlordship in the other world.[65]

Cultural Specificity

The limited relevance of the centralisation/feudalisation issue will also shed light on the contribution of Max Weber with his insistence on cultural factors in the pattern of behaviour of social classes. Weber has two arguments:[66] The rationality of bureaucrats assures the efficient use of the surplus and the frugality in the lifestyles of lower levels of the privileged, the bourgeoisie, limits waste and reserves the surplus for investment. Rationalisation of the bureaucratic command and information systems has been an objective of all rulers of tributary modes of production. Work done by local historians in command of the local official languages shows us that the difference between Western and Oriental bureaucracy is less great than assumed by the Weberians: These 'pre-modern' courts kept files (Jordan 2006: 577 f.; Tyagi 2010: 167 f.). The theory of the dynastic cycle argues that such rationalisation occurs during the more centralised periods of the tributary structures. It does not coincide with increased autonomy of local producers on the basis of expanding markets in periods of feudalisation.[67]

The frugality of the bourgeoisie is underlined by Weber in order to explain why, for the first time in history, a ruling class did not waste surplus but used it productively for investment. This pattern of explanation loses considerably in importance if capitalism does not require an investment effort of the type described as previous or primary accumulation. The argument would hold only if capitalism had to be explained along the lines of a pre-capitalist inefficient estate holder. If any new investment reduces unit costs there is no need for an explanation based on an effort for additional saving considered as constitutive for the transition to capitalism.

The option of investing instead of spending on luxuries can be explained by the strategies of financially and politically weaker elements in opposition to the strategies of the lords. Climbers try to get hold of assets which help them to improve their relative position in relation to others. They strive for prestige, financial resources and power, and opt for an optimal mix between these varieties of assets or, in Bourdieu's words, capital types (Bourdieu 1991: 94; Ouaissa 2004: 45 f.). They privilege assets which allow getting hold of additional assets later on. In case of success of the lower income strata to increase their own consumption, investment in productive capacities, in our pole of popular industry, always yields incomes, as the consumers of mass consumption goods cannot 'eat' the investment goods. There is no such inbuilt safeguard for incomes earned on the basis of power and prestige. The weaker holders of financial assets will be disadvantaged in the struggle for incomes on the basis of power and prestige because with respect to these assets the concentrated access is decisive. A holder of some power or some prestige will always lose to more powerful and more prestigious holders of power. The more powerful and prestigious ones can deprive the weaker holders of such categories of assets from gaining access to surplus, not so different from a pop star in relation to less performing singers as a category of producers of prestige goods in the actual price formation for pop stars (Bourg 2008: 377). In both cases the winner takes all.

When there are expanding large markets which can be supplied only on the basis of expanding productive capacities which can emerge only through additional investment, an investor with state-of-the-art technology is sure to make money even without power and prestige. If demand exceeds the capacity of production of the leader of the industry, the smaller enterprises still can accumulate.

In capitalist market economies based on mass consumption the common man is relatively safe even as an investor to the difference of the powerful who depends on prestige and 'delight'. Provided that the subalterns can increase their consumption, investment in productive equipment for mass consumption goods is safe. If the subalterns succeed in reducing the surplus appropriated through power and prestige by their increasing mass consumption, this shift to productive investment becomes not only the safest, but ultimately the only means of access to surplus. In case of insufficient capacities of production, prices rise and entrepreneurs achieve so high yields that they are able to finance the costs of additional or new (newcomers) investment. It is probable that those who aspire to surplus but have only smaller amounts of resources will turn more rapidly to this type of use of their resources. As they will be more successful, they will be able to disempower less productive holders of resources who try to base their claims on power and prestige. As long as mass consumption increases and markets are maintained in competition, the strategy of investing in technology and equipment is superior to any other use of surplus. Obviously, the patterns of behaviour of those who thrive by following this strategy will be upheld by this group and, in parallel with their rise in the socio-economic and political system, gain influence.

Those who do not follow the pattern of privileging the priority of market-oriented technical efficiency of investment but continue to follow the prestige of conspicuous consumption try to complement their resources by borrowing money. They risk becoming indebted and going bankrupt. Therefore, they try to deprive the holders of productive assets by initiating political regulations (= the constitutional struggles on taxation between the forces of the tributary modes of production and the holders of private assets). If they do not prevail politically, they are ultimately kept from further access to surplus. Among those who have low resources, the non-innovative ones are the first who will early on be eliminated as failures. If they happen to have inherited larger amounts of resources, they lose more slowly, generation after generation, being not sufficiently modern, or they themselves become entrepreneurs, as did large parts of the English[68] and Prussian aristocracies (Küttler 1985: 246).

There no need for a specific cultural heritage in order to explain the shift to capitalism. No process of cultural change generated by cultural mechanisms has to be conceived to explain the impact on behavioural patterns of the mechanisms triggered off by rising mass incomes and rising mass consumption.

The issue whether European absolutism was the highest form of feudalism or, instead, a stage in the transition to capitalism[69] can be resolved on the basis of the different patterns and conditions for access to surplus. Access to surplus on the basis of power is facilitated on the basis of relatively more power. Access to surplus on the basis of productive efficiency does not require concentration of assets as shown by the permanent emergence of new waves of small and medium enterprises especially in connection with the discovery of new technologies (Mantoux 1905: 39). If the growth of a pole of popular industry reduces the surplus available for the holders of power and prestige, there are two possibilities: Those among them who hold more concentrated power succeed in further concentrating the power. They will then centralise the class of power holders and develop a more centralised tributary structure: This structure was called in Europe 'absolutism'. If they fail in this attempt they have to give up their predominant role to those in control of productive equipment: This was called in Europe 'the bourgeois revolution'.

It has often been shown that the owners of assets which yield surplus through markets tried to convert their market-based surplus yielding assets into political power through monopoly and purchase of office[70] and land[71] (especially assets acquired through long-distance trade). Especially the struggles between small businesses and large monopolistic trading companies during the English bourgeois revolution (Brenner 1973: 55; Croft 1975: 25 f.) show that this tendency to transform commercial profit into monopoly earnings was counteracted primarily by the rise of new strata of market-oriented entrepreneurs. They were capable of caring for new mass needs by developing new products and became prosperous by being successful on the market.

Absolutism, that is, the return to more efficient forms of politically based patterns of surplus appropriation and the bourgeois revolution of the removal of politically based surplus appropriation are equally forms of dealing with the incipient growth of a pole of popular industry.

The return to more efficient forms of politically based surplus appropriation can also occur at the end of any other form of a temporary weakening of a tributary socio-economic structure. Its emergence under the specific circumstances in Europe during the 16th–18th centuries shows, however, that even an incipient form of growth of a popular role of an industry in periods described by Goldstone as efflorescence triggers off the vitality of tributary socio-economic structures. In most European countries which experienced Goldstone's efflorescence the ultimate outcome was absolutism, also in the benign form of enlightened absolutism which was accepted by many of those ideologically or culturally close to the aspirations of the rising bourgeoisie. This renders doubtful the claim of a specificity of the European culture.[72]

The well-documented tendencies of autonomy turning into restrictions against market-oriented petty producers with even city governments being captured by the patricians against plebeians (Italy, Germany) show that political autonomy may well lead only to more oligarchy but not to more openness to capitalist development (Berthold 1977: 167 f., 1982: 220). The rise of capitalism took place in the most institutionalised form of oligarchical government,[73] England. This is a demonstration that decentralisation and oligarchic government may just not have been more than a weak obstacle to capitalist development. There has been never a demonstration of how the empowerment of oligarchs through suffrage for minorities could lead to the empowerment of labour on the labour markets. As well, it cannot be shown how the empowerment through elections with the suffrage only of minorities created empowerment of labour in its dealings with employers. What can be observed is that labour was able to impose the extension of suffrage after it was already empowered on the labour market, first in the United States[74] then in Britain (lately; Engerman & Sokoloff 2005; Green 1961: 6 f.). Labour used this newly acquired power to decisively restrict the freedom of the contracting parties in defining labour contracts to the benefit of the weaker part, labour (10 hours day, safety regulations: Social policies are largely implemented through restrictions for labour contracts; Marx 1867: 312).

The growth of capitalism precedes the political empowerment of labour. Empowerment of labour has, therefore, other origins. They lie in the demand for labour by the growth of a pole of popular industry. This pole of popular industry in turn could base its growth on large and expanding often rural markets, the growth of an urban market constituted by urban lower income strata, and also by external markets. The emergence of capitalism may then be tracked to the vitality of a pole of popular industry. For the first time in history the process of better mastery of nature, technical progress, could not be exclusively captured by a ruling class with its innate tendencies to consume better and more luxuries but had to accept growing rural and urban mass consumption.

The only possible explanation is the incapacity of the European ruling class to establish and then to centralise tributary modes of production as had occurred in all other societies. This failure is due to the incapacity of some parts of the European ruling classes to overcome their internal difficulties in centralising themselves with sufficient speed so that the pole of popular industry could not be suffocated in time.

Many factors, those I have already mentioned and others currently proposed in literature to support the argument of a European distinctiveness, may have rendered the process of concentration of power in Europe more difficult. Their simultaneous existence may have constituted especially difficult challenges for the ruling classes. The population decrease during the great plague created possibilities of peasant resistance[75] (but did not help in Italy); Christianity allowed peasants to consider themselves to be ritually equal to the nobles, but all tributary modes of production had their axial periods:[76] Buddhism[77] but also reformed Hinduism[78] claimed equality of all human beings before God against the areopaguses of Gods' tributary ruling classes normally developed in order to fight against the egalitarian natural religion of the communitarian socio-economic structures.[79] Islam and Judaism share with Christianity the view of the equality of all human beings before God.

Other aspects can be mentioned. Some authors maintain that there are special patterns of gender relations with females being more independent in Europe than elsewhere.[80] Marriages were based less on family alliances so that women were freer. Although the mechanisms of mediation between the resulting family structures and the capacity of the subalterns to impose higher incomes and to direct the employment of factors of production to higher degrees of satisfaction of their needs are difficult to establish, I feel sympathy with such views. Such greater cohesion and autonomy of the nuclear households may explain the unruliness of the subalterns in parts of Europe as an essential condition for their capacity to stand up in social struggles (MacFarlane 1978a: 163, 1978b: 268).

The European case is said also to be characterised by the high degree of institutionalisation of property rights. The role of trade in Greece led to the commercialisation of land in the extended city precincts.[81] Rome's expansion was characterised by the sharing of the conquered territories among its ruling class which, at least in the western part of the Empire, created large estates (Sarris 2006; Wickham 2005: 57 ff.). In very varied forms Medieval Europe inherited aspects of these property rights and married them to the high importance of family in less differentiated immigrating populations (Hintze 1962: 89). Inheritance by direct descendents became dominant which even limited the freedom of those who had something to bequeath (with limits also to the right to adopt). Such structures may have favoured the establishment of property rights against the discretionary powers of lords. The struggle for hereditary rights in feudal fiefs seems, however, not to have been greatly influenced by abstract principles of property rights. Lower lords had to fight for hereditary rights as they did in Asian tributary modes of production. Also in Asia the discretionary power of the central authority, so often highlighted in the comments on the opposition between the European feudalism and Asian centralisation, has only rarely been really exercised.[82] The right of peasants to the use of land seems, however, not to have been stronger under feudalism in Europe than in Asia. Not Asian, but European history is full of reports on the struggle of peasants to keep the rights of use in their lands (Buszello 1984: 48; Korn 1873: 23).

I propose, therefore, that there are no specific traits in Europe's tributary structures, European social organisation, European political arrangements within the class of lords or European culture which cannot be found in other tributary modes of production or which have not been at least periodically put into question also in Europe. Neither of these traits can explain the rise of a pole of popular industry in Europe which triggered off the massive use of equipment a class of entrepreneurs could own and use as an instrument of further access to surplus provided that this surplus was spent on more investment goods production.

This corresponds to the argument about the accidental character of capitalism even if there may have been enabling circumstances and mechanisms which can be quoted as favourable to the emergence of capitalism. Probably, other elements which are unknown to me can be added. For example, the technical possibilities of using machines for increasing production had to exist. Such possibilities were linked to an orientation of increased technical knowledge to mechanics as a precondition of the combination of non-human energy, motion of tools and repetitive operations, all of which are not privileged by all forms of improved technical knowledge (Bekar & Lipsey 2004: 710). If there are no costly instruments for improving the efficiency of work they cannot be bought and cannot serve as the basis for future incomes.

But the decisive factor was the emergence of a relationship between the subalterns and the overarching socio-economic structure, in which the subalterns were able to impose rising mass incomes. Rising mass incomes made investment in such machinery rewarding for the owners of machinery to such a large degree that a class could emerge which reproduced itself as the bourgeoisie on the basis of the ownership of such means of production without political ad-hocist state protection, because the simple disposal over such means of production created safe income opportunities. The very reproduction of these means of production created empowerment of labour via employment, hence a powerful working class.

This has an important implication. All those factors mentioned can be classified as enabling. No one is causal in itself. Consequently, there is no explanation of the emergence of capitalism by any of these factors beyond the argument that capitalism needs the empowerment of labour, which under very specific conditions becomes possible within tributary modes of production. This implies that capitalism can emerge where labour is empowered. In England as the special case, in tributary modes of production with weak centralisation, but also today when export opportunities create scarcity of labour because of massive external demand (South Korea, Taiwan, but also China), capitalism can go with the most diverse inheritances. Some pre-existing factors may come into play that may render the transition easier because they are favouring labour. They are, however, not causal.

The patterns of transition are, hence, varied. The British case is characterised by a combination of the extension of the internal market and increasing exports of simple manufactured goods (Esteban 1997: 879; O'Brien 1985: 774 f.). In the Northwestern part of continental Europe, the massive demand for labour through the railway revolution played an important role.[83] In the settler societies of North America and Oceania, the open frontier contributed by absorbing labour directly and by rendering labour scarce in the already settled areas.[84] In Japan, the ruling class transformed feudal dues into a monetary land tax which subsequently was devalorised because of inflation in the wake of excessive state financing of investment in industries and infrastructures, and this increased the real income of the agriculturalists (Grabowski 1994: 443; Hayami 1972: 29).

The variety of the enabling structures implies that the adaptation of tributary socio-economic structures to requirements created by a dynamic capitalist centre may allow the transition to capitalism. Two mechanisms transmit such requirements. The growth of productivity in the capitalist centre changes comparative advantages of the leading economies and, hence, also comparative advantage of all others. Increasing productivity in the capitalist economy creates new opportunities for ruling classes of capitalist economies in their dealings with ruling classes of non-capitalist economies which lose also in relative military power. The ruling classes of non-capitalist economies have to face these new challenges by doing something to maintain their own power bases. One aspect of this is the necessity to combine such efforts with efforts to avoid general revolt in their own societies, hence proceed to reforms.

Notes and References

1. Dalton 1967: 73; Graf 1973: 110; Suret-Canale 1964: 27.
2. Benz & Wächtler 2006: 479 f.; Boehm 1993; Dème 1966: 19; Dugast 1995: 431; Karlström 2004: 595; Oki 1984: 281.

Stratification Without Transition to Capitalism 55

3. Aaby 1978: 34; Dossogne 2007; Hindess 1975: 67; Meillassoux 1964: 217; Tignor 1972: 288; Lancaster 1974; Willame 1973: 352.
4. Alagoa 1971: 274; Augé 1978: 395; Coquery-Vidrovitch 1981: 439; Diallo 1994: 366; Ki-Zerbo 1978: 176; Meillassoux 1964: 59; Schade 1986: 78; Soret 1965.
5. Chandra 1982: 458; Lentz 1998: 639; Moreland 1987: 451; Savonnet 1980: 42.
6. Berghe 1983: 225; Dittmer 1967: 327; Lombard 1967: 73; Schlenther 1961; Strickland 1976: 376.
7. Godelier 1978: 767; Håkansson 1998: 275; Hallett 1970: 268; Mair 1977: 78; Suret-Canale 1964: 31.
8. Breysig 1955: 380; Olivier 1966: 372; Posnansky 1968: 1; Schoenbrun 1993; Thibon 1989; Turton 1975: 536; Wolf 1982: 42.
9. Anthony 1986: 302; Fisher 1972: 385; Ki-Zerbo 1978: 98 ff; Law 1975: 1.
10. Goody 1963: 8; Hill 1984; Rounds 1979: 75; Southall 1988; Stein 1985.
11. Anderson 1971: 24; Benz & Wächtler 2006: 475; Gilman 1981: 7.
12. Igbafe 1975: 409; Safari 1972: 44; Suret-Canale 1964: 34.
13. Brara 1994: esp. 208 illustrates this permanent conflict in the marriage relations between superior and inferior princes.
14. Dodgen 1999: 816; Kennedy 1976: 3; Kulke 1997: 244 f.; Nath 2007: 31; Sinha 1997: 332.
15. Jaspers 1948, 1974. Cf. also Alam 1979: 213; Bonner 2005; Contursi 1989: 451; Fusé 1982: 109; Gohain 2010: 41; Prasad 2009: 73.
16. Clauss 1986. Cf. on similar orientation to popular mysticism as political resistance in Egypt Haarmann 1978: 381.
17. Diener & Robkin 1978: 505; Gunasekaran 2007: 103; Hall 1985: 201; Hamm 1964: 43; Srinivas 2003: 458; Thapar 1979: 187; White 2006.
18. Cf. the literature in Chapter 2, note 17, and Njammasch 1978.
19. Oxfeld 2004: 965; Steininger 1962: 163; Ufen 2001: 181.
20. David 2006: 1294; Dodgen 1999: 816; Ebrey 1984; Gossaert 2010: 1005; Pomeranz 2007: 28.
21. Ahmed 2005b: 43; Fairbank 1956; Kim 2007: 1018; Moore 1966: 457; Mukhia 1997: 130 f.; Perdue 1986: 198; similar observations in the Arab world: Zubaida 1972: 329.
22. Indeed we observe such very diverse forms of self-organisation already in the less stratified structure of Subsharan Africa, cf. Anquetil 1973: 9; Brandewie 1971: 205; Diop 1998: 94; Iliffe 1984: 43; Kawada 1977: 145; Ubah 1987: 134.
23. Bentley 1998: 247; Critical Inomata 2001: 331; Habib 1980: 37 ff.; Lin 1995: 279.
24. Çizakça 1980: 145; Karwal 1966: 395; Liu 1988: 37; Pamuk 2000: 106; Roy 2008.
25. Gadgil 1971: 45; Habib 1995: 221; Roy 2008: 100.

26. Salt as an early gate for tax collecting: Cartier 1973; Danielewski 1993: 81; Hsu 1965: 369; Lovejoy 1986: 163, 250; Thiemer-Sachse 1987.
27. Brown & Goodman 1980: 76; Chorley 2003: 509; Goldthwaite 2003: 527.
28. Munro 1991: 134; Vries & Woude 1997: 289; Wee 1975: 209.
29. Cameron 1963: 328; Kindleberger 1982; Roehl 1976: 258; Nef 1958: 139; Stürmer 1979: 496.
30. Allen 2009: 903; Berg 2004: 130 ff; Chorley 2003: 509 f.; Thirsk 1978.
31. And which were oriented to luxuries and military products, cf. Eltis 1988: 278; Henderson 1984: 591.
32. Brasseul 2004: 943; Hilton 1978: 18; Jones 1968: 61; Pollard 1964: 530; Stobart 2004. On Germany: Barkhausen 1958: 235.
33. Commander 1983; Guha 2004: 83; Washbrook 1988: 63.
34. Deron 2007: 17; Sédov 1968: 84; Thion 1973: 37.
35. Crafts & Ireland 1976: 623; Howell 1975: 476; Huzel 1969: 451; Wrigley 1966: esp. 85.
36. Chaunu 1972: 17 f.; Dupâquier & Lachivier 1969: 1402; Elsenhans 2007a: 218 f.
37. Cunningham 1990: 115; Mendels 1972: 252; Rosenplänter 2000: 321.
38. Milonakis 1995: 345. Further: Bailey 1998; Hilton 1949: 135; Kosminsky 1955: 33; Schlauch 1940: 421.
39. Blum 1957: 822; Chirot 1974: 69; Kaak 2007: 73; Korn 1873: esp. 17 ff.; Millward 1982: 547; Sundhausen 1983: 562.
40. Abraham 1971: 714; Bosl 1961: 139; Harnisch 1979: 357; Pirenne 1951: 220–227.
41. Dekker 1975: 27. Further: Bavel 2001: 3 ff.; Brenner 2001: 229; Vries & Woude 1997: 345 ff.
42. Epperlein 1962: 71 ff.; Kluge 2007: 128; Sweezy 1976: 44, shows severe limitations to this option of the rurals.
43. Malowist 1966: 27; Pach 1966: 142 f., 1968: 644.
44. Becker & Gehrisch 1977: 1377; Gericke 1966: 929; Laibman 1984: 275
45. Not only in Germany had the feudal rulers turned to the clergy for administering their territories, without having to concede autonomy to other feudal princes. Bloch 1961: 402; Thompson 1993: 55.
46. Hall 1985: 218. Further: Beech 1998: 27; Jones 1981: 91; Lachmann 1985: 360; Morillo 2003: 545.
47. Wittfogel 1931: 411, 1932: 590–596. The early Wittfogel is less militant in his critique of state-organised economies than Wittfogel 1957: 177–188.
48. The earliest comprehensive critique of the mechanism of irrigation leading to and being the basis of state building in pre-capitalist societies is Price 1971: esp. 27. Further, Hauser-Schäublin 2003: 167 f.; Leach 1959: 5; Ludden 1979: 357; Olds & Liu 2000: 417.
49. Facchini 2008: 78; Otayek 1997: 819. Counterfactual argument in: Mo 1995: 101.

Stratification Without Transition to Capitalism 57

50. On the Anglo-saxon misunderstanding of Weber, cf. Ghosh 1994: 105; Kantowsky 1981, 1985.
51. Ali 1997: 271 f.; Guha 1994; Husain 1980: 27.
52. Angermeier 1966: 336; Markoff 1975: 498; Tillotson 1974: 15.
53. Brentjes 1973: 282; Dardess 1970: 541; Mousnier 1967: 194.
54. Alavi 1965: 256; Kiernan 1971: 10; Moore 1966: 479; Mousnier 1967: 327.
55. To mention just a few: the Hussites in 15th century Czechia or the German peasant war 1525–1526, cf. Saberwal 1991: 121; Töpfer 1982; Vaubel 2005: 190.
56. Chesneaux 1972. Further, Bari 1995: 133; Scott 1977: 239; Smith 1969: 149.
57. Landes 2006: 7; Nolte 1996: 34; Teschke 2005: 592.
58. Gottlieb 1984: 18; Mumenthaler 1998: 46; Pellicani 1987: 61.
59. Bowden 2007: 1367; Eickelman 1974: 274; Ertl 2006: 21; Hatejar 2003: 127 f.; Lakshmi 1979: 26; Lapidus 1969: 73; Paskaleva 1982: 55. Dissenting, Mardin 1969: 265.
60. Bindseil & Pfeil 1999; Werner 1987; Zanden 2000: 14 ff.
61. Benadusi 1995: 158; Langer 1979: 370; Osiander 2001: 278.
62. Kantorowicz 1963: 177. Further: 506 f.; Abulafia 1988: esp. 44 f.; Ahmed 1975: 63; Hentsch 1986: 529; Jacoby 1984: 40; Lieberman 1997; Maschke 1966: 303; Thoran 1999: 621.
63. Boshof 1987: 87; Powis 1983: 513; Saberwal 1991: 121.
64. Alam & Subrahmanyam 1994: 193; Barendse 2000: 110; Bayly 1984: 187; Brara 1994: 207.
65. Gommans 1998: 141; Inden 1981: 103; Kulke 1997: 244 f.; Nath 2007: 31; Sharma 2004: 413 f.; Sinha 1997: 332.
66. Trompetter 1982: 272; Vries & Woude 1997: 166 f.; Weber 1934: 84 f.
67. As Ibn Khaldûn 1967: 324, moral decay through luxury consumption and implicit exploitation.
68. Brenner 1977: 78; Dobb 1964: 45; Overton 1995: 52.
69. Anderson, P., 1974: 34–40; Lublinskaya 1972: 90; Parker 1990: 297.
70. Ash 1999: 639; Blanquie 2004: 472; Gongora 1975: 439; Mardin 1969: 267.
71. Aurell 2000: 49; Hocquet 1979: 295; Holderness 1974: 974; Jones 1974: 176–179; Kamen 1984: 123; Leicher 1958: 159; Lublinskaya 1972: 66 f.
72. Ingrao 1998: 11; Mittenzwei 1980; Riley 2003: 199.
73. Brewer 1989; Buck 1964: 81; Harris 1993: 56; Klaveren 1958: 441 f.; Sayer 1992; Vries 2008: 37; Wellenreuther 1982.
74. Cox & Ingram 1992: 552; Phillips & Wetherell 1995: 417; Tholfson 1961: 228.
75. Ashtor 1970: 19; Biraben & LeGoff 1969: 1500; Bridbury 1973: 583, 1974: 551; Mieck 1994: 15.
76. 'When Adam dalf and Eve span who was thane an gentlemean' (preacher John Ball, around 1381), quoted in Dobson 1970: 376.

77. Lewis 1989: 51; Njammasch 1978: 123; Oommen 1984: 49; Thapar 1979: 193.
78. Chattopadhyaya 1997: 209; Dumont 1960: 57; Heuzé 2003: 105; Nadkarni 2003: 4787; Prasad 2009: 73.
79. Morris 2004: 732; Kristiansen & Larsson 2005: 984; Schmidt-Glintzer 2004: 158; Stöber 1965: 134.
80. Kreile 1993; Spengler 1968: 433; Zanden 2000: 19.
81. Kreissig 1969: 363; Morris 2004: 732; Meikins Wood 1990: 71 f.
82. Ali 1997: 272; Cosmo 2002: 220; Goldschmidt 1971: 1065; Husain 1980: 29.
83. Broadberry et al. 2008: 170; Fremdling 1977; Kocka 1990: 68.
84. Coelho & Shephard 1976: 221; Karabel 1979: 212 ff; Sombart 1906: esp. 136; Webb 1952: 57 ff.

3

Pre-capitalist Origins of Culture: The A-cultural Character of Capitalism and the Cultural Turn

In the creation of conditions favourable to the growth of a pole of popular industry the pre-eminence of the configuration of social power structures over behavioural patterns derived from culture, values and norms has a major meta-theoretical implication: The proposed modelling depends on the validity of the argument that capitalism is a-cultural. This is the old issue of 'realism', often in the form of 'economic reductionism', against 'idealism'. However, in my approach there is no simple choice between these patterns of explanation. The conception configured by idealism can only exist in the absence of dire scarcity as following values and norms require freedom from need. Such choices are available in those societies in which there is a plentiful surplus for those in control of the surplus. Here, culture can matter: Where there is scarcity the range of choices inevitably becomes narrower. Characteristic of capitalism is the phenomenon of 'artificial' scarcity: Those in control of surplus have the opportunity to produce 'artificial' scarcity via the desire resulting from their research into efficient technologies and new products which create new needs among consumers. The realm of choices is limited to the 'households' and individuals who are free to expend their rising incomes whichever way they deem fit. Returning to culture, this becomes simply one aspect in the area of their consumption. Culture is not required for maintaining social cohesion. Individuals will seek identity in cultural activity.

However, by arguing that capitalism, contrary to all other social systems is 'a-cultural', I do not pretend that there is no culture in capitalism. Indeed there is a lot. And even if large domains of culture have increasingly been subsumed under 'capitalist' logics of money-making, in principle culture has become liberated under capitalism, as culture is no longer an indispensable element for providing social cohesion. Capitalism does not need a sacred king for the superior unity of the social system. Where kingship has survived, is but an incidental additional element for crystallising feelings of identity, a function which also can be performed by a national football team. The concentration of cultural production on the individual as described by the theoreticians of the post-modern world[1] reflects this disconnection of culture from the main components of stabilisation of the social system.

I argue that capitalism is a-cultural because the economic system can be (but not necessarily is) capable of producing social actors who create the conditions for stability at the political and social levels within the economic system itself. They do so by privileging their selfish economic interests, even by ruthlessly pursuing these interests. This argument is not identical with the argument about the self-steering capacity of market economies. The actors may achieve the result by just acting individually on markets but may have, in addition, to influence the performance of markets by other means: in collective struggles for shaping the signals which are sent by markets to the participating actors.

I maintain, however, that all these 'additional factors' are complementary to the basic relation, rising mass incomes which create profitability of investment and scarcity of labour through higher employment. This implies that the most diverse patterns of embeddedness may go with capitalism:[2] Anglo-Saxon capitalism, Rhenish capitalism, corporatist structures of the Japanese style, but also dominant party systems from single party systems (China) to at least apparently more open dominant party systems. Some of such arrangements may be more compatible with specific forms of growth: Rhenish capitalism is said to be less innovative in totally new technologies than Anglo-Saxon capitalism. On the one hand, such environments are malleable, that is, they can compensate their shortcomings by gradual adaptation without converging with those systems which are temporarily more efficient.[3] On the other hand, patterns of growth and requirements for innovation change. These changes may render previously less adapted systems of embeddedness more appropriate. Totally differing systems may be appropriate equally to sustain catching up processes as shown by the parallel overtaking of Britain by the United States and Germany at the end of the 19th century.

Origins of Culture in the Constraints of Communities

The origins of culture are to be found in the necessity of communication for cooperation. The realm of community privileges children and relatives as we are sure that they react to us with understanding, fairness and reciprocity. When contacts increase, we will try to extend community, with reciprocity and understanding also to other relations. If communities become larger, the easy contact within primary communities becomes more difficult. Fairness and reciprocity as well as understanding are malleable concepts on which we enter into dialogue with others. Transaction costs rise. Even in our more complicated societies we tend to react to difficulties by establishing 'direct human contact'. When the customs officer catches us smuggling slightly more cigarettes than allowed, we try to win his understanding by presenting us in a way appropriate to trigger off his sympathy. Even more so, there are increasing interactions between separate communities. Communities are not societies with society-wide cleavages on which trans-community solidarities can be developed. Communities are comprehensive in their embedding of members and, hence, project on each other their parochial outlooks. This implies further dialogue as exemplified by the African palaver. The focus of anthropologists on reciprocity reflects the real importance of reciprocity in decentralised relations within communities.[4] In their relations with other external communities, these decentralised communities try to follow those rules to which they are accustomed from their internal relations. Reciprocity can be interpreted as the search for rules where neither anonymous markets with options for all players nor a centralised authority can establish rules of exchange (Davis 1996; Gregory 1975: 82). Reciprocity can, therefore, be interpreted as unstable: All players will favour a central authority whenever they expect that they can influence it in their favour (Benz 2006: 456; Zambrano 1998: 483).

It is very improbable that such dialogues can lead to universally accepted agreements which satisfy all participants to the same degree. Participants have, therefore, to decide up to which point they want to commit resources in order to prevail on which principles. They will take into account their own costs of voice and exit and compare them with the costs and intentions they suspect with their contenders. This will imply that they ultimately take into account their always uncertain perspectives of power. Therefore, stable hierarchies which reduce transaction costs but provide only second-best solutions in their eyes are preferred and accepted in the form of institutionalised arrangements. Under the coverage of an acceptable degree of solidarity and reciprocity, hierarchies develop (Benz & Gramsch 2006: 433; Gregory 1975: 82). These hierarchies are sanctified and integrated into the system of distinction and appear as legitimate in order to avoid further continued contest, discussion and conflict. More so, maintaining community with other communities implies the protection of communitarian rules of interaction against other communities. This requires that these principles are rendered into a hierarchy as not all of them can be imposed by one group on the other. The institution of a hierarchy is attempted and defended and leads to institutions based on relative power in order to defend more cherished institutions. The internal interaction, as well as interaction between communities, trigger off a process of reducing the costs of transaction. The reduction of transaction costs succeeds if stable hierarchies are mutually recognised as well as the legitimate exercise of power.

There is a basic difference between dialogue and market exchange which we can observe on any flea market: in exchange we do not need a common definition of the usefulness of the product. In dialogue, we try to find one and to discuss the definition of the partner. In market exchange, we buy elsewhere if we do not agree, in dialogue we do not. This does not imply that economic interests do not matter in communitarian interactions. Many of the rules for interactions are related to distributional issues. There is a complicated system of gradation for the exchange of benefits in reciprocal interactions within communities (how much juniors have to give to which seniors, how much seniors to other seniors depending on age, distinction, etc). But the argument implies that such economic interests have to be negotiated and defended within a framework of regulations established and justified on the basis of culturally agreed rules.

Communities appear to most Westerners as being characterised by solidarity and warmth. They are, therefore, admired. However, also in communities humans are forced to cooperate and, therefore, have to find mechanisms for distributing in a fair manner their efforts where exchanges do not concern easily comparable benefits: Forecasting the future may be very important for many members who are able only to make tools. The member who asks for a forecast can rarely address himself to suppliers outside the community who would be able to provide it more cheaply.

So within communities there are different degrees of monopoly which in principle would allow some of these monopolists to increase their price up to the level of the 'utility' of their service for a customer like an excellent doctor with superior healing capacities can do in our societies. This contradicts the claim to equality within the group and would create different possibilities for the group members to indulge in laziness. Communities, therefore, will regulate the value of such services by power. This is the origin of the 'just' price in any doctrine of moral economy.

Communities or larger groups which follow some communitarian principles will define what is fair within the framework of a worldview of valuation of behaviour and distinction justified on tradition. The whole literature on reciprocity tries to seize such structures and draws from them interpretations on the culture of such communities.[5] Communities, therefore, cannot do without culture.

At the level of the internal structure of communities and their relations to other communities, culture appears as a sphere which allows cooperation in those spheres where equal exchange determined by the opportunity cost of the service cannot be achieved by unlimited possibilities of choosing alternative suppliers.

The innate tendency of community to hierarchy and the incapacity of community to organise larger units on the basis of shared communitarian identities create the necessity of bringing communities together by means of political power on the basis of strengthening overarching and largely shared elements of culture. Here, communities are trying to project the communitarian principle of agreeing on rules to the outside by developing perspectives of a common culture. The projection of reciprocity in relation to others is an example. When communities fail to agree on such common principles with other communities, they can resort to purely commercial relations where differences in monopoly power and use values of their commodities determine the terms of trade or to the imposition of their 'moral' norms through naked power.

Extending the sphere of communitarian structures constitutes a safeguard against unforeseeable consequences of the resort to violence. The elites of structures based on communitarian rules which have grown into larger units such as tributary modes of production will favour the extension of their culture. This coincides with the interest of the dominant 'communities' of such a structure in increasing the productive base from which they can draw surplus. Empire building and the integration of local cultures (local gods) into overarching trans-local and trans-regional structures are complementary.[6]

Culture as an Instrument of Domination

An elite, a minority, can dominate a majority by having greater military means and institutions such as armies and bureaucrats. The concentration of naked power in the hands of a minority is, however, shaky, even if together with other arrangements such as the disarming of the mass of the population. In case of generalised escalation of conflict, the coherence of the hierarchically structured ruling minority suffers: Lower ranks and more peripheral leaders are always tempted to take sides with the revolting majority in order to establish their own minority power against the old apex of the power structure. Minority power consists in the minority's capacity to repress a fragmented majority by defeating some elements in originally limited regions (Mukhia 1997: 130 f.; Thapar 1979: 191) or in the capacity to isolate the more revolt-prone elements before these have been able to raise the whole majority in rebellion (Thapar 1979: 192; Zurndorfer 1983: 317): This is the old principle of 'divide et impera'. It implies that minority power is accepted at least in large parts of the empire. This requires legitimacy.

Non-capitalist structures require a mechanism of concentrating repressive resources. This mechanism is the political system. The political system comprises mechanisms of ensuring the participation of lower or peripheral elements which can command allegiance or docility. Local communities can be destroyed but in this case do not supply resources. The alternative consists in maintaining them through the creation of bridgeheads in their own structures and through their own leaders. The dominating political system co-opts within a framework of shared culture (David 2006: 1294; Dodgen 1999: 815 f.). Allegiance is embedded in a cultural system. The cultural system legitimises the political system and the mechanisms through which it mobilises the resources needed to maintain itself.[7]

At the economic level, political systems are based on the extraction of resources. There are varieties: Trade-based empires rely on the monopolistic control of scarce goods, the local communities cannot produce themselves.[8] Land-based agrarian empires rely on land taxes if sufficiently monetised.[9] If not, they would tend to rely on services transferred to the hierarchical apex—the example of European 'feudalism'.[10] Most really existing structures are mixes of both. In order to appropriate economic surplus other than profit, political means are necessary. With the exception of capitalism, economic interests are inevitably defended on the basis of a struggle over political power. Trade may be propelled by the market, as shown by trading cities surrounded by agriculturally rich areas. Trade can also be promoted by the politically powerful as shown by trading cities with rectangular streets which are observed in the Indus valley but also in Yoruba kingdoms (Mabbett 1977: 145; Ratnagar 2004: 46 f.)

In such a scenario, local culture can be respected provided that it lends itself to the process of integration via bridgehead building within the framework of an overarching value system which legitimises the power of the centre. Therefore, non-capitalist empires can go with cultural diversity provided that the 'local gods' are not normally utilised for challenging the legitimacy of the centre. There is no need of a uniform collective identity, but only for ritual supremacy of the representatives of the centre. The notion of a nation, a homogeneous body politic which comprises of all members of the Empire, is not necessary.[11]

Some of these tributary structures have organised the political system by creating a centralised bureaucracy. Even then they have tolerated local leaders, sub-kings, and most of them comprised areas of one or the other types even with varying degrees of autonomy of different ranks of sub-kings, the weakest among them being barely more autonomous than bureaucrats appointed by the centre.[12]

There is no doubt that the contents of those worldviews which create legitimacy can influence social structures. Ibn Khaldûn's açabiya (1967: 55) of the tribesmen was a permanent challenge to the centre. The notion of the mandate of heaven of the son of heaven was the basis of legitimacy which underpinned central power in China; it could serve as the basis of revolt if orderliness, protection and the basis of the biological reproduction of the majority were no longer guaranteed.

Thus, culture, politics and economics are interwoven and this interwovenness distinguishes non-capitalist from capitalist socio-economic structures.

The Liberation of Culture by Capitalism

In capitalism the 'mute constraints' (Baehr 2002; Marx 1867: 765) of economic relations make cultural and political systems much less important than in any other socio-economic system, even if there are of course political structures and cultural systems also in capitalism. The rise of capitalism is linked to the capacity of the economic system to create structures of exploitation and production, which force all its members to pursue primarily economic goals in the economic realm. They pursue these goals within an economic system which because of the reckless pursuit of economic goals of all its members maintains its stability and marginalises culture and politics as subservient systems for its own logic whenever culture and politics come in touch with economics. At the same time, the interaction of these systems is limited as the appropriation of profit does not require political intervention and political negotiation within worldviews based on culture.

Capitalism is, therefore, estranged from the realm of discussion which members of society in capitalism will still entertain in all those types of interaction which have nothing to do with economic exchange. There are obviously social and political spheres which are not under such direct influence of capitalism. International relations[13] with their focus on security and political intervention into the market mechanism is an example of the limited social dominance of capitalism outside the economic sphere, even if there are markets[14]. Not yet capitalist societies which interact with capitalist systems are another case as I demonstrated in my theory of the state-class-dominated bureaucratic development societies where I have insisted on the non-determination of the behaviour of state classes by economic interests.[15]

Capitalism is an economic organisation which allows a self-sustaining process of empowerment of labour on which in turn it depends. This relation is a frail equilibrium. Cultural factors then may contribute to the emergence and stabilisation of capitalism by strengthening and triggering-off mechanisms of empowering labour but it is not culture as such and probably also not the culture which capitalism generates which stabilise this equilibrium. This explains the failure to develop a uniform theory of the enabling characteristics of culture on the transition to capitalism as shown by the complete change in appreciation of the Buddhist factor on East Asian non-development and development in the last 70 years (Chan 1996: 44; Dirlik 1994: 51).

The Problems of the Cultural Turn

It is doubtful whether the literature which claims to promote a cultural turn in the last three decades takes into consideration the relation between culture and socio-economic systems. Instead of dealing with this link the cultural turn literature rejects the importance of the socio-economic bases of social structures, presents a revised idealism and opposes not only the North American version of realism in international relations theory but also realism in general in the theory of human action. It privileges the manifestations of high culture against the probably much more decisive mass cultures. It underestimates those secondary quasi-incidental expressions of mass culture such as anxieties and psychological suppression and ultimately concentrates on oppositions between rationalised worldviews in elite cultures which, in my view, are of minor importance for social analyses (for example, Huntington 1993: 45 f.). This was ultimately the consequence of a movement to access cultural phenomena as practised in the literature departments and its often close relatives which are contemporary history departments, both far removed from cultural sociology and anthropology. This was in my view an instrumentalisation of the importance of culture and crucially avoided socio-economic analysis with its requirement to comprehend political economy.

The theory of a clash of civilisations does not reflect the role of culture in the development of societies. It privileges a particular aspect, the instrumentalisation of worldviews by ruling classes in order to prevail in the class struggles in their societies.

The profile of culture which I describe here as pertinent for the relation between cultural phenomena and capitalism largely corresponds to a reduced role of culture in systems where the market allows to solve such problems as equal exchange (hence, the content of reciprocity) and fair price (the issue of moral economy). In all other domains, Asian and African cultures I became acquainted with in my field work were basically similar to the culture in which I had been brought up in Central Europe. The codes of communication were obviously very different, as well as the details of the worldviews they were based on, but the functions of these divergent codes were similar and the dynamics which resulted from their application turned out to be not too different. Where there were major differences, they were due not to different contents of culture but to different functions of culture. Where exchange values cannot be checked on the basis of anonymous markets, there are specific patterns of engaging communication. Situations such as the rejection of protest, discrimination against innovation, a lack of accuracy in communication and a lack of orientation among discourses about the perceived world in relation to the reality of this world—including the rejection of any type of systematic reference as to the appropriateness of one's own perception of the world of real things—served as instruments for achieving a common ground and those subjects about which communication could take place. In rent-dominated socio-economic settings the 'perceived' reality was the result of negotiations between the powerful. Truth in the rent-based societies is negotiated in order to preserve social relations by means of which reality is constituted and can be changed (Elsenhans 1987: 83 ff.; Phlix 2009: 14).

The difference between intensively culture-dominated non-capitalist socio-economic structures and a-cultural capitalism is not to be found in a greater homogeneity of capitalist cultures in comparison to non-capitalist ones. In both systems, producers of cultural products create items of beauty. Cultural items are launched like products for conspicuous consumption. Competition for audiences leads to product differentiation on the market for cultural products. Cultural items are valued because of their uniqueness.

Cultural items or values are appreciated because they impress. Some provoke positive reactions because they reflect orientations and feelings widely shared in the audience, others because they are provocative in relation to majority positions. Some reflect social and economic interests. There are, therefore, large variations and also cross-cultural identities. Princes in the 15th-century Italy probably did not read Machiavelli in order to follow the principles he suggested and Frederic II of Prussia read him, rejected him and behaved very much according to his principles (Meinecke 1963: 325 ff.). The 4th-century (BC) Kautiliya's Arthasastra (1987: esp. 556 ff.) was written in a totally different social setting of an ancient and centralised empire and was nevertheless so close to Machiavelli. Cultural items may reflect society, contradict it or sustain it: Many positions followed in the cultural realm have survived because minorities adopted them without their being socially influential.

The principles of product differentiation make different perceptions of one's own societies in relation to other societies and their cultures equally paying, so there is always a competition between those who assert uncompromisingly their own superiority and more universally oriented ones. Whether the more aggressive stances or the more conciliatory ones prevail in any given point of time or place depends on their instrumentalisation in the internal dynamics of the conflicts in the respective societies with a lot of mediations. Despite very strong racist exclusion and a past of slavery in the United States, it was not possible for the United States to achieve the national cohesion necessary for a world power without rejecting racism. The 15th-century Spanish society drew cohesion from the principle of racial solidarity (limpieza de sangre) against Jews and Muslims despite class solidarity between the Muslim, Jewish and Christian traders in the newly conquered cities of the Spanish South.[16] Germany opted for a racial definition of nationhood against the pro-French leanings in its Western marches with a rejection of Western political values but was assimilationist on its eastern border.[17] Czech nationalism succeeded in marrying pro-Western political orientation and an ethnic definition of nationhood (Boldt 2004: 18; Sugar 1969: 47). To the difference of the inclusivist definition of nationhood in the United States despite a racialist past, France with its universalist values in the official discourse consistently rejected equal citizenship for its (numerically not so large, especially during the Algerian war) colonial population (Dronne 2009: 252; Elsenhans 2010: 33). I agree, therefore, with Senghaas (1998: 189) that there is more conflict within civilisations than between them.

So also the notion of identity is absurd if it relates to collectivities: The multiple bases of nationhood have already been demonstrated by Renan (1996: 228 f.). In the realm of international relations, identity, therefore, cannot be more than an allegiance to a decision-making centre which in a world of states is territorially limited. States are privileged targets in the need for identity because they are beacons in the landscape for individuals who perceive states as a means to reduce transaction costs. In addition, states are identified with a set of legal rules which are parameters for the behaviour of all individuals who live together in a space defined by borders. The possibility of identity creation through the rejection of any specific identity is illustrated by a standard dictation for Indian school children where the glory of India is praised on the basis of the 'incredible diversity of cultures, religions, languages, etc., living peacefully together in the country'.[18] Compare this to the practice in Western Europe where immigrants have to prove allegiance on the basis of an arbitrarily selected canon of knowledge in history, culture and geography of a European 'province' in order to become eligible for citizenship.[19] One does not find in the constructivist literature on the emerging European identity any suggestion to grant European citizenship alternatively on the basis of the knowledge about European history, culture or the geography.

Cultural items play important roles in creating political identity when the market does not provide equality within 'national' societies. National societies become national, precisely, because labour is mobile and as such it can participate in the whole of the labour market, which is called national, because any labour belonging to this nation can participate without discrimination in relation to other labour of the same condition with respect to skills and economic characteristics. In cases where there are high levels of employment, all participants will interact on markets and consider the results as an illustration of equality in exchange. This perception follows from high levels of employment, and therefore, equality does not need to be negotiated or, that is, mediated through culture.

Identity is an aspect of the attempt to define oneself. Collective identities in the form of cultural identities serve the most different purposes. They have been instruments of social emancipation (Algerians against France,[20] Poles against Germans,[21] Czechs against Austrians[22]), but also instruments of justifying dominance as in the case of the minority sects and religions adopted by trader communities which wanted to maintain exclusiveness of their trade routes.[23] Identity formation is always linked to economic interests which have to be imposed in a struggle over market imperfections, either in a struggle against rentiers or in the service of rentiers as all studies of large conversion processes demonstrate (for example, the maintenance of Buddhism in those areas of India where elephants could not be used for conquest as in the upper valleys of the Himalayas or the Ganga delta[24]). Class is a limitational case as class is the least comprehensive type of collective identity. It addresses only economic interests and reflects, therefore, the liberation from community to society as conceived by Marx (1843: 388) in his argument about the disappearance of pre-capitalist fetters and by Tönnies's (1935: 40–48) distinction between community and society. A class, therefore, reflects the fact that in capitalism the sphere for not freely chosen cooperation is limited to the economic realm but even here regulated by mechanisms which exclude naked power. In capitalism, in the economic realm the rule at arm's length has to be respected. In all other spheres, like the satisfaction of cultural and religious needs we may cooperate with whomever we want to because the 'blossoming of thousands of flowers' does not disturb the reproduction of the whole and especially not the economic process. Liberation in all other spheres can become in capitalism an issue of individual perfection provided that labour is empowered on the labour market.

Hence, culture does not disappear with capitalism but the generalisation of capitalism with empowerment of labour delivers culture from the functions it performed together with its genuine purposes in pre-capitalist societies. In capitalism, culture can limit itself to these functions and satisfy our needs of beauty and understanding of the human condition, and finally of acquiring consciousness of ourselves.

The relevant problem of a cultural turn consists in the easing of this transition to freedom of culture by linking culture to the struggle for the embeddedness of capitalism in a society where labour is empowered, without having to own individually the means of production. Under perfect competition and where labour is empowered, the rules for the use of private property in the means of production are so restrictive that the private ownership of the means of production is just a veil for its real socialised character. Under the appearance of private property de facto socialisation of the means of production is imposed by competition in perfect markets. Joint control of means of production, for example, the German models of co-determination were appropriate for improving the relation between capital and labour, but could not fundamentally change the growth strategies of the companies under co-determination.

My impression is that, by neglecting the character of the link between culture and economic basis in different modes of production, the cultural turn in the literature risks a conception of capitalism which blocks it from contributing to the dissolution of pre-capitalist power-based socio-economic formations by weakening labour in its struggle for empowerment through a meaningful appropriation of capitalism. I share with others the fear that the rise of the non-governmental organisations (NGOs) at the global level, with their principled adherence to neoclassical economics[25] and their neglect of the question of power, ultimately contributes to the disempowerment of labour, whether the NGOs want this or not. The NGOs provide tools for a new wave of imperialism.[26] The parallel to the missionary societies which called for colonial intervention in order to suppress slavery in Africa in the late 19th century seems obvious, despite the good intentions in both cases.

Notes and References

1. Bogason 2001: 170; Davis & Robinson 1999; Hechter 2004: 412 f.
2. Albert 1991; Shonfield 1965. Further, Barton 1980: 18; DeWit 2009: 11; Gambarotto & Solari 2009; Jackson & Deeg 2008: 680; Panuescu 2004: 56; Rueda & Pontusson 2000: 373 ff.; Soskice 1999: 205.
3. Abelshauser 2001: 522; Cantwell 2000: 161; Faust 1993: 20; Kaiser 2008; Papadakis 1994.
4. Goodell 1985: 257; Mauss 1947: 129 f.; Mizuno 1976: 18.
5. This implies a multiplicity of possible diverging definitions which require negotiation, cf. Sethi & Somanathan 2003.
6. Bauer 1996: 334; Beattie 1964: 33; Hall 1981: 394 ff.; Hill 1984; Sharma 2004: 413 ff.
7. Dieterich 1982: 125; Ramaswamy 1985: 417; Sutton 2007: 15 f.; Szonyi 2007: 66; Talbot 1991: 332.
8. Beaujard 2005: 451; Evers 1987: 751; Heesterman 1989: 10; Liu 1988: 122; Ray 2006: 89; Wink 1988: 57.
9. Bayly 1988: 47; Mabbett 1977: 148; Morony 2004: 172; Wink 1988: 35.
10. Claessen 1984: 370; Demel 2001: 43; Kaviraj 2000: 144.

11. This excluded attempts to linguistically homogenize the subject population as shown by the diversity of languages practised (Dimitrov 2008: 42), but not the homogenisation of ritual practices, cf. Chapter 3, note 7.
12. Aydin & Özel 2006; Bello 2005; Brara 1994.
13. As I show later, the local cost of labour is only indirectly related to competitiveness because of being mediated by the exchange rate. So, many patterns of distributions can go with international competitiveness, cf. Chapter 5, note 3. This allows differences in the importance of private versus public consumption and also subsidies for not yet profitable exports in order to change comparative advantage, so that the state can play a positive role in shifting comparative advantage, Page 1991: 58; Stein 1994: 302.
14. Protectionism, state financed promotion of innovation in order to change comparative advantage. At the international level the process of homogenisation of productivities as described in Chapter 2 does not automatically work; appropriation of rents in order to increase incomes and to pursue industrial policies becomes possible.
15. I constantly stressed that influencing this process by arguments and, hence, from the cultural sphere was possible. The demonstration of the superiority of some strategies of reordering the economy in comparison to others could have a direct political influence with important economic consequences. My own contribution was considered as important enough to convince the Algerian planning ministry to invite me to show by an empirical analysis that its model of planning followed until then was unnecessarily state oriented and unnecessarily opposed against small-scale industry and the market and, therefore, inefficient in relation to a strategy of overcoming underdevelopment based on my own explanation of capitalism. Cf. Centre National d'Etudes et d'Analyses pour la Planification 1986: 31–36.
16. Bodian 1994: 57; Fayard & Gerbert 1982: 65; Walz 1995: 727; Zuñiga 1999: 428.
17. Chirot 1996: 11; Dann 1994: 60 f.; Lepsius 1985; Plessner 1959: 47, 68.
18. Class 4 dictation of an English medium school in Sikkim, India.
19. There are not many questions on Europe in comparison to the questions on Germany, 11 out of 310, in the test for German citizenship, cf. http://oet.bamf.de/pls/oetut/f?p=514:1:3427299612702767::NO (downloaded on 22th June 2011).
20. Abbas 1962: 314.
21. Noun 1998: 412 f.
22. Hroch 1996: 134; Koralka 1976: 132; Ther 2003: 164.
23. Abraham 1982: 1; Alagoa 1971: 277; Aslanian 2006: 393 ff.
24. Ahmed 2005a: 15 f.; Gohain 2010: 41; Omvedt 2003: 215.
25. Chatterjee 2008: 70; Hearn 2001: 47; Hoksbergen & Madrid 1997: 48; Levy 1995: 17 f.; Powell & Seddon 1997: 9; Shivji 2006: 44.
26. Hearn 1998; Kothari 1986: 2177; Petras 1997: 11.

4

The Nature of Capitalism

World system theory debates on the date of emergence of a world system. Frank (1993: 38) and others interpret the appearance of long-distance trade as proof for their view of a nearly perennial world system at least since the neolithical revolution. Wallerstein (1988b: 582) defends his 16th century as the incubation period of the capitalist world system. In my conception of the importance of a pole of popular industry for capitalism, we are just on the way of achieving a capitalist world system, without perhaps succeeding in establishing capitalism at the global level.

Indeed, the regionally only limited emergence of capitalist zones was linked to the expansion of capitalism into not yet capitalist areas but this did not necessarily create capitalism. The normal outcome of capitalist penetration in Africa, Asia or Latin America and even some European regions (East Central Europe) was underdevelopment. An only limited penetration of capitalism which resulted in underdevelopment triggered off reactions which tried to overcome underdevelopment by using rents for industrialisation. At best they created better conditions for the transition to capitalism but not capitalism itself.

Capitalism is expansionary but not contagious and the argument presented here rejects those theories which claim an inbuilt necessity of capitalism to expand in order to maintain itself by exploiting other structures or by using the absorptive capacity of non-capitalist markets. In these theories, capitalism is expected to transform non-capitalist structures into capitalist ones. Capitalism gets into crisis when there is no longer anything non-capitalist which can be transformed into a capitalist structure and, hence, be exploited for the maintenance and reproduction of capitalist structures.

Suppose, however, that capitalism is self-contained and in principle it produces the surplus necessary for its reproduction internally. Provided that labour is empowered, the markets for absorbing total production emerge inside capitalism. Nonetheless, it may be easier to cream off super profits or extra profits (in Marx's terminology) resulting from production in low-cost areas outside the geographic area where capitalism has developed. There may be still very rich untapped mineral deposits in non-capitalist areas when rich deposits near the traditional centres of industrial production are already exhausted. There may be comparative advantage which allows for the profitable sales of products manufactured under capitalism to those less advanced countries which are not yet capitalist. There may be cheaper labour outside capitalism which can be taught to produce manufactured goods for the markets in capitalist countries. All this appears to result from the search for profit. As capitalists need profit the search for profit, such as by the means just outlined, appears as a necessity for capitalism.

The fact that capitalism expands into non-capitalist areas does not, however, necessarily imply that capitalism needs such areas in order to reproduce itself. The fact that capitalism tends to expand into non-capitalist areas because of its inherently superior qualities does not imply that capitalism transforms these non-capitalist areas into capitalist ones in order to draw from them contributions for its own maintenance.

Capitalist expansion can be accidental, with capitalism being attracted into these areas without drawing substantial benefit from this expansion in terms of its own reproduction. There may even be substantial transfers from these areas to the capitalist centre, but they would be important for the reproduction of capitalism only if capitalism could not replace these additional resources by similar resources, surplus and markets, generated inside capitalism. The relativisation of the importance of a periphery for capitalism despite the instrumentalisation of any existing periphery through capitalism is not a purely theoretical issue. It is of the utmost practical importance. In theoretical formulations where the periphery is central for the reproduction of capitalism liberation movements can win only if they are capable of smashing the capitalist centre. The chances of liberation movements prevailing are much greater if capitalism can reproduce itself without any periphery. If capitalism can exist without reliance on the periphery, then capitalism will not transform the periphery into a capitalist economy. Liberation movements in the periphery may have their social bases outside the transformations that a capitalist centre may have imposed on them, as well as outside the capitalist 'counter forces' which capitalism is assumed to produce. The struggle of the periphery for emancipation has, therefore, a very weak link with the rise of capitalism and the creation of socialist counter forces in the periphery.

The Pre-capitalist Character of European Expansion

The development of capitalism in some limited regions of the world triggered off expansionary tendencies which were largely linked to previous pre-capitalist forms of expansion. They strengthened both non-capitalist structures as well as (at least in some places) poles of popular industry in contradictory manners.

The expansion of Europe has to be viewed in the perspective of then universally existing tendencies of expansion of tributary socio-economic structures. Recent research on tributary systems distinguishes between trading empires and agricultural empires (cf. Chapter 3, note 8) but confirms for both types the interests of the ruling classes in products of foreign origin to be consumed as luxuries for purposes of distinction (Liu 1988: 5, 115). In dealing with sub-Saharan Africa, Hufman and Coquery-Vidrovitch had early on insisted on the role of external trade and the control of the prestige goods it provided to the privileged for the transition from more egalitarian still largely communitarian socio-economic structures in a way of social differentiation to early forms of tributary socio-economic structures with state formation.[1] Such mechanisms have been shown later on also in operation in other regions.[2]

Trade is universal before capitalism. It would be difficult to explain the spread of Islam otherwise than on the basis of the control of the traditional trade routes of the ancient world and, therefore, by the search to monopolise 'profits' on long-distance routes and to protect these routes against outsiders. The same results would be achieved if the spread of Buddhism along the caravan routes from India to Central Asia and China or the sea routes from India across the Bay of Bengal and the South China Sea were more seriously investigated.[3] The European expansion to Asia and America was initially nothing else than the attempt to circumvent the routes controlled by the Muslim states of the Near and Middle East. This European trade expansion was organised and financed initially by the crowns. When it was handed over to private companies, these companies were closely associated to the crowns which granted protection and monopoly in exchange for incomes accruing to the crowns and members closely associated with the political centres of the states which supported them.[4]

There was an expansion of Europe in the 16th century, but this was not an outgrowth of capitalism nor had it been pushed by those regions of Europe which had been leading in the extension of market relations. It has been called capitalist later on by the protagonists of the paradigm of capitalism originating in external trade. They used it as a proof for their theory that external trade was the decisive motor for the growth of capitalism in Europe.[5]

Those who underlined the importance of the contribution of the periphery to the growth of capitalism through the easing of primary accumulation emphasised the plunder of the riches of Latin America in the form of the inflow of precious metals into Europe. Where the resulting price revolution (which also had other causes[6]) was the strongest, there was no Industrial Revolution (Spain, Portugal).[7] Those who benefited least from the incoming bullion had to earn bullion by other means than monopoly. They increased their exports, that is, had to mobilise additional labour in order to produce manufactured goods for exports to countries with easier access to this bullion. The imports from the newly discovered overseas countries did neither increase the availability of investment goods nor of mass consumption goods at least until the middle of the 18th century. Only then increasing shares of the English working class started to drink tropical beverages and to wear cotton cloths.[8] The food for the pole of popular industry in Britain was produced locally and decisively contributed to revolutionise English agriculture, ultimately also strengthening local labour in Britain. The productivity increasing innovations in English agriculture were realised by large farmers and also by yeomen.[9] The raw materials necessary for the industrial revolution, coal and iron, were produced in England. The capital invested in mines did not come directly from the overseas trade.[10]

The inflow of bullion from overseas fed the attempt of the Spanish monarchy to once more try to establish universal monarchy. All crowns tried to participate in the Atlantic slave trade with its monopoly profits in order to earn money for their war chests, as money became the sinews of war (Cole 1939: 3). The London city and its overseas companies stood at the side of the monarchical power and to such an extent that even the English East India Company lost at least temporarily its monopoly on the Indian trade when the would-be absolutist English monarch was overthrown by the Glorious Revolution.[11] Those segments of business which were in favour of the (bourgeois) Glorious Revolution fought constantly against monopoly (Dutt 1970: 99; Williamson 1965: 309). Monopolistic trade interests, the overseas companies and also the planter interests in the slave-holding plantation colonies tried to limit popular participation in Britain, for example, by buying constituencies, the rotten boroughs which were abolished only in the 1832 parliamentary reform.[12]

There is, however, a contribution of the periphery to the growth of the pole of popular industry. When through this growth some of the participating economies acquired comparative advantages in simple mass consumption goods, these economies were able to conquer the markets for such goods all over the world. Their ruling classes may have been as contemptuous of their own masses as all other ruling classes and were interested in luxuries to be imported from other tributary modes of production for which, due to their comparative advantages, they paid with simple products. The pole of popular industry in their home economies could grow disproportionately.[13]

Such a favourable specialisation was not the objective of traditional long-distance trade: The most coveted routes, the control of the intra-Asiatic trade, were characterised by self-sustained 'isolation'. The Europeans tried to have nothing to supply but only to serve as intermediaries between different Asian societies and to send the surplus earned from this trade in the form of luxury products to Europe without any European compensation.[14] African slave exports during the 18th century were increasingly paid by Indian textiles supplied by the English East India Company.[15] On the other hand such favourable specialisation did not necessarily work in favour of the centres of European expansion: Spain and Portugal paid their imports—to the extent they paid them at all—with manufactured products they received mostly from Northwestern Europe and, thus, contributed to early export-oriented industrialisation of that region.[16]

Such patterns of specialisation did not work only in the relations between Europe and the rest of the world but also within Europe. In Britain and also in Germany or Switzerland, the poorer regions with higher shares of marginal populations had to specialise in manufacturing (Kisch 1959: 543; Müller 1938). Proto-industry emerged in poor regions: for example, in the hilly areas of the Bern and Zurich cantons of Switzerland and also in the Jura or the Black Forest with their clock industries or in the Sudeten Mountains in Silesia with their weavers. The German hill areas with their small-scale manufacturing or the location of English rural industries in the midlands and the North show the regionally concentrated development of early manufacturing in poorer areas for export to agriculturally richer areas. Here peasants had managed to limit their exploitation so that they could become markets for these products (Thirsk 1978: esp. 62 ff.).

The access of the European ruling classes to the luxuries of the rest of the world on the basis of payment using European mass consumption goods created an additional demand for these small manufacturing sectors. These manufacturers did not care for the luxury orientation of their own ruling classes, but these ruling classes unintentionally promoted them because they had nothing else with which they could pay for their luxuries other than the products of these small producers. Europe's low level of sophistication in luxury production (which is admitted by those who claim Asia's superiority) implied that the European ruling classes had either to conquer foreign lands or to increase their local production of industrial mass consumption goods.

This necessity was incompletely understood even by the protagonists of European trade expansion: When England sent a choice of its excellence in manufacturing to China at the end of the 18th century, luxuries were selected because machine-produced simple products were deemed as not to be attractive for the Chinese court (Berg 2006: 271–276).

The Pole of Popular Industry and Free Trade

Unequal specialisation between Europe and Asia resulted in differences in interest concerning trade regimes. There is no way to increase earnings from sales of mass consumption goods through monopoly because in case of high prices local handicrafts remained cost competitive as they continued to be until the late 19th century in the more remote areas of China, India and Latin America (until the railway revolution).[17] In order to be competitive, such exports had to be cheap and higher earnings had to come from larger quantities sold. Traditional long-distance trade in luxuries, benefits on the contrary from quantity restrictions. Price elasticity of demand rapidly declines when quantities sold increase because the products lose their distinguishing character. Britain relatively early on, therefore, favoured competition and, hence, quantity over quality. Learning to produce more cheaply simple products goes with developing more sophisticated machinery. More sophisticated machinery makes new products thinkable. The lineage from the bicycle and the sewing machine to the car has been mentioned (p. 16). The chemical industry owes its origin to the attempt to get cheaper dyestuffs for mass-produced textiles (Headrick 1996; Streb et al. 2007). The electrical industry acquired a large market by equipping cities with lighting and transport for masses and machines which produced mass consumption goods (DuBoff 1966: 431; Newfarmer 1978: 23 ff.). The absence of tramways in many Third World cities because of the preference of the richer strata for individual transport removes collective consumption of transport as a market for electrical industry.

The pole of a popular industry produces as a by-product the emergence of new products, some of which are initially luxuries (car, aircraft) but the consumption of which is democratised,[18] some of which are initially rejected by the better off (most of the household equipments, such as the vacuum cleaner, as the better off had maids; Heßler 2001: 209; Pierenkemper 1988: 201).

From Luxuries to Raw Materials

By producing new products to capture the demand of the higher income brackets, the pole of popular industry renders obsolete many of the luxuries in which the more sophisticated tributary socio-economic structures were specialised. They could no longer sell these older luxuries and were crowded out from the export markets. By imposing a distribution of incomes favourable to the lower and middle classes, the growth of the pole of popular industry triggered off cheaper substitutes for the luxuries of the more sophisticated tributary socio-economic structures, as shown by import substitution of high-quality textiles, china and silverware in England since the 18th century (Berg 2004: 87). This continued until the demise of the distinguishing role of old luxuries in the regions of recent European settlement where the import of Asian luxuries seems never to have been as important as in Europe.

As well, the new products the pole of popular industry made available were increasingly consumed by the privileged in the more sophisticated tributary socio-economic structures because they satisfied completely new needs. The increasing access of lower income households to car ownership or air travelling are good examples.

The original comparative advantage of the more sophisticated tributary socio-economic structures was no longer sufficient to provide enough export earnings for paying the increasing imports of new modern luxuries and mass consumption goods. Other items with comparative advantage had to be found.

Capitalist economies were characterised by the coexistence of industrial poles with growing productivity in manufacturing on the basis of technical progress in machine production with disembodied technical progress (higher increases in productivity than increases in the machine costs).

They interacted with a stagnant rest-of-the-world economy where such progress did not take place. Comparative advantage of this rest of the world had to shift to products where the element of nature, the so-called natural conditions of production, was important. The higher the share of nature in total value creation, the less is the share of those productive operations in which innovation in the advanced economies has occurred.

Although technical progress in Europe may have been especially high in raw material production (and transferable to non-developed countries), there were two supplementary factors for a systematic comparative advantage in the non-developed regions of the world. In the industrially advanced regions of the world, natural resources were exhausted and consumption became diversified.

The Industrial Revolution started on the basis of the rich mining deposits in Europe, especially in Britain. With the progression of industrial production, the richest deposits near the centres of industrial production progressively were depleted. More distant, deeper or poorer ore deposits had to be developed in order to maintain a continuous flow of mineral resources. With the transport revolution of the 19th century, it became interesting to exploit the rich deposits of non-ferrous metals outside Europe where transport costs mattered less to the difference of coal and iron which are more bulky.[19]

As well, since the beginning of the 20th century, oil, first discovered in North America, was searched for worldwide, first on the grounds of being less bulky than coal (this increased the radius of oil-fired battleships),[20] then as the only fuel for the combustion engine. Oil became the basis of modern navies and then of mechanised armies and air forces.[21]

Many countries without industry acquired comparative cost advantages in mineral production with copper and tin as the starters (Chile, Peru, Zambia, Zaire, Malaysia, Nigeria). In the new raw material economies, those deposits near the coasts were developed with priority. In the leading industrial countries, mineral deposits are dotted all over their territories. In the non-industrial countries, mining is concentrated in regions near the coasts.

Rising mass incomes in Europe and North America implied also an increase in the demand for non-mineral raw materials. Output for basic foodstuffs did not expand initially with rising mass incomes. This led to increasing costs of production with improving terms of trade for agriculture. In Britain the share of industry in the total production had risen so fast during the first half of the 19th century that the home production of grain was sacrificed (repeal of the Corn Laws 1846; Kindleberger 1975b: 24;

Lusztig 1995: 399). In Britain this favoured on balance employment because of an increase in real consumption in the wake of cheaper food for the working class (Sau 1979: A45). Rapidly rising exports allowed to absorb additional labour shed in agriculture. Bairoch (1972b: 228–234) has shown that ultimately the only weak agitation of the continental European working classes for the liberalisation of food imports can be explained by the much larger importance of agriculture as a market for industry and as an employment creating sector. In continental Europe, agriculture also indirectly protected the labour markets of industrial labour. In some sectors the deficits of European consumption of agricultural raw materials were especially pronounced: fibres and fats (for soap: Lever's West African offensive for coconut fat production).[22]

With rising mass incomes the demand for amenities increased: tea, coffee and cocoa,[23] with tea becoming a mass consumption good already in 18th century Britain (Devèze 1970: 537; Gilboy 1932: 632).

The increasing demand for tropical goods laid open the existence of marginality also in non-European societies. In order to maximise the marketable surplus, those with property rights of the European capitalist type, whether locals or foreigners, shed marginal labour and created a labour surplus.[24]

Visibility of Surplus Labour

A structural labour surplus without the possibility of its absorption through demand-driven industrialisation triggered off further demographic growth in the non-industrial world. Households wanted to have a satisfactory number of children probably also because this was their only instrument for economic safety in their old age in pre-capitalist societies. This implied demographic growth in case of sufficient resources and medical care which limited the precocious loss of human lives.

As long as there are no major crises, pre-capitalist societies grow demographically as long as famines are not frequent enough to counteract.[25] Because of the already mentioned mechanisms of redistribution in pre-capitalist societies (p. 21), the level of population in relation to agricultural resources seems invariably to lie beyond the level where additional labour in food production produces still at least as much as it consumes. Less productive additional labour can be sustained if there is agricultural surplus. The total product is increased by egalitarian structures. Redistribution allows the employment of marginal labour whose product is lower than its needs but still positive. Surplus labour does not starve and is higher in the form of the so-called 'hidden unemployment'. Surplus labour is released when principles of the maximisation of the surplus are introduced. Both types of pre-capitalist socio-economic structures—those rather egalitarian structures of communitarian type and the rather inegalitarian structure of a tributary type—will face the problem of intensified labour surplus.

In a relatively egalitarian structure, the share of those with a marginal product lower than the needs of subsistence is high. The dissolution of communitarian bonds is slow but inevitable if newly emerging small farmers opt for market rationality.[26] An owner-operated agriculture of small and medium farmers emerges and at least medium-scale farmers opt for production increasing technical progress, reduce their unit costs, may undersell small land-deficient farmers on markets and keep them from having access to modern inputs because of their low earnings.[27] Ultimately, the middle farmers become capable of buying out the smaller ones because of the latter's incapacity to improve production methods. Agriculture tends to lose labour if there is no empowerment of shed labour which increases the demand for food. This is probably the most visible difference between home-grown capitalism as *desarrollo adentro* (development based on the internal market) and capitalist penetration as *desarrollo afuera* (development based on exports) (Furtado 1965: 167). In Europe initially the demand for labour in agriculture increased, although at a slower rate than population increased.[28] In the 'underdeveloped' economies labour declined in agriculture under the impact of capitalist penetration. It seems that this process is actually accelerating in the areas where communitarian structures prevailed but are now dissolved under cultural modernisation, especially in sub-Saharan Africa.[29]

When tributary socio-economic structures are opened to the world economy on a massive scale with comparative advantages in agricultural products, landlords shed labour which produces less than it consumes in addition. Share cropping arrangements and labour inputs are 'rationalised' and 'adapted'[30] to the new possibilities of increasing production with industrial inputs (where chemicals—fertilisers—are less dangerous for employment than mechanisation).[31] Both processes are reflected by the 'premature' increases in urbanisation, first in Latin America and Asia (since the mid 20th century) and nowadays in sub-Saharan Africa.

With comparative advantages in agriculture and relatively good prices for agricultural products, the industrial sector also declined (de-industrialisation) especially in places which were well-connected to the increasingly expansionary production system of the capitalist centre. In most cases, these are also the places in strategically central positions of the local transport systems. Local industrial production was undersold, pushed back into the hinterlands or consigned to some sectors where imports remained still costly.[32] The argument is not that there was general de-industrialisation as maintained by the critics of colonialism and neo-colonialism[33] but that because of the tendencies of shedding labour in primary production and world market competition for industry, the employment effect of restructuring became negative so that labour remained disempowered, and this in the more inegalitarian and the more egalitarian structures alike.

Under colonial rule measures in favour of labour concerned especially health (since the late 19th century) and contributed via demographic growth to further disempowerment of labour on the labour market.[34]

Most sectors which grew through trade did not develop new equipment using technologies because of the continuing low cost of labour or the availability of imported inputs and equipment from abroad because of comparative advantage. However, the implied dependence from abroad was also forced upon the underdeveloped economies by Western enterprises through their monopolistic practices (Körner 1963: 473).

New Possibilities of Rent Appropriation in Capitalism

Integration into the world economy on the basis of agricultural raw material exports implied the extension of market relations which increased the visibility of already existing marginality of labour. Improvements in the security from internal wars which colonial powers imposed after initial often terrible wars of conquest (which often led to demographic decline: Algeria; Elsenhans 2000b: 147; Meynier 2000: 20 f.) increased the already existing surplus of labour (Campbell 1991: 419; Chandavarkar 2007: 449). Mining did not create much employment. The integration into the capitalist world economy, therefore, implied the non-transfer of an essential condition for the transition to capitalism through a pole of popular industry, the emergence of scarcity of labour. Where labour was locally scarce, it was subject to repressive practices (mine workers in South Africa).

From the demand side there were few incentives to transform available surplus into investment and, hence, profit. There was an unprecedented degree of globalisation under the colonial system which took over most of the non-yet occupied areas of Africa and Asia, and despite the opening up of Latin America to British influence called 'informal colonialism' even before.[35] Capitalism did not impose the conditions of its reproduction on not yet capitalised areas, but only tried to draw as much rent as possible, often by using non-market forms of exploitation (forced labour, Ahuja 1999: 176 f.; Nickel 1976; monopoly, Kaplow 1978: 330; Lehmann 1965: 299). It can be said that capitalism even preserved pre-capitalist power structures (Schiel 1992: 78).

From the supply side the tendency to block the emergence of profit received additional impetus. In case of agriculture being based on owner-operated farms as in the case of the second wave of European colonialism in the late 19th century,[36] the limited flexibility of small-scale farmers implied that such farmers reacted to deteriorating demand conditions on the world market. Good prices in the industrial centres due to rapid growth in demand in the wake of rising mass incomes triggered off a worldwide increase in tropical agricultural production from the late 19th century (Chayanov 1966: 235; Mathur & Ezekiel 1961: 399). Overproduction became visible after the First World War. Agricultural producers had to accept falling prices from the mid-1920s. Hence, this experience pre-dated the Great Depression.[37] Financial surpluses were low, leaving little room for expanding consumption or engaging resources in productivity increasing investment which could have become a market for local investment goods production. Where agricultural export production was organised by landowners, these landowners tried to adjust to lower prices by cutting the cost of labour as there was always a surplus of labour available, without committing funds to increasing labour productivity through investment. Surpluses they earned were not invested in economic diversification as long as there were no expanding local markets, especially local mass market for the products where these economies may still have had comparative cost advantages or at least very low disadvantages. Surpluses were used for luxury imports or exported as financial assets to the financial centres in the developed world.[38]

Mineral exports implied the possibility of earning differential rents, incomes which did not only cover the costs of labour and inputs as well as average profit rates for capital employed, but additional incomes, because prices were high. These rents were based on the fact that mineral exports from the South competed with mineral production in production sites with less favourable natural conditions of production, less rich deposits, greater difficulties of extraction, lower mineral contents, etc. The takeover of mining deposits started in the last third of the 19th century.[39] Never the South could, however, eliminate mineral production in the North. So, rents were based on the fact that the South had no monopoly in the supply of such minerals, but only had better natural conditions of production. Until the 1940s, the share of the South in world mineral production was high only in copper and tin.[40] It increased in crude oil production with a high and for security reasons still protected oil production in the US and a high share of an increasingly expensive coal production in Europe. American oil and European coal kept energy prices high.[41] Low production cost producers could earn differential rents on markets where prices had still to keep high cost production producers economically viable. These differential rents had been the basis for concentration processes in favour of multinational raw material enterprises against less internationalised national producers in the developed world, for example, the so-called independents in the American petroleum industry (Sampson 1975; Shaffer 1968: 13). Since the 1930s for political reasons Western companies which owned the raw material concessions in the South accepted increasing participation of the elites in the South in these rents through royalties and taxes (Hamilton 1975: 100; Koppes 1982: 72). With political decolonisation this share increased (1946, 50/50 agreement in Venezuela; Gardner 1964: 209; subsequently extended to the American sphere of influence in the Middle East, Stocking 1970: 145). The struggle over this share constituted the main issue leading to the foundation of Organization of the Petroleum Exporting Countries (OPEC) in 1960.[42]

Rents could be appropriated, however, also in the export of those products where the South had a de facto monopoly. The South specialised in agricultural and mineral raw materials which had low prices and faced an income-inelastic demand, similar to the old luxuries of the sophisticated tributary modes of production. Exporters could agree on quotas or export taxes and earn higher incomes despite the (slightly) smaller quantities sold. Already the colonial powers had established marketing boards in the late 1930s (Akude 2006: 36 f.; Joseph 1983: 22) in order to get resources for their late colonial reform strategies that they deemed necessary in order stop the anti-colonialist movements (1929 Colonial Development and Welfare Act).[43] Hence, also in those products were the South did not compete with high-cost producers from the North on the basis of its lower production costs, strategies of state intervention into the market in order to appropriate (consumer) rents were followed.

Specialisation of the non-developed world on products with low price and income elasticity is the consequence of uneven development at the world scale. With rising mass incomes in the industrially developing countries, the relative share of food and, hence, of those products which are used for food production decreases. This applies to such items as sugar, coffee, cocoa, tea and fats which constituted about three quarters of the exports of the South since the late 19th century until around 1960.[44] As well, with rising mass incomes the share of textiles, another important export item of the South (especially cotton) in consumption, decreases. In addition, the share of fibres in the value of textiles decreased as fashion became more important and natural fibres were replaced by synthetics since the 1940s.[45] The share of minerals in total production decreases as one of the achievements of capitalist development consists in economising raw materials by making their use more efficient (Mommsen 1962: 765; Qu 1992), including energy efficiency.[46] Under capitalism, the specific consumption of raw materials, that is, the consumption of raw materials in relation to production decreases.[47] There would be no environmentally sustainable growth if raw materials consumption rose in parallel with the total production.

With the thriving of the pole of popular industry in the capitalist world new products were discovered. These new products had their more dynamic markets in the mass consumption-based capitalist economies but enjoyed also increasing demand from the richer strata in the lagging behind economies. Innovators from the advanced capitalist economies could capture these markets. The small amount of dynamism introduced through world market integration into the South, that is, expanding demand originating from the rent-fed privileged strata, contributed to the growth of the pole of popular industry in the North. It is normally the banalisation of these products which greatly contributes to the transferability of the production technology into technically less advanced economies. The lagging behind economies may enjoy later on comparative cost advantages in the production of mature products as described in the theory of the product cycle (Galtung 1980: 189; Vernon 1966: 203), although it can be shown that this is not a stable mechanism. It worked over long periods but to different degrees in the case of different underdeveloped economies. Even if the South acquired comparative cost advantages in industrial products, these were once more normally products which enjoyed no longer dynamic demand expansion and for whom the demand on the world market was characterised by low price and low income elasticity.[48]

Because integration into the world economy makes the already existing surplus labour in the South visible and transforms it into an additional offer of labour, there is no mechanism in the South which renders labour scarce. An increasing mass of shed off labour in unstable working conditions keeps labour from being empowered. Final demand is, therefore, not dominated by expanding mass markets. As the pattern of specialisation implies specialisation on price and income inelastic products, integration into the world economy does not lead to massive additional increases in the demand for labour. The weak position of labour on the labour market is but mildly corrected.

Because there is no dynamic employment creation, a dynamic industry for the supply of new products for an increasing mass consumption does not emerge. Because rents from raw material exports are available, the import of new products is not blocked by scarcity of foreign exchange. The structural weakness of the rent receiving economies does not translate into pressures on their foreign-exchange markets which would lead to devaluation and higher competitiveness of local suppliers.

The described phenomena are the basic characteristics of underdevelopment: the existence of surplus labour (Fei & Ranis 1964: 13; Lewis 1954: 171), the disappearance of large parts of what had existed as industrial production, generalised poverty, the West became aware of in the 1930s (cf. Chapter 4, note 43). From the tendencies to immiserisation only those groups were protected which were allies of an external power, or necessary for maintaining political stability locally (bridgeheads) or had access to differential rents because they were owners of specific assets. As also the appropriation of differential rents depends on the access to those markets where the higher prices for raw materials were paid (you cannot eat oil), practically all the better off depended on an external power. This explains the later association between underdevelopment and dependency in the critique of capitalist exploitation in the post-1945 theories of imperialism and the dependencia theory.

Dependency appeared to the anti-imperialist movements as linked to capitalist exploitation often in association with colonialism. It was thought to have even been created by the pattern of penetration of capitalism in non-yet-capitalist societies. But this link is not the result of capitalism having been effectively transferred to the underdeveloped world. Quite to the contrary, the link between dependency and underdevelopment reflects the fact that capitalism has not been transferred (Baran 1952: 67). Exploitation was possible without mobilisation of labour to levels where labour became scarce. 'Superexploitation', that is, productivity increases without wage increases was possible because capitalism had not been transferred.[49]

Classical theories of imperialism before 1914, therefore, had privileged quite the opposite perspective of imperialism as a pioneer of capitalism (Lenin 1899: 42 f.; Warren 1980), as they assumed that labour also in underdeveloped countries was per se surplus producing. If, however, only limited sectors of the economies in the underdeveloped world became competitive on the world market, only a small percentage of peripheral labour became surplus producing through its integration into the capitalist world economy. Export sectors could serve the transfer of capitalism only to a limited degree, the so-called bridgeheads or enclaves. The transfer of capitalism could occur only if this external impact led to the rise of a local demand for products which locally could be produced by means of an appreciable share of locally produced equipment. As long as the employment impact of the external sector was too weak to achieve this, it could not create a local mass market. At best it created a labour aristocracy[50] which may have been politically progressive but not a basis for a domestic industrialisation process. If local mass demand was weak, the existing local demand was highly skewed in favour of higher incomes.[51] This led to imports or relatively inefficient and non-dynamic local production based on imported investment goods so that demand for locally produced equipment was nearly non-existent (Lustig 1982: 368; Singer 1976: 983).

Local bridgeheads of privileged strata and tiny labour aristocracies were both created through integration into the capitalist world economy. For some time, they were open allies of the external powers. Since the 1930s, they were no longer capable of maintaining their hold over the dependent economies even with the help of external powers. The general tendency towards the immiserisation of the masses in the wake of the extension of surplus labour led to political protests, the control of which these bridgeheads could no longer capture through rent-based clientelistic networks. Often the existence of these bridgeheads themselves was threatened. The world economic depression of the 1930s with the massive decline in raw material prices decisively weakened the old patron client networks of these local bridgeheads and led to the weakening of rents available to fuel these networks.

The Crisis of the Colonial and Semi-colonial Economies

Whenever capitalist enterprises expand into non-capitalist ones, they try to cut costs, and the prime motive for an entrepreneurial decision is the desire to have access to products at the lowest possible price. This had an impact on the strategies of the colonial powers.

The raison d'être of tributary modes of production consists in extracting surplus for the benefit of maintaining a ruling class in glory and luxury. Such a ruling class could only be respected by the colonial powers to the extent that it reduced the costs of creating a political, economic and social environment, including the physical aspects of production, in order to reduce the cost of access to products. Colonial powers have nearly always considered that local allies were cheaper than an imported bureaucratic structure of their own. Where local allies were not available (especially in the case of self-sufficient communitarian socio-economic structures), the colonial powers eliminated the unruly local populations they were unable to control in order to have access to their natural resources.[52] They removed such populations to reservations and even imported more docile labour. This had been the case of the Atlantic slavery of the 16th–18th centuries or of the 19th century migration of Asian labour as coolies to Oceania, the Caribbean or South Africa.[53] Where they succeeded to strike a deal with local allies, the political structure was called indirect rule (Crowder 1964: 199; Fasseur & Koeff 1996: 38) which indeed comprised very different forms: the indirect administration with traditional local chiefs as agents of the colonial administration (in the French case in sub-Saharan Africa),[54] delegation of authority to local chiefs who applied customary law (instrumentalised often to their own needs and interests, Lentz 2000: 598; Ubah 1987: 137), nomination of subservient elements as chiefs by fiat of the colonial authorities[55], maintaining local pre-existing state structures under the supervision of colonial residents, protectorates (which to the difference of princely states could still claim to be a subject of international law like the trucial states in the Arab Gulf, or Morocco and Tunisia) with more visible formal independence when there were rivalries between external powers as in China after 1900[56] or the status of an Empire with the international administration of its finances (such as the Ottoman Empire since 1881[57]).

One can argue legitimately that this still important formal independence of all non-formally colonial countries of the South at the end of the 19th century was in reality highly limited, if it could not rely on legitimacy based on local body politics and international rivalry between major powerful nations (Brailey 1999: 514; Brown 1978: 211). The autonomy which, however, was provided through rivalry decisively increased since the rise of the Soviet Union as a great power, at first in the proximate vicinity of such states since 1918 (Iran, Afghanistan) and then worldwide since 1945.

Capitalist powers did not respect the appropriation of rent for just the glory of the rent-based ruling classes in countries under their control. Since the 18th century they reduced the consumption of the courts in India or Indonesia (Gilbert 1977; Remmelinck 1988: 121), in order to increase their own share in the available surplus. This did not exclude that they justified these policies with the necessity of improving the lot of the poor. The decline of the spending of the courts led to a decline of the old luxury goods industries and, hence, disturbances in the old social structures (Dutt 1992; Gadgil 1971: 39). This plays a role in the increasing but still sporadic emergence of resistance movements beyond the attempts of the old ruling classes to defend their taxing rights. However, resistance was early on triggered off also by large social reform movements such as the Taiping in China 1840–1857.[58] The Sepoy movement of the Indian military servicemen in the colonial army in Northern India 1853–1857 shares some of these characteristics.[59]

The Rise of Anti-colonialist Liberation Movements

Although the integration of the non-capitalist economies did not create full employment and capitalist development, it created new social groups which we may consider in the perspective of their possible contribution for creating enabling conditions for capitalist development. Early on the challenges of penetrating capitalist structures and powers led part of the elites, among them especially lower rank members of the service structures of the ruling classes, to the conviction that the preservation of their own interests and the interests of the socio-economic systems they felt to be members of depended on more or less radical reforms. These elites evolved between two poles: revolution or innovative restoration.[60] They wanted to use state power of a re-established and reinforced more centralised state in order to correct or abolish the market with the aim of getting hold of their own modernities. Some defined them as revolutionising renewal of their societies, others viewed themselves as following the old attempts to correct the exploitative practices of decaying old dynasties according to the practices in the processes usually to be observed within the framework of the dynastic cycles (cf. Chapter 4, note 68). These lower ranks of the old tributary modes of production had for long been oriented to the state as the locus of power and reform. This resistance was based on strata close to the old ruling classes which could rarely conceive of the transformation of their societies through the market. Some imported Western legislation (Horowitz 2004: 459) in order to make their entrepreneurs, but in priority their bureaucracies[61] and their armies,[62] more efficient. I do not know of any case where mass demand was taken into consideration as an instrument of economic dynamisation.

After the 'primary resistance' under the leadership of the old dynasties had been crushed by superior Western artillery, naval power and machine guns, new groups emerged.[63] The colonial rulers and also local traditional classes needed support in order to maintain political order and to benefit from the integration of the respective economies into the capitalist world system. These were the educated the French called 'évolués' and the Portuguese '*asimilados*' in the bureaucracies, but especially also amongst the teachers,[64] army officers and non-commissioned officers[65] with the leaders (also the lower rank leaders) of the emerging trade union movement in the modern economy which developed especially in the export sectors and in infrastructures related to them (railway workers).[66]

New strata saw themselves in line with the bourgeoisie as progressive promoters of enlightenment and rationalism (Hawthorn 1989: 21 f.). The values of the Western bourgeois revolution were never more enthusiastically adopted by intellectual elites outside Western civilisation than between the late 19th century and the demise of the Third World development states in the 1980s. A unique apex could be observed in the years immediately following the defeat of fascism in the Second World War. At that time only a minority group within the developing world expected salvation from a return to an old idealised past of their societies.[67] Its members wanted to achieve this return by purifying their cultures and religions from obnoxious elements acquired because of the particularistic interests any fragmented ruling class of a tributary socio-economic structure acquires. They were critical of the permanent threat of moral decay of such classes, described brilliantly in the Chinese theory of the dynastic cycle[68] or in the work of Ibn Khaldûn (1967: 597–602).

This 'new middle class'[69] was addressed in quite a similar approach by the Komintern (Kunze 1979: 663; Mährdel 1967: 1413) since Lenin's prescription of creating large class alliances (without a predominant role of the still numerically weak proletariat; Imam 1969: 279–292; Lowe 1963: 146). These new middle classes were vexed by Western racism which increased in the colonies since the 1890s as an offshoot of the use of racism as an ideology to combat the socialist leanings of labour in the capitalist world.[70] The new middle class was further activated because it was most hit by the world economic crisis of the 1930s.[71] The crisis not only reduced the financial resources of the politically independent but also that of the dependent state structures (the colonial administrations) in the South from which these middle classes drew most of their financial means.

These new middle classes explained 'backwardness' with the most easily visible mechanisms which kept their economies from diversification: the drain of resources (in India already in the 19th century),[72] the illegitimate enrichment of powerful foreign enterprises through monopoly profits from raw material exports which were not reinvested,[73] the penetration of their markets for industrial products by foreign suppliers,[74] the bones of the weavers bleaching the fields of Bengal.[75] They identified the old 'feudal' aristocracies as the essential supporters of the external influences (Marx 1867: 455). The new middle classes rejected Western domination, admired the West and asked for independence in order to achieve equality with the West in the name of the ideals of the Western bourgeois and socialist revolutions.[76]

The prestige of the West was not really diminished when Japan as the first Asian country was able to defeat a European power in the technically most advanced domain of military technology, the naval battle of Tshushima in 1905.[77] This battle demonstrated not only that you had to learn from Europe but also that by learning from Europe you could catch up. But the First World War, when Europe engaged in mutual slaughtering, destroyed the European aura of an also morally superior civilisation (Adas 2004: 49). More so, the October Revolution in Russia demonstrated the possibility of a development which no longer relied on profit-making private enterprises but claimed to put technical progress at the service of the general good also of the deprived masses.[78]

The new middle classes together with the workers in the modern sector as well as cash-crop-producing agriculturalists who had engaged in modernisation were severely hit by the slowdown in the expansion of raw material production subsequent to the First World War. This slowdown turned into massive decline of the raw materials sector during the world economic depression of the 1930s. Raw material earnings were halved in real terms, with exported quantities remaining at nearly the same levels. The South was hit by deteriorating terms of trade which it could not compensate by a shift from imports of manufactures to their local production. Despite a fall of world prices for industrial products by one third, very few of the industrial capacities of the South were able to grow by substituting their production to hitherto imported goods. [79]

Because underdevelopment was explained by external causation, the leaders of the new middle classes demanded the overcoming of external dependency: stopping the outflow of resources through taxes for the colonial powers,[80] taxing of monopoly profits in raw material exports of foreign companies, protection against unnecessary imports in order to increase the local production also through state support from new financial resources to be acquired by removing colonial and capitalist dependency.

In the 1930s, major parts of the hegemonic capitalist economics criticised the hitherto unquestioned idea of self-regulating markets and became open for state intervention into the economy, often adopting ideas expressed by

Keynes. The Soviet Union demonstrated that state-led growth was nearly unaffected by economic crisis in the West, despite its cooperation with the West in order to benefit from its technical advance.

Although the subsistence peasantry was relatively unaffected by the crisis (Brown 1986: 1022; Chaudhuri 1975: 117 ff.), the new middle classes were able to capture also the support of the peasantries. The new middle classes had, however, split into two political orientations on the issue of how to deal with those who previously occupied the middle of the society. Were the traders and craftsmen as well as the local echelons of the bureaucracies the colonisers had inherited from the previous tributary modes of production supports of the 'feudal' order? Could the servants of the old 'aristocracies' be won over for liberation or were they just part of the old order which had to be overthrown? The new middle classes had to decide to what extent they wanted to respect the property rights and the status of these old middle strata (Sarkar 1983: 241, 274 f.).

This issue was at the basis of the split of the national liberation movements between a communist and a nationalist wing (which also had often social-revolutionary aspirations).[81] The Chinese and the Vietnamese revolutions stand for the first tendency. The Indian National Congress (founded in 1885) is the protagonist of the second.

In China and East Asia, religion was closer to the old natural religions of the communitarian modes of production with little focus on very systematically elaborated belief systems. Here, religious convictions did not contain views of world history being governed by the permanent intervention from the other world in an unfolding process of the salvation of humankind.[82] Therefore, the strongly secular nationalists based on Marxism and its world historical perspectives did not offend religious feelings of the masses. Very radical tendencies could, therefore, capture the peasantries.[83] These were the communists in China and Vietnam. They waged peasant insurrections since the 1920s, in Vietnam already in the 1930s.[84] In all other countries the communists were also those among the new middle classes who were ready to follow the Narodniki (Russian populists of the late 19th century) strategy of going to the peasants and mobilising them by uplifting their political understanding and widening their horizons.[85]

Others among the new middle classes had less revolutionary leanings for the rural world, did not comprehend a quasi-metaphysical historical worldview which opposed them to the old religions and, therefore, were able to capture the support of the economically and culturally most diverse middle strata, including important parts of the traders, craftsmen and even lower levels of the bureaucracies, Amin's third estate (1973: 218, 265), in the name of national self-determination (Fitzgerald 1990; Nouschi 2005: 363).

Outside China and Vietnam, these more inclusive nationalists with milder revolutionary leanings became the undisputed leaders of the national liberation movements.[86] They became leaders of large class alliances. They normally excluded only the big landlords and the compradors, those businesses which were active in export–import trade.[87]

Communists in East Asia (including Korea) and nationalists in the rest of Asia won independence in the wake of the Second World War. Britain's war effort in India had been possible only because the Indian nationalists in the Congress Party tolerated it.[88] In the countries Japan had occupied, the Japanese defeat led to the de facto power of the nationalist movements.[89] Those European powers which did not recognise the new power relations and foolishly tried to reoccupy these countries suffered bitter defeat (Netherlands in Indonesia 1946–1949, France in Indochina 1946–1954 with the defeat of a modern Western army by a national liberation army in Dien Bien Phu 8th May 1954).[90]

A parallel development took place in Latin America where new social forces (the young officers) similar to these new middle classes had disestablished the old oligarchies (Wirth 1964).

Development-oriented State Classes: Rise and Failure

The political movements which drew their origins from the new middle classes had largely converging views about the requirements of overcoming underdevelopment. At the political level, they wanted to concentrate power at the political centre, a strong state often yet to be created, by limiting particularistic interests through a dictatorial exercise of power in various forms, military dictatorships, one-party systems, etc., pretending to be an enlightened avant-garde which had to lead the still backward masses.[91] The concentration of the state power was meant to allow the concentration of financial resources to be channelled into economic diversification in order to reduce dependency. The strategy consisted in state-led import-substituting industrialisation which would exclude the import of products which could be locally produced in order to save on scarce foreign exchange, would increase employment and would allow acquiring technical skills. Cooperation with international enterprises was not rejected because it was considered as a source of technology and capital.[92] In such a state-led industrialisation, available or accessible surplus could be used for investment which otherwise would not have been realised because demand conditions did not indicate profitability to a private enterprise. As profitability depends on demand conditions, a coordinated transformation of the economy can render an investment profitable which previously might not have been profitable. Complementary investments could create linkages and also final demand which would make individual investments profitable in creating an outlet for new products. This is described in Rosenstein-Rodan's (1943) model of simultaneous investment in a large variety of branches which provide employment and full capacity utilisation for large-scale enterprises after short delays. Private entrepreneurs are reluctant to base their expectations on expected decisions of others who they cannot decisively influence.

Investments are selected if they fit into an inter-industrial (inter-branch) structure of linkages which the leading body wants to realise until a given time horizon.[93] This can be broken down into steps where due to indivisibilities for some time overcapacities emerge with temporary underutilisation of equipment. This implies that microeconomic inefficiencies are bound to emerge at least temporarily. The criterion for profitability sent directly by the market cannot, therefore, be applied as a yardstick for sanctioning those in charge of executing a projected plant. The profitability criterion can only be 'simulated' and has to be tempered by taking into account the extent to which the programmed steps of realisation of this industrial structure have already been achieved: Failure or success in the realisation of a project does not only depend on the plant where inefficiencies occur. The problem is not insurmountable as shown by the methods of sector-wise planning of South Korea where overcapacities had been consciously accepted.[94]

However, there is a problem of asymmetric information. The central authority knows only the targets to be achieved.[95] It can at maximum avail itself of information about the cost-output relations of comparable projects in other economies. Its aim is to transform an underdeveloped economy which by its own definition and the definitions of all other participants lacks that essential factor of productivity increases. There is not yet any experience and learning by doing, so that plant-level management has always the argument that the specific adversities encountered in its own field are incomparable and larger than foreseen. I have described elsewhere that this leads to systematic misinformation (Elsenhans 1987: 83–86). Plant-level decision-makers influence target setting in production where potentials are deliberately underestimated and in financial planning where requirements are systematically overestimated.[96] This issue is not a technical problem of management but a political problem because it leads to alliance formation among the decision-makers. In order to increase their share in the total which is targeted for investment, sectoral administrations cover the behaviour of their plant managers and replicate it. All managers, at plant and at sector level, look for allies in other sectors of the economy in order to support their arguments at the central level. They accept and support deliberate misinformation of their allies in order to be covered in their similar attempts by them. Alliances try to protect their own misinformation and to unmask the misinformation of the opposing alliances by collecting information from all walks of society, which their opponents naturally try to manipulate. Rivalries between the alliances within the state classes inevitably cross institutional lines of organisation.

Behind the official organisational charts there is a second reality. The state classes appear as centralised, seemingly bureaucratic structures but can function in the struggle over rent only if their segments build alliances across formal divisions within the political set-up called administration. Despite their external appearance as Weberian institutions, the state classes appropriate the surplus as rent by political means and arrive at decisions by political means. In this process, they distort information deliberately in order to increase their political clout (influence) and prestige in order to increase their share in the collectively appropriated rent. Own failures are interpreted as caused by adverse structures inherited as underdevelopment. This 'clothing' of reality becomes possible as it increasingly turns out to be the essential instrument on which participants in these struggles have to rely in case of difficulties. Interpretation grids are tacitly agreed on and openly justified on meta-theoretical grounds comparable to the fairy tale on the emperor's new clothes where the capacity to see the clothes and to accept misinformation is a proof of intelligence and qualification for the job. When the strength of economic sanctions and incentives is weakened and made subject to political negotiation, moral principles and ideological global views are instrumentalised in order to arrive at decisions.

In the case of rent-based underdeveloped economies, the failure of these state classes to efficiently invest resources results from the following biases in their concept of economic diversification: The state classes tried to maintain national cohesion and were reluctant to engage in divisive social reforms with few exceptions (Viola & Mainwairing 1985: 207; Scheffler 1988: 510). They avoided radical agrarian reforms. When there is a large surplus of labour, the only readily available instrument for employing this labour productively at least to some extent consists in agrarian reform with redistribution of the cultivable land.[97] By endowing a large number of agriculturalists rather equally with always scarce land, agricultural production—and, therefore, a decisive element of mass consumption—increases via growing in-farm consumption (Elsenhans 1979a: 537 ff.). According to the decline of marginal product of labour in line with increasing inputs of labour, the owner-operated farms produce already a large amount of food with only a small share of their total labour time, but have to commit all their labour time to further production in order to make ends meet, even if the additional returns to their labour are low. They increase production in comparison to a surplus maximising agriculture of landlords. With an important part of their labour time, households can expect already high yields which are, however, too low in order to survive. In order to make ends meet, such owner-operated farm households have to increase their labour spent on their fields but receive only low additional yields according to the 'law' of diminishing returns. Agricultural surplus, however, decreases (Furtado 1966: 8; Ghose & Griffin 1980: 569).

In this sense, an egalitarian distribution of land is indeed a redistribution of poverty and does not create dynamic farms which are viable in the long term (Minhas 1970: 113; Moene 1992: 59). Peasants deliver the relative unproductive labour time as long as they have no better earning opportunities. They may even use their otherwise non-marketable labour time for investments in the form of labour intensive improvements which raise production.[98] If they are economically rational and not capable of preferring leisure (because they are poor), they engage in additional investment if the additional output is higher than the costs of the inputs to be bought without counting their additional labour time. An egalitarian agrarian reform appears costly at the economic levels as it reduces the surplus. At the political level, it creates conflict in the countryside because it limits not only the earnings of the landlords but also those of middle peasants. The middle peasants have often been an important element of the nationalist coalitions,[99] even in those countries where the national liberation movement was under communist leadership (Durau 1983: 77 ff., 243; Wright 1951: 265).

Radical agrarian reforms have, therefore, been undertaken only in the communist countries or in countries which were under the threat of communist takeovers (South Korea, Taiwan) which might have been supported by the rural poor. Where leftist governments implemented radical agrarian reforms, they combined them with a strong orientation against the market so that farmers could not reap the benefits they could hope to achieve by more efficiently using the land (Elsenhans 1977a: 71–74; MacKintosh 1987: 249). State-controlled organisations for the commercialisation of the marketable surplus were imposed. The full potential of agrarian reforms implied a commitment to radical redistribution and at the same time to the principles of market economy. Such a configuration was stable only in Taiwan and South Korea, and accepted by the communist regimes only in the initial phases of their seizure of power in the countryside and as an early step when introducing economic liberalisation.[100]

The state classes underestimated also the importance of mass consumption because of the necessity of using rent parsimoniously. In most cases the bulk of the rent was available in the form of foreign-exchange earnings. This rendered plausible the idea that shortcuts in the acquisition of new technologies were possible. If technical progress depends on 'disembodied' 'learning by doing', then the local construction of even an outmoded technology in a backward economy with no experience in technology production is relatively expensive if compared to the import of technology. Backwardness in the production equipment is higher than average backwardness in relation to more advanced economies. Productivity in equipment production is, hence, comparatively lower than the average productivity in relation to more advanced economies. Therefore, any equipment production is relatively expensive in relation to the production of final goods. The local construction of an obsolete technology appears as wasteful in relation to the import of a more performing technology which could be paid from the receipts of better earning exports. The argument was often made that there is no use of inventing the wheel a second time (Emmanuel 1981). The purchase of the new technology will allow increasing production more rapidly than the local construction of a less performing equally expensive technology. It is, however, not sure that the increase in skills is higher by operating the imported technology in comparison to the local construction of an earlier technology. Even by constructing an outmoded technology locally, the basis may emerge from which the construction of a better technology can be launched at a later date. Especially the richer among the state classes have systematically imported technology instead of promoting local equipment production as this increased the availability of products.[101]

Such a choice of technology limited employment especially for the mass of the population and, hence, the markets for which dynamic small entrepreneurs could produce. Often such enterprises, nevertheless, thrived because of the unintended inefficiency of the public industrial sector which distributed incomes but did not supply products. The rise of the so-called informal sector in highly rent-dependent economies invigorates the long standing argument that Keynesianism is not applicable in underdeveloped economies. The argument was that there is no idle capacity.[102] Unemployed factors of production exist only in the form of 'raw' labour (Raup 1967a: 275) which could not be brought into production merely by creating additional demand.

Scarcity of rent implied that the public sector, just as the modern sector built up by foreign enterprises, had to be 'maintained' against the devalorisation of its capital by more efficient competitors in order to preserve the capital goods bought at high expenses for its construction. Hence, competition had to be 'regulated', for example, by not admitting potentially competing investment projects to government development programs. In economies with high custom barriers, this excluded such projects of private investors even from the access to imported machinery and made them economically impossible.

Inefficient investment led to increasing CORs.[103] Further, growth required ever increasing amounts of investment. Inefficiency of investment implied that the state-promoted industrial sector did not earn the financial resources for further increasing investment. Employment expansion remained limited. State-led industrialisation lost in dynamics.

The hope for ever increasing transfers from the rest of the world through an alliance of Third World governments did not materialise: The new international economic order launched as economic decolonisation after the independence of nearly all the former colonies in the early 1960s could not be implemented. The Soviet Union and its allies supported only half-heartedly higher raw material prices (Knirsch 1978: 106). Western enterprises could not be forced to transfer most modern technology at low prices.[104] The extraordinary success of OPEC in raising oil prices tapered off in the early 1980s when technical innovation reduced the cost of alternative sources of oil (Blitzer et al. 1985: 296; Champlon et al. 1991: 211). Discipline among the petroleum exporting countries could not be maintained. Saudi Arabia with the highest reserves considered the American military guarantee for its regime as vital. It acted as a swing producer in order to limit further price hikes (Cooper 2008: 570; O'Brien 1986: 1313). Saudi Arabia and its allies refused to support the extension of cartelisation strategies to other raw materials where world demand would have allowed price rises as shown by the rise of coffee prices in the wake of frost in Brazil during the mid-1970s (Elsenhans 1982; Elsenhans & Olschewski 1976). Non-oil exporting countries of the South had expected price rises also for other raw materials and engaged in indebtedness for following rent-based industrialisation strategies.[105] The recycling of the petrodollars had made credit internationally cheap (Jayawardena 1983: 54; Lütkenhorst & Minte 1979: 89).

In the early 1980s, Great Britain and the United States abandoned Keynesian policies of demand expansion which they had previously been following in order to maintain high levels of employment, despite inflation. They shifted to monetarism with tight money policies. Especially the more industrialised underdeveloped economies which had been eligible for bank credit had to abandon the strategy of creating a front of the underdeveloped 'wretched of the earth' and to ask for debt rescheduling and debt forgiveness (Hojman 1987: 214; Holler 1989: 90). The condition of the West and its international institutions consisted in the South accepting a new wave of economic liberalisation and the end of 'inefficient' state intervention into the economy including a downsizing of the loss-making state-owned enterprises.[106]

Against the now universally shared criticisms of the wastefulness of this state-led development processes, I have always argued that the state classes which were in charge were ambivalent and torn between two poles. They struggled between an inclination to strive only for self-privileging and the necessity to legitimise themselves with respect to a larger public, their national constituencies which at least originally had been mobilised for a project of national liberation.[107]

I add that the contemporary processes of globalisation do not necessarily remove rent.[108] Quite to the contrary, they lead under certain conditions to configurations where still rent-based state classes conform to the Western discourse of the inefficiency of state economic activities and at the same time just shamelessly pocket rents for the own privileges.[109]

Rent-financed investment tends to be less efficient in contexts of 'managed' competition than investment realised by private enterprises under perfect competition. It is, however, still more efficient than no investment (Elsenhans 1994b: 410, note 21). Rent-based microeconomically inefficient state-led industrialisation can lead to higher growth than economic liberalisation if the amount of rent invested is higher than the amount of private profit-based investment. Economic growth and diversification in underdeveloped economies had been blocked under the conditions of underdevelopment because there were no internal incentives to invest even if resources were available (Bagchi 1972: 20). Under conditions of underdevelopment available rents were just used for consumption or transferred to foreign economies, as shown by the caricatures of rentiers spending their money in Paris nightclubs and lighting their cigars with banknotes in the 1920s. Such caricatures reappear today as Saudis and Russians pushing up the prices in hillside resorts. Neither prices nor rents appropriated by Western consumers in the form of low raw material prices contribute to overcoming underdevelopment in their countries of origin.

Rent-based investment has often blocked private investments because of the tight regulations of economic activity it accompanied, but often it created also new outlets for private investment. Some but obviously not all private investments the state sector encouraged or tolerated, even sometimes in the form of a shadow economy, were not 'distorted'.[110] These tolerated investments could become the basis for a market-oriented accumulation process. Even if inefficient, state-owned enterprises contributed to skill formation (Evaluation 1983: 20 f.; Pasara & Santistevan 1973: 142). Much public investment for infrastructures could contribute to industrial development. The success of most of these state-class-dominated regimes in putting their youths to school most favourably compares with the failure of the previous oligarchies and colonial regimes in this domain. The supporters of export-oriented industrialisation often admitted that import-substituting industrialisation was a condition for the subsequent opening to the world market on the basis of the export of manufactured goods.[111]

The failure of state-led development consisted in an ideologically determined pre-Keynesian underestimation of the market and of mass consumption. The market was not seen as an instrument which disciplined those who had access to financial surpluses. It was much more considered as an arena for power play under conditions of imperfect competition and information asymmetries. These representations of the market are not entirely different from the views currently put forward by ideological supporters of oligopolies and which are presented as natural.

There are reasons for this biased perception of the market. All these countries had suffered from exploitative practices of enterprises from the colonial metropolises. They got specialised on raw materials where foreign companies with economic alternatives could appropriate rents, whereas the underdeveloped countries had no alternatives because their economies had been distorted by the pattern of penetration of market relations. The lopsided development (Issawi 1961) was caused by the capitalist enclaves, so that market imperfections which allowed rent-seeking were attributed to the dominance of markets, although ultimately they were the result of the pattern of market penetration. It was not market penetration but the absence of local mass empowerment. This absence of local mass empowerment created distorted market structures which led to structural unemployment so that labour could not share in the fruits of technical progress through higher mass incomes.

Because of the denunciation of the outflow of resources (colonial super profits and declining terms of trade for price-inelastic products) as the primary cause of underdevelopment, the benefits of declining the terms of trade and even 'superexploitation' in case of specialisation on price-elastic products could not be conceived. The possibility of growth by 'being exploited' in the specialisation in products that lead to higher rates of growth was discarded as long as there was hope of increasing rents in the export of traditional products.

The neglect of this possibility is tightly linked to the classical and the Marxist theories of growth. Both theoretical approaches consider that growth depends on increasing amounts of the value of investment. Any decline in export prices and any rising consumption imply a reduction of investible resources and lead to a loss in possible growth. The neglect of mass markets has to be seen in parallel to the disregard for the development of internal mass markets. To the neglect of the internal mass market austerity policies correspond. They were imposed on the whole population by those state classes which considered themselves more committed to the improvement of the weaker sections.[112] Obviously, the less committed and less disciplined state classes provided even more of this medicine but especially for the poorer sections of the population. So poles of popular industry could not emerge on the basis of market incentives even in cases of commitment of the state classes to the improvement of the plight of the poor. In no case the state classes could reach an understanding of the market which instrumentalised its disciplining function as a means of imposing parsimoniousness and mass orientation on those who managed the surplus. Nothing demonstrates this failure more than the rise and demise of real socialism.

The Rise and Demise of Real Socialism

Real socialism was a mode of production established by political forces which claimed to represent mass interests, the working class, and replaced market regulations by central planning. Invariably, real socialism created a 'bureaucracy', a state class, even if it tried to limit its tendencies to self-privileging by powerful avant-garde parties with egalitarian ideologies and carefully selected memberships.[113]

Also here, there was no automatism comparable to the market which sanctioned inefficiency in the choice of technical processes, investments, managerial shortcomings and mistakes in the choice of new products. There were certainly efforts to improve technology and search for innovation but no automatic sanctions for those who were less committed to them.

Real socialism became attractive at the world level during the great depression of the 1930s (Elsenhans 2000c). With high levels of investment, real socialism was able to grow, even to grow faster than capitalism. Lower efficiency of new investment in real socialism than in capitalism did not matter. The growth rate can be defined by the capital productivity (b) (the inverse of the ICOR) and the rate of growth of investment (i). Capitalism is assumed to be more efficient than socialism in using scarce resources. This is described by definition (1):

$$b \text{ (cap)} > b \text{ (realsoc)} \tag{1}$$

Despite lower capital productivity, real socialism can grow more rapidly than capitalism if it devotes more resources to investment. This is described by the two definitions:

$$b \text{ (cap)} > b \text{ (realsoc)} \tag{2}$$

$$i \text{ (cap)} < i \text{ (realsoc)} \tag{3}$$

Provided that the rate of growth of investment is higher in real socialism than in capitalism, real socialism can grow more rapidly than capitalism despite its lower efficiency. This will be the case, especially, during crisis in capitalism when the rate of accumulation may even become negative. In this case, real socialism may appear to be efficient. If capitalism, however, returns to full employment with the rate of growth of investment corresponding to the rate of possible technical progress in full employment capitalism (so that growth rates correspond to the golden rule: the rate of capital accumulation converging to the rate of growth of net national product[114]), then the following holds:

$$i \text{ (cap)} = y \text{ (cap) and } b \text{ (const)} \tag{4}$$

In that case, real socialism can keep up with capitalism only if it raises the growth of investment i (realsoc) above the rate of growth of national income, so that

$$y \text{ (realsoc)} = y \text{ (cap)}; i \text{ (realsoc)} > i \text{ (cap)}; c \text{ (realsoc)} < c \text{ (cap)}. \tag{5}$$

A higher rate of growth of investment implies a lower growth of consumption, also in relation to the rate of growth of income. This will lead to a declining share of consumption. The rate of growth of consumption (c) in capitalism equals the rate of growth of income if the golden rule assumptions are fulfilled, so that the rate of growth of consumption in real socialism must be lower. Consumption grows in real socialism less rapidly than national income. With increasing shares of investment in national production, this configuration may even lead to stagnating consumption.

The planners of the Comecon interpreted the low efficiency of investment as the result of historically determined backwardness due to the fact that the October revolution took place in the 'weakest' chain of imperialism. They, therefore, resorted to massive technology imports since the Conference on Security and Cooperation in Europe (1974) and its basket 2.[115] In order to finance these imports, they further restrained consumption and contracted debts in the West. Both ultimately led to the downfall of real socialism.[116]

State-led Development in the Periphery: An Element of Stability of Capitalism

The shift of major areas of the world to state-led development despite globalisation which precedes the actual globalisation discourse had been nearly unconstrained in the colonially dependent economies. This shows that the resistance of capitalist socio-economic structures against rising state intervention is rather limited. Although capitalism is expansionary, it does not seriously attempt to pull down barriers to its expansion which countervailing social forces may erect. Capitalist enterprises could well accept also the emergence of real socialism and even cooperate with these systems. The Cold War was not a consequence of the withdrawal of about one third of the surface of the globe from capitalist expansion, but the result of the rivalry between two superpowers which tried to increase their influence in the world by exporting their socio-economic models. Capitalism can go along very well with structures which restrict the operation of the market mechanism. We are far from the classical theories of imperialism. Lenin's (1916: 245) forecast of an inevitable shortage of surplus in relation to capital did not materialise and so imperialistic expansion was not imposed on capitalism but resulted from other causes. Luxemburg (1912: 115 ff.) deduced a similar scenario of decay on the basis of an inbuilt under-consumptionist threat which according to her for political reasons could not be overcome under capitalism through increasing real wages. It was Hobson (1938: 88) who initially showed the possibility of a reformist solution. He was reviled by Lenin and subsequently by all leftists and ignored by the Keynesians.

The critics of state-led development under real socialism, often committed leftist intellectuals, have argued that state-led development did not really challenge capitalism and even supported it.[117] Indeed, according to my argument, socialism can but create the conditions for mass-income-based capitalist development. This is the argument developed by Barone (1935: 269) and Lerner (1935: 60) which becomes important today because business itself seems to be less and less able to maintain the conditions of capitalist development. In this perspective the question of the readiness of real socialist economies to cooperate with capitalist ones is not even pertinent. Socialism does not consist in the overcoming of the microeconomic rationality of capitalism but of its lack of macroeconomic rationality, that is, its neglect for maintaining the bases for high levels of employment and, hence, empowerment of labour.

Indeed, also the state classes of the South cooperated intensively with multinational enterprises in order to buy technology and to attract foreign direct investment. They were a nuisance as they tried to cream off super profits at largely above average profit rates. They respected, however, profits and constituted increasingly important new markets for capitalist enterprises as did the countries of real socialism.[118] This was, however, not the reason for their failure. But this demonstrates that rent-based state-led industrialisation was no challenge for capitalism in the centre and was viable as long as the state classes were able to extract resources from the West (higher raw material prices) and to serve their debts. Capitalism thrives not only internally on the basis of rising mass demand with powerful labour because of full employment but also internationally if there are countervailing forces.

In the absence of such state-led strategies, there was no important development of capitalism in not yet capitalist economies. Examples are czarist Russia with an insufficiently dynamic capitalist development despite high government support for modern industries[119] or the South despite its openness to foreign direct investment and trade during the colonial period and also until the 1930s in the politically independent countries. The absence of economic dynamism in all these cases demonstrates that capitalists cannot create themselves the conditions for capitalist development. Only in the case of favourable structures which capitalists often do not even contribute to bring into existence, high levels of employment create the conditions for capitalist development. Where these conditions are created, perhaps even by other forces, labour or substitutes such as high government spending on the basis of the appropriation of rents, capitalism can grow and structures favourable to capitalist development can emerge even inside the initially rent-dominated structures.

The final outcome of the new expansion of capitalism under the conditions of the late 20th century globalisation depends, therefore, on the impact of this new capitalist expansion on the social structures which it draws into its orbit. Can the empowerment of labour with high levels of employment be achieved or promoted by complementary measures which would include appropriate state intervention? The state-classes-dominated model in the South and real socialism in the East have shown that they rarely achieve the empowerment of labour but rather the emergence of a 'bureaucracy' which inefficiently represses labour in the name of accelerated accumulation. The worldviews of the capitalists and their academic supporters stabilise the privileged classes in these state-dominated systems as they share with them the despise for the masses and their consumption as well as the glorification of spending on investment.

The crisis of the state-based growth models of the 'periphery' and the shift of these socio-economic structures to market regulation under the pressure of the new wave of globalisation will not solve the dilemma of the absence of the conditions for capitalist growth by just spontaneously establishing these conditions. These processes will not necessarily lead to growing mass consumption. They will not overcome the inability of the ruling classes of capitalism and of the would-be capitalist structures to realise these conditions.

In arguing that capitalism can survive along with resistance against the exploitation it engenders, I certainly do not want to deny the crimes committed by European colonial powers, the slave trade, forced labour, population displacements and political regimes based on violence. Furthermore, the extent of these cruelties was magnified significantly in the 20th century by the increasing technical capabilities which capitalist technical development was able to put at the disposal of colonial powers.

The undeniable reality of these crimes is, however, no argument for the inevitability of their existence in the case of capitalist regulation of the economy. Capitalism depends on checks and balances as do other social systems. In capitalism, these checks are depersonalised, there is a scarcity of labour and the collective organisation of wage labour, but there is no systematic structure of ethical responsibility among the ruling class implied by capitalist relations because this ruling class is fragmented with ethics belonging to the sphere of private life. As a fragmented class where each member competes with each and all other members in an anonymous market, capitalists have difficulty developing collective responsibilities. If ethical discourses become important, there is a clear sign that capitalists seek to avoid structural change, as is the case today. The previous inflation of valueless financial assets requires a cut, not so much for deficit governments, but for the speculators, in order to preserve the savings of households, who acquired their financial assets through work.

Wherever the underprivileged do not dispose of empowerment because of their not being scarce, they have only very limited possibilities for resistance. This applies to the immense mine of cheap labour outside the regions of capitalist development.

Those who suffered in the periphery of the world system had little or no possibility to effectively resist capitalism until the success of the national liberation movements. The national liberation movements lost hundreds of thousands of their fighters in order to win independence from the Western rule. Wars of liberation have been at least as bloody as the Second World War in terms of the size of the populations which participated and the number of lives lost.

The people in the periphery have suffered terribly from European colonialism, but the real scandal is that this suffering did not contribute to capitalist development. Some historians argue that the development of capitalism is a contribution to human civilisation and ultimately to human happiness. Even if such arguments are admitted, they cannot serve to justify any suffering which was caused by capitalism in the periphery. Unfortunately, the exploitation of the masses in the colonialised world, the violence and human rights violations against the people in the colonised countries were just meaningless for the development of capitalism. Capitalism did not require external surplus nor external markets, although it was utilising both, if and where they existed.

The human suffering caused by capitalism in non-capitalist regions belongs to the realm of useless suffering, of meaningless history. It is a Newtonian idea that the 'macro' is the sum of all 'micros' but in reality very few events in the 'quarry of life' become stones which contribute to build a story. Most of it is discarded and left by the wayside. Most of human history, including colonial exploitation and violence among it, belongs to the realm of useless sufferings. So the injustices linked to capitalism. Superexploitation and the violence connected to it are just a threat to capitalism, not a support for its development.

Notes and References

1. Alagoa 1971: 273; Coquery-Vidrovitch 1969: 65; Huffman 1972: 364.
2. Alden 1982: 628; Anthony 1986: 303; Klengel 1978: 218; MacGaffee 1986: 17; Shaw 1979 [Shaw/Heard]: 365; Wilson 1972: 588 f.
3. Aris 1987: 137 f.; Liu 1988: 107; Miller 1961: 198; Samuel 1982: 219.
4. Blaut 1989: 281; Brasseul 2004: 963; Jones & Ville 1996: 912; Masselman 1961: 459.
5. Sweezy 1953: 10, 1959: 235 ff.; Wallerstein 1974: 76 ff., 1988a: 104.
6. Day 1979: 312; Gould 1964: 265; Hamilton 1942: 267; Hammarström 1957.
7. Drelichman 2005a: 532, 2005b: 374; Forsyth & Nicholas 1983: 603; Hamilton 1938: 177; Kamen 1978: 44.
8. Braudel 1967: 189; Elsenhans 2007a: 186 (note 1072).
9. Allen 1992: esp. 310; Kircheisen 1987: 988; Tribe 1981: 85. German parallel: Müller 1964: 638.
10. Bairoch 1972a: 1129; Bose 1988; Chapman 1970: 252; Donnachie 1977: 271; Heaton 1937: 4.
11. Ames 1991: 25; Brenner 1973: 55; Jones & Ville 1996: 912; Sheridan 1976; Unwin 1927: 51.
12. Williams 1964: 90 ff., 133; Williamson 1965: 289, 310.
13. Chorley 1987: 377; Digby 1901: 262; Dutt 1970: 119; Field 1983: 417; Jevons 1865: 3; Pares 1937: 132 ff.; Temin 1966: 190; Toynbee 1969: 51; Wilson 1963: 176. Similar on the US: Sawyer 1954: 371.
14. Ariyasajsiskul 2004: 92 f.; Barendse 1988: 32 ff.; Blussé 1988: 209 f.; Vries & Woude 1997: 386 f.
15. Eltis & Jennins 1988: 943; Emmer 1975: 249; Lovejoy 1983: 103 f.
16. Mauro 1958: 239; Morineau 1978: 6; Pike 1962: 363.
17. Brötel 1971: 251; Feuerwerker 1970: 347; Johnson 1978; Krishnamurty 1985: 415; Lewkowski 1959: 348; Morris 1968: 9; Murphey 1972: 258; O'Hear 1987: 521; Platt 1973: 81; Yanagisawa 1993; 25.
18. Eichengreen & Mitchener 2004: 211; Fischer & Carroll 1988: 1172; Mishkin 1978: 931; Olney 1989: 145.
19. Hillman 1984: 412; Lamicq 1975: 195; Mamalakis 1978: 851; Matthews 1990; Phimister 2000: 40.
20. Carmoy 1971: 18 ff.; Fabricant 1940: 235; Harms 1916: 44; Regul 1937: 56.
21. 3% before 1914, but 25% of all ships in the late 1930s were fired by oil, cf. Sayers 1967: 96; Stocking 1970: 12 f.
22. Brooks 1975: 37; Fieldhouse 1994; Wilson 1954: 37.
23. Bucharin 1929: 32; Gilboy 1934: 685; Sarkar 1972: 3 ff.; Ukers 1935: 502 f.
24. Campbell 1977: 434; Dovring 1967: 173; Fernando 2010: 318; Harnetty 1971: 407; Langer 1985.

25. Malthus 1958: Vol 2, 48. For a recent discussion cf. Clark 2008; Persson 2008: 170; Voth 2008: 150 ff.
26. Ellis 1981; Hugon 1967; Todaro 1968: 353.
27. As examples cf. Ahmad 1972: 11; al Khafaji 2002: 320; Boeckx 1971: 387; Gaiha 1987: 33.
28. Collins 1967: 356; Devine 1999: 183; Jones 1965: 16; Mendels 1976: 204; Timmer 1969: 392.
29. With new but now urban potentials for endogenous growth, cf. Kappel 1999: 434.
30. Keyder 1983: 136; Kikuchi & Hayami 1980: 36; Otsuka et al. 1992: 2007; Pertev 1986: 27–31.
31. Ahmad 1972: 28; Blyn 1983: 719; Byres 1972: 106; Grabowski 1990: 48.
32. Feuerwerker 1958: 342; Platt 1973: 81; Rott 1979: 36.
33. See Baer 1982: 74; Bagchi 1976: 185 ff.; Chaudhuri 1971: 205; Harnetty 1991: 473; Issawi 1966: 9; Komarow & Grasche 1959; Simmons 1985: 600; Yen 1961 to compare with the more nuanced positions, quoted in Chapter 6, note 44.
34. As an example: Kaur 2006.
35. Adewoye 1971: 609; Bethell 1969: 128 ff.; Cross & Brading 1972: 557; Fall 1993; Gallagher & Robinson 1953; Landes 1961: 500.
36. This followed the shift of the British raj from establishing large landowners to the taxing of farmers in India who got their rights in land confirmed, as ryotwars, cf. Majumdar et al. 1978: 796; Rao 2006: 57.
37. League of Nations 1933: 109 ff.; Svennilson 1954: 218; Timoshenko 1933: 578 ff.
38. Blakemore 1979: 297; Mathew 1972; Moutoukian 1992: 911; Sunderland 1999: 305.
39. Harvey & Press 1990: 100 f.; Lutz 1939: 9; Yamada 1971: 243; and the literature quoted in Chapter 5, note 19.
40. Coal 7.8%, oil 21%; Dresdner Bank 1930: 52. Cf. also Elsenhans 2007a: 342; Lamartine 1959: 226, 240; Schmitz 2000: 97.
41. Elsenhans 1974b: 21; Hartshorn 1969: 147; Tugendhat 1972: 117 ff.
42. Amuzegar 1975: 73; Cubertafond 1976: 32 ff.; Elsenhans & Werde-Bräuniger 1974: 91; Tugendhat 1972: 173 ff.
43. Abbott 1971; Albertini 1989: 604; Dimier 2006: 339.
44. In 1970, industrial products represented only 22% of the exports of developing market economies, food 24%, agricultural raw materials 18%, but fuels 33% already before the 1973 oil price increases, UN Monthly Bulletin of Statistics, 38, 5 (May 1984).
45. Ettl 1982; Goode et al. 1966: 464; Kurth 1965: 60; Manes 1964: 161; Meyer et al. 1971: 71 f.; Varon & Takeuchi 1975: 175.
46. Janosi & Grayson 1972: 242; Kander & Lindmark 2004: 309; Kmuche 1982.

47. Scrivenor 1854: 312 reports a reduction of coal per ton of iron by a factor of 10 during the first half of the 18th century. Clough & Marburg 1968: 20 report a reduction of coal per kWh by a factor of 7 from 1899 to 1968.
48. Krugman 1997: 114; Phillips & Henderson 2009: 43 f.
49. This is the relevant part of Emmanuel 1969: esp. 171.
50. Anderson, R., 1974: 111; Arrighi 1966: 57; Bacha & Taylor 1978: 291; Boeckh 1978: 262; Deeb 1979: 191–201; Harris 1986: 286; Henderson 1970: 597; Ingleson 1983: 475.
51. Angeles 2007: 1157; Gibson 1963: 388; Green 1974: 23; Ho 2006: 186.
52. Bloom 2002: 497; Edelman 1998: 378; Levene 2000: 317; Samarin 1992: 68; Stannard 1992.
53. Galenson 1984: 19; Kenwood 1972: 70; Tinker 1974.
54. The distinction between direct administration in French colonies and indirect administration in British colonies has to be nuanced; there were many elements of indirect rule also in the French practices of colonial administration, Barrows 1974: 270 ff.; Meister 1971: 136; Zucarelli 1973: 224.
55. For example, princely states in India, Grischow & McKnight 2008: 103, or Indonesia, North Nigerian emirates, Afigbo 1971: 447; Lugard 1922.
56. Brown, S., 1978: 192; Esthus 1959: 454.
57. Bootsma 2005: 56; Brett 1982: 18 f.; Hallgarten 1971: 263; Issawi 1966: 10 f.; Platt 1963: 502; Thobie 1977: 718; Woolf 1920: 73.
58. 1854–1861. Cf. Chesneaux 1958: 172 ff.; Levenson 1962; Willing 1971: 268. Similar process in Iran: Keddie 1962: 269.
59. 1857–1858. Dasgupta 2007: 1729; Malik 1973: 103 f.; Roy 2007: 1724.
60. Bhattacharya 1979: 95; Chandra 1979: 82; Keddie 1966: 80; Reid 1974: 190.
61. Bergère 1984: 334; Burçak 2008: 69; Chu 1963; Eastman 1968: 702.
62. Cronin 2008; Elman 2004: 302; Hou 1961: 33; Karpat 1972: 245.
63. Baker 1991; Büttner 1975: 301; Chesneaux 1972: 86; Parsons 1976: 91; Wakeman 1972: 67 f.
64. Lutchman 1974; Markovitz 1977: 183; Nworah 1974: 7; Rankin 1971: 3; Sadria 1986: 59; Tai 1983: 82.
65. Blasier 1972: 27; Davies, T., 1971; de Carvalho 1982; Tejapira 2006: 18; Wirth 1964: 161.
66. Affonso 1972: 48; Bradford 1984: 310; Deeb 1979: 191; Mukherjee 1981; Reddy 2006: 118 ff. In this context the deterioration of the terms of trade in 1937 seems to be most relevant. When the world came out of depression, first the industrial prices rose and then the agricultural prices followed. This lead to worldwide resistance, without any coordination. Cf. Abdullah 1995: 212; Baños 1994: 143; Korzeniewicz 1993: 35; Lindberg 2001; Menon 1980; Reddy 2007: 129.
67. The Islamic world is most prominent: Burke 1972: 99; Dobbin 1974; Hodgkin 1962: 325; Lapidus 1997: 447; but other cultural regions experience the rise of similar movements: Choe 1986: 226 ff.; Duara 2001: 101; Ip et al. 2003: 492; Kuntowidjojo 1986: 186; Subramanian 2009: 30.

68. Barendse 2000: 210; Habib 1985a: 48; Reischauer & Fairbank 1960: 117; Wakeman 1977: 204 f.
69. Halpern 1969; Jones 1998: 148 ff.; Perlmutter 1967.
70. Conklin 1998: 441; Duffield 1981: 258; Jewsiecki 1976: 49; Morlang 2001: 501.
71. Akude 2006: 26; Bhattacharyya 1978: 627; Clarence-Smith 1985: 321; Eckert 2006: 475; Goswami 1984: 359; Gould 2004: 19; Jewsiecki 1976: 57; Potter 1973: 49 f.; Thirumali 1994: 236 f. .
72. Banerji 1984: 1283; Ferguson 2002: 47; Majumdar et al. 1978: 800 f. Critical position Chaudhuri 1968: 45; Subramahnjam 1984: 135.
73. Jalée 1965: 78; Lanning & Mueller 1979: 493 f.; Magdoff 1969: 45; Peter 1990
74. Habib 1985b: 361–364; Simmons 1985.
75. Bill 1963: 412; Bosma 2004: 658; Desai 2008: 650.
76. Duiker 1973: 187; Hunger 1968: 4 f.; Kaviraj 2000: 147–150; Kulke 2008: 27 f.
77. Mao Tse-tung, quoted by Snow in Craig et al. 1965: 481; Davies 1971: 72; Dua 1966; Keddie 1970: 239; Lenin 1962: 216; Matsumura 1997; Sinha 1975: XI.
78. Dua 1966; Geyer 1968: VIII, 47; Jaisingh 1983: 47; Kohn 1928: 115; Madjarian 1977: 42.
79. On the development of the terms of trade for the South, cf. Chapter 5, note 37. The share of the South in industrial production ('Other countries' in the League of nations definition) decreased from 14.6% in 1926–1929 to 13.6% in 1936–1938, League of Nations 1945: 13.
80. Majumdar et al. 1978: 925; Neil-Tomlinson 1977: 128; Shaloff 1974: 359; Smith 1972: 122.
81. Bradley 2004: 82; Chandra 1979; Fitzgerald 1997: 426; Kaviraj 2000: 151; Wakeman 1977: 224.
82. David 2006: 1291 ff.; Dodgen 1999: 816; Ebrey 1984: 221; Oxfeld 2004: 965; Sutton 2007: 12.
83. Gillin 1964: 277; Liu 1971: 9; Luong 1985: 167; Wakeman 1977: 234.
84. Brocheux 1976: 665; Dirlik 1997: 363; Duiker 1973. Similar processes in Cuba: Carr 1996: 129; Grobart 1975: 101.
85. Affonso 1972: 65; Josh 1981: 187; Little 1967: 31; Mukherjee 1981: 12; Selden 1995: 36.
86. As evident in the option for the popular front tactics as a junior partner. Cf. Erdmann 1964: 179; Goldenberg 1966: 396; Gough 1969: 32; Josh 1981: 171; Leclerc 1981: 795; Raouf 1990: 20.
87. Chandra 1979: 84; Chenntouf 1977: 227; Frank 1962: 372; Ghosh 1988; Gould 2002: 625.
88. Banerjee 2004; Bhattacharyya 1978: 613; Ray 1969: 97; Veerathappa 1965: 537.

89. Gardner 1998: 61–63; Hess 1972; Homan 1990; Venkataramani & Shrivastava 1964: 2.
90. Anderson 1983: 481; Bridier 1968; Fasseur 1982: 111; Goto 1999; Popkin 1985.
91. Kaviraj 1989: 15; Rathmann 1967: 1373; Sandbrook 1981: 206.
92. Delacroix & Ragin 1981: 1339; Evans 1977: 59; Ndongko 1985: 246.
93. Délégation Générale du Gouvernement en Algérie 1960: 275 ff.; Elsenhans 2000b: 646.
94. Kwon & Cordell 1985: 261; Lukauskas 2002: 393 ff.; Sunoo 1978: 323.
95. A l'origine des projets industriels les prévisions sont toujours optimistes. La réalisation est différente. Les plans de productions ne sont pas atteints, Révolution africaine (When projects start, the forecasts are always optimistic. Execution is however different: Production targets are not achieved, cf. Révolution africaine [This is a newspaper]), 30 May 1979: 19.
96. Oksenberg 1974: 97; Pye 1985: 243; Reda Mezoui 1986: 286–289.
97. Ansari 2001: 5 ff.; Autin 1973: 153; Gordon 1981; Raup 1967b: 54 f.
98. Ahmad & Sternberg 1969: 175; Ardant 1963: 20; Thiesenhusen 1966: 292.
99. Bhatt 2001: 162; Charlesworth 1980: 274 f.; Fuhr 1987: 48; Petras 1975: 297.
100. Durau 1983: 269. On the later return to free marketing, Agarwal 2007: 4263.
101. Berry & Sabot 1978: 1214; Clark 1978: 129; Fritz 1973; Havrylyshyn 1978: 217–223; Robinson 1979: 32; Thiesenhusen 1974: 41.
102. Ardant 1975: 239; Perroux 1966: 516; Vakil & Brahmananda 1956: 219.
103. Islam 1979: 9; Reza et al. 1987: 72; The I.I.P.O. 1979: VI; Winston 1970: 418.
104. Holthus 1975: 362; Lund-Thomsen 2008: 1017; Menck 1975.
105. Anell 1981: 77; Kitching 1980: 428; Le Guay & Royer 1985: 127; Stallings 1979: 249.
106. Bulow & Rogoff 1990: 32 ff.; Dornbusch 1987: 812 f.; Ebenroth & Bühler 1990: 23 ff.
107. This tension was highlighted even in the title of one of my first contributions to the subject, cf. Elsenhans 1977c.
108. Beeson 2009: 734 f.; Brown 2006: 960; Chang et al. 1998: 740.
109. Blundo 2006: 805 ff.; Ibrahim 1994: 439; Ihonvbere 1995: 150.
110. Ayubi 1982: 269; Lofchie 1978: 458; Steel 1997: 54 f.; Vadi 2001: 131; Wils 2000: 386.
111. Ahmed 1976: 295; Bina & Yaghmaian 1990; Datta 1987; Donges 1976: 647; Schatz 1983: 11.
112. Green 1976: 22 ff.; Sklar 1967: 8; Spairs 1991: 105.
113. Markov 1970; Müller 1967; Roeder 1989: 876; Zawodny 1966: 368. Cf. also the literature on the single-party state in developing countries, Bayart 1973: 144; Benakezouh 1985: 673; Jones 1976: 221.

114. Equality of the rate of interest and the rate of growth of the capital stock and the rate of growth. This implies a stable COR and a stable share of wages in national income, cf. Phelps 1965.
115. Baufeldt 1978: 291 ff.; Hanson & Vogel 1978; Hewett 1975.
116. Kornai 1996: 1007; Monkiwicz 1989: 120; Schröder 1987: 171.
117. Ake 1985: 105; Kaplan 1978: 823; Kim 1984: 844; Wallerstein 1990: 136. For a criticism, cf. Elsenhans 1996c: 134–151.
118. Clark 1978: 129; James 1987: 202, 222; Rogerson 1990: 93; Thiesenhusen 1974.
119. Nolte 1984: 324 ff. Cf. Laue 1953: 444; on the relevant controversy between the Narodniki and the proponents of accelerated industrialisation led by finance minister de Witte.

5

Globalisation and Its Contradictions

Globalisation is the name given to a new wave of capitalist expansion, following many other waves, such as colonialism in the 19th century. It became possible because those non-capitalist forces described in the previous chapter failed to deliver economic growth. The colonialist extensions from the 16th century until the end of the 19th century were all intimately linked with superior Western military power. The new wave, which is called globalisation, is no longer linked to the use of military power. It develops and takes place at the invitation of local elites. It is ultra-imperialist in the sense of Kautsky (1914). In all participating countries, it is based on those who benefit from the market against those who need empowerment in order to correct the effects of the market. Globalisation does not create lines of resistance for those who need them in order to form counterweights against individualistic capitalist strategies.

Globalisation is, therefore, ambiguous. The economic and social consequences of globalisation are controversial. Where opportunities for resistance exist or are established accidentally through increasing employment, globalisation promotes the transition to development and welfare style capitalism. Wherever such opportunities for resistance do not exist for large numbers of people, globalisation leads to increased rent-seeking and inequality.

China has managed its transition to development through globalisation. It has become the second economic power next to the United States and the world's most important exporter of manufactures. Critiques argue that China has become a deeply inegalitarian society. With an undervalued currency and a high share of imports in the consumption patterns of upper income households, the statistical distribution of income becomes distorted through currency parities. High-income households consume products priced at international prices. Low-income households consume locally produced products which, in comparison to other economies, are underpriced because of currency undervaluation. In China, mass hunger seems to have largely been overcome. This distinguishes China favourably from some less globalised highly populated economies in Asia, especially South Asia.

China's economy is now flexible enough to allow for a redirection of production. In addition to exports the development of the Western provinces has become a major motor of growth.

Together with some other export-oriented industrialising countries, more than one third of the underdeveloped world benefits from globalisation. Hence, the link between globalisation and development in the interest of masses is mixed.

A major part of the underdeveloped world benefits from globalisation because of two mechanisms: internal reforms, especially land redistribution, which has created a minimum of real income, and the pattern of liberalisation which has favoured labour-intensive manufacturing.

The effects of globalisation are independent from the extension of capitalism and depend more on internal structures and their impact on the empowerment of labour. Even with a better negotiating position, labour can avail itself of the additional demand for its services, increase its income and contribute to the emergence of an internal market. Such an internal market for mass goods becomes the basis for accumulation and self-sustained growth.

I argue, however, that the impact of globalisation is too weak to ensure that these positive tendencies prevail. My argument is that the contemporary wave of globalisation will not lead to a capitalist world system. I will break this down into five propositions:

1. The success of the catching-up economies which grow with export-oriented manufacturing is based on their increase in performance not only in world-market-oriented activities but also in the local-market-oriented wage goods production which allows them to support their exports with an implicit subsidy. These achievements in the wage goods production will not necessarily lead to a parallel expansion of their home consumption capacity.
2. There is no assured possibility of leading countries to maintain leading positions. In defending their leading positions they might be

tempted to resort to industrial policy and state-subsidised strategic trade behaviour.
3. Catching-up economies accelerate the process of catching up by industrial policies which are based on rent.
4. Leading economies develop tendencies of rent-seeking in order to protect social equilibriums and thus weaken their own capitalist structures.
5. Underconsumptionist tendencies in many areas of the world economy lead to the dominance of finance capital which reinforces rent-based structures.

Export-oriented Growth in the Underdeveloped World: A Dependency on Cheap Labour?

Mainstream interpretations of the push of (some, but major) hitherto underdeveloped and technically lagging behind economies insists on the emergence of a world labour market with large supplies of cheap labour which is ready to work at very low real wages because of the lack of other earning opportunities.[1] This labour can be employed with modern technology which has become available in production sites outside the industrialised economies because technology has become mobile: Transnational corporations can use cheap labour in countries by bringing their technology. Local private and public enterprises have access to foreign technology on commercial bases and are able to manage these technologies at high levels of efficiency and productivity.

These possibilities do not lead to increases in real wages as long as this labour is not scarce in line with my argument that it is not productivity but scarcity of labour which determines real wages quite in line with the neoclassical wage drift.

Cost competitiveness and, hence, specialisation is based on comparative advantages, and never on absolute advantages. Absolute advantages are difficult to define and in any case are irrelevant. China has many absolute advantages in tropical products in relation to Europe, but export manufactures. Ricardo (1951: 135–149) shows that an economy which leads in productivity in the production of all tradable goods has still an interest to specialise, provided that its advances are higher in the production of some goods than in the production of other goods. Comparative advantage is transformed into cost competitiveness by adjusting the labour cost of production, in Ricardo's demonstration by adjustments in the relative price levels between the respective economies in relation to gold through movements of bullion, under the contemporary conditions of scriptural money through adjustments of the exchange rates. The actual drive for export-oriented manufacturing is not based on low real wages but on the capacity of the hitherto underdeveloped economies to devalue their currencies below purchasing power parity (Elsenhans 2000a, 2002, 2004, 2005). Labour in catching-up economies is cheap because of the exchange rate (Gala 2008; Suntum 1986: 502). The real wage rate influences the exchange rate only in so far as imports matter for the real consumption of the wage earners.

The role of the exchange rate has been belittled in the Latin American discussion during the 1960s as it had been argued that the share of imports in mass consumption was high so that devaluation of the currency could not lead to improved international competitiveness: Higher prices for imported products in the wake of devaluation would lead to local inflation.[2] The share of imported goods in the consumption of poorer people in most of the population-rich countries of Asia seems, however, to be limited today not only because of their poverty but also because of the success of import-substituting industrialisation in these simple goods.

There is broad evidence that real wages in export-oriented economies of the South are much higher if measured in the products which can be purchased locally in comparison to the basket of goods which can be bought abroad on the world market if their income is converted into international purchasing power. Already at first sight, it is obvious that labour paid less than 1/50th of the average wage in an industrial country could not survive there. Cheap labour paid in international currency at the rate reported from the catching-up economies of the South has to have access to the basic-needs goods at cheaper prices than practiced in the industrially advanced world. The World Bank regularly compares per capita income not only at the exchange rate but also on the basis of purchasing parity. Purchasing power parity is for most of the Asian countries four times higher. Twenty years ago, a Chinese household could buy for its income in Beijing up to 10 times as much as in Canada after converting its earnings into Canadian dollars, depending on the definition of its basket of consumption goods, including housing and services, or not (Chen et al. 1994). Our students who travel to Asia are well aware of the differences in purchasing power parity: For them India is cheap and the Gulf emirates are expensive. Not poverty stricken sub-Saharan countries, but Asian countries where poverty is less blatant, have succeeded in export-oriented growth. The lengthy discussion on the Chinese exchange rate and the ever increasing pressures of the West on China to put an end to the 'undervaluation' of the Yuan[3] are an ultimate proof for the argument that the new competitiveness of Third World industrial production sites is the result not of low real wages but of currency parities. Third World labour is cheap because of the low exchange rate for their national currency. There is a race between currencies for low labour costs—rather than between labours in various regions of the world for the lowest real wages.[4] The real wages are often not known to investors who care only for the cost of this labour in international currency (Kenney & Florida 1994: 31).

Higher real wages than purchasing power of these wages in international currency imply that there has to be a supply of products which are not imported but are locally supplied in the exchange for the local currency income of the workers in the export sector. This additional supply of products can only come from the local economy. In order to increase exports on the basis of additional workers whose share in the receipts of the export sector (their wages) does not pay for the import of goods which cover their additional consumption requires that this difference in real consumption is supplied by the local economy. The local wage goods production has to be able to react flexibly to the additional purchasing power which accrues to these additional export sector workers.

At low levels of real income, the bulk of household expenditure goes to food, up to 70%. The share of food remains nearly constant around 50% until real incomes reach the double of bare subsistence. The additional items are to nearly equal shares clothing, housing and shelter, household equipment (furniture, dishes, pots, cutlery) and 'various items' (transport, some amenities).[5] Most of these items, but also modern products, amongst them household equipment (priority: refrigerator, then TV),[6] are produced locally in most Latin American and Asian countries or in neighbouring countries showing similar signs of low levels of development. Feeding additional export sector workers in an export-oriented manufacturing sector in order to make it competitive on the basis of an undervalued currency depends on the production of a surplus of the local agriculture. Devaluation depends on the availability of a locally produced agricultural surplus. The requirements for successful export-oriented manufacturing are quite identical to the requirements for the so-called self-centred development.

The Green Revolution is at the origin of this surplus of food production. By reducing the growth period of some cereals, especially rice, it has increased not only yields per surface but also useful surface.[7] It is, therefore, no accident that the rice growing economies of East and South East Asia where the Green Revolution has had its greatest impact are at the forefront of export-oriented manufacturing. Those regions where the Green Revolution has not really worked, sub-Saharan Africa (Masters 2005: 43–51) and the Arab world, have not succeeded in adopting this development path. All countries which were successful in export-oriented manufacturing were at least initially self-sufficient in food production.

Where the Green Revolution was complemented with agrarian reforms, an additional effect was achieved. Farm households directly mobilised agricultural surplus for subsidising industrial labour and keeping wage rates low even in the local currency. Agrarian reforms have been shown to force owner-operators to supply additional labour for only low increases in production. Whenever industry offers higher wages than the declining marginal returns in owner-operated farms, the households will offer labour. The wage rates which trigger off this supply can be lower than the wages that industry would have to offer to workers without links to agriculture. Workers without any link to agricultural production have to cover the whole of their subsistence from industrial employment. Off-farm labour still has access to the income provided by the most productive 'hours' spent by themselves or by members of their family on the farm (Dasgupta & Ray 1987: 177; Elsenhans 1996a: 96). Workers without some link to agriculture have to earn at or above the average wages per hour which cover the cost of living. Workers with access to some form of agricultural production need only earn above the marginal earnings they would achieve on their farms. Hence, the young females work for some time in export industries in Korea or Taiwan until their marriage: They need to cover only their costs of their on-going subsistence, but not their costs of reproduction which have to cover child rearing and old age.[8] The same applies to many migrant workers in today's Mainland China (Croll & Ping 1997: 128).

If cheapness of labour is based on devaluation, the more advanced industrial countries cannot get protection from competitive pressures from low-cost economies by cutting their own wages. The cost difference to low-cost labour countries with self-sufficiency in mass consumption goods can be maintained unilaterally by the low-cost economy by simply further devaluing, and this is quite in line with neoclassical economics (Suntum 1986: 504). This will not be perceived as illegal as the Bretton Woods institutions constantly favour devaluation if an economically backward country experiences difficulties in its external equilibriums. As well, wage cuts in the leading economies do not decisively affect their comparative cost advantages.

By devaluation-driven growth, catching-up economies put on the world market additional quantities of products without providing additional demand by themselves. The additional demand has to come from the more advanced economies. These economies experience already difficulties in keeping their wage increases in line with the neoclassical textbook prescription where real wages should follow increases in productivity. Neoclassical authors now argue that this rate should be calculated not on the basis of the observed productivity increases but on the basis of the average which includes the productivity of the increasing number of unemployed.[9] Their productivity is assumed to be near zero. Taken as a whole, this demonstrates the confusion of mainstream economics and the tendency to no longer follow this yardstick in the West.[10] The theoretical mess reflects the fact that capitalism does not work without empowerment of labour here because of the disempowerment of labour in the low-labour-cost economies. Correctly, formulated within the framework of an open economy, the productivity orientation of wage increases implies that wages should rise not only according to increases in productivity but also in line with the improvement of the terms of trade. Obviously, in cases of competition and interaction with economies which systematically engage in devaluation, the terms of trade of the non-devaluing economies have to improve. The hitherto expensive products produced by high cost, high wage labour in the advanced economies are replaced by imports produced by low cost (and not necessarily by low real wage) labour in the catching-up economies. The prices of the products which are de-localised decrease in relation to the prices of the products which continue to be produced in the high-income economy. A deterioration of the prices for one category of products in relation to others constitutes a deterioration of the terms of trade for the products with falling prices and an improvement of the terms of trade for the products with stable prices.[11] In order to absorb the rise in production available without additional demand from the newly industrialising countries, the more advanced economies would have to increase their consumption and their real wages more rapidly than the increase of their own productivity. This in turn would intensify the tendencies of industry to migrate to low-cost economies (and increase their employment, that is, contribute to the empowerment of labour).

Even catching-up economies with balance of trade deficits may produce less than they consume. The balance of trade deficits result primarily from declining prices for industrial exports which in turn translate into improving terms of trade of the industrially leading economies.

More rapid growth of production from low labour cost areas has the same consequences as productivity increases. More imports from low-cost areas combined with the slow expansion of production in the advanced economies increases the availability of goods in relation to factors of production employed, hence productivity but not income. This is the standard definition of underconsumption.[12]

There are two limits to devaluation-driven growth: the exhaustion of the local surplus of wage goods, ultimately of the surplus of agricultural production on the one hand, and full employment on the other hand. We can disregard the first limit for our issue of how to get catching-up economies to contribute to increased world consumption. Nobody would dare to fall behind the achievements of the Green Revolution and to once more risk dangerous famines in the South. Hence, the achievement of high levels of employment is primordial in order to transform export-oriented catching-up economies into capitalist ones. The more equal the distribution of incomes, the higher the multiplier of additional employment in export-oriented manufacturing. Agrarian reforms, therefore, not only contribute to ease the entry into export-oriented manufacturing but also accelerate their transition to capitalism. There is no need to discuss here the old issue whether the import share of low-income households is really lower than the import share of high-income households (who consume services and local luxuries).[13] Without a low share of imports in low-income household consumption, devaluation-driven growth with export-oriented industrialisation would just not have taken place.

Additional exports in case of high levels of employment lead to scarcity of labour. Nominal wages increase. An economy with undervalued currency imports inflation in case of high levels of employment and the rise of its cost advantage if it rejects currency appreciation. Germany in the late 1950s and Japan in the late 1960s provide the examples.[14] When Korea reached high levels of employment through export-oriented manufacturing, wages no longer increased only in the export branches but also in the rest of the economy. Korean economists call this the turning point.[15] In addition, after 10 years of high levels of employment, a Korean working-class movement had emerged which later, after initially violent strikes, turned into a reformist movement which contributed to stabilise democracy and a capitalist market economy.[16] China shows similar developments which are encouraging:[17] Even a large economy may reach rapidly employment levels through appropriate combination of export-oriented manufacturing and poverty eradication[18] which empower labour.

The essential question is therefore: Can we complement the drive to globalisation based on trade and foreign direct investments by the implementation of the empowerment of labour before we can rely only on the mechanism of empowerment constituted by high employment levels, and this under conditions where more and more still underdeveloped economies acquire the capacity to devalue as a result of development efforts even reactionary governments cannot avoid to implement?

Established Leading Economies Risk to Be Overtaken

Processes of de-localisation on the basis of changes in comparative advantages are inextricably linked to the relation of a growing capitalist centre and an at least previously less dynamic periphery. Productivity growth rates differ from branch to branch in the capitalist economy. This leads to changes in the relative prices between branches and ipso facto to changes in comparative cost advantages of any periphery, even if there has been no productivity increase at all. Often such processes undermine the power relations in the capitalist centre. Already in the middle of the 19th century, Marx reported that the English entrepreneurs threatened their English workers with the argument that Belgian workers were ready to accept lower wages and harsher work conditions (Marx 1867: 700). Bismarck is quoted for having argued: 'A normal work day could be established by Germany alone, if Germany was surrounded by a Chinese wall and was economically self-sufficient' (Huberman & Meissner 2010: 665). At that time (in the last quarter of the 19th century) Germany was considered as a new threat: the label 'Made in Germany' was introduced against the German low-quality products[19] as today everybody warns against the shoddy products from China.

As the hope to block this competition through wage cuts is unrealistic, a rational reaction of a leading economy could consist in intensifying specialisation in technically more demanding products. A large spectrum of theories of growth, including the theory of the product cycle,[20] the theory of endogenous growth,[21] the theory of imperialism[22] and the theory of dependency,[23] considers technical progress as path dependent. Hence, the technically leading country is not only best placed for technical innovation but has also comparative advantages in the newest and technically most demanding products. Such a protection through specialisation on high technology branches is, however, not possible if we assume it to go together with the new endogenous growth theory,[24] the post-Keynesian theory of a stable COR (cf. Chapter 2, note 13), the theory of the importance of disembodied technical progress,[25] the theory of learning by doing[26] and the strategic trade theory.[27] These theories assume that technical progress is not only the result of better investment goods, but also of an invisible element which is mainly produced without additional costs through the process of improvement discovered and implemented in the production process itself. If an economy acquires productivity increases by its experience in producing a product or a family of products, it is most implausible that it will enjoy the same advance in productivity when it engages in production of a new product or family of products at the same time as an economy which has not yet been active in both families of products. The theory of the product cycle and all other theories of a path-dependent technical progress have argued that learning by doing in a high-technology product allows reducing the cost of discovery and exploiting new technologies. Here, technical progress is viewed as a discovery process which incrementally shows new possibilities at the frontier of technical knowledge and skills based on the 'acquis' acquired in already practiced production processes. This incremental character of technical progress and this dependence of innovation and productivity on acquired skills and knowledge are not denied. But it is highly improbable that a leading economy has the same advances in productivity in a new production process, it has not yet been active in before, as in old processes where it has already acquired experience in relation to an economy which has not been active in neither of the two production processes. The essential term is 'same'. The more advanced economy is more productive also in the new production process, but its advance is not equally important but smaller. It has, therefore, comparative advantages in the old production process although it is also more productive in the new one. It is not 'competitive advantage', a very unclear notion, but 'comparative advantage' which shapes specialisation.

The mechanism can easily be illustrated by the division of labour between two students coming to Europe from Asia. We assume the first has already passed a year of studies in Amsterdam. He dislikes the plains and goes to Austria where he is able to have his girlfriend from his home country joining him. They have to work for their living by filling forms where Dutch and German language is needed. Although the boy, having already started to learn Dutch is rapidly much better than his girlfriend in German, so that he is able to fill more rapidly both the Dutch and the German forms, the boy would first fill the Dutch forms, leaving the German ones to his girlfriend and only filling German forms if he has time left.

The specialisation on old products despite higher productivity in new products has often occurred in history. It has allowed catching-up economies to overtake former leaders especially in branches with new technologies (Dormois & Bardini 1995: 100). France was very advanced scientifically and technically in the 18th century but left the production of mass consumption industrial products to Britain.[28] The inventions of the second industrial revolution (electricity, chemistry) were all made simultaneously in Britain and Germany.[29] Britain was earning so well with the old products (textiles) that it did not care for developing electrical machinery and chemical industries which were left to Germany and the United States.[30] Both countries overtook Britain in industrial production in productivity during the interwar period.[31] The complaint that nowadays Germany is specialised on old industries (machine building, vehicles, chemistry) and has ignored the microelectronics revolution has been largely advanced in the last decades.[32] The fax machine has been invented in Germany but has been developed and produced in Asia as it seemed not to be profitable in Germany (Kremendahl 1995: 971).

The increasing transferability of technology makes this danger more threatening as it reduces the importance of immobile elements in productivity increases and makes productivity increases less path dependent.

Threat of being overtaken becomes more relevant in an underconsumptionist situation. Let us assume a truly capitalist world economy where all participating economies achieve high levels of employment. Assume now that there is an innovation in one of these economies, we may call 'A'. Its balance of trade improves. The new branch attracts capital from other walks inside the own economy but also from outside. Its exchange rate appreciates. The exchange rate of the rest of the world falls. Branches without innovation lose their competitiveness to producers in the rest of the world which I call 'B'. The amount of depreciation depends on the relative backwardness of the non-innovative branches in 'B' in relation to 'A', as the falling exchange rate of 'B' makes branches competitive in 'B' which previously could not sell abroad (Elsenhans 2001a: 62 ff.).

If 'B' is a capitalist economy, devaluation will lead to increases in its production for its home market and for the world market in those branches where its lag in physical productivity is lowest. 'B' will increase its exports rapidly in those branches where there was no innovation in 'A'. As 'B' is a capitalist economy, there will be wage increases because of increases in production, also in the 'old' branches. Italy captured large part of the world market for labour-intensive shoes and textiles produced by its small-scale industries of the Third Italy, Emilia Romagna with high wages by Italian standards.[33] This is a good example for high levels of employment with low levels of productivity increase in old industries. High levels of employment will in addition favour productivity-increasing innovation even in old industries as the entry of information technology in many of these old industries in the last three decades has shown (Elsenhans 1990: 15). High levels of employment on the basis of still well-earning workers maintain internal demand on which further innovation can be based.

If 'B' is a capitalist economy, the tendency to full employment triggers off adjustments between relative prices as described in Chapter 2 (on the capitalist mechanism homogeneous factor productivities created through competition on factor markets (p. 21). The expanding production in branches with low productivity lags leads to more employment and competition for labour: Wage rates increase also in the non-affected branches. The capitalist mechanism of growth on the basis of high mass incomes is maintained with some shifts of employment to the 'non-innovative' branches of production and a continued pressure for reducing labour costs through innovation because of the continued scarcity of labour. Branch wise productivities converge through changes in relative prices of products. Productivity differences in monetary terms in relation to the economy 'A' tend to become identical. In case of further innovation in 'A', 'B' becomes competitive in new branches with new employment effects and new export possibilities. If 'B' maintains high levels of employment, any new even unfavourable specialisation allows new specialisations with new employment possibilities. There may be (limited) losses in export earnings but no threat to high levels of employment. As 'A' enjoys improving terms of trade in the wake of its innovativeness, the lower levels of international costs of production in 'B' may result in 'B' having lower costs in exploiting the next generation of innovations. 'B' catches up with 'A'. 'B' has lower international costs for its immobile factors of production, maintains its possibilities for growth via the internal market, remains a flexible economy because the capitalist mechanism of productivity convergence continues to work and maintains its possibilities for participating in the exploitation of the next generation of innovations.

Let us now assume that the 'rest of the world' is no longer a relatively homogeneous economy 'B', but divided between a capitalist area with high levels of employment and a non-capitalist area which I call 'C'. Because of a large amount of workers who are unable to produce at least their subsistence in agriculture, there is structural unemployment. 'C' is able to compete with 'B' after 'B' has to focus more on older products with higher wages as assumed in the benign model without the existence of 'C'. 'B' will not be able to expand its employment on the basis of old industries in case 'A' innovates and destroys the competing productions of the innovative sector in 'B'. 'C' will be able to supply the non-innovative products on the basis of its cheap labour and reduce their price so that 'B' can no longer compete in non-innovative products on the basis of its to high labour costs.

If there are high levels of employment in the whole world economy, the danger of being outpaced or overtaken in productivity is not seriously felt because the falling behind economy can maintain high levels of employment on the basis of its specialisation on 'non-innovative' products. It can even hope to acquire later on comparative advantage in new branches on the basis of still high levels of economic activity which are supported by its own home market.

The emergence of a C-world has no influence on this configuration between advancing, falling behind and once more catching up and overtaking economies as long as one of the two following conditions is fulfilled:

1. The C-world has comparative cost advantages in a very limited spectrum of products on the basis of high productivity levels in comparison to the advanced industrial countries. The market-based exchange rate reflects this high productivity (low-productivity differentials) and renders all other productions of the tradable goods in the C-countries uncompetitive. This was the case when Third World countries specialised in mineral and tropical raw materials.
2. The C-world has comparative advantages in some manufacturing products, but its productivity lags are still high so that the costs necessary for the transformation of comparative cost advantages into cost competitiveness cannot be covered. Causes may be high transport costs which are not affected by devaluation or a low surplus of the local production of wage goods which does not allow supplying the local labour in the export sector with locally produced wage goods. This corresponds to the actual situation of the internationally marginalised areas of the Third World, for example, sub-Saharan Africa or landlocked countries in Asia.

The challenge of actual globalisation consists in the weakening of these barriers: transport costs have decreased; raw material prices have fallen until the recent import drive of the threshold countries so that high raw material prices do no longer keep exchange rates high for the C-world (this means the end of Dutch disease); the Green Revolution has worked in large parts of Asia and Latin America.

It is the danger of being overtaken in also very modern products which keeps the most advanced countries from playing the game of continued adjustments in their specialisation with the catching-up world. As long as the most advanced economies have their comparative advantages in the most modern products (and hence also technologies), they can maintain high levels of employment by pushing the expansion of their internal demand. The demand for the newest products is highly demand elastic and benefits the home industry. This is the configuration on which the product cycle theory was based. Rising mass incomes in the leading economies lead to the de-localisation of the production of older products to technically less advanced economies which are catching up without endangering the capitalist growth mechanism in the technically more advanced economies. If, however, catching-up economies early on acquire comparative advantages in the most innovative products, leading economies with their higher wage costs due to high real wages and high exchange rates feel threatened from competition of low labour-cost countries: the 'ugly ants' working without interruption first in Japan than in China.

The reaction consists in strategic trade (Krugman 1979: 479, 1986) and industrial policy.[34] Independently from the initial comparative cost advantages, lasting comparative cost advantages can be acquired on the basis of early entry into the production of a new product, the early capture of the world market and the development of economies of scale on the basis of this capture. The followers can enter the production of this product only by overcoming high barriers to entry with initially high costs. They have to pay for initially sub-optimal sizes of plants and high degrees of underutilisation of plant and equipment, as initially their production capacities are oversized in relation to the share of the market which they can achieve at an early phase of entry into the production of the new good.[35] Strategic trade requires industrial policy. Industrial policy implies investment, the profitability of which can neither be foreseen nor be guaranteed. On a large scale, industrial policy requires protection of those industrialists who invest in uncertain industries of the future. This does not necessarily mean state planning, as governments in leading economies do not know better than industrialists which are the industries of the future.

As well, non-governments also do not: Half of the predictions of the institutes of futurology of the second half of the 20th century have been wrong.[36] But even if industrial policies are applied with restraint in not putting one's eggs in only one basket, industrial policy implies rent. The necessary government guarantees for early risk takers have to be paid by somebody who does not benefit from their success of promoted new branches. Burdens have to be limited and so has to be the number of promoted projects. There has to be a rationing process which is not based on an anonymous market but on political negotiation processes. Industrial policies, therefore, cannot avoid bureaucratic target setting whatever the attempts to limit bureaucracy. Because of the difficulties in forecasting, the inevitable infringements on competition may not only endanger technical leadership but may also lead to intensified rent-seeking (Amsden & Singh 1994: 654; Weiss 2005: 732).

One way of guaranteeing competitive advantage consists in concentrating on quality. This was the solution of the old tributary modes of production. It is adopted now by some leading industrial countries. The pattern of specialisation of the German motor industry illustrates such an attempt (Abelshauser 2001: 522). The technical sophistication of cars is increased. Gadgets are added. Germany even keeps major motorways from speed limits in order to increase the interest in high-powered high-speed cars. Many of the characteristics on which the attractiveness of such cars is based are not due to special skills of German workers. The production can be realised in a less advanced economy, in the German case in the Central European countries (Dudenhöffer 2005). The car is only assembled in the technically leading country in order to convey to it the image of the high-technology trade mark. Price formation is linked to distinction like in old luxury products. Sinn's (2005b: esp. 26) argument about of the development of a bazaar economy in Germany reflects this increasing share of a luxury rent in German export earnings. The threat of being overtaken by low-income but rapidly growing markets is normally not perceived. Continued superiority in luxuries appears as a guarantee of good earnings (Kuntz 2007). This is quite similar to the late 19th-century British belief that the new industries of the second industrial revolution of the 19th century did not matter.[37]

Luxury orientation implies unequal distribution of incomes in major markets. In the technically advanced world sales of still leading enterprises increasingly depend on higher degrees of inequality of distribution.[38] The technically leading world develops a luxury pole of industry whereas mass production is transferred to less developed world without creating there necessarily high levels of employment. The West is happy to sell luxuries to a tiny minority in China, but China develops the new mass-consumption-oriented industries.

The tendencies to infringe on the principles of market competition because comparative cost advantages are not being distributed along the hierarchy in productivity growth can best be limited if the hitherto underdeveloped economies achieve rapidly a high level of employment. As the possibilities of enlarging their own internal markets are limited until marginality is overcome or at least decisively reduced, the advanced industrial countries are the main resort for providing a rising world demand in order to ease the transition to a global capitalist system.

Rent-seeking in Export-oriented Industrialisation of Catching-up Economies

Devaluation is not cheap. The critics of devaluation have often insisted on the high losses in foreign exchange.[39] Industrial policy is less risky for a catching-up economy as the task is to imitate more advanced economies (Leff 1985: 347). Upgrading exports is possible by promoting the acquisition of known skills and to gauge the success on the basis of achievements elsewhere. The money required for subsidies can be obtained by taxing export products which are already competitive at a higher exchange rate. This corresponds in substance to the pattern of industrialisation based on taxing raw material exports in order to launch import-substituting industrialisation. Such rent appropriation is also possible on the basis of specialisation in price-inelastic and income-inelastic manufactured goods.

South Korea had been so successful in exporting textiles and clothing that its exports became price and income inelastic. Further increases in quantities exported could be achieved only with deteriorating terms of trade (by further devaluating the currency). Instead, South Korea blocked textile machinery imports.[40] South Korean textile exporters had to turn to the local producers of spare parts and ask them to produce complete machines obviously at an initially higher cost than the machinery until then imported. The textile exports had low price elasticities of demand. Their higher international prices because of higher machine costs did not lead to compensatory decreases in quantities. The import content in export earnings decreased and overall employment increased. The South Korean share in value formation increased. In addition, the local construction of textile machinery increased the local skills in machine-making and contributed to the emergence of a South Korean machinery production, for other branches. Any machine is an assembly of metal parts conceived for executing repetitive movements and power transmission in order to work on a workpiece. Learning in textile-machinery-making improved the capabilities in any machine-making.

In strictly economic terms, the solution adopted by South Korea was only slightly different from the policies of oil countries to appropriate rent in oil exports from which to finance programs of industrial development. Financial support was given to undertakings which were expected to contribute to the diversification of the economy. In the South Korean case, the rent was incorporated in the higher export prices which followed the 'artificial' increase in the cost of the machinery. The rent was directly paid to the diversifying industry in the form of the prices for the equipment the new machine makers had to charge. Competition was maintained amongst the machine makers as they were protected only from foreign competition, not from local competition. There was no moral hazard between the funding agency and the promoted enterprises because all machine producers had access to the rent in the form of market prices under competition. The customers of the machine shops were themselves businesspeople with a clear knowledge of the technologies required. They knew the cost effectiveness of different choices of substitution of labour and equipment in their plants. They were probably better extension agents for the machine producers than government officers and remote from corrupt practices. The rent was appropriated with a minimum of administrative costs and channelled into a subsidy for diversification of industrial production with practically no moral hazard.

Such practices of diversifying the local industrial apparatus on the basis of export charges are most varied. Singapore (Holtgrave 1987: 59–81) has levied special payments on its low-skill industries. Enterprises which paid low wages were taxed on the basis of their declared wage bills. The proceeds were used to finance training programs for labour to be employed in technically more demanding industries. Many export-oriented countries adopt the mechanism already applied in import-substituting industrialisation of requiring foreign investors to gradually raise the local content of their production.[41] Affiliates of foreign enterprises will address local producers to start the production of new inputs and even equipment. In order to limit their own costs they will provide these producers with knowledge they own themselves. The strategy is acceptable to foreign investors as long as they achieve the same profit rate they would get elsewhere. In the foreign enclave normally high profit rates (extra profits) are achieved because of structural heterogeneity, a major characteristic of underdevelopment.[42] In these enclaves, multinational enterprises produce with their own technology at productivity levels close to their home countries, but with cheap local factors of production. As long as prices stay high, they earn extra profits.

Even when having to pay additional burdens, the investors still earn ordinary profits so that they do not run away. It may be difficult for such companies to find equally yielding investment opportunities in the underdeveloped economy. As long as the companies dispose of these extra profits, they might be tempted to export them. With import content rules which link the further access to profit to new investment in less profitable activities, the average profit rate goes down in the original line to ordinary profit rates because of at least initially higher cost inputs. The local production of these inputs may contribute to industrial diversification and can help to improve the overall efficiency of the local economic environment. Brazil's automotive supplier industry is a good example.[43] Taiwan has used the same mechanism early on.[44]

Raw material rents have not played such a role because especially oil countries were hampered in two ways from benefiting from such a diversification strategy. High rents led to high exchange rates which made all other exports and despite protection many import-substituting industries uncompetitive. These countries suffered from the 'Dutch disease'.[45] In addition, raw material production, especially oil production, is characterised by specifically sophisticated and very costly equipment. The cost of starting production of this type of equipment is comparatively high (Sid Ahmed 1995: 77 f.) in relation to the cost of production of equipment for manufacturing, especially for technically less demanding labour-intensive products with which export-oriented manufacturing normally starts.

Where competitiveness of the leading industrial countries depends on the employment of special-purpose machinery, simpler substitutes can normally be used in economies with lower labour costs. The higher quality of the manufactured goods precludes the employment of lower quality investment goods, but the expansion of the market for lower quality final products through the catching up of the less developed world creates new markets also for lower quality machinery and the resulting products. China's export offensive in the underdeveloped world is a good example. In India or Africa, Chinese products have become competitive despite their very low quality because of their price.[46] The concentration of the leading machinery producers of the world—Germany, the United States and Japan—on special-purpose machinery leads to the emergence of a local machinery production in the more advanced of the still technically backward economies. The leading machinery producers give up these less sophisticated production lines.

This modification of the international division of labour in technology production will probably not put an end of the overall hierarchies of unequal development in technology production. This is in opposition to my argument that because of comparative cost advantages, the long-time assumed tendencies to stable hierarchies in the international pattern of specialisation cannot persist. There are special mechanisms in technology production which make this sector resistant to overcoming inequalities in the international division of labour. They provide at the level of theory a good example for the paradigms of continued inequality at a world scale. This is due to the fact that productivity increases in equipment production affect productivity in the production lines which use this equipment.

A machinery producer can introduce new machinery if it reduces costs by saving on inputs, labour or machinery costs. Most machinery achieves this effect by reducing the amount of labour directly used in the production process. It substitutes direct labour by more intelligent labour used in the design and production of the machinery. This use of higher quality of labour may be the empirical background for the usual prediction of a rising capital intensity of production. The net effect of these cost changes (reductions in the cost of direct labour, higher costs of machinery and, hence, higher costs of labour in the production of the machinery) may lead at constant labour remunerations to savings. In that case, it is a rationalisation investment (Bonhoeffer 1967: 25; Bourlès & Lorenzi 1998: 240). It may be that the new machine saves quantities of direct labour by expending high amounts of indirect labour so that overall labour does not decrease. It can, however, still reduce costs if the cost of less skilled direct labour employed in using the machine increases during the lifespan of the machine in relation to the cost of highly skilled labour in the production of machinery at the time of its production. This is a defensive investment. This type of equipment is, therefore, competitive only in economies with rising real labour costs and should be less attractive in economies where real labour costs stagnate because of stagnating real wages.[47]

An innovating machinery producer is normally unable to capture the benefits that the new technology provides to the user. He has to transfer the economic benefit of the innovation to the user of the machinery through a lower price of the machinery. He can sell his new machinery only if he reduces its price to the level where the user receives a benefit from opting for the new technology (Cohen & Levinthal 1990: 135 f.; Elsenhans 1984: 552). The producer of the technology is ready to lower the price of his product as long as they earn average profit rate including the cost of development for the next generation of machines, otherwise he would compromise his future chances for growth and disappear from the market. If he undersells competitors by not charging these costs in the sales price of the machines actually produced, he jeopardises the future of his business.

The innovative machine producer confers a benefit to the machine user. Any user of the new machine realises an increase in his productivity and has lower unit costs of his production, in principle without having acquired any new skills himself. The producer of the machine, and only he, has acquired the skills of not only using this better technology but also of producing the next generation of machines. He has earned an invisible resource that he no longer has to pay for but which reduces the cost of conceiving a new generation of machines in comparison to a competitor who newly engages in machine production.[48] As machine costs are only a share of the machine user's total cost of production, these invisible cost reductions in machinery production have a greater impact on productivity in machine production than in the branches that apply the machines. Productivity increases due to these invisible gains in machinery production are higher in machine production than in the machinery using branches.[49]

If a machine user in a technically less advanced economy is able to operate the new technology at the same level of efficiency as the users of the new technology in the technically more advanced economy, the technically less advanced economy acquires comparative advantages in the machine-using branch. The productivity advance in the technically more advanced economy is higher in machine building (no productivity advance in the less advanced economy) than in machine using (same productivity advance in the less advanced economy).

The possibility of catching up in new industries without having enjoyed learning by doing and the tendency to stabilise leaderships positions in most advanced investment goods production have an important consequence for the promotion of technical learning. In the Korean example it was shown that machine users could become competitive to such degrees that they faced declining earnings because of low price elasticity. Declining prices through worsening terms of trade did not change comparative advantages. In such a situation, total earnings can increase through the strategy of climbing up the ladder from final good to machinery production. Earnings can increase despite comparative disadvantages in machinery production because a further decline in prices for final products is avoided. Perhaps in the case of further devaluation, local machinery production would have become competitive, but only in the wake of losses of foreign exchange earnings.[50] Climbing the ladder before competitiveness is achieved may, therefore, be rational. The best solution for a technically less advanced economy would then consist in looking for export opportunities on the basis of comparative advantages and promoting the local capacities in technology production against the rules of comparative advantage.

The conflict about World Trade Organisation (WTO) rules is a direct emanation of these possibilities. The protection of national innovation systems which always combine competition and government promotion is a consequence and manifestation of this contradiction.[51] This can include the protection of national enterprises which specialise in the development of technologies. Catching-up economies which engage in devaluation and the promotion of their internal mass markets are better placed in this race than the leading economies which seek shelter in the excellence of their technology and of their final consumption goods. Catching-up economies have only to learn about the latest knowledge and skills from elsewhere. Even if this knowledge is protected, they know what to learn and what to search for. Leading economies do not know what they should learn: They have to discover what they could learn.

The Export of Rent-seeking into the Capitalist World

If the capitalist world is not able to transform the non-capitalist world into a capitalist one, the limited expansion of capitalism into the non-capitalist world hits back unto the capitalist world. The capitalist world develops itself as rent-based structures and imports social structures of the non-capitalist world and this despite the appearance of globalisation of its own social and political structures. Market relations can go with many social and economic structures, not only the ones which had preceded the emergence of capitalism, but also the ones which we may become acquainted with in the future. We may perhaps be not even aware of the change in the quality of market relations from perfect markets to markets based on a multitude of rent situations. The same is true with participation: Non-capitalist structures were not devoid of participation as claimed by the theorists of Oriental despotism (cf. Chapter 2, note 47). 'Defective democracies' (Herbst 2001: 358; Merkel et al. 2003) of the third wave of democratisation mostly have formally free electoral regimes. We may live in political and economic systems also in the West which continue to exhibit formally many elements that we are accustomed to associate with bourgeois democracy and capitalism. It can, however, not be excluded that in reality we have already lost the social contents of capitalism and democracy because of the disempowerment of labour.

The leading industrial countries cannot apply the strategy of devaluation cum rising mass incomes to any a large degree, because any devaluation will lead to further devaluations by the catching-up economies as long as they have not achieved high levels of employment. The leading industrial economies, therefore, try to keep their costs low by reducing real consumption. They contribute by this way to the intensification of the underconsumptionist tendencies triggered off at the global level by devaluation-driven export-oriented industrialisation of the catching-up economies.[52] It is misleading to attribute these problems of maintaining employment and international competitiveness in the West to wage levels which are too high as the developing economies rely on devaluation-driven growth and shifting comparative cost advantages. The new competitiveness of low labour-cost economies is, however, used by business in the West for imposing wage restraint. Such wage restraint is, however, economically inefficient as it does not decrease Third World competitiveness. It further intensifies the tendency to underconsumption in the technically leading economies as well as in the world economy and further reinforces the emergence of rents.

If the new competitiveness of emerging countries was due to too high wages in the technically leading countries, then wages in the export sectors and the import competing sectors would have to be low in relation to wages in the non-tradable sector.[53] In fact, in technically leading countries like Germany, wages especially in the export sector are high in relation to the average wage level. In these sectors of the leading economies there is no competition from low-labour-cost production sites. The pressure for wage restraint is high not where there is worldwide competition, but where there is no competition at all such as in non-tradable services.[54] Hence, it cannot be argued that the pressure for wage restraint is triggered off directly by international competition but only indirectly. The transmission belt is created by the interpretation of joblessness by the powerful ones, the ruling class, in the technically leading countries. It is argued that lower wages would lead to more jobs, and the isolated cases of plants migrating to low-labour-cost areas are highlighted in support of this argument.

The loss of jobs in the technically leading economies to the periphery is much less due to a running away of industries to low-labour-cost countries than to a higher increase in productivity in relation to the increase of production in the developed world. Productivity outpaces production (cf. Chapter 5, note 12). The resulting underconsumptionist tendency may have various aspects, but the essential characteristic consists in real wages not growing in line with productivity increases. This lower rise of real wages in relation to productivity cannot be explained by the neoclassical criticism of Keynesianism as also according to neoclassical economics, wages have to increase in line with productivity increases plus/minus changes in terms of trade and the ICOR.

I have already referred to the tendency of neoclassical economists to abandon their own theory of the wage drift arguing that shed off workers have zero productivity (cf. p. 120). The production of an unemployed worker has, however, to be evaluated also within the framework of neoclassical economics on the basis of a full employment level of demand. In a Keynesian world, the level of full employment demand is itself a function of the wage rate. Only in the case of full employment the neoclassical calculation of the marginal product can avoid the tautology that the wage rate enters both the right and the left side of the equation which compares marginal product and marginal cost of labour (Irsch 1979: 47). The issue of unemployment in the leading industrial economies has, therefore, to be dealt with in the light of the causes for unemployment and not vice versa, especially if the economy is characterised by a balance of trade surplus as in the case of Germany. This balance of trade surplus clearly indicates that the economy is so competitive that it sells more to the rest of the world than it buys from it. An increase of its consumption and, hence, its wage bill with a reduction of its exports are compatible with overall equilibrium.

This issue is of central importance: It shows that under globalisation the neoclassical (not the Keynesian) model can no longer be maintained because, to the difference of Say's world, the partial disequilibria on national labour markets are an aspect of disequilibria on a transnational market with adjustment processes elsewhere, but not within the same national economies. At a given exchange rate, wages for one industrial sector 'B' may be too high in relation to a foreign competitor. Labour in this sector is shed when due to increases in average productivity either the average wage rate increases (and this leads to an increase of the wage rate also in sector 'B') or if the exchange rate appreciates due to productivity increases in a more dynamic sector 'A'. Only in the case of rapid growth it can be hoped that the innovative sector 'A' can absorb this additional labour. The demand for 'A' cannot, however, come from sector 'B' in the own economy because this sector is under competition from the catching-up world. Demand for sector 'B' from the catching-up world may, however, also be insufficient due to the strategy of devaluation. In a Keynesian world, it can be shown that full employment can be maintained if the advanced economies grow because also the less advanced economies increase their demand for the products of the dynamic sector 'A' and their own internal mass consumption so that even competitive pressure on sector 'B' is reduced.

We are not at the end of Keynesianism, but at the end of national Keynesianism and need a worldwide Keynesianism. In order to prepare worldwide Keynesianism, we have to behave at national levels in ways in which we do not intensify the challenges to be solved at the international level. Each country should avoid aggravating underconsumptionist tendencies.

It is not a lack of productivity which keeps real wages from rising at national levels. Other causes have to be looked after in order to explain why the neoclassical wage drift is disestablished. They are to be found in the general Keynesian argument about a lack of demand. The link between globalisation and the disempowerment of labour focuses on the question that how globalisation disempowers labour, although it is not a lack of productivity and competitiveness which are the causes. Why does globalisation disempower labour and does globalisation only complement other tendencies to the disempowerment of labour?

In the Keynesian framework, capitalism is always unstable because the neoclassical wage drift only operates in case of full employment. Globalisation in its form of intensified de-localisation of production to low-labour-cost production sites could cause by itself a lower level of employment in the leading industrial countries only if it would lead to balance of trade deficits. Such balance of trade deficits cannot be observed for the already industrialised world in its overall relations with the catching-up economies. The argument of an increasing share of imports in the export of leading industrial economies which Sinn criticizes as a bazaar economy is empirically valid only if there is an overall balance of trade deficit, not if exports are characterised by an increasing share of imports. There is no such increasing balance of trade deficit in Germany's relations with the rest of the world.

With respect to possible internal causes for unemployment in the leading industrial countries, I see three main causes:

1. Investment necessary for the expansion of production is reduced due to the composition of production and the nature of the technical progress.
2. An increasing heterogeneity of labour reduces not only its stability but also its solidarity.
3. An increasing propensity to save out of workers' household incomes which constitutes a claim on the profit earnings of capitalism entrepreneurs.

These three mechanisms disempower labour and lead to new arrangements which weaken the capitalist growth mechanism. Globalisation reinforces but does not create these tendencies.

There is a shift in the mix of production in technically advanced industrial countries and a shift in the composition of value formation. With increasing services,[55] the amount of capital needed for increasing production tends to decrease. Services are not capital intensive.[56] The share of industrial employment in total employment decreases. Industry has been hitherto the main outlet for the use of financial resources for investment.

With less investment required for the extension of production, the share of profit in the real economy would have to decrease. If financial markets existed only for the provision of finance to the real economy, their volume would also have to shrink. This functionally based requirement for a shift in the distribution of income stands across the claims of social groups for maintaining their share in income distribution. The redefinition of the relation between financial wealth and the real economy is resisted by the 'powerful' and successfully resisted if they are able to appropriate 'profits' on the basis of oligopolistic market structures which allow mark-up pricing.

Despite rapid innovation, the new technical wave of microelectronics has not yet led to massive investment outlays in the economy, especially in industry (Bryson 2001: 183 f.). The information revolution contributes to productivity increases but does not lead to a sizeable even temporary increase in investment spending. The COR does not increase, to the difference of other major innovations in history such as the steam engine, the railway or the car with the infrastructures connected to it (Fagerberg 2000: 409; Gordon 1999b: 8, 1999a: 21–23). With a decreasing rate of growth of investment spending, new investment is increasingly financed by amortisation. In the 1960s, amortisation accounted for about one third of the gross investment, in the last decade in Germany for more than 75%.[57] This implies that the net profit in the real economy had to decrease and so also the net rate of profit as the relation between the net investment and the net capital stock. The parallel increase in low-capital-intensive services and relatively low-capital-intensive industrial branches indicates new causes of productivity growth which are independent from accumulation of physical capital. Physical capital could be easily owned as an asset in a balance sheet despite the inflation of assets through the incorporation of immaterial assets. Human capital is difficult to organise in ways which allow its appropriation by individuals other than the person who applies the skills called human capital. When fixed capital becomes less important for the growth of production, the share of profit would have to decline. As long as high profit rates are, however, the mechanism on which the privileged position of the capital owning class is based, the capital owning class interprets such developments in the real economy as a disadvantage imposed on it by the powerful position of labour. It will interpret objectively favourable conditions for growth as seemingly unfavourable conditions. Indeed, high production increases per unit of the additional capital invested are favourable for growth, but unfavourable conditions for the class position of the owners of capital. As a result, the capital-owning class will be reluctant to invest.

This further contributes to low investment spending even if this does not disempower only labour but also the owners of the capital.

Labour has achieved in technically leading economies a position of material well-being where material needs decrease in importance in relation to non-material needs. One aspect is largely discussed under the heading of post-materialist value orientations (Block 1985: 157 f.; Inglehart & Baker 2000: esp. 49). It is not the pursuit of non-materialist values which constitutes the challenge, but the implications which this new orientation triggers off.

Public goods become important, such as the environment. If these goods are consumed as publicly owned goods, especially also if they are produced as publicly owned goods, the share of publicly owned fixed assets increases (Block 1985: 95; Kamieniecki 1991). This constitutes a reduction of the areas where profit-yielding assets can be owned and reduces the possibility of using profit and, hence, privately owned assets as part of the portfolio of private capitalists.

As well, with an increasingly post-materialist orientation, material benefits from selling one's labour power become less important. The flexibility of the labour market in capitalist economies is based on the interests of workers in such material benefits. Either labour is deprived of such benefits and this intensifies the underconsumptionist threat or it participates in such benefits. As they become less attractive, their amount has to be higher in order to have a microeconomical effect, especially in the domains of labour mobility and flexibility.[58]

Labour markets become inefficient or demand becomes insufficient for provoking growth and in addition structurally growth impeding because of diversification. New forms of labour management may emerge: Hierarchical structures develop with a boss who controls the resources to be distributed and logic of 'divide et impera'. Not only there is an opposition between those in relatively protected jobs and those with increasingly precarious employment, but also a hierarchy of grades of skills inside the plant. This hierarchy is often artificially engrossed.

Labour loses its homogeneity and more so the overarching consciousness of its solidarity.[59] The majority of labour explains its economic success increasingly not in terms of class relations and collective organisation but in terms of individual efficiency.[60] Business first sheds unskilled workers in times of low activity. Skilled workers move increasingly into jobs with low-skill requirements and relatively low incomes.[61] The preference of business for highly skilled workers even in jobs with relatively low-skill requirements results in unskilled workers being particularly hit by unemployment

(Bloom & Freeman 1992: 544; Feenstra 1998: 32). A low-income sector of workers emerges which suffers from casualisation of work.[62] An opposition between the still protected sector and the workers with casual work emerges. Joblessness, especially long-term joblessness is increasingly explained as being caused by a lack of skills and commitment to hard work.

This is different from an economy with high levels of employment where unskilled workers earn relatively high incomes if their job is painful. The example of rising haircutter wages (1950–1959 by 86%) in relation to metalworker wages (only by 60%) when levels of employment increased and labour became scarce in West Germany can be quoted as the empirical demonstration of the existence of negotiating power of unskilled workers if there is full employment.[63] The interaction of a tendency of levelling worker incomes and periodical pushes of incomes of some workers with scarce skills (for example, the microelectronics sector until the crisis of the new economy) and casualisation of employment for all those with plentifully available skills is at the basis of the shift from Schelsky's[64] levelled middle-class society to the two tier society (Glotz 1999). Here, all those without scarce skills and without integration into units which require firm specific learning by doing, often in reality 'loyalty', that is, discipline, are marginalised in the economic sphere.

Capitalism becomes socially disembedded but not in the perspective of Schumpeter (1950: 180). Capitalism does not suffer from a lack of entrepreneurial talents and increasing bureaucratisation, but from the lack of the countervailing power of a working class which can no longer exercise such a role when it becomes more heterogeneous with less shared perception of values, interests and worldviews.

Organisational structures and inherited ideologies and values may delay the demise of the Western working class, but not prevent it: Labour had been complaining of being exploited, hence producing a surplus and, therefore, being politically powerful. It now becomes fragmented (Döring 1989: 267 ff.). Some of its better-off parts engage in corporatist participation in distribution, its majority turns to the state from which guarantees for its survival are expected, not so different from the attitudes labour developed in tributary modes of production in relation to the 'good emperors'. Employers are no longer considered as exploiters but perceived as providers of jobs to whom labour has to be grateful (Boyer 1990: 30; Yamamura 2008: 84). Labour aristocracies are no longer the avant-garde within a labour movement which struggles for the emancipation of the working class as this had been the case in the 19th century.[65] Labour aristocracies become a privileged stratum which is rather fearful of violent action of the less well-off masses.[66] They assume a similar function in the power structure as the better off in the fragmented communities of the tributary modes of production.

Labour in the most advanced countries is still confident to benefit from this benign, in relation to the ancient tributary modes of production democratically much more controlled 'emperor': When the financial crisis broke out in 2008, labour in Germany did not react with restraining its consumption, because at least the more skilled parts of it still believed in the corporatist arrangement that the state would not let them down.[67]

Nevertheless, labour in many countries, among them Japan and Germany (since the 1960s), has adopted an alternative of seeking shelter in the market economy by increasing household savings. Household savings of workers in Germany grew of from next to nothing (2%–3%) to about 15% in the 1970s and remain at such a high level.[68] The savings of private households destroy capitalism. Savings of average private households are primarily the costs paid as part of the wages by enterprises to workers, for which they do not get demand. Quite comparable to a shift of the working class to imported products, there is a lack of demand.

On the basis of the link between profits and workers' incomes, profits were shown to be dependent on the demand for consumption goods in excess to the wages paid in consumption goods production (cf. pp. 7–10). A decrease in the demand of households because of savings implies that the total amount of profits earned in consumption goods production decreases by the amount of household savings.[69] Household savings cannot push up the rate of growth of investment, as investment is financed either by retained profits or by credits from the banking system (Pasinetti 1974: 109–132). Savings may ease the liquidity of the bank system, but will not decisively create it. Decreasing profits in the consumption goods production implies a decreasing rate of profit in this department which impacts on the profit rates achieved elsewhere. Liquidity preference increases. Other things being equal, the rate of accumulation decreases in case of higher household savings.

Western capitalist economies have reacted to such decreases of the propensity to invest by policies of cheap money. Enterprises were expected to increase their propensity to invest when bank credits became cheap. However, at no level of non-negative returns on liquidity, an entrepreneur will invest in other projects than rationalisation, if there is no expanding demand (Patnaik 2009: 8; Siebert 2000: 235). The rationalisation investment decreases the income paid out in relation to production. An increase of final demand in the wake of such investment spending in relation to productive capacity can be expected only if there is 'herding' of investment—many investors simultaneously spending money on expansion of future capacity. Cheap money policies may turn inflationary before they reach this critical level where simultaneous investment becomes so important that a scarcity of labour emerges in the labour markets. Only then will real wages rise. Only then an investment boom would lead to a longer term demand-led growth process and a demand-led boom would emerge.

Private savings threaten business profits as the latter are more difficult to achieve if overall household demand decreases as a result of private household savings (Elsenhans 1999: 116–128). In case of real savings of households, the equality of investment on the one side and profits on the other side is modified. Investment has to equal the sum of profits and real household savings (demand foregone). In an economy where workers save, full employment equilibrium requires investment spending in excess of expected profits, hence a rising share of debt-financed investment in the case of a rising propensity to private savings, especially among the households of workers. With a rising share of savings in national income, the Keynesian macroeconomic equilibria can only be achieved at the price of high inflation which would destroy liquidity and devalue financial assets in relation to fixed capital. Such a solution is, therefore, rejected. The problem, however, is that there is no other solution except for mildly combining expansionary monetary policies while trying to limit inflation. This implies stagflation, that is, stagnation with some inflation where neither growth nor stability is achieved.[70]

Inflation is also rejected because with a higher propensity to save the better-off part of working, population rejects inflation. The principle of prefering 5% of inflation over of 5% of unemployment proposed in 1972 by federal chancellor Helmut Schmidt (1972) is not supported by labour when only one part of it, the last tier, suffers from casualisation of employment. The development of productivity under capitalism on the basis of the increasing importance of labour leads to its differentiation. This definitely removes the basis for labour's idealisation by Marx and Engels (1969: 69) as a general class which has nothing to lose but its fetters.

Within the framework of this integration-fragmentation position in a new power configuration, labour does not develop a comprehensive concept of how to manage the capitalist economy in a Keynesian manner.

Labour accepts the ideological hegemony of the existing structures of power and shares with them the ideological dominance of a microeconomically determined perspective, close to the view of business, as the background for a corporatist deal with the 'providers of jobs', at best. (Bergman 2011: 24; Boggs 1997: 747). The fundamental separation between ideology and real socio-economic processes through which capitalism has achieved the empowerment of labour despite opposing ideologies and through which capitalism was able to dissolve tributary modes of production is removed. The relation between ideology and real social process is reversed.

In the transition to capitalism, labour could tolerate any ideology of the organicist type which stressed the social functions of the privileged strata. Ideology did not matter because rising mass incomes reduced the amount of surplus available to the amount effectively spent on investment. Labour had not have to care for ideological hegemony if free competition, scarcity of labour, free labour markets and the absence of political power to force labour to work were guaranteed.

If, however, labour loses this power because of changes in its social and economic position, in its internal structure, and the structures in the demand for labour, labour would have to gain ideological hegemony. Cultural theorists of the prevailing version of constructivism would probably link this requirement to some process of learning and getting access to an appropriate understanding of the conditions for full employment. Marxists have dealt with this issue long before in their analysis of the formation of class consciousness. [71] They followed the obvious aim to establish the conditions for the emergence of a revolutionary conscience which did not take place except in severe crises of capitalism. Marxists had to accept with disappointment that mass revolutionary conscience was not produced on the basis of class positions. Keynesians in turn have to accept that voters will not develop a macropolitical view on how to maintain the conditions of capitalism. Voters are a-cultural and ultimately accept 'fetishised' positions according to which further growth and employment depend on a pattern of distribution of national income which favours capital, a view which is ultimately the particularistic view of business.

Capitalism could thrive in the interest of the masses as long as ideological hegemony was irrelevant for maintaining capitalist growth.[72] When the automatisms of capitalism are weakened, labour is unable to develop a hegemonic ideological position for preserving its negotiating power and with this, capitalism declines politically and economically.

In the case of the disestablishment of the capitalist growth mechanism through lack of demand, capital is sanctioned in the real economy under perfect competition. In case of open crisis, net profits become negative (Kreps 1935: 594; Levadoux 1980: 968). Under perfect competition, capital has to lower prices or to stop production because of lack of demand. There are two mechanisms to fight this challenge, increasing market imperfections and the shift to financialisation.

By eliminating weaker enterprises, those who can still hold on can survive even on the basis of lower demand. As long as gross profits are still positive, existing enterprises have the competitive advantage of disposing of financial resources from amortisations, which new entrants do not have. Concentration of production increases (cf. Chapter 6, note 57). Permanent tendencies to oligopoly develop on the basis of product differentiation in boom and crisis because of the growing complexity of products in the wake of higher levels and greater diversification of consumption (Rauch 1999; Wright 1978: 631). Market power increases and allows mark-up pricing (Choudhary & Orszag 2007; Vickrey 1995).

The actual drive to globalisation is characterised by concentration at the world level. The number of groups at the world level producing cars from industrial countries is today not significantly higher than before the opening of the German economy in Germany.[73] In many other branches the degree of concentration is similar and only moderately lower due to the emergence of new transnational enterprises from the emerging countries (Nolan & Zhang 2002: 8). Oligopolistic groups follow mark-up pricing and are only marginally affected by changes in their cost structures. Major changes in exchange rates lead to pricing through,[74] that is, fixing the prices in the importing economies in function of the now higher cost in their local currencies of the goods sent to them.

Oligopolistic groups exhibit profit margins out of proportion with the rate of growth of real world capital, the national capital stock or their own capital stocks. The rate of growth in profit is disconnected from such elements contrary to the expectations of the neoclassical golden rule of accumulation[75] which Keynesians would, in principle, accept as a yardstick. There is no growth rate of 10% of the world capital stock, but many enterprises in the oligopolistic sector of Western economies want to achieve profit rates of more than that. This can be achieved only by market imperfections, by accumulation to the detriment of other capitalists (the *Mittelstand* with its weak capital basis) and financialisation, the possibility to shift assets from the real economy to the financial markets (accumulation by dispossession).[76]

Rise of Financial Markets and the Weakening of Capitalism

Financial markets are a necessary element of any capitalist economy. Capitalist economies are money economies. It would be very burdensome to transfer by direct contact a saving of an enterprise or a household to an enterprise which wants to invest without having accumulated savings in a bank account. Credit and money creation are mechanisms which emerge much earlier than capitalism in order to reduce transaction costs in market exchange. Without state intermediation, paper money or token money was invented not only in Europe but also elsewhere (China, West Africa) in order to settle operations.[77] Signs which document exchanges are invented in the form of token money, so that at the end of the day only the balances of all the operations have to be cleared in the form of commodity money. Only commodity money has itself a labour value on the basis of its cost of production. Traders on Asian fairs even before the European expansion inscribed their debits and credits on documents sanctioned by the market authority and received at the end of the market period their balances (Juk 1984: 60 f.; Ray 1987: 213). Token or paper money is a paper in itself without value, which provides its holder with purchasing power inside the community which adheres to common legal rules on the basis of trust. The bill of exchange[78] is the promise to pay at an agreed date and place. It is accepted as a means of payment by all those who trust the emitter of the bill of exchange. If a public institution, for example, the state, issues a banknote, the state is responsible for its purchasing power. Where there is a state which can impose taxes and which accepts to be paid for its taxes with the banknotes it has issued, these bank notes are generally accepted as a means of payment. Anybody can use the banknotes for paying taxes so that even non-taxpayers can settle payments if somebody at the end of the line of exchange has to settle taxes (Mosler 1995: 5, 1998: 8).

Whenever there are banks which have access to paper money, they can create money. Banks accept deposits in order to lend them. Any lending to a debtor will lead to payments of this debtor to other market participants who once more give the money they receive as a deposit to banks which in turn will lend it out. Each credit handed out becomes afterwards a new deposit within the banking system. As credit can be produced in an economy with paper money at nearly no cost and is produced as long as there are market participants ready to take loans, control of money creation is necessary. If the banks create money which enjoys public trust because this money is accepted by the state, ultimately the state is responsible. If the banks created money on their own, for example, in offshore banking places, which the hard currency states would not accept as a means of payment for their taxes on their own territory, an exchange rate between this bank-created money and the hard-currency area would have to develop and reflect the trust of the public in the solvency of these banks. Control could be private, if the money is not directly public money. This had been the case of the bill of exchange. It could also apply to the case of means of payment nominated in a currency guaranteed only by banks in offshore banking places.

The privilege of the banks to create money which the state accepts as taxes led to the creation of central banks since the mid-19th century. Such central banks intervene in the economic freedom of banks in order to influence the volume of money created (discount rate, minimum reserves). The goal is the adjustment of the volume of money to the need of the means of payments for transactions and the solvency of the emitting institutions, banks and the state. Money circulates in transactions outside the real economy. In case of transactions in the real economy there are always real assets behind the transactions. In transactions outside the real economy, assets which cover the circulating credit money are ultimately financial assets, hence financial claims of the emitting institutions. If the volume of money expands, more money may enter the exchanges in the real economy, triggering off inflation. If the money remains in the financial circuits, the relation between such financial assets and volume of money decreases with rising prices for assets but not for goods and services. [79] There may be interlinkages between the financial markets and the real economy. In the real economy these linkages need not to be very direct or automatic, for example, through demand for real products out of gains from speculation for goods and services. Expanding financial markets do not lead to inflation in the real economy, but may even raise effective demand in case of a too low expansion of demand from incomes more directly linked to the real economy, such as wages, state demand or enterprise demand for real investment.[80]

The expansion of financial markets may, therefore, be welcomed by the real economy if the expansion of demand from other types of incomes does not clear the markets for goods and services at stable prices. Therefore, the expansion of financial markets often appears as a palliative for an already existing disequilibrium between productive capacity and mass demand. As the deteriorating relation between assets of the emitting institutions of financial titles and the volume of money is not revealed immediately as long as speculators on financial markets believe that there is no such disequilibrium, the expansion of financial markets may aggravate disequilibria in the real economy.

Central banks may follow different goals (price stability, high levels of employment, stability of the external accounts, stability of the exchange rate) but until now have never interpreted rising values of financial titles on the stock markets as inflation, if such increases in values caused worry at all. They were interpreted as speculative bubbles. Price stability is interpreted on the basis of the prices for goods and services in the real economy. Rising prices for financial titles, especially shares, normally are interpreted as a sign of good health of the economy.[81]

Those who buy shares are not only considering the actually paid dividends. They buy in expectation of future rises of the values. Rising prices of shares may reflect the expectation of rising dividends in the future and this on the basis of the expectation of a high growth potential of the respective firm. But the 'investor', a word never used for speculators as long as the real economy was in the focus of interest, can realise a higher future price of the share already, if many believe that the price of the share will rise. The earning potential of the firm whose share is traded may in reality not have risen; it is sufficient that the course of the share rises because a sufficient number of speculators believe that it will rise. Who expect rising courses may adjust on the basis of these expectations of rising value and assume that they are able to sell them before the prices fall when it will become clear that the firm has lower earning capacities. They must only expect that they are able to forecast the development of values more accurately than others, similar to a poker game. The expansion of the financial markets is, therefore, called casino capitalism (Paula & Alves 1998: 11; Strange 1986).

On financial markets expectations are traded. Banks can provide credits for such operations. Who correctly predicts the future is able to repay. If the banking system keeps credit expanding, all speculators correctly predict rising values because all titles traded in the financial markets rise when additional liquidity is supplied and their expectations do not change. If the expectation that financial titles will continue to increase in value ultimately collapses, then it immediately becomes visible that the financial wealth which was recorded in stock markets was just a bubble—literally an illusion, a fiction. The wealth which was registered on the stock market was nothing more than a fictive wealth. It was only paper money for which no value had been created in the real economy. In this respect, everything is merely psychology. The over expansion of money is inevitable if financial markets are left unregulated. Nevertheless, the necessary destruction of fake money is difficult because social groups have believed in this illusion and the destruction of this illusion hurts these social groups (Crotty 2009: 577).

The expansion of financial markets in capitalism corresponds to a large interest coalition. An active monetary policy which reduces the interest rate in periods of low economic activity is advocated by Keynesians because it helps to reduce liquidity preference of potential investors in the real economy (Keynes 1930: esp. 182). The true liberals, such as Hayek (1941: 34), have argued against Keynes that this creation of artificial money ultimately only aggravates the crises it tried to avoid. For Hayek, crises result from excessive or ill-directed accumulation in the wake of which the profit rate decreases. The destruction of capital serves to clean up the market and restores profitability. For Keynes profit and, hence, the average profit rate will not depend on productivity of investment, but on the amount of net investment in relation to the capital accumulated and not yet amortised. High investment spending, therefore, can improve the profit rate.

An expansive monetary policy corresponds to those variants of social democratic reform policies which hoped to reach sufficient final demand without social conflicts and without curbing the expansion of artificial wealth. They may be called monetary Keynesians.[82]

Obviously, earnings on financial markets in the wake of speculation benefited the finance industry. As any other branch of industry it welcomed higher rates of growth provided by measures of the state. There was no reason for the finance industry to warn against such measures. The experts of the banks and the intellectuals who believed in non-Keynesian neoclassical economics could all the more loudly express their support. Neoclassical economists and bank experts have no reason to doubt the viability of a mere expansion of financial markets as long as the money illusion is not challenged. The context for such a challenge would require that economics realise that money is merely a fictive value which becomes a real value only when the entitlement it provides over goods in the real economy is translated into an act of purchasing a produced good with the result of the creation of the corresponding value.

Criticising the bankers with moral indignation as greedy and demanding of them to return to the principles of the honourable merchant is, therefore, a fake struggle and not only an illusion but an instrument to maintain illusions. It dispenses from accepting both the principle of the merely regulatory function of money and the decisive foundation of capitalist economies in their labour value basis. The Marxian attempt of deriving prices directly from labour values has obviously failed but his sociological insight that goods are either free (without price) or are produced, and hence based on those costs of production that an average producer has to incur in their production, ultimately direct and indirect (investment) labour, is however pertinent.[83] There may have been excesses of financial market institutions in their ingenuity in expanding the volume of book money with little amounts of own capital and, hence, high leverage (like derivatives). Even the arguments against hedge funds (locusts) are misplaced that they may not be interested in the long-term viability of enterprises they acquire and resell, but they are interested in the long-term viability of their own hedge funds (Guttmann 1998: 647; Welzk 2007: 59 f.). It is this ongoing viability for which they have been formed.

The money illusion on which the activities of bankers are based cannot be put to their discredit as long as they do not pretend that they are experts not only in speculation and in evaluation of debtors and their projects but also in macroeconomics, which they are not. The great advantage of capitalism to the difference of non-capitalist socio-economic systems lies in the fact that the only partial rationality of any social group with necessarily partial interests in principle is not dangerous in capitalism. For its operation as a system, capitalism does not depend on the predominant influence of any particularistic group but on some equilibria which are brought about by the struggle of contending social and economic forces. These groups can either block the system with negative consequences on themselves or achieve, if they are successful, nothing else than full employment and profit rates depending on the propensity of entrepreneurs to net investment.

The money illusion has, however, been increasingly shared by other social groups. Because of the increasing welfare of workers' households, workers at least started to share in the financial markets. Better-off workers believed that the finance of the future consumption, especially in their old age was possible on the basis of financial assets (for example, capital-based pension funds).[84] They hoped to avoid the transfer of income implied in contribution-based solidarity funds which financed the consumption of the elderly with their actual contributions and their own old age consumption from contributions of the next generation. They feared that they might not get their own money back, not only if in the future there were too few to contribute. They feared that such openly redistributive mechanisms would entail not only intergenerational redistribution but also some intragenerational redistribution in favour of those who had not contributed enough during their working time.[85] Time and again, it was argued that the taxing of contributions for the old today kept the actual working generation from benefiting from the increase of financial titles they would be able to enjoy if they could use their contributions to social security for capital-based old age pension funds. No saving produces today the products the old person will have to consume in the future. The real value of such financial assets on the future markets for goods and services does not depend on their actual purchasing power but on the share of such titles in the global purchasing power of means of payment in relation to the output of the real economy in the future. Like in a contribution-based system, it is ultimately the productive capacity of the economy of the future which determines the value of financial means (Elsenhans 1999: 140 f.). An expansion of the financial markets for feeding the balances of pension funds reduces the actual purchasing power through withheld consumption. In the future the purchasing power of the funds may be reduced because of an oversupply of dis-savings in relation to the productive capacity of the economy. Such a reduction is predicted by those who criticise the unfavourable age structure of the population.[86]

The counterargument that the increasing volume of financial assets supports the growth of productivity can be turned down as investment in the real economy does not depend on financial markets but on liquidity which the central bank can provide even in crisis as shown by the 2009–2010 management of the Western economies (Stolz & Wedow 2010; Wagner 2008: 29). Quite to the contrary, rapidly growing financial markets are characterised by high rates of return in excess of the rate of profit which can be achieved in the real economy. This tends to crowd out real investment. Holders of liquidity prefer to place their money on the financial markets in order to avoid lower rates of return on investment in the real economy (Behr 2000; Frank 1991: 215 f.).

The growth of the financial markets has eased the conflicts which emerged from a deceleration of effective demand in relation to productive potential. The growth of financial markets pushed the inevitable conflict into the future when the bubble broke down. The growth of the financial markets did not remove the disequilibria between the growth of productive capacity and consumptive capacity. When the bubble collapsed, the conflict over the character of the money emerged: Had it been only artificially created? Either those who held this money had to get now real titles or their (until then only fictive) values had to be adjusted to what they could really claim. As the banks are an integral part of the mechanism of regulation of a capitalist economy, their breakdown could be accepted only if part of the banking system could be maintained in order to supply the real economy with means of payment in order to ensure the continuity of activity. If such banks are identifiable and can be protected from the repercussions of the collapse of other banks, this is a viable solution which explains that some economies with tighter regulations for their banks have been more or less largely protected from the impact of the world financial crisis.

If such an isolation is not possible, the banks have to be sheltered from having to pay for the expansion of the financial markets. This is the purpose of government policies, not only since 2008 but already during the Third World debt crisis of the 1980s (Elsenhans 2003: 332–333). At that time, the banks were allowed to proceed with rescheduling debt. Rescheduling allowed an increase in the amount of the principal (the amount of money rented out) of the debt to high levels without further fresh money by adding to the principal new credits to cover the interest which debtors (practically in default) were no longer able to pay. Indebtedness rose through bookkeeping operations. Interest which was not paid was not only foregone income but a loss of the principal. As a part of the principal they became losses which could be deducted from other bank earnings. Interest for the new money provided by rescheduling was high because of the low quality of the debtors, although the principal goal of the operation was to secure the principal by guarantees from the governments of the industrial countries. By transforming unearned income into losses the banks succeeded in reducing their tax burden from other operations. As a result, inflated provisions for losses shifted the real losses from the banks' foregone income to the taxpayers in the West. By such procedures fictive money was converted into real values by means of state interventions.

If the state is able to tax the banking system, the state can subsequently recover its means. If by globalisation this capacity of the state or a group of states is rendered inoperative, the holders of financial means succeed in a real redistribution of wealth by the political instrument of their systemic importance. This is why the actors on financial markets can be called a new rentier class (Elsenhans 2000d). They make money on the basis of power without being exposed to the disciplining mechanisms of the market as other holders of surplus in capitalism. They are not exposed to the disciplining mechanisms of the real economy as shown in the dependence of profit on real investment spending. They create fictive money they can transform into real value on the basis of the power relations.

The Financial Crisis: An Opportunity for Strengthening Capitalism

The main issue of the current financial crisis is whether this pattern of recovery by increasing fictive money will succeed. It would imply the creation of an immense overhang of financial assets. Due to the limited amount of real assets it would result either in an increase of public debt or private debt of households or just deflation through compression of demand for the real economy. Both increases in debt imply the readiness of the state and private households to live on debt on which they would have to pay a permanent tribute to the holders of financial assets. If they refuse to do so, they would have to reduce spending and trigger off deflationary processes in the real economy which in an extreme scenario would further increase the debt as the nominal principal would not decrease despite a decrease in price level. The result would be a serious breakdown of the real capitalist economy. Globalisation would lead to a simple underconsumptionist crisis.

In order to keep capitalism alive, the two patterns of crisis resolution until now experienced should be avoided: The purifying crisis and military Keynesianism. The classical solution is the purifying crisis:[87] the financial assets are massively devalued, even destroyed, the deflationary process with prices declining more rapidly than wages so that ultimately consumption becomes resistant in relation to production despite a period of high unemployment.[88] The share of consumption in national spending increases ultimately and this provides the basis for a new process of accumulation after a longer period of disinvestment.

The Keynesian solution was made possible in a perverse form during the 1930s: the fascist preparation[89] for war pulled also the non-fascist economies, including the US economy after the American entry into the war, from unemployment. Military spending created demand and finally also destroyed the monetary overhang (Brown 1956: 869; Jensen 1989: 574). This solution proved that the restructuring of the major elements of national income utilisation in favour of 'wasteful' demand is economically viable. Politically, it could be realised only under the condition of national danger. It could be implemented only in favour of a goal accepted, if not actively promoted by the holders of financial assets, in the German case territorial expansion through war, in the American case the resistance against this German attempt to hegemony.

Can the then economically successful and not only viable solution be applied in favour of social goals? Has globalisation provided political structures which allow a solution of the crisis in favour of the subalterns even if the negotiating power of labour is severely constrained in times of crisis? Can capitalism be saved even if the spontaneous economic processes at its foundation—the empowerment of the subalterns—have been hollowed out? The transition to capitalism was possible because it did not depend on 'culture', 'norms' or a process of 'civilising'. We have not yet experienced the capacity of social transformation of capitalism with its tremendous increase in productive forces and material well-being even in poor countries. We have seen its disastrous consequences wherever it has only partially penetrated, with the motor of growth being the capitalist centre. Does the intensification of this capitalist penetration into the as-yet noncapitalist world today lead to new perceptions and new experiences? Can these changes create the possibility today to build world-wide alliances in order to create the political structures from which the countervailing power to capital can be built by launching investment and consumption and ultimately the empowerment of labour, now on a worldwide basis? Or does the new wealth primarily benefit the emergence of new rentiers in the North and in the South?

Notes and References

1. Allais 1994: 18; Oman 2000: 9; Scharpf 1987: 307; Sinn 2005a: 8 ff.
2. Braun & Joy 1968: 871; Dunkerley 1968: 129; Felix 1965: 146 f.; Gafar 1982: 235; Marquez & MacNeilly 1988: 313.
3. Guillaumont-Jeanneney & Hua 1996. Further: Bowles & Wang 2006: 237; Drezner 2006: 6; Faujas 2008: 2; Gu 2010: 17; Jungnickel & Schüller 2008: 14; Kaplan 2006: 1184 ff.
4. Asikoglu & Uctum 1992: 1511; Diehl 1996; Hsing & Chen 2004; Intal 1992: 92–96; Page et al. 1993: 126.
5. Banerjee & Duflo 2007: 145; Bardhan 1970: 135; Gujral 1980: 6; Khan 1963: 404; Lokanathan 1935: 376; Oshima 1990: 63. To compare with the household budgets of the early phase of the English industrial revolution: Shammas 1983: 91.
6. Banskota 1985: 56; Hammouda 1984: 72 ff.; Lembke 1980: 56. Cf. also Marsden 1970: 479 ff. On the productive capabilities of the informal sector. Therefore deliberate import substitution policies in mass consumption goods are advocated: Tran 1999: 415.
7. Estudillo & Otsuka 2006: 140; Lewis 1976: 86; Tran & Kajisa 2006: 172.

8. This not imply that capitalism depends on this 'superexploitation of labour', it just exploits it, Boles 2002; Boyd 2006; Cohen 1987: 38; Jomo 2009: 38.
9. Giersch 1983: 13; Landmann & Jerger 1993: 713; Lehment 1999: 81; Leibfritz 1998: 27; Sinn 2007: 57.
10. However such workers have some productivity as is demonstrated in case of subsidised employment in the second labour market. Whitley & Wilson 1983.
11. Giersch 1967: 164; Kendrick & Sato 1963: 982; Long 1966: 143; Salter 1960: 161.
12. Appelbaum & Schettkat 1995: 611; Begg et al. 1999: 229; Burck & Silberman 1955: 97 f.; Dauderstädt 2004: 6; Gerstenberger 1999: 14; Hsieh 1973: 16; Rawthorn & Ramaswamy 1999: 18 ff.; Schumacher 1981: 187 ff.; Semmler 1998: 565.
13. Elsenhans et al. 2000: 13, 2001: 17, with large documentation of the literature.
14. Berthelot 1983: 21 f.; Iwami 1992: 459; Milward 1992: 485; Schatz 1976: 654; Shinohara 1961: 137.
15. Bai 1982; Manning 1995: 77; Osborne 2000: 128. With respect of Japan, cf. Blumenthal 1968: 24.
16. TAZ 2010, and http://www.labournet.de/internationales/bd/index.html, downloaded on 4 June 2011; Clemens 2007: 17; Gray 2008: 111; Sonn 1997: 117; 2007: 528.
17. Barroux 2010; Lee & Selden 2008: 35; Pedroletti 2010; Yuchao 2004: 1021. TAZ 2010, or Bouissou 2010; and Cambodia, Le Monde, 17 September 2010: 10.
18. Bardhan 2007: 3851; Biau 2007: 3370; Bramall 2008: 44; Chandra 2009: 44; Chun 2007: 14; Gustafsson & Zhong 2000: 984 ff.
19. Weiher 1987: 177; Howard 1907: 91; Kindleberger 1975a: 482.
20. Bairoch 1972b: 242; Balogh & Balacs 1973: 242; Chichilnisky 1981: 161; Linder 1961: 57 ff.
21. Cantwell 2000: 149; Frantzen 2000: 207; Krugman 1979: 479; Posner 1961: 329.
22. Majumdar et al. 1978: 810. As an example, cf. Chapman 1938: 49; Dobado González et al. 2008: 759; Osterhammel 1989: 171. And a critique: Warren 1973: 41.
23. Amin 1970; 79 ff.; Broeze 1984: 456; Costa & Robles Reis de Queiroz 2002: 1431; Senghaas 1977: 177.
24. Grossman & Helpman 1989, 1994; Helpman 1984; Sala-I-Martin 1997.
25. Denison 1964; Fabricant 1959: 8 f.; Griliches 1996.
26. Arrow 1962; Foster & Rosenzweig 1995: 1196; Lucas 1993: 251; Sheshinski 1967: 576.
27. Bergelijk & Rabels 1993; Bhagwati 1989: 40; Cowling & Sugden 1998; Helpman 1999; Krugman 1986.
28. Kindleberger 1964: 88, 157 f.; Markovitch 1968: 567; Root 1982: 303; Stürmer 1979: 496.

29. Andersen 1999: 86; Broadberry 1997: 265; Chandler 1992: 19; Harhoff 2008: 51; Headrick 1996: 9, 15; Krause & Puffert 2000; Milward & Saul 1973: 229.
30. Bairoch 1989: 243; Brown 1995: 502; MacCloskey & Sandberg 1971: 107; O'Brien 1999: 69.
31. Aukrust 1964: 32; Broadberry 1993: 773, 1997: 249; Fremdling et al. 2007: 353.
32. Cantwell 2000: 161; Harhoff 2008: 54 f; Hild 2005: 41; Hummel et al. 1996: 10; Penzkofer et al. 1989: 17; Vieweg 2002: 24 f.
33. Bruno 1982; Piore & Sabel 1984: 19 ff.; Rinalsi 2005.
34. Barbet & Benzoni 1993: 766 ff.; Jungnickel & Schüller 2008: 13; Lafay 1975: 433.
35. Baldwin 1988: 229; Bergelijk & Rabels 1993; Helpman 1987.
36. Kuran 1991: 8–12; Schanetzky 2010: 161; Seefried 2010: 109.
37. Aldcroft 1964: 128; Berghoff & Möller 1993: 359; Botticelli 1997: 281; Court 1965: 83; Hobsbawm 1968: 131–146; Kemp 1969: 189; Levine 1975: 306 f.; Musson 1978: 160; Payne 1967: 538; Platt 1972: 124 ff.
38. Curran 2009: 266; Hild 2005: 41; Vieweg 2002: 24.
39. Cf. 5, note 2, and Agénor 2004: 203; Berument & Pasaogullari 2003; Godfrey 1985: 37; Shafaeddin 2005: 1135; Wang 1986.
40. Dahlman & Sercovitch 1984: 8; Haggard 1983: 83; Kim 1980: 273; Mytelka 1986: 258; Westphal et al. 1985.
41. Desai 1984: 1267; Lee 2001: 22; Lemoine & Ünal-Kesenci 2004: 840.
42. Elsenhans 1981a: 45, 1996c: 94 f.; Nohlen & Sturm 1982: 95.
43. Baranson 1970: 30; Belderbos et al. 2001: 201; Halbach 1985: 36; Jenkins 1985: 65. Cf. also Le Monde, 12 June 2007: 14.
44. Jacobsson 1985; Lowe & Kenney 1999: 1439; Shih 1968: 121 f.
45. Sid Ahmed 1989 is the best summary of the issue area. Karl 1997 is not well informed about the struggles for escaping Dutch disease and follows at best the political science simplification observed in most of the contributions to Beblawi & Luciani 1987.
46. From 2000 to 2009 world exports in manufactures rose by 7% p.a., from Asia to Asia by 9%, from Asia to Africa by 18%, and from Asia to Latin America by 14%. During the same period, China's exports to Latin America rose by 25% p.a., to Brazil even by 32%, to Africa by 25%, to Asia by 18%, but to Japan only by 13%, and the 'Six Asian Traders' only by 18%, Data from WTO 2010: 75 f.
47. This explains the maintenance of a constant average COR despite quite different paths of technical innovation in different branches. The interaction of differential evolutions of CORs in different branches is described by Stürmer 1968: 22 ff.
48. As long as he is not able to defend an above average profit rate in comparison to the users of machinery, in his country or in other countries, he cannot capture his achievement as a rent but has to transmit it to the users of machinery.

As a result, his physical productivity in relation to his price increases in comparison to a non-innovative producer in the Third World. If all users are equally performant, the productivity increase in machine using is equal in the economy where the machine has been produced and in the economy where innovation took place only in the form of an import of the new technology. In the economy with machine production the advance in machine production is higher than the advance in the using of the machine in relation to an economy where no machine production has occurred. The economy with no machine production has, therefore, comparative advantage in the branches which use the new machinery.

49. The increase in productivity of the machine producer is measured by the improvement in performance and the cost of the machinery. The improvement in performance is comprised of savings in labour, inputs and machine costs in relation to an identical amount of output of the machine user. This reduction of costs in relation to the costs of production (wages, input, machine costs) measures the productivity increase of the machine user. This reduction of costs also measures the productivity increase of the machine producer, but in relation to his own lower cost of production. His costs of production are not more than the price of the machinery he sells and which covers his own costs of production. It is evident that there is an identical numerator for both, the machine producer and the machine user, but a lower denominator for the machine producer, whereas the denominator of the machine user is higher (machine costs plus other costs).

50. Indeed, at that time the leading machinery producer may already have achieved additional advances so that entering the local production of machinery at the lower level of performance may once more become possible for the catching-up economy with further devaluations or subsidies. This is the basis of the rise of Third World producers in standard machinery production, Fukuchi & Satoh 1999: 272; Ochel 1984: 73; Sapir 1986: 609. In this case, the leading machine producer has a better performance in his labour input ratio in his advanced types of machinery, but a less good relation in the production of an old type of machine in comparison to a catching up economy.

51. Asam 1988: 199; Brimble & Doner 2007: 1021; Desai 1983.
52. Elsenhans 1981b: 89–91; Peet 1987: 782; Ross & Trachte 1983: 411.
53. Chase 2008: 657; Dauderstädt 2004: 5; Freeman & Schettkat 2001: 583; Gerbier 1999: 15; Jones 1997; Landmann 1999: 141.
54. Poor people's jobs are not threatened from foreign competition, Laaser & Schrader 2009: 198 f.
55. Appelbaum & Schettkat 1995: 622; Berman et al. 1994: 392; Dahrendorf 1964: 266.
56. Cadoret & Guéguen 2004: 93 ff.; Gregory et al. 2001: 35; Husson 2001: 1309; Kaplinsky 1981: 85.
57. The net investment was but 21.7% of the gross investment from 2001 to 2008, the last years for which data were available. Data from Statistisches

Bundesamt 2011: 14, 40. The statistical yearbooks document this trend. Gross investment/amortisation billions of DM until 1990, in billions of Euro 2001 and 2008: 1960: 83/24, 1989: 488/277, 2001: 412/316; 2008: 480/363, Statistisches Bundesamt 1990: 754, 781, 2009: 644.
58. Agell 2001: 378; IZA 2003: 7; Jessop 1993: 18; Kregel 1998; Schmid 1997: 334.
59. Esping-Andersen 1997: 243; Gerbier 1999: 16; Groff 1997: 108.
60. Turowski 2010: 73 ff., 139; Wagman 1995. On differences even within one branch, cf. Boggs 1997: 747; Töpper 1993: 178; Yates 2001: 29–31.
61. Brodkin 2000: 241; Heylen et al. 1996: 26; Puhani 2004.
62. Gerbier 1999: 15; Hudson 2001: 44; Turowski 2010: 139.
63. Own calculations based on Statistisches Bundesamt 1960: 525.
64. Bevers 1994: 46; Braun 1989: esp. 220; Schelsky 1955: 218.
65. Engelsing 1970: 304; Geary 1999; Holding 1987; Rancière 1983: 3 f.
66. This starts with the observation of the rejection of the necessity of a revolution, Dawson 1979; Walker 1985: 393. Cf. also Barbalet 1987.
67. Statistisches Bundesamt für die Bundesrepublik Deutschland: Volkswirtschaftliche Gesamtrechnungen, Fachserie 18, Private Konsumausgaben, downloaded on 9 June 2011; Räth et al. 2010, report saving rates of private German households of 10.8% (2007), 11.2% (2008), 11.2% (2009).
68. Although household savings have fallen, they still remain largely above the 1960s levels, cf. Bardt & Grömling 2003; Harvey, R., 2004; Hornung-Draus 1989: 26; Masubuchi 2006; Meyer 2005: 311. Deutschmann 1996: esp. 336, presents a similar argument about the limited capacity of absorption for financial resources = savings in mature knowledge-driven capitalist systems.
69. Keynes 1930: 172. Cf. also the following observation: 'The USA combine rising investment outlays with decreasing shares of saving, whereas Germany is characterised by decreasing net investment despite high and only slightly decreasing savings. Savings of private households do not seem to be a precondition for higher investment (translated by HE)' Bardt & Grömling 2003: 5.
70. Argy & Spitäller 1980: 108; Malinvaud 1987: 57; Bronfenbrenner 1976; Akerlof 2007: 6.
71. Chakrabarty 1988: 30; Diggins 1977: 375; Gallissot 1995: 83–85; Moorehouse 1978. On the formation of bourgeois class conscience, there are wonderful texts neglected by contemporary 'constructivists', cf. Borkenau 1934; Lukacz 1960; Goldman 1967.
72.
> The society of the Netherlands distinguished itself not by being filled with rational actors who would not neglect to pick up five-dollar bills from the street, but by its advancement of processes that assisted those rational actors in increasing the efficiency of economic activity. Those modernising, dynamic processes included urbanisation, education, mobility, monetisation, and political and legal development. These

features of the Dutch society in the 17th and 18th centuries placed the rational actor, the homo-oeconomicus, in a dynamic setting conducive to innovation. This is the basis on which we argue for the modern character of the Dutch economy long before the double blows of the French and British revolutions could be felt.

Vries & Woude 1997: 715. Cf. also Akeredolu 1971: 200; Bradley & Baigent 2009: 1101; Trompetter 1982: 271.
73. The 10 largest companies produced in 2007 59.4% of all vehicles and 69.5% of all cars, http://oica.net/category/production-statistics/2007-statistics/, downloaded on 11 June 2011; Haipeter & Banyuls 2007: 377.
74. Athukorala & Menon 1994; Betts & Devcreux 2000: 216; Knetter 1993; Kopits 1976; Wechselkurs 1997: 51.
75. Hengsbach 2007: 5; Nuti 1970: 43; Weizsäcker 2010: 248.
76. This is the title of Harvey 2004. Cf. also Altvater 2004: 43; Arrighi 2005: 85; Vakulabharanam 2009: 147.
77. For example, cowry and *badam* (almond), cf. Barendse 2000: 176; Lovejoy 1983: 103 ff.
78. Gascon 1971: 239 f.; Rubin 2010: 213; Vilar 1969: 344.
79. Andrade & Silva 1998: 1; Bichler & Nitzan 2004; Dale 2005; Gowan 2009.
80. Baily & Elliott 2009: 210; Belke & Wiedmann 2005: 275; Kumar 2009: 22 f.; Wagner & Berger 2003.
81. Fay & Nordhaug 2002: 89 f.; Hampton & Christensen 2002; Illing 2011: 9.
82. Krugman 1999a: 140. And a slightly differing view Krugman 1999b: 58, 69. For a critique cf. Fine & Waeyenberge 2006: 149; Foster 2009: 5.
83. If prices are determined by demand and supply, the adjustment of supply to demand implies that prices tend to conform to synchronised labour costs, cf. Wolfstetter 1973.
84. Baillin & Reisen 1998: 706 f.; Blackburn 1999: 5 ff.; Gompers & Leiner 2001: 147.
85. Bonoli 2003: 403; Müller 2000: 513; Pitelis 1989: 3.
86. The battle for the reform of old age pensions in most of Western industrial countries shows that monetary illusion prevails over the requirements of the real economy. The battle for preserving capitalism through its embeddedness into social structures which preserve it from the desire to accumulate fictive wealth has already been lost. It was lost because the mechanism of steering the economy at the micro level, the search for financial improvement of individual households, has been misinterpreted as the mechanism of capitalist growth.
87. Hayek 1976: 55; Hawtrey 1933: 428; Lescure 1933: 393–397; Phillips et al. 1938: 9.
88. Hanes 1993: 745; Keynes 1939: 36; Richardson 1939: 430 f.; Tucker 1936: 81.
89. Erbe 1958: 34 f.; Nathan 1944: 288; Petzina 1968: 11.

6

Alliances for Imposing Capitalism: The Globalisation of Profit Against the Globalisation of Rent

There is a threat of erosion of the capitalist model of regulation in our times. New varieties of needs in the developed world do not support the capitalist mechanism of demand expansion. The control of surplus within the capitalist system of regulation becomes weaker. With this the realm of rent grows. In the periphery there are blockages to the implementation of capitalism. Between major political forces in different regions of the world, there are political and ideological distances which make alliance building difficult. Governments have a clear advantage in relation to other forces in alliance building because they concentrate on the balance of power in order to preserve security. From this concern for security they deduce state responsibility for preserving the core areas of innovation in the economy. The current tendency to a multipolar state system with conservative state elites playing the dominant role works against the creation of opportunities for transnational alliances between social and political forces. The scenario which hopes for the rise of a world civil society seems unrealistic in these circumstances.

The Rise of Collective Needs, the Struggle Against the Money Illusion and the Importance of Democratic Management of Rents

The transition to capitalism depends on a configuration of power in the socio-economic structures which makes culture quite irrelevant. The maintenance of capitalism, especially when the rise of mass incomes is achieved, does, however, not depend on culture. The privileged strata may prefer to create structures which allow them to appropriate surplus by social, political and economic power also for consumption and not for investment. However, they can be hindered in this endeavour if the scarcity of average skilled labour raises wages to levels where they can appropriate only that part of the surplus which is invested in profitable projects. Investment projects are profitable when they allow for a reduction in the cost of production of products for which there is demand on the market under perfect competition. This constraint on the access to surplus implies that incomes paid to labour are used for products produced by the capitalist economy. If this simple reciprocal empowerment of labour and capital is wrecked by the behaviour of labour, the owners of capital suffer because they do not make profit under perfect competition. Either the socio-economic structure suffers from underemployment of resources or finds a way of channelling resources by other means into demand for the real economy. Such other means invariably imply a weakening of competition as a mode of regulation of the utilisation of economic surplus. Such other modes of regulation imply by necessity political or social power and, hence, rent.

As long as real incomes of labour were low, a low propensity to save made the maintenance of capitalist competition dependent only on the fight against open collusion between private enterprises. If there is surplus for which there is no demand from investors, labour or the state, labour and the privileged strata have either to accept an under-consumptionist crisis or to collude in order to find another mechanism of bringing effective production to the level of potential production. In this collusion, political and social powers matter. Both depend on belief systems of the interacting players. The views of the protagonists influence their capacity to present their solutions as conforming to the overall collective interest. Those views which society believes to be correct influence the capacity of protagonists to mobilise their own political bases and to win credibility among those elements of society which are not directly concerned. Such views and belief systems as well as the fears and anxieties they can be linked to constitute the realm of culture.

Alliances for Imposing Capitalism   161

The uneven development of capitalism at the global level creates new sources of rent, even if some rents disappear. The increasing demand for final products has increased regularly the demand for raw materials despite decreasing raw material consumption per unit of the output produced (cf. Chapter 3, note 20). New deposits had to be discovered with rising costs of production. This created rents for the owners of the new, less costly deposits. The rising demand for raw materials quickly led, however, to overcapacity in production which could not react to limits in demand expansion. At least in the 'periphery' of the system where the only limited penetration of the dominant capitalist system had not led to the overall productivity increases including technical progress in other branches of production than raw materials, the capacity to adjustment remained limited. Rent-seeking was preferred to losses in incomes in the wake of this shift to branches where productivity lags were higher. Often this shift to rent-seeking was justified by the requirements of implementing new productive capacities in order to become more flexible. Such a preference was shown to be relevant in the context of specialisation on manufactured goods where price elasticity of world demand also was low.

The increasing satisfaction of needs in the technically most developed regions of the world was shown to erode the consumptive behaviour of labour which guaranteed profit. New needs implied political regulation as in the case of collective goods (environment) and even delayed material needs (saving for the future). The economic adjustment to new situations presents additional challenges for the disempowerment of labour which work in the same direction. Once the mechanism at the centre which empowers labour is weakened, competition from low-cost labour—which is low cost because of devaluation-driven growth—increases the gap between consumptive and productive potential. The dominance of finance capital is, initially, just a mechanism for dealing with the threat of under-consumption.

Capitalism continuously produces new possibilities for the appropriation of rent. It does so increasingly when productivity rises but capitalism is unable to create of its own accord the necessary countervailing demand or capacity to consume the new output. Capitalism does not produce the conditions for its own reproduction in the decisions regarding private investment made by those in command of the actual or potential surplus (because of the existing lack of demand). This leads to the permanent emergence of opportunities, both old and new, to shift from the logic of profit to the logic of rent. These possibilities are seized by those whose capacity to earn profit is threatened. They perceive in these possibilities new opportunities of being saved by their relatively better access to resources, political decision-making processes, audience in society and even cultural definition power, which they use to defend their rents. The greater the achievements of capitalism in raising productivity and in expanding its clout territorially over societies where labour has not yet succeeded in achieving empowerment, the greater the possibilities for rent-seeking.

Under which conditions can labour re-establish its empowerment? This comprises two problems. Under which conditions can labour maintain its negotiating power in developed economies as economically homogeneous labour? This implies that labour can avoid to be fragmented into small groups which are tied in clientelistic dependence as 'sectional' interests, who benefit from specific market failures regarding their scarce skills. Under which conditions can marginality in technically backward economies be overcome?

The first problem needs an extension of Keynesianism: How can a full employment demand be guaranteed if non-individual needs become more important? The success of capitalism in freeing ever increasing parts of the population from immediate needs has led to the emergence of new needs. Some of them do not lead to direct demand for goods and services. These needs cannot be fulfilled within the proper functioning of the capitalist mechanism of demand which triggers off investment spending. This can be shown with the example of two types of needs, provisions for the future and the protection of the environment.

The products an old age person will consume can only be produced when this person has reached old age. Savings today cannot serve to produce these products but can only reserve production for the elderly today. The actual lack of demand through savings benefits the actually elderly provided they enjoy entitlement. The future demand the saver is entitled to can be served only by the production of future workers, often not yet born. If there are no producers in the future due to demographic decline, the savings realised today will not allow buying anything in the future. Savings are not values, but only claims. As any system of old age provision depends on redistribution in the actual economy, its actual impact on the growth of demand is decisive. The build-up of claims to be transformed into demand only in the future cannot launch actual growth. An increasing importance of such future needs has to be dealt with in a way which does not decelerate actual growth. Hence, the claims for the future production have to be established today on a basis which does not negatively affect the actual demand. Contributions for the upkeep of the actual elderly, as in non-capital-based compulsory systems have this effect. Also, in a capital-based system the only guarantee of the last resort for claims for future production can be the 'state' which credibly commits itself to look for old age provision.

Saving is just a lack of demand. It creates safe entitlement only when there is somebody who is prepared to take on debt. If private households reduce their overall level of indebtedness due to higher incomes and their increasing preference for future consumption, then the state has to increase its indebtedness. This is certainly a major element in the recent increases in public debt. As private household savings increased, governments had to resort to deficit spending in order to maintain employment through demand management. Due to their increasing material wealth, more people may want to save for the future compared with people who want to take on debt. Therefore, increasingly the real economy does not provide any counterpart for this increase in savings, as we have seen in the current financial crisis. The options are: We either create disincentives to save or we have to extend the financialisation of the economy. One disincentive would be to ration the right to save and would consist in fixing an upper limit to which governments and the banking system guarantee private savings. To this extent, money continues to have the quality of preserving 'value' for the future. Extended financialisation with subsequent banking crises which are, at best, overcome through government money creation and inflation will not preserve even this limited protection for ordinary savers with limited financial resources.

The state becomes central in the provisions for the future in rationing the right to provisions in a manner that the actual economy does not suffer. Under such conditions, capitalism can be preserved only if the fragmented individual households succeed in complementing it not only by full-scale participation in the form of democracy but also by ideological hegemony of the masses. This implies the democratisation of also the non-economic spheres. This demand was formulated as the necessity of real democracy which extends beyond merely electoral democracy.[1] Capitalism would have to be understood as based on delegated property rights, and not on natural property rights. Delegation implies the possibility of limiting such rights with a view to overall balances. Extent and orientation of such interventions can be determined either by power of the few or by equal participation of the many. In case of the intervention of the many, a new view of capitalism is necessary, practically a sort of Cultural Revolution. This implies ideological hegemony and intervention from other spheres of social regulation. As these other spheres are characterised by different logics, for example, in the cultural sphere by mechanisms described in the economics of star earnings

(Bourg 2008: 377) where the winner takes all, democratisation of some of these other spheres to extents and in patterns still to be determined requires a restriction of the pure play of the market.

Another major area is environment. The protection of the environment is obviously in the interest of the masses, but gives rise to two mechanisms of their empowerment. The search for environmental improvement and protection implies measures for which there is no demand of decentralised agents like households or enterprises on competitive markets, although these agents may desire improvements in the environment.

This has an international and a national dimension. There are many mechanisms which can be employed in order to create incentives through the market for an environment-friendly behaviour of enterprises, but the ultimate decision to create this demand, its direction and its volume, is a political one and has to be formulated by political alliances and implemented through political action.[2] This action may take the form of bureaucratic or participatory action and has to follow the logic of these types of regulation. Some groups which are better placed and can get better earnings for their services may receive an exceptional share of the fruits of the realisation or the absence of actions for their own privileged consumption. In that case, they appropriate a rent. In case of optimal democratic processes, the additional resources are used for the benefit of all.

Due to the power to be transferred to the required collective actor, there is the possibility of moral hazard like in the tributary modes of production where the protective and managerial services of the ruling class implied the simultaneous emergence of the possibility of rent appropriation in favour of the ruling class.

At the international level, the necessarily global framework for protecting the environment creates possibilities for rent appropriation for all those ruling groups which are in control of the attributes of state sovereignty and which are less under the pressure of local environmentalist movements. Environmental rules have a similar impact as differences in the quality of raw material deposits. Some governments will prefer to have weaker regulations in order to have lower costs. They can appropriate these cost differentials as rents and use them as subsidies for their local industries. In countries with stricter rules, environment-dangerous products will no longer be produced but be imported.[3] More lax rules may be an instrument of employment creation via higher exports and be supported by local business and labour.

Globally operating environmentalist groups have difficulties in creating mass-based coalitions at the world level as long as standards of living do not converge. They have to face the argument widely shared in less advanced economies that the more advanced economies are able to apply stricter rules because they are not only richer, but because they owe their higher levels of income to the exploitation of poorer countries in the past (Chen 2008: 148 ff.; Pataki et al. 2008: 69). The poorer countries ask for compensatory financing which are rents of sovereignty.[4] They can be linked to performance but at first contribute to the financial resources of governments which are not necessarily controlled by their constituencies to which they should be accountable.

Whenever the capitalist mechanism cannot work, the alternative consists of either the emergence of rent structures or of non-market-operated empowerment of the many. This second alternative can be called the conscious appropriation of society by itself. Given the international dimension, the ultimate aim would be the achievement of the society appropriating itself at the global level. I have argued that the capacity of the society to appropriate itself has been greatly facilitated by the a-cultural character of capitalism. Capitalism freed vast areas of individual consumption from social regulation. Historically, capitalism has provided the society with the breathing space to create the conditions for the society to appropriate society itself by liberating the economic sphere from the influence and permanent intervention of other spheres which were still characterised by hierarchies of power. The autonomy of the economy made it possible to liberate these other spheres from the permanent colonisation by the privileged. Such colonisation is useless for correcting the results of the market (but not necessarily of new oligopolistic structures). Capitalism, therefore, was and continues to be an instrument to combat rent. It works as long as individual consumption prevails in the hierarchies of the needs of the many.

When the structure of needs changes, capitalism has to be complemented by democracy as a principle of organising all spheres of society and this historically, to the difference of the real socialism of the East European countries, has been originally defined as socialism (Marx 1843: 370). It can be argued that both mechanisms of regulation, market and democratic participation, are twin sisters. Capitalism is a means of establishing equality in the reign of individual consumption. It has to be complemented by democratic and participative socialism when more and more needs emerge which cannot be satisfied within the capitalist framework of priority to mass consumption.

The Threats to Capitalism at the Centre

A tension emerges in capitalism's modes of economic regulation such as between actual needs and actual production, on the one hand, and the provision for future needs, on the other. These needs ultimately cannot be satisfied by goods actually produced and purchased out of the income actually earned. As long as money is considered as a means of preserving value, it can be used as an instrument for protecting against future risks and providing for future needs. But saving is possible only if there are debtors. Preserving against future risks by accumulating wealth in the form of money requires state indebtedness or a state guarantee for the provision of services required in case such future risks eventuate.

Where many households become wealthy enough to privilege security and other future needs, there need to be either private households which enter into the obligation to provide for these future needs or the state must provide this guarantee to supply services for such future needs. Property as a means of guaranteeing against future risks is also of limited value as there are limits to the amount of property which will have economic value in the future and from which a liquid supply of income can be drawn to pay for the mitigation of these risks and future needs.

With an increase of the share of those needs which are scheduled to be fulfilled only in the future, a cultural change in the perception between the private and the public is required which runs against property individualism and the focus on social struggles related to distributional issues about the actually achieved national income. Instead, the development of a democratic consensus on how to manage the appropriation of the potential of society is required as this consensus is the basis of trust. It is this trust in the future which allows the households to understand that they cannot use their monetary income which they achieve actually for providing goods of the future. Without such trust, the mechanism of transformation of actually received incomes into demand for products which, in turn, triggers off investment, is suspended and, with it, the auto-regulation of capitalism.

Capitalism is an arrangement which empowers the mass of individual independent households without their cooperation on the basis of the scarcity of labour and actually consumable products. Households need other systems of regulation than capitalism if they aspire to other goals. If these goals require production in the future and, hence, entitlements for future products, households can get such entitlements only insofar as other actors are ready to consume or invest now in exchange for payments to be realised only in the future. Capital investments now have been considered as such a form of spending to counterbalance the increased savings of the households.

The actual financial requirements of the capitalists for financing investment tend to become limited in relation to the future needs the households perceive as priorities over expenditure for currently consumed products. On the one hand, the process of development of productive forces is not particularly capital absorbing; on the other hand, the role of these future needs in the preferences of the households increases. There are two alternative scenarios: By not taking seriously this tension, households will wreck the actually existing capitalism by oversaving and under-consumption. The foreseeable reaction is the development of rentiers who provide the necessary demand for economic activity in exchange for shelter behind market imperfections, ultimately monopoly or oligopoly situations to the benefit of private entities outside any market or democratic control. They will fight against democratic control by arguing that they enjoy property rights in these situations and that the criticised market imperfections are just natural. The alternative scenario consists of a clear distinction of what the capitalist structure can do and the development of comparably democratic structures in all other spheres of the social, economic and political system which take care of these newly important future needs and goals. In this context, property as a basis of guarantees has to be complemented by other institutions which can enjoy trust because of their being embedded in structures based on social forces which the members of the society consider as counting also in the future.

Connecting capitalism to these other spheres on the basis of the principles of capitalism, equality, fairness and freedom of options implies democratic socialism, the democratic appropriation of the society by itself. By cutting down the issue of socialism or capitalism to questions of property relations and by rejecting the market in an undifferentiated manner, neglecting its role as an instrument to fight inequality, the political left in the West is not well placed to contribute to the cultural change I assume to be necessary. By focusing on technical problems of demand management, Keynesian macrotheory has not contributed to distinguishing between the realm where market competition of private enterprises is efficient and the realm where other regulations have to be established.

If democratic structures for these other spheres cannot be established because of the simple fact that these areas are not even defined, non- or less democratic structures will emerge. Society even unconsciously will respond to the new challenges, following the principle of the lowest degrees of change. With this principle, those who are better placed for creating these structures will be those who are the earliest to develop them and to shape them according to their interests. The actual financial crisis provides a wonderful example: When the banks wanted to draw on public resources, they focussed on their systemic relevance and behaved as if they were public institutions nearly like elements of the constitutional order of the West. When the possibilities of enrichment re-emerged because of state support, the bankers argued that they earned disproportionately because they were private entrepreneurs. There are non-market institutions which the actual system pushes into emergence in order to digest new challenges in a nearly 'natural' manner. There will be, therefore, many 'innovating groups' which want to participate in this nearly spontaneous process. The 'better-placed' ones will draw advantage from their relatively close access to the respective issue areas and create arrangements where they are sheltered by a common consensus from perfect competition so that they can build rentier situations.

Two visions of capitalism will confront each other in this struggle for cultural change: There are those who defend economic freedom for all operations which take the form of exchange. This comprises also the exchanges which do not only concern the formally interacting partners but also formally unrelated third parties. Take, for example, the expansion of financial markets. Deals between formally private speculators who are completely free of links to the real economy may threaten the viability of the monetary flows in this latter sphere. This example can be compared to a parallel situation where the adoption of an environmentally dangerous process of production has important effects beyond the immediate sphere or branch of production. Most people in the West nowadays consider that such decisions can no longer be an affair simply between the investing enterprise and the supplier of the technology. Therefore, the state intervenes in the name of the public interest in private property rights. In the case of regulation of the embeddedness of capitalism into other spheres, such a group of supporters of only the market form (with unlimited property rights) will stand against those who admit non-intervention from the political and social spheres only in those areas where there are 'free' markets with low barriers to entry and equal access for all concerned in addition to an imperative process which guarantees that all are responsible for the costs the occasion to others and all having their costs paid by the contracting parties.

Such a transition of capitalism to a new relationship between a further restricted capitalist realm and a realm regulated by the struggle between rent-seeking and participation occurs in a phase where not yet capitalist economies enter into the international division of labour on the basis of devaluation-driven growth. The state-led import-substituting industrialisation models collapsed because of the exhaustion of rent. Export-oriented manufacturing which has replaced them may be characterised by lower amounts of rent. But rent may become even more pervasive: It is directly associated through rent-based market imperfections in the form of subsidies and policies of technology promotion with the competitiveness of branches which operate on international markets.

It can be argued that the mechanisms of the market are fundamentally restricted at the international level through the embeddedness of labour in national settings and that these restrictions will not be overcome in the foreseeable future. Despite a decrease in transaction costs for transborder operations we are far away from the law of one price for most products (Goldberg & Knetter 1997: 1270) and naturally also from uniform wage rates for equally skilled labour (D'Costa 2003: 218; Erber & Sayed-Ahmed 2005: 108 ff.). There would be no possibility of devaluation-driven growth if the rule of one price prevailed: In that case, cheap subsistence goods in devaluing countries would be just exported. An essential aspect of and cause to this limited convergence of prices is the limited mobility of even high skilled, but especially average skilled and unskilled labour. Even if all administrative barriers were removed, barriers of language and habits would continue to exist. The discourse on the importance of culture reflects these barriers. The Samuelson (1948: 183) argument that international specialisation is a substitute to international migration has some empirical basis but only little impact even in the sphere of highly skilled labour. The massive outsourcing of software production has reduced wages in this speciality in the United States but has not led to the rise of Indian wages in software production to the US level (Chaganti 2004: 2222 ff.; Lakha 1994).

As long as there is no uniform worldwide labour market with uniform wage rates, the mechanism of empowering labour through employment will work only in an imperfect manner. Where markets are imperfect, capitalism needs additional, mostly political embeddedness. This embeddedness is all the more difficult as there are still many not yet capitalist structures, especially but not only in the catching-up economies of the South. In non-capitalist structures the relationship between the economic sphere and other spheres, especially politics and culture, differs from capitalist ones without any worldwide agreement on the precise character of these differences and their implications for the transfer of capitalism, hence development.

'Development' and Achieving Worldwide Capitalism

The worldwide expansion of capitalism has not led to the transfer of the basics of political and social power relations to the economies which are newly participating in the international division of labour in manufacturing organised by capitalism. This applies to those socio-economic structures which attempted to overcome underdevelopment by state-led import-substituting industrialisation financed from rents and to those economies which tried to reach high levels of employment by devaluation-driven exports of manufactured products. Success in the second strategy depends on the readiness of the already capitalist world to accept increasing exports of the catching-up world (even if the catching-up world enjoys already export surpluses). Both strategies imply increasing risks of rent-seeking either internally or through their impacts on the disempowerment of labour in the West. Both are more successful with respect to the goal of limiting the emergence of rent, if they give importance to the internal mass markets in the newly competitive countries. This is facilitated in the absence of scarcity of labour if, within the framework of these strategies, redistributive mechanisms in favour of the poor are put in place.

Given the limits of both strategies in achieving high levels of employment, governments remain important for collecting revenue in order to promote measures for improving employment, growth and some sort of social security for the poor in different combination of measures. These 'assortment of measures' are designed according to the economic philosophies that governments follow in the context of their internal political power relations and the desires of foreign partners, donors, multinational enterprises, etc., they may consider as relevant. Without transformation of the world into an integrated capitalist world system, where the rule of one price for products prevails, there are large varieties of rent, not only in case of state-led import-substituting industrialisation but also in case of export-led growth[5] and large varieties of philosophies which govern the struggle over rent and the justification of their utilisation for politically chosen purposes.

Under which conditions can it be expected that those with access to these rents spend them in priority on overcoming underdevelopment. In a nutshell, this is the question of how capitalism based on rising mass incomes and the empowerment of labour can be brought about in underdeveloped economies where labour is disempowered. This has been the realm of development theory since its inception.[6] How can surplus which private investors cannot appropriate through sales on competitive markets be transformed into investment? Underdeveloped economies have a low marginal product of labour. This leads to openly visible surplus of labour in the form of structural unemployment if market regulations are imposed and pre-capitalist structures are dissolved. The introduction of market relations often negates the obligation of those with access to rent to redistribute it along clientalist lines.

I immediately admit that development theory tends to concentrate on the way on how to succeed in the transition to capitalism (Mattick 1969: 341). This is in line with my interpretation of democratic socialism as the completion of capitalism through the embedding of the other social spheres into structures governed by the principles of capitalism, that is, empowerment of the many. Many of the political movements which were most committed to the endeavour of overcoming underdevelopment called themselves socialist and claimed to promote socialism in the name of development: This reflects the fact that the basics which led to the spontaneous emergence of capitalism are absent in underdeveloped economies. Where these basics are absent, the transition to capitalism needs support from other spheres of economic and social regulation. As long as there is scarcity of goods in relation to wants, there is no more rational regulation of exchange of value and labour than can be achieved by full employment capitalism with perfectly competitive markets (Barone 1935: 269; Lerner 1935: 60). Development theory is no playing ground for romantics who oppose the rationality of the market. The market has to be corrected only in those areas where the empowerment of labour does not take place due to structural deficiencies in underdeveloped economies.

Development theory became victim of two oppositions. On the left it was accused of neglecting dependency and imperialism. The argument said that because of dependency and imperialist exploitation markets cannot lead to development. The fact that many economies became capitalist with high growth rates and 'shared growth'[7] because of dependency and even 'imperialist' penetration has relativised this criticism and led to a culturalist condemnation of capitalism which was said to dissolve and destroy pre-capitalist settings and their (more humane) cultures (Chakrabarty 2005: 4814). Capitalism was opposed in the name of identity, but where the poor got better incomes and the advantage of full employment, often even before these achievements were fully provided but existed only as a certain hope, identity was a minor preoccupation of the poor. The rich associational life in the American society demonstrates the compatibility between capitalism and community. But, to the difference of pre-capitalist societies, capitalism leaves the individual free to choose. Sociology of modernisation has since long described the importance of achieved roles, in opposition to ascribed roles for individual freedom and self-realisation. The praise of community is rarely a topic developed by authors who have lived as ordinary members in such communities.

On the right, complementary but especially compensatory non-market measures were discredited as inefficient. Rent per se does not exclude its use in for promoting economic structures on which capitalism can be based (cf. Chapter 4, note 44). It is simplistic to attribute to improving terms of trade, rent appropriation and Dutch disease the absence of economic diversification and development. Rent is an income which is managed by non-market, political means and actors. Its reasonable employment depends on the preferences and capabilities of these actors, that is, preferences outside any imposed by market forces. State classes adopted wasteful policies and created often repressive political structures but in some places consciously or unconsciously under social pressures adopted industrial policies and structural reforms which allowed to use the market in order to increase employment via the production for mass needs.

There are different paths by which development policy can create the conditions for self-sustained capitalist growth via mass production for mass needs. Some basic issues of development theory can, however, be restated. Where the endowment with technology and investment goods is limited, agrarian reforms are an essential element of incorporation of marginal labour into the production process so that gainful activity, agricultural output and the share of low-income household demand in the total demand increase. More low-quality products can be produced. More products can be produced in larger series. More simple technology can be used and a higher share of such technology can be produced locally.[8]

The local informal sector is the true capitalist sector. Its performance depends on the environment it is embedded in. If the demand for its products expands, it improves, modernises and triggers off the demand for the investment goods of low-quality type. Exchange rates should be low enough to keep it competitive (Baldwin 1961: 603; Broda 2006: 53).

Export orientation is a support for development if it creates mass employment, especially of low-skilled labour. Specialisation on products where there is comparative advantage promotes development. Low technology specialisation may not directly promote skill acquisition but contributes to employment and, therefore, to the expansion of the internal market.

In case of specialisation on rent-generating products which imply the danger of Dutch disease, compensatory measures are indicated like keeping the exchange rate low by (intelligently, see p. 129) taxing these exports or by protecting emerging new activities.[9] Exploitation by foreign trade and investment partners is preferable to marginalisation.[10] Exploitation should be preferred to the defence of the terms of trade in case of export-oriented branches with high multiplier effects and linkages. Exploitation should, however, be controlled in case of low multiplier industries by means of government appropriation of rents, especially in the case of mineral raw materials, but as a second-best option.

Industrial policies should aim at the promotion of local technology production by concentrating on branches where an expanding local mass consumption and increasing export orientation provide expanding demand.[11]

On the supply side, priority should be given to the capacity to produce mass consumption goods and employment creating exports as well as the technologies required for these sectors. On the demand side, mass demand and employment which generates mass demand should be the central focus. In the case of technical dependence, there may be a trade-off between austerity cum investment versus mass consumption. But austerity for the masses promotes rent-generating political structures, as austerity has to be politically imposed: Those who impose it become able to impose a cost for their services in the form of high incomes for them, which normally lead to higher imports and inefficient local luxury production.

This is not a plea for basing a theory of development on criteria as dissociation from or integration into the market. Market and state should be used in an instrumental manner in order to promote mass employment and mass consumption. The choice of the relationship to the world economy is not an art as believed in some benign West German development discussion (Senghaas 1989: 59) but can be determined on the basis of the opportunities provided by the world market for employment creation, preferably directly through exports, or at least through rents which can be used for employment creation.

Development strategies have to be formulated today in a world where the possibilities of devaluation-driven growth increase the danger of reaction in technically leading, already capitalist economies which threaten capitalism worldwide. Insufficient demand expansion in the leading economies not only threatens capitalist growth in these leading economies but also the transition to capitalism via devaluation-driven growth in the catching-up not yet capitalist world.

The Political Crisis of the Development State and the Emergence of New Political Forces in the South: New Cultural Identitarian Movements

The counterweight in the capitalist world has tapered off because the subalterns became increasingly better off and increasingly heterogeneous. It was not replaced by an empowerment of labour in the South. The defence of capitalism against an increasing influence of the privileged which have inevitably turned and continue to turn into rentiers, hence the struggle for capitalism against the pursuit of rent-seeking requires new political resources.

Therefore, the impact of the actual drive to globalisation on political structures and attitudes in the South becomes crucial with two aspects: On the one hand, the emergence of new political forces which I call the new cultural identitarian movements and, on the other hand, the end of serious efforts of achieving development through development policies are conceived as supporting the transition to capitalism by restructuring the deformed but not yet capitalist structures in order to promote mass consumption.[12]

The a-cultural character of capitalism implies large varieties of political utopias on which subalterns base their political activities. Internationalist cosmopolitanism within the framework of the priority of class solidarity was one version. This version was important in the emergence of modern Western nations. Many demands of labour have been realised in the struggle over the wage bargain in class against class patterns of interaction. Many others were realised by political pressure and action which addressed the legislative process within the framework of institutions the subalterns found in place, the states, which created identities on the basis of invented histories, mostly together with shared languages and the belief of common ethnic descent.[13] Within these structures the body politic was, however, organised on the basis of conflicts which emerged between social classes even if trans-class identities mattered. Western political structures are shaped largely by class struggles (Badie & Hermet 2001: 332) and communication for mobilisation in such struggles. This is the basic reason for the importance of language in identity formation as shown by the European way of nation-building (Hayes 1927; Sayer 1996: 175 ff.). The forces of the established order who defended in European constitutional history the royal prerogative and, subsequently, the status quo moral order against change (the famous distinction of Goguel between the '*parti de l'ordre*' (the party of conservation of the existing order) and the '*parti du progrès*' (the party of changing the existing order) in France; Goguel 1946: 553) were opposed by the liberals. The liberals wanted to open the non-economic domains of the society to the innovations which originated from the revolutions in the economic realm, rationality, enlightenment, rule of law and constitutionalism, human rights. The deepening of capitalism transformed the resistance of labour based on its scarcity into the emergence of labour movements which demanded certain restrictions on discretionary power to form contracts in order to defend the 'true' liberty of those who had nothing else to sell but their labour power.

In the South there were not always large-scale pre-capitalist states and often rarely sufficiently large ethnical groups for the emergence of markets capable of supporting the division of labour and industrialisation. Where such large ethnic groups existed there were low degrees of mobilisation along class lines so that parochial, communal and other outlooks remained important. So the structuring solidarities of class and shared economic interest could rarely constitute the mould into which social struggles could be embedded in the pre-capitalist 'periphery'. Such a mould had to be created in the non-Western world by instrumentalising structures which had survived from ancient times, the old tributary states as in most parts of Asia, the colonial administrative structures of the second wave of colonialism such as in South Asia (India) or in sub-Saharan Africa, or even provincial administrations such as in Latin America. The Western class-based configuration of political camps could not apply to structures where the main opposition lay between an external prospering world and a local world where economic and social conditions were deteriorating often absolutely for the great mass and in any case relatively. As tributary modes of production comprise many identities with at the apex a respected sacralised top, the king in command of a centralised structure of exploitation and repression, there were no other centralising institutions comparable to market or class. The 'nationalisation' of identities such as ethnic descent had been an important element of nation-building in Europe in destroying really existing ethnic units (in France: Brittany, the conflict between the [southern French] Occitan and the [dominant and Northern French] Oïl languages; Boulard 1999: 47). Such a nationalisation of identities was totally inapplicable in societies which, in their nation-building, were decisively shaped by the imperialist expansion (tributary modes of production of Asia; Oommen 1997: 151 f.; Mukherji 2009: 7) or migrations and linguistic diversity (sub-Saharan Africa).[14] The (re-)creation or adaptation of statehood in the South in order to manage the new socio-economic structures had either to be considered as impossible as the diehards of colonialism maintained (Indians cannot govern themselves[15], Algeria has never been a state[16]) or be accompanied by a new concept of nationhood.

The new states had to be multiethnic empires. They could not base their 'national' identities on ethnic criteria. The identities on which the national liberation movements could organise themselves in this supra-ethnic mould could draw on two criteria, the solidarity of Fanon's (1965) 'wretched of the earth'[17] and religion.[18]

Those who wanted to recover identity and autonomy by primarily modernising their societies in order to stop exploitation are called the secular nationalists.[19] They were opposed by those who expected the end of exploitation by the removal of the 'corruption' of their societies caused by the intrusion of the Western culture. They call themselves cultural nationalists.[20] Mobilisation against the West was achieved by secular nationalists who affirmed the opposition between the exploited class in the colonies and semi-colonies against the West. The West was perceived as largely owing its technical advance to this very exploitation, such as the 'drain of India' (Ferguson 2002: 47; Majumdar et al. 1978: 800), the 'black ebony' of Africa (Canu 1951: 81), the deteriorating terms of trade of Singer (1950: esp. 482), Prebisch (1962: 6, and others) and dependencia with the extra profits of multinational enterprises.[21]

The cultural nationalists defined the communities they tried to represent and to mobilise on the basis of cultural otherness from the West. This appears as a return to the past, as the only model of the good society available to them had to be identified in some historical past, a paradise of an uncorrupted social live in a period before the contact with the West. All these cultural nationalists initiated, however, important steps to remove the cultural dimensions of pre-capitalist social hierarchy. In India they tried to remove the barriers created by the caste system (Jaffrelot 1998: 22 f.; Lohda 2004: 5461). In the Islamic world they fought against superstition and the clannish structures under the label of removing superstition (Bayat 1998: 160; Chikh 2003: 95).

Secular nationalism comprises basically two tendencies: those who saw in the existing local structures the main cause of foreign exploitation and those who were more accommodative with respect to their local societies in which, however, they also wanted reform.[22] Both drew their main followers from among new social strata which had emerged through the contact of their societies with the West, hence from the 'modern sectors' of their societies (Bhattacharya 1979: 19; Chandra 1976: 82). These were especially the Western-educated intellectuals, a modern either openly colonial bridgehead or indirectly but still dependent bridgehead created in their societies in order to allow colonial exploitation: teachers, clerks, modern sector manual and white collar workers, but also cash crop farmers. Those among them who were able to rally behind them the large class coalitions of workers and the property-owning middle strata became moderate nationalists, flirted with Marxism and rejected the principle of class struggle as shown by the political theories of Arab socialists,[23] African socialists (Hopwood 1982: 99; Nicolas 1981: 93) or the socialist wing of the Indian Congress party.[24] Those who entered into conflict with such reformist political practices had to turn to the peasantries in order to build strong political bases.[25] Very often, they adopted Marxism.[26] Wherever national alienation was intense, the middle strata component was strong within these movements. Consequently, the moderates prevailed, as in India (Nayar 1997: 14; Paranjape 1964: 173). Where the local middle strata and the old elites had more autonomy, the conflict between the two tendencies became more open. Cultural identity was less important. The socially conservative forces had to oppose the radical nationalists more openly. Examples are China or Vietnam (Scott 1979: 109; Selden 1995: 29).

The more radical forces with their Marxist positions comprised comprehensive worldviews, and not only social and economic demands for reforms. In the world of Islam and Hinduism they had difficulties in penetrating into the villages with such worldviews.[27] The Indian Congress party suffered from competition by the Communists but more so in urban areas than in the countryside, although the moderate Indian nationalists cared very little for organising the rural poor.[28] The Communists remained weak in the countryside of Hinduism or Islam and could not develop peasant-oriented mass mobilisation before independence.[29] Where the Marxist worldviews did not antagonise elaborate systems of religion as in the Chinese world, communists could penetrate the rural world with an adapted version of the Marxist theory of revolution. The turn of the Chinese Communist Party from its working-class-based activities to the mobilisation of the peasantry between 1926 and 1935 is a good example (Albrecht 1977: 365 ff.).

In societies which are penetrated from the outside, the polarisation between a political right and the political left is difficult, although these terms are often employed. The forces of the established order of the tributary modes of production had either been crushed by colonialism or transformed into bridgeheads of the external powers who fed the oligarchies, old feudals and dynasties, and international competitive land or mine owners with rents. Against this colonialist bridgehead, the national liberation movements had to mobilise large class coalitions or strong rural support.[30]

The moderate alliances comprised national bourgeoisies, small shopkeepers and craftsmen, exploited workers and farmers under various forms of labour contracts. Because of this heterogeneity, they were limited in their economic programmes mostly to issues like the recuperation of national wealth, stolen by the foreigners. They were kept together by insisting on their distinctive cultural identity, so that they invariably comprised of at least some cultural nationalists.[31] Their discourses included moderate economic programmes of reform and the assertion of cultural identity in various and often changing mixtures.[32]

The national liberation movements took power in the wake of the crisis of the great depression of the 1930s. They were led by the secular nationalists. Both tendencies of secular nationalism, moderates and Marxists, had privileged class and economics. They had deduced from their critique of colonialism and imperialism the concept of state intervention in the economy. They developed their state-based approaches into a wide pattern of often heterogeneous strategies of planned development (Nayar 1997: 27; Schaller 1986: 430). Where moderates were strong, they adopted gradualism which allowed the large majority to join them. They proposed only cautious measures against the propertied classes and basically preserved and even protected small enterprises, traders and middle peasants.[33] Where the moderates were weak as in East Asia, the communist-led national liberation movements were able to launch peasant wars as in China or Vietnam.[34]

Changes in power relations within the industrialised West after the outbreak of the Second World War made the preference of the US for politically independent countries under the leadership of the most Western-oriented movements hegemonic in the Western strategies.[35] For remaining hegemonic against more revolutionary movements, the partners chosen by the West could be as much revolutionary as accepted by the West. The moderate nationalists became the privileged partners of the West (Clymer 1988: 344; Sherwood 1996: 412 f.) and could impose the retreat of the colonial powers and even force these powers to contribute to their establishment as the new leaders of this not yet capitalist world in the South. The West favoured 'true' nationalists against the communists.[36]

When state-led industrialisation collapsed, the state classes' control over political power became endangered. In many cases, cultural nationalists rose to power (Elsenhans 1994a). They were able to break their relative isolation and to conquer new social bases. With the gradual exhaustion of rent, the state classes increasingly appeared to the small and medium businesses as a purely rapacious fiscus from which they had nothing to expect.[37] In a quite Keynesian pattern, these small businesses had grown during the state-led industrialisation because of the inefficiency of the public sector.[38] The public sector spent more money on wages and services than it provided goods. It operated as a state engaging in deficit spending with a large share of its deficit appearing as wages of average income households. The small and medium businesses grew by producing for these strata. In order to continue this growth, they wanted to disband state regulation, in India the license raj (Lubell & Zarour 1990: 395; Mizrahi 1994: 151). With dwindling resources, the state tried to spend its rent on politically useful audiences. Those kept from such favours accused the state of corruption which anyhow had to arise as a consequence of the rigidities of bureaucratic coordination in the economy.[39] They turned to the cultural nationalists who had since long criticised the statisation of the economy and the statist economic basis of the secular nationalists and their state classes.[40]

In addition, to varying degrees the cultural nationalists became attractive to the marginalised. They had been seduced by the secular nationalists with the promise of improving conditions for their lives but, in reality, had been neglected in most cases.[41] State-led industrialisation did not, however, provide them with sufficient jobs as shown above. Moderate agrarian reforms privileged middle farmers and did not remove rural property for the landless. In most cases agrarian reforms kept additional demand for (new) non-family rural labour low, although the labour input in such reformed agricultures rose, mostly to the benefit of the families of the owner operators.[42] The marginalised, especially those who had migrated to the cities in order to find new jobs created by rent-financed spending, opted increasingly for the cultural nationalists.[43]

The secular nationalists can, however, take pride in their success to put their populations to school.[44] Ever increasing numbers of school leavers faced, however, a declining rise of demand of the modern sector for educated labour (Hanf 1969: 303; Roussel 1971: 515). At the start of state-led industrialisation, the state-financed modern productive sector and the administrations (because of state building) were short in supply of qualified staff. The early generations of school leavers came from families with a relatively intensive contact with the foreign bridgehead and were often well-acquainted with the languages of the ex-colonial powers and even often educated in these languages. New generations were drawn from the countryside or the provincial towns and were less acquainted with these Western languages. In order to fight the earlier generations who blocked the seats in the limited modern sector, the only advantage of the new climbers was their higher familiarity with the local culture and the 'vernacular' languages. Insisting on the importance of the restoration of the national culture was a suitable argument for asking for more places in the modern sector and even for replacing those already in place which were accused to be too Western.[45] Amin's (1973: 218)[46] third estate—the old middle strata—and Ouaissa's (2011) effendiyya—a combination of the historical and newly formed middle strata, often in alliance with the marginals as storm troopers—gave rise to new cultural identitarian movements. These movements grew under the leadership of intellectuals who had, in the competition over ideas, adopted cultural nationalism.[47] They became powerful in those regions of the South where there were chances to develop on the basis of more autonomy from the Western world, where the secular state classes had failed and where the reference to cultural heritage could allow marking the difference from the dominant Westernworld and its previous dominant bridgehead.

The new cultural identitarian movements are, therefore, absent from a variety of regions of the South. In Latin America, cultural difference from the West is perceived by the masses primarily as conflict between a westernised established privileged class with conspicuous consumption on the one side and culturally and politically excluded poor which belong to the indigenous people on the other side (Canessa 2000: 115; Madrid 2008: 507). The state classes had been relatively conservative in Latin America with the exception of Mexico. The challengers to these established westernised classes are new forms of populist movements.[48] Although there is a rise of religion,[49] there are no political movements which use religion as a mechanism of political integration.

In sub-Saharan Africa the established state classes are challenged mostly by segments of state classes which happened to be excluded from sinecures and members of newly emerging urban middle strata.[50] There is very little connection to the rural world where the old traditional families maintain their influence.[51] The urban informal sector is relatively weak as compared to Asia or Latin America. There are no really expanding dynamic rural and urban markets. Discontented segments of state classes and newly rising middle strata opt for the disempowerment of those segments of state classes which are in power. They adopt a discourse which is oriented to the values of the Western bourgeois revolutions of the 18th century.[52] They hope to please Western donors and are trying to gain their support in the form of development assistance in order to reopen the tap of rents flowing from the West.[53]

Where radical secular nationalists had followed strategies of radical reforms including agrarian reforms with land redistribution, they were able to create the conditions for removing poverty via market regulation.

They were able to introduce economic liberalisation against the wastefulness of bureaucratic regulation and to mobilise the labour force. They favoured the trickling down of productivity improvements to the poorer sections which previously had been given some entitlement (especially through agrarian reforms). This success was achieved also in those socio-economic structures where anti-communist state classes feared the political competition of the communists and introduced themselves far-reaching land redistribution such as in South Korea (Kim 1976: 13; Lee 1979: 513) or Taiwan.[54]

The new cultural identitarian movements are, therefore, powerful in the world of Islam and in South and parts of South East Asia, but not in sub-Saharan Africa (Green 2006; Harnischfeger 1995). In the world of Islam and these parts of Asia, state-led import-substituting industrialisation has created new middle strata and promoted (indirectly) the informal sector without integrating the subalterns into production so that the mechanism of growth via expanding internal mass markets was blocked.

Those political forces which emerge on the basis of the impact of the West on the not yet capitalist South are only partially available for strategies of co-ordination between the West and the South: The space shrinks for coordinated strategies which could aim at compensating the disempowerment of labour (in the West) in relation to capital in this period of the rapid integration of the as-yet non-capitalist periphery into a worldwide international division of labour.

It is even tempting to give up the project of development through restructuring. The shift in Western thinking on development policy towards an expectation that this can be achieved simply by orientating the economy around exports contributes to the downplaying of development issues. It leads to a pattern of international relations oriented around power.

A Non-development Pole in West-South Relations

Those political forces in capitalism which are close to business interests are actually unable to transcend the immediate interests of business in cost reduction and to impose at the political level the countervailing interest in market expansion through rising mass demand. They are, therefore, no partners for an alliance to preserve the bases of capitalism. They favour economic liberalisation and the dismantling of state-controlled institutions of rent appropriation and rent allocation. Under their influence development, policies have lost their macroperspectives and been limited to private sector promotion, better 'good governance' against wasteful use of rents and some rather limited social measures.[55] The conflict between Japan and the World Bank over the role of the state in development was a manifest example (Moore 1999: 63; Watanabe 1997: 315). Those conservative forces in the West which concentrate on the preservation of national security interests formulate general views in line with such limited measures on the desirability of overcoming underdevelopment. They focus, however, on cooperation with all well-established powers which share with them the interest in the maintenance of the balance of power at the level of the global state system. There is, therefore, little political pressure for correcting this shift to non-development (Tammen 2006: 577).

There is a convergence in interests which contributes to maintaining stability at the interstate level such as avoiding major social break-ups of the established order at the level of any individual state.[56] As long as the powers in place are capable of maintaining social stability, they are welcome partners. They are expected to avoid the instrumentalising of internal conflicts to achieve aggressive foreign policies ends, that is, a strategy to enhance their 'national' legitimacy. External pressures aiming at imposing on them empowerment of their subalterns with the result of launching their internal markets are limited. Really occurring measures in this direction which took place during the current financial crisis in many countries of the South are favourably commented by experts, but not understood as a change in orientation in the direction of capitalism.[57]

Difficulties of Western and Southern Mass-based Political Forces

Possible strategic actors for the creation of a worldwide alliance against the global under-consumptionist threat of the current pattern of globalisation in the West, the Western parties with a large mass support, are not well placed for cooperation with the newly emerging political forces in the South which can command large mass support. This applies not only to the social democratic and communist parties (where they still exist) but also to the Christian Democratic parties. The Western Labour movement has certainly been less associated with the aggression of the West against the non-capitalist world during the expansion of the West since the 16th century. Those Christian churches which were close to Western subalterns like the Methodists were prominent in fighting the slave trade.[58] Labour organisations were often opposed to colonial expansion but often also accomplices.[59] Labour parties were partners for the secular nationalists in implementing colonial reforms and even decolonisation (Albertini 1989: 616; Holland 1996). But Western labour participated in the belief in the superiority of Western political norms which were often instrumentalised in order to justify Western military intervention against national liberation movements. The social democratic support for France's Algerian War[60] and the launching of the Vietnamese war by the US Democrats[61] are outstanding examples for the belief of Western labour that the resistance movements of the South had to be taught which political goals they should pursue. The advice that they should privilege individual liberation against their collectivist ideas is well-known. These collectivist ideas were, however, necessary in order to mobilise widespread support on the basis of the promise to completely reorder growth-inhibiting social structures. In rent-dominated societies the use of the rent for the many requires intelligent 'collectivist' structures, whereas markets (under conditions of market imperfections) protect the rentiers, and hence privilege. Rents are the expression of market imperfections which freedom of contract cannot remove.

As capitalism emerged regionally in an uneven manner, countervailing powers were also organised regionally. Especially after the first successes in the organisation of labour movements, labour became nationally restricted in its political practices. The areas in which it had to gain influence were organised as states (Gallissot 1995: 83–87). The literature on the types of capitalism typically describes national differences in the various restrictions on the operation of the mechanism and structure of competition and then goes on to develop typologies of business behaviour (Albert 1991: 117). Nevertheless, these differences are limited: The capital relies on worldwide relatively uniform rules of behaviour which are patterned by a-cultural competition on markets.

In contrast to this, labour relies on the resource of organisation: Organisation of political movements depends on national conventions labelled as culture and state-related 'national' institutions. Labour may have been cosmopolitan in outlook when it rose as a political force, but its immediate interests and, therefore, its political praxis are shaped by the existing organisational set-up in national societies and states (Ritter 1980: 360; Stearns 1997: 69). The need for communication in order to achieve organisation is facilitated by a shared language. Global strategies are broken down into concrete goals which are formulated and perceived by members on the basis of the existing institutional settings. A good example is the social security systems which were established within the boundaries of existing states. So, the regionally uneven spread of capitalism creates a multitude of incentives to privilege the national level in the organisation of labour. The attempt of labour to protect the national instances in the European integration process and the preference of business for the Union institutions,[62] also through the so-called negative integration, are good examples.[63]

Where the state classes of the South had succeeded in imposing redistribution at the world level during the oil price crisis, the progressive elements of the state classes in the OPEC countries did not find partners in the Western social democratic parties. These Southern state classes had seen the success of OPEC as a first step in a more general transfer of resources to the South via taxing the raw material exports of the South. This had been proposed in the demand for a new international economic order.[64] The United States supported oil-price increases in order to become less dependent on cheap Middle East oil,[65] but it did not intend to contribute by such an outcome to the political legitimacy of the more radical political forces in the Arab world which since long had demanded better oil prices. Indeed, they wanted their conservative allies to reap the fruits of the achievement of higher oil prices, which they deemed necessary in order to diversify their supplies of oil (Elsenhans 1974b: 20). They intensively cooperated with the most conservative oil monarchies of the Arab world.[66] Their probably common objective was that the oil dollars could not be used to finance other raw material cartels (Sirc 1978: 322; Toye 2005: 157). The conservative oil monarchies wanted to support the Islamist forces against the Godless Marxists in other Muslim countries, with the well-known results in Pakistan and Afghanistan.[67]

Other outcomes proposed by the then *tiersmondiste* (thirdworldist) Algeria[68] failed because not only the US but also the European social democratic party leaderships were hostile (Gosovic & Ruggie 1976: 317 f.; Sabkani 2005). The social democrats could not adopt their own principle 'as much market as possible—as much state as necessary' (SPD 1959) to the specific challenges of overcoming underdevelopment. First World social democrats had been unable to formulate a differentiated critique of the dangers implicit in an overextension of the state. [69] Therefore, they could not strike an alliance with those segments of the state classes which limited rent by raising mass consumption. Instead, they indulged either in an uncritical approval of the role of state planning or an equally uncritical accusation of its wastefulness and oppressiveness.[70] The Soviet Marxists were not better in evaluating the 'national intelligentsia' on the basis of their usefulness for implementing Soviet foreign policy goals (Jeffries 1968; Mährdel 1967:

1413). Alternative Marxists usually were adamant in the critique of the state classes for their cooperation with the imperialists,[71] which was, however, the only means of appropriating rents from raw material exports.

Today, social democrats simply do not exist as partners for strategic alliances outside the Western industrialised world. The secular nationalists have reacted to their failure in state-led industrialisation with the wholehearted adoption of economic liberalism and close cooperation with international capital and the institutions which share the latter's views.[72] The undoubtedly valuable contribution made by social democrats in the training of trade unionists and social activists in Third World countries does not compensate for the absence of coalitions for implementing alternative paths of development. Those communists who have succeeded in developing their own underdeveloped countries (China, Vietnam) prefer competition for external demand impulses (admittedly with some demand creation at their national levels) from the world economy by devaluation-driven growth. This allows them to negotiate further access to rent in apparently close cooperation with the Bretton Woods institutions.[73] The secular forces based on labour do not exist anymore at the global level

The Christian Democrats of continental Europe share some characteristics with the new cultural identitarian movements of the South. Both take their origins in the failure of the secular 'Marxist' (in a broad definition) to attract all strata of the subalterns. The Christian Democrats are directly heir to the populist parties which tried to present an alternative to the secular socialists in the late 19th century in creating a counterweight against the strategies of business to reduce costs. They chose a discourse based not so much on intensifying the class struggle but on moral principles deduced from religion. After 1945, the Christian Democrats inherited the electoral bases of those forces which had tried to limit the influence of the labour movement among the subalterns by addressing it with chauvinistic, organic and even racist ideas of community building. They had audiences among those parts segments of labour which social democratic parties could not easily reach (that is, employees, white-collar workers, rural workers, small business workers).[74]

Obviously the Christian Democrats are not the direct ideological heirs of the fascists, but they could take over their constituencies after the catastrophe of 1945: This is useful to remember when the new cultural identitarian movements in the South are linked to fascism and are denied any capacity to become moderate conservative forces.

The bases, the sources of their ideologies, the opponents to check and the overall worldviews of the Christian Democrats and at least the increasingly dominant moderate fractions in the new cultural identitarian movements are relatively similar. But the close identification of all these movements with their respective cultural traditions keeps them from perceiving these similarities. The new cultural identitarian movements are, therefore, locally influential but internationally homeless outside their own cultural regions. They, therefore, cannot realise that they could play a similar role as the Christian Democrats in embedding capitalism. In order to create these movements, cultural traditions have been used as an overarching common umbrella rather without too much and recently also decreasing practical relevance (Sharma 2014).

In order to enlarge their bases among the three constituencies I mentioned above, these movements have to complement this umbrella by practical programmes. These practical programmes are inspired by pragmatism as they do not have a precise and coherent economic and social theory. They have principles, which can be summarised as moral economy,[75] an imprecise term which describes a fundamental commitment to market and private property combined with an overall responsibility for state intervention to maintain social norms of equity and fairness. In order to enlarge their audiences, these movements have increasingly to relegate their cultural goals to the second level and to concentrate on their pragmatic stances.[76] This often leads to considerable tensions between their constituencies and their core memberships (Schwecke 2011: esp. 121 ff.). The more these movements move towards the centre of their societies in order to become influential, the more they have to address much less culturally committed middle strata which reject some of their more purist goals. These middle strata have a lot to lose in case of disorder. They are more powerful and more committed in these movements, the more their businesses grow on the basis of growing demand and the implied empowerment of labour. This does not preclude a return to aggressive identitarian policies by the new cultural identarian political movements[77] but limits this perspective especially in case that the growth of employment counteracts tendencies to economic depression.

The main representatives of the West in the South have very little contact with these new cultural identitarian movements: The Western labour movement rejects them in the name of secularism and cosmopolitanism because of their nationalism and their foreignness, hence cultural distance. The Christians do not find common ground with the religiously based organisations due to the divisive influence of the differences in cultural identification.

The Isolation of the Non-governmental Organisations

NGOs occupy at the international level the space which in national capitalist settings is occupied by the political organisations which mediate and alleviate the conflict between capital and labour. This space is not occupied at the global level by mass organisations because the impact of capitalism is too weak to create uniform conditions of labour. Labour in production sites with poor conditions cannot easily migrate to locations with better conditions as in the case of national economies. Without such migrations there is no homogenisation of work conditions on the basis of labour becoming scarce in regions with poor conditions. This place is, therefore, occupied by elite organisations without large memberships.

NGOs have no mass base and are not financed by those in the name of whom they pretend to realise improvements. They are in a double relationship (with their sources of funds and their target groups) which is characterised by rent. Those whom they help would not receive the same benefits if they refused to cooperate. NGOs, therefore, have the power to successfully 'advise' their target groups. However, in the case that a target group refuses such advice they would be worse off (Elsenhans 1995, 1996b). In order to acquire the resources necessary for their activities, NGOs have to convince donors about the quality of their work, particularly their successes.[78] Donors are invariably those who belong to the hegemonic block in power in the capitalist countries as other groups have much less money to spare, even if well-intentioned members of the capitalist societies contribute. The latter's contribution will never be large enough to engineer strategies to restructure underdeveloped disarticulated economies which lack the economic capacity to provide for mass needs. NGOs can be successful in acquiring resources if they conform to those overall views which donors value about successful development strategies. In order to show a good profile to donors, target groups as recipients of NGO assistance have to behave in ways which are presentable to donors (Baierle 2003: 323; Fowler 2000: 641). NGOs 'sell titles to moral well being', hence a sort of certificates of good conscience (Elsenhans 1991b: 211, 1995: 158 f.) and impose the required patterns of behaviour because in this way they acquire a non-material asset which gives access to a rent distributed by a donor. They acquire their resources neither from mass membership fees nor by selling their certificates of good conscience on anonymous markets regulated by perfect competition, but oligopolistic markets where they create the demand partially themselves by influencing the political audiences to which the rent distributing planners refer. They participate in the creation of the demand like many other oligopolists who sell less noble products than NGOs.

There is no need to extensively report on the shortcomings of NGOs but two implications should be mentioned. NGOs escape even less than organisations with mass membership the iron law of oligarchy[79] and the emergence of the self-interest of any organisation in its own survival.[80] They will, therefore, employ power and influence to shape target groups to their needs for acquiring new rents. Transparency and the free flow of information will constrain these tendencies, but the Third World is remote so that the results achieved by the NGOs and their targets groups are always amenable to 'presentation', finally masquerade.

Their rivals are truly mass-based organisations which may exhibit other preferences. Some NGOs even subvert existing mass organisations (Petras 1997: 12) by co-opting their leadership or by providing more benefits which are attractive at least in the short run.[81]

It would be suicidal to attack openly the philosophy of major donors. As these major donors have no incentive to directly oppose capital on side issues such as development policies, NGOs cannot go beyond curative practices. Their policies are supposed to not enter into decisive conflict with established powers in the capitalist West. The parallel between their role and the role of missionary societies during the period of colonialism has already been mentioned. The stepping in of the NGOs into the role of quasi-governments with responsibility for entire territories is an observable tendency and greatly promoted by the European Union and its 'civilian' foreign policy.[82]

NGOs are typically without close contact with those organisations which posit themselves as independent from the West. As long as the secular nationalists had powerful local social bases and in so far as they still have them, they do not cooperate with the NGOs who do not accept their terms.[83] With the demise of the secular nationalists, some of their cadres have joined the NGOs (Elsenhans 1991c: 277; Vaughan 1995: 518). As well, the NGOs do not have contacts to the new cultural identitarian movements. They consider them as competitors and tend to present as politically dangerous and opposed to the values of development and democracy.[84]

Despite globalisation, in the realm of transnational political and social organisation there is globalisation only in appearance. Neither the 'civil society' of the West nor its political organisations in the sector of the representation of mass interests have contact with the really existing—perhaps, however, in reality—'uncivil',[85] sometimes even violent civil societies of the not yet capitalist world.[86] This really existing civil society is quite powerful and vigorous due the importance of rents in all walks of society.

The relative isolation of the NGOs is reinforced by the recruitment basis of the organisations. In the capitalist world, they recruit from the same supply of university graduates as transnational enterprises or governments.[87] In the South, the recruitment comes to a large extent from those strata from which also governments and transnational companies recruit (Le Naëlou 2004: 792; Werker & Ahmed 2008: 79). A Bangladeshi civil servant described this mechanism as follows: 'You go into government administration for 10 years in order to learn how the government ticks. Then you try to be hired by a transnational enterprise and, if you fail, by an NGO. If you do not succeed in both ways you will remain a civil servant and try to collect bribes.'

There is, therefore, at the global level no mass-based political structure which constitutes a counterweight against the strategies of business to reduce costs. Under the conditions of still continuing structural underemployment, the absence of political mass organisations leads to the admittedly highly decentralised appearance of rent. The discourse about cultural and social globalisation is, therefore, misleading. Globalisation in these walks of society might be interpreted as the constitution of an efficient countervailing power against the strategies of business comparable to the negotiating power of scarce labour in capitalist social structures.

Maybe the discursive impact of these organisations, as they try to represent general human interests, develops an impact of its own by the strength of its argument. This comes back to the question whether ideas matter. I admit that my own appreciation is influenced by a materialistic interpretation of history. Interests may lead to different formulations and these interpretations may transcend inherited worldviews but there are no worldviews which become powerful in history without being related to deeply felt interests nested in the anxieties and perspectives of identifiable social groups with a distinguishable embeddedness in social conflict structures.[88] The failure of so many attempts to democratisation to go beyond electoral democracy (Merkel et al. 2001: 68) and the parallel inability of their subalterns to acquire and organise real influence shows the importance of rent (Zinecker 2009: esp. 325). Capitalism can go with many political regimes but democracy probably only with a socio-economic system where capitalism removes or at least decisively reduces the possibilities of rent appropriation.

Notes and References

1. Boron 1999: 222; Carothers 2002: 10; Levitsky 2002: 52.
2. It is, therefore, not absurd to see a tension between the environmental challenge and democracy, although the conclusion of downplaying the environmental issue is ridiculous, cf. Klaus 2007: 28.
3. Atteh 1993: 281; Clapp 1994: 23 f.; Logan 1991: 61; Rublack 1989: 364.
4. Take the case of taxes on energy-intensive goods in more energy conscious countries, Goh 2004: 399; Mathy 2004: 95.
5. Elsenhans 2001b. Cf. also Baer et al. 1999: 1743; Bello & Rosenfeld 1990: 443; Chang 1993.
6. Take the classics, Bhatt 1964; Hirschman 1958; Nurkse 1953.
7. Ahluwalia et al. 1979: 324 ff.; Amsden 1991: 283; Bello & Rosenfeld 1990: 456; Klasen 2009: 326; Page et al. 1993: 160.
8. Clayton 1970: 440; Cortázar & Downey 1977: 705; Dorner & Felstehausen 1970: 228; Elsenhans 1979a: 540–544; Janvry 1981.
9. Agosin & Ffrench-Davis 1995: 35; Bienefeld 1988: 23; Koenig 1967: 382; Pant 1972; Balassa 1974: 178.
10. There is no theory of 'deformation' through underdevelopment in Lenin 1977; Lenin (277 f.) observes above average growth in the colonies. Warren 1980: esp. 177 argues in favour of an appropriate (and, hence, lower) exchange rate, and hence, in favour of the acceptance of exploitation.
11. Abdel-Fadil 1971: 621; Alcorta 2000; Bhagavan 1985: 409; Casar & Ros 1983: 266.
12. The feuilletonnistic approach, followed in Pieterse (2001), is a good illustration of the disinterest of this development literature for overcoming underdevelopment; in Germany the position of Menzel (1991, 1992) can be quoted.
13. Gallissot 1995: 83; Reinecke 2009: 44; Wallerstein 2003: 664.
14. Dunn 2009; Kohn & Sokolsky 1965: 10 f.; Nigam 2006: 177; Rotberg 1966: 37.
15. Bridge 1976: 184; Lütt 2006: 274; Moore 1966: 458.
16. Elsenhans 2000b: 403. Cf. the speeches of de Gaulle on 4 November 1960 and 11 December (Blida) as reported by le Monde 6 November 1960, p. 2, and 13 December 1960, p. 4. In the deep embeddedness of this conviction in the French concept of nation, cf. also Meynier 2001: 32, 2002: 242.
17. Boahen 1966: 222; Brunschwig 1970: 416; Frank 1975: 445 ff.; Gough 1977.
18. All resistance movements started with a religious reform, cf. Büttner 1985; Chesneaux 1958: 172 ff.; Fox 1984: 467; Houtard 1977; Isichei 1978: 467; Keddie 1962: 269 ff.; Lapidus 1997: 451.
19. Desai 2008: 650 ff.; Leclerc 2000: 59; Tinker 1969.
20. Chakrabarty 2005: 4817; Desai 2008: 655; Deshpande 2008.
21. Most prominently Galeano 1973: 247 ff.
22. Arslâne 2008: 46; Bhatia 1965: 351; Fox 1984: 468; Keddie 1966.

23. Dodge 1966: 98; Inukai 1974; Kühne 1986: 71 ff..
24. Menon 1990: 206 ff.; Mukherjee 1981: 12 f.; Sarkar 2006.
25. Bernal 1981: 168; Carr 1987: 385; Chatterjee 1986: 203.
26. Brehme 1985; Chandra 1988: 4; Etienne 1987: 177; Wang 2003.
27. Bhagwan 1981: 171; Chowdhuri 1976; Das Gupta 1987: 447; Pavier 1974; Upadhyaya 1980: 230. Nuanced about Patiala and Hyderabad: Mukherjee 1979: 24; Prasad 1986: 243. But: Ram 1973. Further: Low 1981: 77; Carrère d'Encausse 1964: 338, 1965: 338. Indonesia: Kahin 1952: 67 ff.; Sadria 1986: 57 f. Arab world: Abbas 1973. In Algeria, the Communist party had no peasant organisation, Elsenhans 2000b: 526, fn. 701.
28. Crawley 1971: 95 f.; Robb 1991: 186; Sharma 1999: 53.
29. The fact that the Communist party ultimately split over the issue of the peasantry after independence confirms this appreciation. What has to be explained is why the Communist Party of India (M) became able to penetrate the villages after independence, such in West Bengal, cf. Banerjee 1996: 212.
30. Chandra 1979: 75; Kerr 1962; Nayar 1997: 14.
31. Bhagavan 2008: 39; Jaffrelot 1996: 25 ff.; Julien 1972: 101; LeTourneau 1962: 317 f.
32. Dekmejian 1980: 5; LeTourneau 1962: 314; Majumdar et al. 1978: 955.
33. Couland 1964: 174; Mercier 1965: 153 f.; Nicolas 1981: 93; Petras 1975: 297.
34. Harrison 1965; Lockard 1994; Thaxton 1977: 54; Wolf 1968.
35. Gardner 1998: 61 ff.; Hess 1972; Homan 1990; Kent 2005; Louis & Robinson 1994: 463; Nissimi 2001: 827.
36. Greenfield 2005: 173; Kinda 1992; Srinivasan 2006: 262.
37. Atasoy 2008: 127 f.; Bugra 2002: 192; Heuzé 1999: 739; Mazaheri 2008: 592 f.; Moaddel 1991: 335.
38. Elsenhans et al. 2000: 218; Hugon 1980: 421; Liedholm et al. 1994.
39. Kothari 1984: 217. Further: Ayubi 1982: 268; Fernandes 2006: 25.
40. Müller 2002: 9 ff.; Rudolph & Hoeber-Rudolph 1982: 140; Rutten 2003: 79 f.
41. Faksh 1984: 141 ff.; Lieten 1996: 242; Wankhede 2008: 50.
42. Ahmad & Sternberg 1969: 171; Boeckx 1971: 387; Byres 1972: 110.
43. Bayat 2002: 14; Chowdhry 1994; Clark 2004: 966.
44. Anshuman & Chandrashekhar 2004: 835; Chhibber 1996: 134; Mansouri-Acherar 1996: 179.
45. Grandguillaume 1977; Jaffrelot 1993: 160; Pulsfort 1996: 534.
46. Cf. also Kupferschmidt 1987: 409; Shechter: 572.
47. Nasir 2004: 3; Tétreault 2011: 18; Waldner 1994: 4.
48. Dorraj & Dodgson 2009: 149 ff.; Petras & Veltmeyer 2007: 392; Roberts 1995: 83; Sylvia & Danopoulos 2003; Tejapira 2006: 15; Viguera 1993: 64.
49. Almeida & Sánchez 2000; Corten 2005: 172; Gifford 1991: 15 ff.; Longman 1998; Löwy 2001: 36 ff.; Ströbele-Gregor 1989: 60.
50. Adejumobi 1996: 421 f.; Akude 2006: 55; Elsenhans 2001a: 162 fn. 286.
51. Barchiesi 1996: 351; Elsenhans 2001a: 162, fn. 287; Erdmann 2000: 117.

52. Barya 1993: 23 f.; Baylies 1995: 335; Elsenhans 2011.
53. Brown 2005: 193; Bromley 1995: 341; Dunning 2004: 409; Fatton 1995: 89.
54. Grabowski 1993: 55, 1998: 357; Isvilanonda et al. 2000: 4649; Kay 2002: 1091; Page et al. 1993: 160; Rapley 1996: 128.
55. Ben Hammouda 1998: 98; Chakravarty 1987: 125; Dollar 1992; Pieterse 2001. Is a nice example of adding many sidetours including the cultural turn in order to avoid discussing the turn to the neoliberal paradigm, so that this really existing turn can be hidden to the observer.
56. Bhattacharya 2010: 72; Cheru & Obi 2010: 3; Iida 2007: 30; Lind 2005: 33; Mohan 2003: 75; Virmani 2006: 4601–4604.
57. Artus & Mistral 2010; Chaponniere 2008; Edes 2010.
58. Anstey 1981: 211; Emmer 1973: 173; Kaufmann & Pape 1999: 643.
59. Bédarida 1969: 5; Bertrand 2007: 121; Cohen 1987: 33; Eley 1976: 272; Harrison 1957: 105.
60. Elsenhans 2000b: 933; Ouaissa 2009; Quilliot 1972: 604–625, in the interviews with Robert Lacoste (111–134), Max Lejeune (140–153), Daniel Mayer (164–175) and Christian Pineau (189–207).
61. Hoffmann 1970: 137 f.; Krippendorff 1970: 40 ff.; Lumer 1987: 307.
62. Caporaso 1996: 44; Cocks 1980: 31; Isenberg 1998.
63. Bieber et al. 1988: 313; Cohen 1996: 151; Scharpf 2001: 4.
64. Huber Stephens 1987: 89; Petras 1982: 416; Rothstein 1984.
65. Akins 1973; Elsenhans & Junne 1973: 1312; Krasner 1973: 138; Penrose 1974: 38 ff.; Sarkis 1975: 69.
66. Kissinger addressing the UN General Assembly quoted by BMZ Materialien 51: 7. Cf. also Adelman 1974: 66; Bahgat 2003: 448; Elsenhans 1977b.
67. Gause 2004: 69 f.; Shahin 1997: 10; Tazmini 2001: 75.
68. Cervenka 1976: 197; Le Monde, 23/24th April 1975: 24, 10th January 1974: 2.
69. When I suggested in May 1973 at a Franco-German conference a strategy on how to deal with the coming oil price crisis (hence, before it occurred) on the basis of launching industrialisation in the interest of the Arab masses, the head of the German delegation invited me to no longer participate. The French side imposed my further participation, cf. the report with a summary of my intervention in Levi 1973, 356: '*Peut-être, a fait remarquer un participant, la situation serait différente si des gouvernements ayant des conceptions révolutionnaires et modernisatrices prenaient la place des gouvernements conservateurs actuels, dès lors que de tels gouvernements seraient enclins à poursuivre des programmes d'investissements pour assurer le développement des économies nationales!*' (One participant suggested that the situation might be more favourable if governments with revolutionary concepts for modernisation replaced the existing conservative governments. Such modernising governments would be more ready to pursue investment programmes for developing their national economies!)
70. Destanne de Bernis 1962: 155; Jreisat 2002: 117; Mahalanobis 1953.

71. Alavi 1972; Bienefeld 1976: 5; Duvall & Freeman 1983.
72. Ayubi 1982: 268 f.; Benderra 2003: 24; Case 2005; Zhou & White 1995: 471 ff.
73. Andrieu 1996: 673 f.; Ghosh 2005: 5990; Nitsch & Diebel 2006: 10.
74. Biscione 2008: 175; Elsenhans 2012; Gehler & Kaiser 2001: 786; Kirby 2000: 390.
75. Duran & Yildirim 2005: 231; Fassin 2009; Müller 2002.
76. Khosrokhavar 2005; Rutherford 2006: 726; Seifzadeh 2003: 67.
77. Khosrokhavar 2008: 347; Takeyh 2003: 49; Vahdat 2005: 664.
78. Extreme cases Atlani-Duault & Poujol 2008: 41 ff.; Bano 2008; Barr et al. 2005: 659.
79. Dingwerth 2003: 101 f.; Hanisch 2004: 25; Wegner 1993: 292.
80. Gordon 1997: 60; Hashemi 1990; Kuhn 1998: 79 ff.; Künzler 2006: 8.
81. Sen 1999: 336; Starr & Adams 2003: 20 f.; Stiles 2002: 843.
82. Bowen 1992: 279; Shivji 2006: 39; White 1999: 324 f.
83. Ahmad 2005; Bratton 1989; Deshpande 1986; Fernandez 1987: 43; Wanyama 2006: 98; Wuyts 1996: 745.
84. Arditi 2004; Goonatilake 2006: esp. 279; Mallaby 2004: 52; Rieger 2003; Zaidi 1999: 267.
85. Fatton 1995: 72; Fine 1992: 82; Rahman 2002; Zinecker 2009: 321 ff.
86. Chandhoke 2001: 10; Pereira 1993: 375; Zinecker 2002: 54, 2004: 248.
87. Barkan & Holmquist 1989: 367; Dorraj & Dodgson 2009: 145; Harriss 2007: 2716; Kuhn 2001: 9; Künzler 2006: 8; Schultz 2006: 54.
88. Risse & Ropp 2001: 237 ff. Nobody until now has seriously investigated to which degree these organisations like Transparency International, etc., develop on the basis of the emergence of a reference group with important financial resources, which the Bretton Woods Institutions project into the Third World, cf. Pinto-Duschinsky 2007: 153–161.

7

An International Community of Rentier Governments: Noble Intentions or a Return to the Past

If the economic bases of the civil society at the world level are shaky and weak, the defence of capitalism will depend on the organisation of an appropriate cooperation between governments. In this cooperation, governments will facilitate the transition of additional major regions to capitalism, an option which is open through the emergence of the newly industrialising countries. The vibrant discourse of the elite organisations which pretend to be the world civil society can contribute to this outcome, provided that these elite organisations take cognisance of the conditions for a worldwide transition to capitalism.

The perspective of globalisation leading to an interstate system where even major powers accept increasingly to follow rules developed by international consensus will materialise only to a limited degree. In order to reduce transaction costs, states will certainly, as they did before, accept to extend the areas which are governed by international law. But this will not extend to areas where states perceive major interests. They will not give up their quality of sovereign states which can be bound only by their consent. This applies not only to major powers but also to most of the minor powers. Rather than the right to participate as a part of the majority in international institutions, these minor powers would prefer to be shielded from the obtrusive influence of major powers. They will continue to consider sovereignty as a major protection from being drowned by external forces. It can be expected that smaller states will be reluctant to relinquish the attributes associated with sovereignty in favour of rules agreed by majority votes.

They see in their sovereignty a better safeguard against encroachments by more powerful states with regional clout than in the possible protection by majorities they can form together with other smaller states.

We are heading for a multipolar system composed of around six major powers (the United States, European Union, BRIC [Brazil, Russia, India, and China]). These are all major powers, also the emerging powers, despite the differences in their capacities to project military power abroad. The Iraq war has demonstrated that even the United States is unable to reduce military resistance without applying nuclear weapons in a mid-sized country. It can be concluded that none of these six powers can be durably occupied by another one with conventional means. Neither of these powers can be forced against their own will to comply with the goal of another one without being threatened by nuclear weapons. In all areas of vital interests of these powers, their interests have to be respected. The emerging interstate system will be regulated according to the principles of building temporary alliances for limited agreements in order to conduct the balance of power. This will resemble the cooperation within the framework of the post-1815 Vienna system during the first half of the 19th century (Mohan 2009; Qin 2009).

To the difference of this period, actual globalisation seems not to trigger off worldwide new social movements, which like nationalism in the 19th century seriously subvert the existing distribution of power. Therefore, this system is composed of existing major powers that are saturated and will not entertain movements for territorial expansion against others. This system will also not be altered by new social forces as all governments are interested in maintaining stability by maintaining their partners in the direction of the other powers of the system with whom they entertain relations.

There are no 'irridenta' territories which have to be liberated. Admittedly, there are areas difficult to handle like sub-Saharan Africa or the Arab world. In sub-Saharan Africa, the previous power configuration in the interstate system with its decolonisation by increased balkanisation created a multitude of weak states. In the Arab world, Britain had followed a similar strategy in order to separate populous regions from oil rich regions wherever possible. It is difficult to imagine that the feelings of Arab identity are weaker in the many Arab countries than the feeling of Indian identity within the multilingual Indian world. All major powers seem to agree that this dispersion of state power in the Arab world is in their interest to avoid the control of a unified Arab state over two-thirds of the cheaper world resources of oil.

The dispute between China and the rest of the world about the appreciation of the yuan (Gu 2010: 17; Kühnlenz & Kaelble 2010), but also

Germany's refusal to raise real wages in order to contribute to economic growth in the Euro zone show that governments (Joebges 2010: 1), even if integrated into a supra-national set-up, are not ready to abandon sovereignty over such issues as their strategy to maintain their international competitiveness.

It cannot be expected that the technically leading economies fulfil the role of a locomotive by accepting permanent balance of trade deficits in favour of catching-up economies. Perhaps they may be forced to do so for some time if the aging of their populations forces them to increase consumption over production (Pfaller & Witte 2002: 129 ff.).

A realistic mode of regulation would consist in all the major governments equally accepting not to resort to beggar-thy-neighbour policies which was intended in the Keynesian draft for the post-war Bretton Woods arrangements.[1] This would take up the Keynesian proposal of taking export surplus earnings from surplus countries and use them to finance the balance of trade deficits of states which contribute more to maintain the global demand.

In the actual financial crisis, some of the newly industrialising countries have maintained growth by launching internal (mass) demand (cf. Chapter 5, note 57). This could augur well for their readiness to conduct their trade relations on the basis of new rules. It also demonstrates that major catching-up economies increasingly become independent from devaluation-driven growth.

The development of the WTO further shows that major powers have regimes to find agreements over eliminating state intervention, especially, in the area where only earning possibilities and, therefore, balance of payments issues are relevant. They are less inclined to give up their means of protecting their national innovation systems which are considered to be much more important than earnings for their growth in the future. They do not accept to be excluded from major new waves of innovation.

I expect, therefore, the management of the threat of rents by government-business cooperation at national levels through intergovernmental cooperation. Governments will not resort to an aggressive capturing of the world market to the detriment of others. Tendencies to unequal specialisation which in the past may have been the source of conflicts will be dealt with by ad hoc agreements where major players will respect each other's interests.

Such structures will be made workable if the main players achieve high levels of employment. This can be achieved if globalisation is intensified: The leading economies would accept to increase their consumption and run further balance of trade deficits as did Britain in the 19th century (MacCloskey 1980: 318) and the United States over much of the second part of the 20th century.[2] There are doubts whether this will happen. It is not precluded, if this is accompanied by parallel measures in the catching-up economies to launch their internal markets. In that case, balance of trade deficits in the leading economies would appear to be temporary.

I argue, therefore, that the best strategy available for labour in the leading capitalist economies consists in intensifying globalisation in order to push the catching-up economies to high levels of employment. This will limit the possibilities of these economies to continue devaluation-driven growth. China, India and Brazil may succeed in their transformation into capitalist economies with labour being empowered by high levels of employment, perhaps together with some other large but not yet fully capitalist economies such as Mexico, Indonesia, Thailand, Vietnam and South Africa. If this proves to be successful, the rest of the world may also reach higher levels of employment, even if the only option open to these countries is devaluation-driven export-oriented industrialisation (although some of them will for long have difficulties in joining such strategies). When these smaller economies will have reached the possibility of export-oriented industrialisation through their capacity to locally produce surpluses of wage goods, there may be the possibility of transforming them on the basis of external demand for their products. When the BRIC states finally reach high levels of employment through the development and extension of their internal markets, the developed world will constitute such a large part of the world economy that it could perhaps absorb the export surpluses of such smaller developing economies on an ongoing basis. There is no real need of worrying about disturbing influences of these smaller economies if the catching-up process and the empowerment of labour will have been successful in those large economies. Within the framework of developing Western Europe, the question whether labour got empowered in Switzerland or the Czech lands was also no issue for maintaining sufficient levels of international demand.

This benign scenario is complemented by some risks which cannot be overseen. Technical progress has led to a mix of activities where industry no longer provides jobs to degrees which characterised Europe's transition to capitalism (Kaelble 1998: 25 ff.). The impact of industrialisation on the empowerment of labour can be expected to be weaker in the future also in catching-up economies. Productivity will rise worldwide but the absorption of the greater wealth by mass demand may not be guaranteed. A scenario can be imagined where consumption increasingly depends on the spending from higher incomes, as the drive to development remains too weak to integrate the mass of the marginalised into the economy via gainful (surplus producing) employment.

Such a scenario can be projected. It removes from my model of capitalism the assumption that the higher income households can receive higher incomes than the average households only in function of the higher costs of training for the skills necessary for technically more demanding jobs. The removal of this assumption implies the removal of perfect labour markets, where those who receive lower incomes are free to acquire better skills on free markets on which all types of skills are provided, certainly on the basis of costs to be paid. A convenient strategy for creating market imperfections is created by mechanisms of job definition which not only comprise formal skills but also social capital. Access to better jobs is dependent on social relations. Enterprises can follow this in principle costly strategy because oligopolistic competition creates barriers to new entrants. Other enterprises follow the leaders in this strategy because it allows them to maintain social hierarchies within the enterprise in the favour of the management. Enterprises can maintain these arrangements because productivity depends on learning by doing with the skill acquired in this process remaining enterprise-specific (Deppe & Lange 1970: 807 f.; Mallet 1969: 84–95). New entrants are unable to produce such skills. New enterprises may get these skills by hiring discontented workers coming from many enterprises, and even with the access to these skills newly founded enterprises cannot become competitive with established enterprises within a reasonable 'learning' period. Alternative centres of learning by doing cannot emerge and workers can apply their acquired additional skills only within the enterprise they belong to. Labour will be tied to enterprises in order to maintain good incomes and certainly refrain from becoming too unruly.

With imperfect labour markets, especially, for jobs where higher incomes are paid and enterprises which because of imperfect markets for their goods can charge mark-up prices, consumption spending out of higher incomes is no longer sanctioned by the market. The Kalecki (1944: 329 f.) scenario of market imperfections allowing enterprises to maximise profits without heading for full employment might become the dominant feature of the economy also because of the behaviour of labour. The economy would then be characterised by the disempowerment of relatively unskilled labour and the empowerment of middle and high-income strata through varieties of imperfections on the labour markets which in turn can go with higher consumption spending out of high incomes. Under such conditions, capitalism will lose its tendency to promote equality. It will become an arrangement characterised by market imperfections. From the demand side, it will appear as an economy of delight[3] where luxury spending becomes important for maintaining high levels of production. From the supply side, technical progress will be geared to excellence, in some economies for a larger, in some for a smaller number of households. If there are no mechanisms through which greater equality can be imposed, the pattern of technical progress will not lead to comparative cost advantages for the more egalitarian economies in new products to be manufactured with mass consumption technologies. The very possibility of a product being based on technologies of mass production may disqualify it for higher income households.

Such a system will be unstable, as it can be assumed that the higher income households will increase their consumption not in line with their higher incomes. They will also desire security in the future so that they increase their savings. These savings will not be required for financing and investment if it is assumed that the decreasing contribution of industry to national income limits also investment in real assets. The expansion of financial markets is the first possibility to avoid crisis but this possibility has limits to be managed by the political system. Therefore, 'investment' in political power becomes probable.

The scenario of the economy of delight based on imperfect labour markets implies oligopolistic restrictions with barriers to entry into new activities and with spending on product differentiation and the creation of images of products. As well, such an economy implies the extension of financial assets without corresponding counterparts in the real economy. The value of such financial assets depends on the protection of the financial assets through regulation. Such regulation will try to limit bubbles on the one hand and on the other hand maintain the nominal value of financial assets which exist. As financial assets do not become automatically demand for the real economy, this is possible in case of a reasonable overexpansion of the financial markets, so that they can function as a sort of potential purchasing power to be available in case of crises. They, however, yield interest for their owners who receive an income because of political protection of their assets very similar to a rent on land holding in the old tributary modes of production. Such a structure is not different from ancient tributary modes of production where markets existed but were limited by political power in the interests of the privileged. There will be relatively protected elites with high incomes which are used for conspicuous consumption. Access to elite positions will be more or less open, but always dependent on conforming to career patterns shaped by the oligopolistic structures in the different industries. Innovators will not be able to exploit innovations themselves but will have to offer innovations to enterprises which follow oligopolistic strategies. As market imperfections are decisive, there will be spending on the creation of such imperfections, that is, on political and social power as in tributary modes of production. Part of the spending will be directed to create images of oneself, the company and the product, not too different from the spending of the lords of tributary modes of production on 'works representing the superior unity of the community' (Marx 1857–1858: 377). Sponsoring is such an activity today.

It is clear that those who have difficulties to enter into the career patterns which are still offered will be told that this is due to their lack of appropriate skills, as the jobless are told today that they are unusable at the price they ask or they have to ask for in order to survive.

Mainstream economists will probably argue that this is still a capitalist economy. Within the multiple imperfect markets, operations take the form of an exchange. But in analysing such a system, at least many future economic historians will inevitably discover that, here, markets are well-entrenched in 'non-market' structures, that is, market imperfections. Some of them will argue that these newly emerging economic and social structures are capitalist. Do the old tributary modes of production of China and India not deserve the label of capitalist as there were markets, as craftsmen sold their luxury products on markets, as there was money and even banks? The only difference would be that the luxuries of the new tributary modes of production are produced with machinery and not on the basis of superior skills of artisans. Machinery produced luxuries imply that achievements in improvement can be transmitted by better machinery, whereas in the case of the old type of artisan skill formation in the old tributary modes of production any new artisan in principle starts from zero. There was knowledge which could be transmitted from generation to generation but the transfer of this knowledge was based not only on the acquisition of knowledge but also on the physical training of workers which always has to start from zero. Theories of history will emerge which no longer treat capitalism as a specific socio-economic arrangement, but as a step in a process of rationalisation of the ancient 'also capitalist' tributary modes by means of a technical revolution based on machinery. The capitalist period of the 16th to 20th centuries will be perceived as an episode of history.

There will be still democracy but highly elite-mediated and limited to the possibility of changing leaders in electoral democracy. Leaders present alternatives as menus. There will be still different menus, however, with many identical items like in a simple fast food shop. Many arguments will be excluded: rent in rent-dominated structures which are clothed as market economies will be defended on the basis of the argument that a reduction of rent through mass incomes will block the trickling down of economic benefits to the poor.

This will go with a parallel re-interpretation of history. The old mechanisms for consultation in tributary modes of production will be considered as forms of still limited democratic participation. Their extension will be considered as having become possible because of improved technical means of participation. The mediation of popular will through organisations called parties in the modern system will be interpreted as an improvement, rationalisation and institutionalisation of ancient modes of participation. The dependence of these modern organisations on financial power which is unevenly distributed will be interpreted as a natural condition for maintaining participation itself, as participation requires order. It will be argued that there is chaos if there is no pre-existing order which flanks spontaneous activities of the disorderly activities of the subalterns. Human rights will be considered as protected as far as the order is not subverted and be, hence, something which is conceded as were the rights in the old system of the ancient times conceded by the good emperors. This ideological turn will put capitalism out of mind, and in the end describe it as a temporary phase of disorderly growth of technology which could have been brought about also without these disturbances. China's progress did not depend on such disorder as such a committed Marxist as Frank (1998: 57 f.) had shown even before the emergence of the politically correct California school.[4] With this ideological turn, a new and stable tributary mode of production will appear as the end of history.[5] Some revolting nonconformists may be tolerated who indulge in describing capitalism full of yearning as a historically unprecedented attempt to disestablish the tributary structures and to create something else.

In some intellectual circles, liberals and socialists may discover their common objective: maintaining and re-establishing capitalism where possible. Liberals would have to accept the importance of empowerment of labour, and socialists the importance of competition. Both together form the basis for the disestablishment of rent.

They will be internationally relatively isolated. The global system will be managed according to the principles of the balance of power as the application of the principles of 'checks and balances' to the global level by the saturated superpowers (Elsenhans 2009: 39–44). They are governed by ruling classes with very well-ordered selection principles not so different from the civil service of the ancient Chinese Empire. These ruling classes tend to support each other in order to avoid unreasonable and especially violent change. The end of history will not be a decentralised bourgeois–capitalist order, but the return to ancient tributary modes of regulation, if we are not able to preserve capitalism by embedding it into social democracy.

The alternative has to be organised. At the conceptual level, there will be a 'marriage' which will consist in the ideological acceptance of the empowerment of labour as a condition for capitalism. It will guarantee high levels of employment. It is this type of empowerment which preserves the option of exit, through which the different possibilities of voice become meaningful. And it is this type of empowerment of labour which can keep the institutions where voice is exercised from falling under the iron law of oligarchy. The 'here I stand, I cannot do otherwise' can be applied only, if it does not lead to personal economic disaster.

Notes and References

1. Agarwal 2006: 204; Boughton 1998: 40 f.; Crockett 2003: 99; Skidelsky 1998.
2. On the basis of an overvalued dollar in relation to the catching-up economies, Kreile 1977: 777 f.; Meier 1977: 613–623; Shinohara 1961: 137.
3. On the concept Nef 1958: 129; Vicens Vives 1969: 174.
4. Pomeranz 2000; Vries 2008; Zurndorfer 2003.
5. And not of the type Fukuyama 1989. But as a threat to capitalist dynamism. I have warned already in Elsenhans 1991a.

Bibliography

Aaby, Peter: *The State of Guinea-Bissau: African Socialism or Socialism in Africa? Research Report No. 45* (Uddevalla: Scandinavian Institute of African Studies, 1978).
Abbas, Ferhat: La France c'est moi. Algiers (1931) quoted from LeTourneau, Roger: *Evolution politique de l'Afrique du Nord musulmane, 1920–1961* (Paris: Armand Colin, 1962).
Abbas, Raouf: 'Labour Movement in Egypt, 1899–1952', in: *Developing Economies*, 11, 1 (March 1973); pp. 62–75.
Abbott, George C.: 'A Re-examination of the 1929 Colonial Development Act', in: *Economic History Review*, 24, 1 (1971); pp. 68–81.
Abdel-Fadil, Mahmoud: 'Modèles dynamiques d'introversion de l'économie dans les pays en voie de développement', in: *Economie appliquée*, 24, 4 (October–December 1971); pp. 619–658.
Abdullah, Ibrahim: '"Liberty or Death": Working Class Agitation and the Labour Question in Colonial Freetown, 1938–39', in: *International Review of Social History*, 40, 2 (August 1995); pp. 195–221.
Abelshauser, Werner: 'Kriegswirtschaft und Wirtschaftswunder. Deutschlands wirtschaftliche Mobilisierung für den Zweiten Weltkrieg und die Folgen für die Nachkriegszeit', in: *Vierteljahrshefte für Zeitgeschichte*, 47, 4 (October 1999); pp. 503–538.
———: 'Umbruch und Persistenz: das deutsche Produktionsregime in historischer Perspektive', in: *Geschichte und Gesellschaft*, 27, 4 (December 2001); pp. 503–523.
Abraham, Meera: 'A Medival Merchant Guild of South India', in: *Studies in History*, 4, 1 (1982); pp. 1–26.
Abraham, Ulrich: 'Zur Frage der Abwanderung westdeutscher Bevölkerung in den ostelbischen Siedlungsraum', in: *Geschichte in Wissenschaft und Unterricht*, 22, 12 (December 1971); pp. 705–719.
Abulafia, David: *Frederick II. A Medieval Emperor* (Harmondsworth: Penguin, 1988).
Adas, Michael: 'Contested Hegemony: The Great War and the Afro-Asian Assault on the Civilizing Mission Ideology', in: *Journal of World History*, 15, 1 (March 2004); pp. 31–63.

Adejumobi, Said: 'The Structural Adjustment Programme and Democratic Transition in Africa', in: *Verfassung und Recht in Übersee*, 29 (Autumn 1996); pp. 417–433.

Adelman, Morris Albert: 'Politics, Economics and World Oil', in: *American Economic Review*, 64, 2 (May 1974); pp. 58–67.

Adewoye, O.: 'The Judicial Agreements in Yorubaland', in: *Journal of African History*, 12, 4 (1971); pp. 607–627.

Affonso, Almino: 'Esbozo histórico del movimiento campesino chileno', in: *Revista Latinoamericana de Ciencias Sociales*, 3, 3 (June 1972); pp. 37–70.

Afigbo, A.E.: 'The Consolidation of British Imperial Administration in Nigeria: 1900–1918', in: *Civilisations*, 21, 4 (1971); pp. 436–459.

Agarwal, Manmohan: 'Issues of Coherence in World Trading System: A Perspective from Developing Countries', in: *International Studies*, 43, 2 (April–June 2006); pp. 203–221.

Agarwal, Ritu: 'Women Farmers in China's Commercial Agrarian Economy', in: *Economic and Political Weekly*, 42, 42 (20 October 2007); pp. 4261–4267.

Agell, Jonas: 'Warum haben wir rigide Arbeitsmärkte? Rent-seeking versus Soziale Sicherung', in: *Perspektiven der Wirtschaftspolitik*, 2, 4 (2001); pp. 363–381.

Agénor, Pierre-Richard: *The Economics of Adjustment and Growth* (Cambridge, Mass.: Harvard University Press, 2004).

Agosin, Manuel R.; Ffrench-Davis, Ricardo: 'Trade Liberalization and Growth: Recent Experiences in Latin America', in: *Journal of Interamerican Studies and World Affairs*, 37, 3 (Autumn 1995); pp. 9–58.

Ahluwalia, Montek S.; Carter, Nicholas G.; Chenery, Hollis B.: 'Growth and Poverty in Developing Countries', in: *Journal of Development Economics*, 6, 3 (January 1979); pp. 299–341.

Ahmad, Mokbul Morshed: 'New Threat to Development? The NGO (Non-Governmental Organisations) Fundamentalist Conflict in Bangladesh', in: *Journal of Social Studies*, 105 (January 2005); pp. 86–103.

Ahmad, Zubeida Manzoor: 'The Social and Economic Implications of the Green Revolution in Asia', in: *International Labour Review*, 105, 1 (January 1972); pp. 9–34.

———; Sternberg, Marvin J.: 'Agrarian Reform and Employment with Special Reference to Asia', in: *International Labour Review*, 99, 1 (February 1969); pp. 159–184.

Ahmed, Aziz: *A History of Islamic Sicily* (Edinburgh: Edinburgh University Press, 1975).

Ahmed, Jaleel: 'Import Substitution and the Growth of Exports. An Econometric Test', in: *Revue économique*, 27, 2 (March 1976); pp. 286–296.

Ahmed, Syed Jamil: 'Machiavellian Centaur and Subaltern Resistance: A (Re)Reading of Three Performance Texts of the Indigenous Theatre of Bengal (I+II)', in: *Journal of Social Studies*, 105 (2005a); pp. 1–34.

Ahmed, Syed Jamil: 'Machiavellian Centaur and Subaltern Resistance: A (Re)Reading of Three Performance Texts of the Indigenous Theatre of Bengal (III)', in: *Journal of Social Studies*, 106 (Mai 2005b); pp. 23–55.

Ahuja, Ravi: 'The Origins of Colonial Labour Policy in Late Eighteenth-Century Madras', in: *International Review of Social History*, 44, 3 (December 1999); pp. 159–195.

———: 'Labour Relations in an Early Colonial Context: Madras, c. 1750–1800', in: *Modern Asian Studies*, 36, 4 (October 2002); pp. 793–826.

Ake, Claude: 'The Future of the State in Africa', in: *International Political Science Review*, 6, 1 (1985); pp. 105–114.

Akeredolu-Ale, E.O.: 'Values, Motivations and History in the Development of Private Indigenous Entrepreneurship: Lessons From Nigeria's Experience, 1946–1966', in: *Nigerian Journal of Economic and Social Studies*, 13, 2 (July 1971); pp. 175–219.

Akerlof, George A.: 'The Missing Motivation in Macroeconomics', in: *American Economic Review*, 97, 1 (March 2007); pp. 5–36.

Akins, James E.: 'The Oil Crisis: This Time the Wolf is Here', in: *Foreign Affairs*, 51, 3 (April 1973); pp. 463–490.

Akude, John Emeka: *Historical Imperatives for the Emergence of Development and Democracy: A Perspective for the Analysis of Poor Governance Quality and State Collapse in Africa. Arbeitspapiere zur Internationalen Poltik und Außenpolitik AIPA 1* (Cologne: Lehrstuhl für Internationale Politik Universität zu Köln, 2006).

al Khafaji, Isam: *Tormented Births: Passages to Modernity in Europe and the Middle East* (Amsterdam: Faculteit de Maatschappij- en Gedragswetenschappen, 2002).

Alagoa, E.J.: 'The Development of Institutions in the States of the Eastern Niger Delta', in: *Journal of African History*, 12, 2 (1971); pp. 269–278.

Alam, Muzaffar; Subrahmanyam, Sanjay: 'L'Etat Moghol et sa fiscalité, XVIe-XVIIIe siècles', in: *Annales. Economie, Société, Civilisation*, 49, 1 (January–February 1994); pp. 189–217.

Alam, Muzahhar: 'Sikh Uprisings under Banda Bahadur, 1708–1715', in: *Studies in History*, 1, 1 (1979); pp. 197–213.

Alavi, Hamza: 'Peasants and Revolution', in: *Socialist Register*, 2 (1965); pp. 241–278.

———: 'The State in Post-Colonial Societies: Pakistan and Bangladesh', in: *New Left Review*, 74 (July–August 1972); pp. 59–81.

Albert, Michel: *Capitalisme contre capitalisme* (Paris: Editions du Seuil, 1991).

Albertini, Rudolf von; Das Ende des Empire: 'Bemerkungen zur britischen Dekolonisation', in: *Historische Zeitschrift*, 249, 3 (December 1989); pp. 583–617.

Albrecht, Dieter: 'Kommunistische Partei und Bauernbewegung', in: Lorenz, Richard (ed.): *Umwälzung einer Gesellschaft. Zur Sozialgeschichte der chinesischen Revolution (1911–1949)* (Frankfort on the Main: Suhrkamp, 1977); pp. 351–404.

Alcorta, Ludovico: 'New Economic Policies and the Diffusion of Machine Tools in Latin America', in: *World Development*, 28, 9 (September 2000); pp. 1657–1672.

Aldcroft, Derek H.: 'The Entrepreneur and the British Economy, 1870–1914', in: *Economic History Review*, 17, 1 (1964); pp. 113–134.

Alden, John R.: 'Trade and Politics in Proto-Elamite Iran', in: *Current Anthropology*, 13, 6 (December 1982); pp. 613–628.

Ali, M. Athar: 'Towards an Interpretation of the Mughal Empire', in: Kulke, Hermann (ed.): *The State in India, 1000–1700* (Cambridge, Mass. et al.: Oxford University Press, 1997); pp. 263–277.

Allais, Maurice: 'La politique de libre-échange, le GATT, et la construction européenne', in: *Revue d'économie politique*, 104, 1 (January–February 1994); pp. 4–23.

Allen, Robert C.: 'Enclosure, Farming Methods, and the Growth of Productivity in the South Midlands', in: *Research in Economic History*, 10 (1989); pp. 69–88.

———: *Enclosure and the Yeoman. The Agricultural Development of the South Midlands* (Oxford: Clarendon, 1992).

———: 'Tracking the Agricultural Revolution in England', in: *Economic History Review*, 73, 2 (May 1999); pp. 209–235.

———: 'Agricultural Productivity and Rural Incomes in England and the Yangtze Delta, c.1620–c.1820', in: *Economic History Review*, 62, 3 (August 2009); pp. 525–550.

———: 'The Industrial Revolution in Miniature: The Spinning Jenny in Britain, France, and India', in: *Journal of Economic History*, 69, 4 (December 2009); pp. 901–927.

Almeida, Lúcio Flávio de; Sánchez, Félix Ruiz: 'The Landless Workers' Movement and Social Struggles Against Neoliberalism', in: *Latin American Perspectives*, 27, 5 (September 2000); pp. 11–32.

Altvater, Elmar: 'Inflationäre Deflation oder die Dominanz der globalen Finanzmärkte', in: *Prokla: Zeitschrift für kritische Sozialwissenschaft*, 34, 134 (March 2004); pp. 41–53.

Ames, Glenri Joseph: 'The Carreira da India, 1668–1682: Maritime Enterprise and the Quest for Stability in Portugal's Asian Empire', in: *Journal of European Economic History*, 20, 1 (Spring 1991); pp. 1–27.

Amin, Samir: 'Le commerce international et les flux internationaux de capitaux', in: *Homme et la société*, 15 (January–March 1970); pp. 77–101.

———: *Le développement inégal. Essai sur les formations sociales du capitalisme périphérique* (Paris: Editions de Minuit, 1973).

Amsden, Alice H.: 'Diffusion of Development. The Late-Industrializing Model and Greater Asia', in: *American Economic Review*, 81, 2 (May 1991); pp. 282–286.

Amsden, Alice H.; Singh, Ajit: 'Concurrence dirigée et efficacité dynamique en Asie: Japon, Corée du Sud, Taiwan', in: *Tiers Monde*, 35, 139 (July–September 1994); pp. 643–657.

Amuzegar, Jahangir: 'The Oil Story: Facts, Fiction and Fair Play', in: Bundy, William P. (ed.): *The New World Economic Crisis* (New York: W.W. Norton, 1975); pp. 69–82.

Andersen, Arne: 'Chemie als Zukunftstechnologie. Teerfarben Industrie vor dem Ersten Weltkrieg', in: *Jahrbuch für Wirtschaftsgeschichte*, 2 (1999); pp. 85–101.

Anderson, Benedict R.O.G.: 'Old State, New Society: Indonesia's New Order in Comparative Historical Perspective', in: *Journal of Asian Studies*, 42, 3 (May 1983); pp. 477–489.

Anderson, Perry: *Lineages of the Absolutist State* (London; Atlantic Highlands, N.J.: NLB Humanities Press, 1974).

Anderson, Robert T.: 'Voluntary Associations in History', in: *American Anthropologist*, 73, 1 (February 1971); pp. 209–222.

Anderson, Rodney D.: 'Mexican Workers and the Politics of Revolution, 1906–1911', in: *Hispanic American Historical Review*, 54, 1 (February 1974); pp. 94–113.

Andrade, Joaquim Pinto de; Silva, Maria Luiza Falcão: *Contrasting or Convergent Views on Currency Crisis: Mainstream or Keynesian Approach*. Paper presented at the Fifth Post Keynesian Workshop: Full Employment and the Price Stability in a Global Economy, organised by *Journal of Postkeynesian Economics*, University of Tennessee, Knoxville, 25 June–1 July 1998. .

Andreff, Wladimir: 'Crises, régulation et réforme dans les économies socialistes, in: *Revue d'économie politique*, 100, 1 (January–February 1990); pp. 1–42.

Andrieu, Jacques: 'Chine: Une économie communautarisée, un Etat décomposé', in: *Tiers Monde*, 37, 147 (July–September 1996); pp. 669–687.

Anell, Lars: *Recession, the Western Economies and the Changing World Order* (London: Frances Pinter, 1981).

Angeles, Luis: 'Income Inequality and Colonialism', in: *European Economic Review*, 51, 5 (July 2007); pp. 1155–1176.

Angermeier, Heinz: 'Die Vorstellung des gemeinen Mannes von Staat und Reich im deutschen Bauernkrieg', in: *Vierteljahrschrift für Sozial- und Wirtschaftsgeschichte*, 53, 3 (1966); pp. 329–343.

Anquetil, M. Jacques: 'L'artisanat, créateur contemporain d'Afrique Noire', in: *Afrique Contemporaine*, 66 (1973); pp. 7–14.

Ansari, Ali M.: 'The Myth of the White Revolution: Mohammed Reza Shah, "Modernization", and the Consolidation of Power', in: *Middle Eastern Studies*, 37, 3 (July 2001); pp. 1–24.

Anshuman, V. Ravi; Chandrashekhar, S.: 'How Contemporary Are IIMs? MBA Curricula in a Globalised World', in: *Economic and Political Weekly*, 39, 8 (21 February 2004); pp. 827–837.

Anstey, Roger: 'Parliamentary Reform, Methodism and Antislavery Politics, 1829–1833', in: *Slavery and Abolition*, 2, 3 (December 1981); pp. 209–226.

Anthony, David W.: 'The "Kurgan Culture", Indo-European Origins and the Domestication of the Horse: A Reconsideration', in: *Current Anthropology*, 27, 4 (August–October 1986); pp. 291–305.

Appelbaum, Eileen; Schettkat, Ronald: 'Employment and Productivity in Industrialized Economies', in: *International Labour Review*, 134, 4/5 (1995); pp. 605–623.

Ardant, Gabriel: 'A Plan for Full Employment in the Developing Countries', in: *International Labour Review*, 88, 1 (July 1963); pp. 15–57.

———: 'Financial Policy and Economic Infrastructure of Modern States and Nations', in: Tilly, Charles (ed.): *The Formation of National States in Western Europe* (Princeton, N.J.: Princeton University Press, 1975); pp. 164–242.

Arditi, Claude: 'Des paysans plus professionnels que les développeurs? L'exemple du coton au Tchad', in: *Tiers Monde*, 45, 180 (October/November 2004); pp. 841–865.

Argy, Victor; Spitäller, Erich: 'The Joint Determination of Changes in Output and Prices in Seven Manufacturing Industrial Countries', in: *Weltwirtschaftliches Archiv*, 116, 1 (1980); pp. 87–113.

Aris, Michael: '"The Boneless Tongue": Alternative Voices from Bhutan in the Context of Lamaist Societies', in: *Past and Present*, 115 (May 1987); pp. 131–164.

Ariyasajsiskul, Supaporn: 'The So-called Tin Monopoly in Ligor: The Limits of VOC Power vis à vis a Southern Thai Trading Polity', in: *Itinerario*, 28, 3 (2004); pp. 88–106.

Ark, Bart van: 'The Manufacturing Sector in East Germany. A Reassessment of Comparative Productivity Performance 1950–1988', in: *Jahrbuch für Wirtschaftsgeschichte*, 36, 2 (1995); pp. 75–89.

Armstrong, Philip; Glyn, Andrew: 'The Law of the Falling Rate of Profit and Oligopoly: A Comment on Shaikh', in: *Cambridge Journal of Economics*, 4, 1 (March 1980); pp. 67–70.

Arrighi, Giovanni: 'The Political Economy of Rhodesia', in: *New Left Review*, 39 (September–October 1966); pp. 35–65.

———: 'Hegemony Unravelling (2)', in: *New Left Review*, 33 (May/June 2005); pp. 83–117.

Arrow, Kenneth J.: 'The Economic Implications of Learning by Doing', in: *Review of Economic Studies*, 29, 80 (June 1962); pp. 155–173.

Arslâne, Chakîb: 'Causes de la régression des musulmans' (Algiers: Haut Conseil Islamique, 2008).

Artus, Patrick; Mistral, Jacques: 'La Chine s'éveille à la consommation', in: *Le Monde*, (27th April 2010); p. 18.

Asam, P.-M.: 'Corporate Requirements for Public Technology Policy. The Siemens Experience', in: *Außenwirtschaft*, 43, 1/2 (June 1988); pp. 191–199.

Ash, Ronald G.: 'Kriegsfinanzierung, Staatsbildung und ständische Ordnung in Westeuropa im 17. und 18. Jahrhundert', in: *Historische Zeitschrift*, 268, 3 (June 1999); pp. 635–672.

Ashtor, E.: 'The Diet of the Salaried Classes in the Medieval Near East', in: *Journal of Asian History*, 4, 1 (1970); pp. 1–24.

Asikoglu, Yaman; Uctum, Merik: 'A Critical Evaluation of Exchange Rate Policy in Turkey', in: *World Development*, 20, 10 (October 1992); pp. 1501–1514.

Aslanian, Sebouh: 'Social Capital, "Trust" and the Role of Networks in Julfan Trade: Informal and Semi-Formal Institutions at Work', in: *Journal of Global History*, 1, 3 (2006); pp. 383–402.

Atasoy, Yildiz: 'The Islamic Ethic and the Spirit of Turkish Capitalism Today', in: *Socialist Register*, 44 (2008); pp. 121–140.

Athukorala, Premachandia; Menon, Jayant: 'Pricing to Market Behaviour and Exchange Rate Pass-Through in Japanese Exports', in: *Economic Journal*, 104, 423 (May 1994); pp. 271–281.

Atlani-Duault, Laëtitia; Poujol, Catherine: 'L'aide internationale en question. Enjeux d'une résistance coloniale, soviétique et postsoviétique en Asie centrale', in: *Tiers Monde*, 49, 193 (January–March 2008); pp. 37–53.

Atteh, Samuel O.: 'Political Economy of Environmental Degradation: The Dumping of Toxic Waste in Africa', in: *International Studies*, 30, 3 (July–September 1993); pp. 279–298.

Augé, Marc: 'Status, Power and Wealth: Relations of Lineage, Dependence and Production in Alladian Society', in: Seddon, David (ed.): *Relations of Production: Marxist Approaches to Economic Anthropology* (London: Frank Cass, 1978); pp. 389–412.

Aukrust, Odd: 'Factors of Economic Development: A Review of Recent Research', in: *Weltwirtschaftliches Archiv*, 93, 1 (1964); pp. 23–43.

Aurell, Cardona Jaume: 'Culture marchande et culture nobiliaire à Barcelone au XV siècle', in: *Revue historique*, 124, 613 (January–March 2000); pp. 33–53.

Autin, Jean-Louis: 'Quelques aspects socio-politiques de la révolution agraire', in: *Revue algérienne des sciences juridiques, économiques et politiques*, 10, 1 (March 1973); pp. 141–154.

Aydin, S.; Özel, O.: 'Power Relation between State and Tribe in Ottoman Eastern Anatolia', in: *Bulgarian Historical Review*, 34, 3/4 (2006); pp. 51–67.

Ayubi, Nazih N.M.: 'From State Socialism to Controlled Commercialism: The Emergence of Egypt's Open Door Policy', in: *Journal of Commonwealth and Comparative Politics*, 20, 3 (November 1982); pp. 265–288.

Bacha, Edmar L.; Taylor, Lance: 'Brazilian Income Distribution in the 1960s: "Facts", Model Results, and the Controversy', in: *Journal of Development Studies*, 14, 3 (April 1978); pp. 271–297.

Badie, Bertrand; Hermet, Guy: *La politique comparée* (Paris: Armand Colin, 2001).

Baehr, Peter: 'The "Iron Cage" and the "Shell as Hard as Steel": Parsons, Weber and the Stahlhartes Gehäuse Metaphor in the Protestant Ethic and the Spirit of Capitalism', in: *History and Theory*, 40, 2 (May 2002); pp. 153–169.

Baer, Gabriel: 'Monopolies and Restrictive Practices of Turkish Guilds', in: *Journal of the Economic and Social History of the Orient*, 13, 1 (1970); pp. 145–165.

Baer, Gabriel: *Fellah and Townsman in the Middle East. Studies in Social History* (London: Frank Cass, 1982).

Baer, Werner; Maneschi, Andrea: 'Import Substitution, Stagnation, and Structural Change: An Interpretation of the Brazilian Case', in: *Journal of Developing Areas*, 6, 2 (January 1971); pp. 177–192.

Baer, Werner; Miles, William R.; Moran, Alan B.: 'The End of the Asian Myth: Why Were the Experts Fooled', in: *World Development*, 27, 10 (October 1999); pp. 1735–1747.

Bagchi, Amiya Kumar: *Private Investment in India 1900–1938* (Cambridge: Cambridge University Press, 1972).

———: 'De-industrialization in India in the Nineteenth Century: Some Theoretical Implications', in: *Journal of Development Studies*, 12, 2 (January 1976); pp. 135–164.

Bahgat, Gawdat: 'The New Geopolitics of Oil: The United States, Saudi Arabia, and Russia', in: *Orbis*, 47, 3 (Summer 2003); pp. 447–461.

Bai, Moo-Ki: 'The Turning Point in the Korean Economy', in: *Developing Economies*, 20, 2 (June 1982); pp. 117–140.

Baierle, Sérgio: 'The Porto Alegre Thermidor: Brazil's "Participatory Budget" at the Crossroads', in: *Socialist Register*, 39 (2003); pp. 305–328.

Bailey, Mark: 'Historiographical Essay: The Commercialisation of the English Economy 1086–1500', in: *Journal of Medieval History*, 24, 3 (1998); pp. 297–311.

Baillin, Jeannine N.; Reisen, Helmut: 'Do Funded Pensions Contribute to Higher Aggregate Savings? A Cross-Country Analysis', in: *Weltwirtschaftliches Archiv*, 134, 4 (1998); pp. 692–711.

Baily, Martin Neil; Elliott, Douglas J.: *The US Financial and Economic Crisis: Where Does It Stand and Where Do We Go From Here?* (Washington, D.C.: Brookings Institution, June 2009).

Bairoch, Paul: 'L'agriculture et le processus d'industrialisation aux XVIIIe et XIXe siècles'siècles', in: *Economies et Sociétés*, 10 (May 1972a); pp. 1113–1132.

———: 'Free Trade and European Economic Development in the Nineteenth Century', in: *European Economic Review*, 3, 3 (November 1972b); pp. 211–245.

———: 'The Paradoxes of Economic History: Economic Laws and History', in: *European Economic Review*, 33, 2 (March 1989); pp. 225–249.

Bairy, Ramesh: 'The Bounds of Agency: Engaging the Space of Brahmin Associations of Karnataka', in: *Journal of Karnataka Studies*, 4, 1 (April 2007); pp. 107–240.

Baker, David: 'Colonial Beginnings and the Indian Response: The Revolt of 1857–1858 in Madhya Pradesh', in: *Modern Asian Studies*, 25, 3 (November 1991); pp. 511–543.

Balassa, Bela: 'Growth Strategies in Semi-Industrialized Countries', in: *Quarterly Journal of Economics*, 84, 1 (February 1970); pp. 24–47.
Balassa, Bela: 'Tariffs and Trade Policy in the Andean Common Market', in: *Journal of Common Market Studies*, 12, 1 (January 1974); pp. 176–195.
———: 'The Changing International Division of Labour in Manufactured Goods', in: *Banca Nazionale del Lavoro*, 130 (September 1979); pp. 243–287.
———: 'Trade in Manufactured Goods: Patterns of Change', in: *World Development*, 9, 3 (March 1981); pp. 263–275.
———: 'Evaluating Strategic Trade Policies', in: *Außenwirtschaft*, 43, 1/2 (January 1988); pp. 202–230.
Baldwin, Robert E.: 'Exchange Rate Policy and Economic Development', in: *Economic Development and Cultural Change*, 9, 4 (July 1961); pp. 598–603.
———: 'Determinants of the Commodity Structure of US Commerce', in: *American Economic Review*, 61, 1 (March 1971); pp. 126–146.
Balogh, Thomas; Balacs, P.: 'Fact and Fancy in International Economic Relations (2)', in: *World Development*, 1, 2 (1973); pp. 71–106.
Banerjee, Abhijit V; Duflo, Esther: 'The Economic Lives of the Poor', in: *Journal of Economic Perspectives*, 21, 1 (Winter 2007); pp. 141–167.
Banerjee, Sumanta: 'Strategies, Tactics, and Forms of Political Participation among Left Parties', in: Sathyamurty, T.V. (ed.): *Social Change and Political Discourse in india. Structures of Power, Movements of Resistance* (New Delhi: Oxford India Paperbacks, 1996); pp. 201–237.
———: 'Remembering M. N. Roy', in: *Economic and Political Weekly*, 39, 27 (3 July 2004); pp. 2957–2958.
Banerji, Arun: 'British Rule and the Indian Economy. Agenda for Fresh Researches', in: *Economic and Political Weekly*, 19, 31/33 (August 1984); pp. 1272–1284.
Bano, Masooda: 'Dangerous Correlations: Aid's Impact on NGOs' Performance and Ability to Mobilize Members in Pakistan', in: *World Development*, 36, 11 (November 2008); pp. 2297–2313.
Baños Ramirez, Othón: 'El protagonismo historico de los sindicatos rurales de Yucatán (1933–1936)', in: *Revista Mexicana de Sociología*, 56, 3 (July–September 1994); pp. 129–150.
Banskota, Mahesh: 'Anti-Poverty Policies in Rural Nepal', in: Islam, Rizwanul (ed.): *Strategies for Alleviating Poverty in Rural Asia* (Dhaka; Bangkok: Bangladesh Institute of Development Studies; International Labour Organization, 1985); pp. 153–174.
Baran, Paul A.: 'On the Political Economy of Backwardness', in: *Manchester School of Economic and Social Studies*, 20, 1 (January 1952); pp. 66–84.
Baranson, Jack: *Automative Industries in Developing Countries* (Baltimore, Md.: Johns Hopkins University Press, 1970).
Barbalet, J.M.: 'The "Labour Aristocracy" in Context', in: *Science and Society*, 51, 2 (Summer 1987); pp. 133–153.
Barbet, Philippe; Benzoni, Laurent: 'Mercantilisme technologique et politique commerciale stratégique: Réflexions sur la localisation de l'industrie

mondiale des semi-conducteurs', in: *Revue économique*, 44, 4 (July 1993); pp. 755–777.

Barchiesi, Franco: 'The Social Construction of Labour in the Struggle for Democracy: The Case of Post-Independence Nigeria', in: *Review of African Political Economy*, 24, 69 (1996); S. 349–369.

Bardhan, Pranab K.: 'On the Minimum Level of Living and the Rural Poor', in: *Indian Economic Review*, 5, 1 (April 1970); pp. 128–136.

———: 'Poverty and Inequality in China and India. Elusive Link with Globalisation', in: *Economic and Political Weekly*, 42, 38 (22 September 2007); pp. 3849–3852.

Bardt, Hubertus; Grömling, Michael: *Sparen in Deutschland und den USA. IW-Trends 3/2003* (Cologne: Institut der deutschen Wirtschaft, October 2003). Available online at http://www.iwkoeln.de/Portals/0/pdf/trends03_03_4.pdf (downloaded on 16.06.2011).

Barendse, René J.: 'The Long Road to Livorno. The Overland Messenger Services of the Dutch East India Company in the Seventeenth Century', in: *Itinerario*, 12, 2 (1988); pp. 15–43.

———: 'Trade and State in the Arabian Seas: A Survey from the Fifteenth to the Eighteenth Century', in: *Journal of World History*, 11, 2 (Autumn 2000); pp. 173–225.

———: 'History, Law and Orientalism under Portugese Colonialism in Eighteenth-Century India', in: *Itinerario*, 26, 1 (2002); pp. 33–59.

Bari, Dominique: 'Chine, Maître Kong et les superstitions: le bras de fer', in: *La Pensée*, 303 (October–December 1995); pp. 125–136.

Barkan, Joel D.; Holmquist, Frank: 'Peasant State and the Social Base of Self-Help in Kenya', in: *World Politics*, 41, 3 (April 1989); pp. 359–380.

Barkhausen, Max: 'Staatliche Wirtschaftslenkung und freies Unternehmertum im westdeutschen und im nord- und südniederländischen Raum bei der Entstehung der neuzeitlichen Industrie im 18. Jahrhundert', in: *Vierteljahrschrift für Sozial- und Wirtschaftsgeschichte*, 45, 2 (1958); pp. 168–241.

Barone, Enrico: *Grundzüge der theoretischen Nationalökonomie* (Berlin; Bonn: Ferdinand Dümmler, 1935).

Barr, Abigail; Fafchamps, Marcel; Owens, Trudy: 'The Governance of Non-Governmental Organizations in Uganda', in: *World Development*, 33, 5 (May 2005); pp. 657–679.

Barroux, Rémi: 'La tension sociale monte dans les pays émergents', in: *Le Monde*, (20th August 2010); p. 4.

Barrows, Leland Conley: 'The Merchants and General Faidherbe. Aspects of French Expansion in Senegal in the 1850s', in: *Revue française d'histoire d'outre-mer* (April–June 1974); pp. 236–283.

Barton, Allen H.: 'Fault Lines in American Elite Consensus', in: *Daedalus*, 109, 3 (Summer 1980); pp. 1–24.

Barya, John-Jean B.: 'The New Political Conditionalities of Aid: An Independent View from Africa', in: *IDS Bulletin*, 24, 1 (January 1993); pp. 17–23.

Bateman, Fred; Taylor, Jason E.: 'The New Deal at War: Alphabet Agencies' Expenditure Patterns, 1940–1945.', in: *Explorations in Economic History*, 40, 3 (July 2003); pp. 251–277.

Bauer, Brian S.: 'Legitimization of the State in Inca Myth and Ritual', in: *American Anthropologist*, 98, 2 (June 1996); pp. 327–337.

Baufeldt, Sabine: 'Umfang, Struktur und Trend der Ost-West-Kooperation 1970–1976', in: *Osteuropa-Wirtschaft*, 23, 4 (December 1978); pp. 274–294.

Bavel, Bas J.P. van: 'Land, Lease, and Agriculture: The Transition of the Rural Economy in the Dutch River Area from the Fourteenth to the Sixteenth Century', in: *Past and Present*, 172 (August 2001); pp. 3–43.

Bayart, Jean-François: 'One-Party Government and Political Development in Cameroun', in: *African Affairs*, 72, 287 (April 1973); pp. 125–144.

Bayat, Asef: 'Revolution without Movement, Movement without Revolution: Comparing Islamic Activism in Iran and Egypt', in: *Comparative Studies in Society and History*, 40, 1 (January 1998); pp. 136–169.

———: 'Activism and Social Development in the Middle East', in: *International Journal of Middle East Studies*, 34, 1 (February 2002); pp. 1–28.

Baylies, Carolyn: 'Political Conditionality and Democratization', in: *Review of African Political Economy*, 23, 65 (1995); pp. 321–337.

Bayly, Christopher Alan: *Indian Society and the Making of the British Empire. The New Cambridge History of India* (Cambridge et al.: Cambridge University Press, 1988).

Bayly, Susan: 'Hindu Kingship and the Origin of Community: Religion, State and Society in Kerala, 1750–1850', in: *Modern Asian Studies*, 18, 2 (May 1984); pp. 177–213.

Bayraktar, Bahar: 'Investigation on Sources of Growth for Turkey: 1968–1998', in: *Canadian Journal of Development Studies*, 27, 1 (2006); pp. 25–38.

Beattie, J.H.M.: 'Bunyoro: An African Feudality', in: *Journal of African History*, 5, 1 (1964); pp. 25–35.

Beaujard, Philippe: 'The Indian Ocean in Eurasian and African World-Systems before the Sixteenth Century', in: *Journal of World History*, 16, 4 (December 2005); pp. 411–465.

Beblawi, Hazem; Luciani, Giacomo: *The Rentier State* (London: Croom Helm, 1987).

Becker, Walter; Gehrisch, Wolfgang: 'Grundzüge der ökonomischen Entwicklung in den vorkapitalistischen Produktionsweisen', in: *Wirtschaftswissenschaft*, 25, 9 (September 1977); pp. 1369–1384.

Bédarida, François: 'The French Working Class Movement and Colonial Expansion', in: *Labour History Review/Bulletin of the Society for the Study of Labour History*, 19 (Autumn 1969); pp. 4–5.

Beech, George T.: 'The Lord / Dependant (Vassal) Relationship: a Case Study from Aquitaine', in: *Journal of Medieval History*, 24, 1 (1998); pp. 1–30.

Beeson, Mark: 'Comment: Trading Places? China, the United States and the Evolution of the International Political Economy', in: *Review of International Political Economy*, 16, 4 (October 2009); pp. 729–741.

Begg, Iain; Fagerberg, Jan; Guerrieri, Paolo: 'Conclusions and Policy Implications.', in: Fagerberg, Jan; Guerrieri, Paolo; Verspagen, Bart (eds.): *The Economic Challenge for Europe: Adapting to Innovation-Based Growth* (Cheltenham, Northampton: Edward Elgar, 1999); pp. 229–237.

Behagg, Clive: 'Mass Production Without the Factory: Craft Producers, Guns and Small Firm Innovation', in: *Business History*, 40, 3 (July 1998); pp. 1–15.

Behr, Andreas: 'Überproportionale Geldvermögensbildung und relativ sinkende Sachkapitalrendite', in: *Jahrbücher für Nationalökonomie und Statistik*, 220, 6 (2000); pp. 642–652.

Bekar, Cliff; Lipsey, Richard G.: 'Science, Institutions and the Industrial Revolution', in: *Journal of European Economic History*, 33, 3 (Winter 2004); pp. 709–756.

Belderbos, René; Capannelli, Giovanni; Fukao, Kyoji: 'Backward Vertical Linkages of Foreign Manufacturing Affiliates: Evidence from Japanese Multinationals', in: *World Development*, 29, 1 (January 2001); pp. 189–209.

Belke, Ansgar; Wiedmann, Marcel: 'Boom or Bubble in the US Real Estate Market?', in: *Intereconomics*, 40, 5 (September 2005); pp. 273–284.

Bello, David A.: 'To Go Where No Han Could Go for Long: Malaria and the Qing Construction of Ethnic Administrative Space in Frontier Yunnan', in: *Modern China*, 31, 3 (July 2005); pp. 283–317.

Bello, Walden; Rosenfeld, Stephanie: 'Dragons in Distress: The Crisis of the NICs', in: *World Policy Journal*, 7, 3 (Summer 1990); pp. 431–468.

Benadusi, Giovanna: 'Rethinking the State: Family Strategies in Early Modern Tuscany', in: *Social History*, 20, 2 (May 1995); pp. 157–178.

Benakezouh, Chabane: 'Centralisme et localisme en Afrique', in: *Revue algérienne des sciences juridiques, économiques et politiques*, 22, 4 (December 1985); pp. 665–687.

Benderra, Omar: 'Netzwerke an der Macht: Implosion des Staates, Raubwirtschaft', in: *Inamo-Informationsprojekt Naher und Mittlerer Osten*, 9, 35 (Autumn 2003); pp. 23–27.

Benelli, Giorgio: 'Die Wirtschaftstätigkeit des Staates und der staatliche Sektor der Wirtschaft in kapitalistisch orientierten Entwicklungsländern', in: *Jahrbuch für Wirtschaftsgeschichte*, 4 (1979); pp. 55–68.

Benería, Lourdes: 'Conceptualization of the Labour Force: The Underestimation of Women's Economic Activity', in: *Journal of Development Studies*, 17, 3 (April 1981); pp. 10–29.

Ben Hammouda, Hakim: 'Les théories du développement du post-ajustement', in: *Economie Appliquée*, 51, 2 (1998); pp. 95–121.

Bennholdt-Thomsen, Veronika: 'Marginalität in Lateinamerika, eine Theoriekritik', in: *Lateinamerika-Analysen und Berichte*, 3 (1979); pp. 45–85.

Bentley, Jerry: 'Cross-Cultural Interaction and Periodization in World History', in: *American Historical Review*, 101 (1996); pp. 749–770.

Bentley, Jerry H.: 'Hemispheric Integration, 500–1500 B.C.', in: *Journal of World History*, 9, 2 (1998); pp. 237–254.
Benz, Marion: 'Zur Bedeutung von Festen während der Neolithisierung im Vorderen Orient', in: *Ethnographisch-Archäologische Zeitschrift*, 47, 4 (2006); pp. 438–462.
Benz, Marion; Gramsch, Alexander: 'Zur soziologischen Bedeutung von Texten. Einführung anhand von Beispielen aus dem Alten Orient und Europa', in: *Ethnographisch-Archäologische Zeitschrift*, 47, 4 (2006); pp. 417–437.
Benz, Marion; Wächtler, Nina: 'Von der Integration zur Distinktion. Die feiernde Elite der Frühdynastischen Zeit', in: *Ethnographisch-Archäologische Zeitschrift*, 47, 4 (2006); pp. 463–483.
Berg, Maxine: 'Small Producer Capitalism in Eighteenth-Century England', in: *Business History*, 35, 1 (January 1993); pp. 17–38.
———: 'From Imitation to Invention: Creating Commodities in the Eighteenth Century Britain', in: *Economic History Review*, 55, 1 (2002); pp. 1–30.
———: 'In Pursuit of Luxury: Global History and British Consumer Goods in the Eighteenth Century', in: *Past and Present*, 182 (February 2004); pp. 83–142.
———: 'Britain, Industry and Perceptions of China: Matthew Boulton, "Useful Knowledge" and the Macartney Embassy to China 1792–94', in: *Journal of Global History*, 1, 2 (2006); pp. 269–288.
Bergelijk, Peter A. G.; Rabels, Dick L.: 'Strategic Trade Theories and Trade Policy', in: *Journal of World Trade*, 27, 6 (December 1993); pp. 175–196.
Bergère, Marie-Claire: 'On the Historical Origins of Chinese Underdevelopment', in: *Theory and Society*, 13, 3 (May 1984); pp. 327–337.
Berghe, Pierre L. van den: 'Class Race and Ethnicity', in: *Ethnic and Racial Studies*, 6, 2 (April 1983); pp. 221–236.
Berghoff, Hartmut; Möller, Roland: 'Unternehmer in Deutschland und England 1870–1914. Aspekte eines kollektiv-biographischen Vergleiches', in: *Historische Zeitschrift*, 256, 2 (October 1993); pp. 383–386.
Bergman, Teresa: *The Transcendence of Difference or Middle Class Pipedreams? A Critical Analysis of the World Social Forum* (Leipzig: Ms., April 2011).
Bergson, Abram: 'Development under Two Systems: Comparative Productivity Growth Since 1950', in: *World Politics*, 23, 4 (July 1971); pp. 579–617.
——— et al.: 'Soviet Economic Performance and Reform: Some Problems of Analysis and Diagnosis', in: *Slavic Review*, 25, 3 (June 1966); pp. 222–246.
Berman, Eli; Bound, John; Gritiches, Zvi: 'Changes in the Demand for Skilled Labour within U.S. Manufacturing: Evidence from the Survey of Manufacturers', in: *Quarterly Journal of Economics*, 109, 2 (May 1994); pp. 367–397.
Bernal, Martin: 'The Nghe-tinh Soviet Movement, 1930–1931', in: *Past and Present*, 92 (August 1981); pp. 148–168.
Berry, Albert R.; Sabot, R.H.: 'Labor Market Performance in Developing Countries: A Survey', in: *World Development*, 6, 9/10 (September–October 1978); pp. 1199–1242.

Berthelot, Yves: 'World Economy: The Rise of Tensions', in: *EADI Bulletin*, 2 (1983); pp. 13–26.

Berthold, Brigitte: 'Innerstädtische Auseinandersetzungen in Straßburg während des 14. Jahrhunderts', in: *Jahrbuch für Geschichte des Feudalismus*, 1 (1977); pp. 157–186.

———: 'Charakter und Entwickung des Patriziats in den mittelalterlichen deutschen Städten', in: *Jahrbuch für Geschichte des Feudalismus*, 6 (1982); pp. 195–241.

Bertrand, Romain: 'La politique éthique des Pays-Bas à Java (1901–1926)', in: *Vingtième siècle. Revue d'histoire*, 93 (January–March 2007); pp. 115–138.

Berument, Hakan; Pasaogullari, Mehmet: 'Effects of the Real Exchange Rate on Output and Inflation: Evidence from Turkey', in: *Developing Economies*, 41, 4 (December 2003); pp. 401–435.

Bethell, Leslie: 'The Independence of Brazil and the Abolition of the Brazilian Slave Trade: Anglo-Brazilian Relations 1822–1826', in: *Journal of Latin American Studies*, 1, 2 (1969); pp. 115–147.

Betts, Caroline; Devcreux, Michael B.: 'Exchange Rate Dynamics in a Model of Pricing-to-Market', in: *Journal of International Economics*, 30, 1 (2000); pp. 215–244.

Bevers, Antonius M.: 'Die organisierte Kultur. Konvergenz zwischen Kultur, Politik und Wirtschaft', in: *Forschungsberichte IWVWW*, 4, 20 (March 1994); pp. 39–49.

Bhagavan, M.R.: 'Capital Goods Sector in India. Past and Present Trends and Future Prospects', in: *Economic and Political Weekly*, 20, 10 (9 March 1985); pp. 404–421.

Bhagavan, Manu: 'The Hindutva Underground: Hindu Nationalism and the Indian National Congress in Late Colonial and Early Post-colonial India', in: *Economic and Political Weekly*, 43, 37 (13 September 2008); pp. 39–48.

Bhagwati, Jagdish N.: 'Is Free Trade Passé After All?', in: *Weltwirtschaftliches Archiv*, 125, 1 (1989); pp. 17–44.

Bhatia, B.M.: 'Growth and Composition of Middle Class in South India in Nineteenth Century', in: *Indian Economic and Social History Review*, 2, 4 (October 1965); pp. 341–356.

Bhatt, Chetan: *Hindu Nationalism. Origins, Ideologies and Modern Myths* (New York et al.: Berg, 2001).

Bhatt, V. V.: 'Theories of Balanced and Unbalanced Growth: A Critical Reappraisal', in: *Kyklos*, 17, 4 (1964); pp. 612–627.

Bhattacharya, Sabyasachi: 'Notes on the Role of the Intelligentsia in Colonial Society', in: *Studies in History*, 1, 1 (1979); pp. 89–104.

Bhattacharya, Sanjukta Banerji: 'Engaging Africa: India's Interests in the African Continent, Past and Present', in: Cheru, Fantu; Obi, Cyril (eds.): *The Rise* of China in India and Africa (London/ New York: ZED Books, 2010); pp. 63–76.

Bhattacharyya, Jnanabrata: 'An Examination of Leadership Entry in Bengal Peasant Revolts 1937–1947', in: *Journal of Asian Studies*, 37, 4 (August 1978); pp. 611–635.

Biau, Daniel: 'Chinese Cities, Indian Cities. A Telling Contrast', in: *Economic and Political Weekly*, 42, 33 (18th August 2007); pp. 3369–3372.

Bicanic, Rudolf: 'The Threshold of Economic Growth', in: *Kyklos*, 15, 1 (1962); pp. 7–28.

Bichler, Shimshon; Nitzan, Jonathan: 'Dominant Capital and the New Wars', in: *Journal of World-Systems Research*, 10, 2 (Summer 2004); pp. 255–327.

Bidard, Christian: 'The Falling Rate of Profit and Joint Production', in: *Cambridge Journal of Economics*, 12, 3 (September 1988); pp. 355–360.

Biddick, Kathleen: 'Medieval English Peasants and Market Involvement', in: *Journal of Economic History*, 45, 4 (December 1985); pp. 823–831.

Bieber, Roland; Dehousse, Renaud; Pinder, John; Weiler, Joseph H.H.: *1992: One European Market. A Critical Analysis of the Commission's Internal Market Strategy* (Baden-Baden: Nomos, 1988).

Bienefeld, Manfred: 'Analysing the Politics of African State Policy: Some Thoughts on Robert Bates' Work', in: *IDS Bulletin*, 8, 1 (July 1976); pp. 5–11.

———: 'The Significance of the Newly Industrialising Countries for the Development Debate', in: *Studies in Political Economy*, 25 (Spring 1988); pp. 7–40.

Bill, James A.: 'The Social and Economic Foundations of Power in Contemporary Iran', in: *Middle East Journal*, 17, 4 (Autumn 1963); pp. 400–413.

Biller, Jürgen: *Zur Entstehung von Herrschaft und Staat. Das Beispiel des indischen Regionalreiches von Orissa* (Freiburg: Hochschulverlag [Hochschulsammlung Philosophische Sozialwissenschaft, Band 18], 1986).

Bina, Cyrus; Yaghmaian, Behzad: 'Post-War Global Accumulation and the Transnationalization of Capital', in: *Review of Radical Political Economics*, 22, 1 (Spring 1990); pp. 78–97.

Bindseil, Ulrich; Pfeil, Christian: 'Specialization as a Specific Investment into the Market: A Transaction Cost Approach to the Rise of Markets and Towns in Medieval Germany, 800–1200', in: *Journal of Institutional and Theoretical Economics*, 155, 4 (1999); pp. 738–755.

Biraben, J.M.; LeGoff, J.: 'La peste dans le haut Moyen Age', in: *Annales. Economie, Société, Civilisation*, 24, 6 (November–December 1969); pp. 1484–1510.

Biscione, Francesco M.: 'La démocratie italienne et ses adversaires', in: *NAQD: Revue d'Études et de Critique Sociale*, 25 (Autumn–Winter 2008); pp. 167–183.

Blackburn, Robin: 'The New Collectivism: Pension Reform, Grey Capitalism and Complex Socialism', in: *New Left Review*, 233 (January/February 1999); pp. 3–65.

Blakemore, Harold: 'The Politics of Nitrate in Chile: Pressure Groups and Policies, 1870–1896: Some Unanswered Questions', in: *Revue française d'histoire d'outre-mer*, 66, 245–246 (July–December 1979); pp. 286–297.

Blanquie, Christophe: 'Fiscalité et venalité des offices présidiaux', in: *Histoire, économie et société*, 23, 4 (October–December 2004); pp. 472–487.

Blasier, Cole: 'The United States, Germany and the Bolivian Revolutionaries', in: *Hispanic American Historical Review*, 52, 1 (February 1972); pp. 26–54.

Blaug, Mark: 'The Empirical Status of Human Capital Theory: A Slightly Jaundiced Survey', in: *Journal of Economic Literature*, 14, 3 (September 1976); pp. 827–855.

Blaut, J.M.: 'Colonialism and the Rise of Capitalism', in: *Science and Society*, 53, 3 (Autumn 1989); pp. 260–296.

Blitzer, C.R.; Cavoulaws, P.E.; Lessard, D.R.; Paddock, J.L.: 'Oil Exploration in the Developing Countries: Poor Geology or Poor Contracts', in: *Natural Resources Forum*, 9, 4 (November 1985); pp. 295–302.

Bloch, Marc: *Feudal Society* (Chicago, Ill.: University of Chicago Press, 1961).

Block, Fred: 'Postindustrial Development and the Obsolence of Economic Categories', in: *Politics and Society*, 14, 1 (1985); pp. 71–104.

———; Somers, Margaret: 'In the Shadow of Speenhamland: Social Policy and the Old Poor Law', in: *Politics and Society*, 31, 2 (June 2003); pp. 283–323.

Block, James E.: 'The Shibboleth of Productivity: The Exhaustion of Industrial Age Strategies in Post-Industrial Societies', in: *Review of Radical Political Economics*, 17, 1/2 (Spring–Summer 1985); pp. 157–185.

Blok, Anton: 'Reflections on City-Hinterland Relations in Mediterranean Europe', in: *Soziologische Geschiedenis*, 19, 2 (1972); pp. 15–125.

Bloom, David E.; Freeman, Richard B.: 'The Fall in Private Pension Coverage in the United States', in: *American Economic Review*, 82, 2 (May 1992); pp. 539–545.

Bloom, Khaled J.: 'An American Tragedy of the Commons: Land and Labor in the Cherokee Nation, 1870–1900.', in: *Agricultural History*, 76, 3 (Summer 2002); pp. 497–523.

Blum, Jerôme: 'The Rise of Serfdom in Eastern Europe', in: *American Historical Review*, 62, 4 (July 1957); pp. 807–836.

Blumenthal, Tuvia: 'Scarcity of Labour and Wage Differentials in the Japanese Economy, 1958–1964', in: *Economic Development and Cultural Change*, 17, 1 (October 1968); pp. 15–32.

Blundo, Giorgio: 'Dealing with Local State: The Informal Privatization of Street-Level Bureaucracies in Senegal', in: *Development and Change*, 37, 4 (July 2006); pp. 799–816.

Blussé, Leonard: 'The Run to the Coast: Comparative Notes on Early Dutch and English Expansion and State Formation in Asia', in: *Itinerario*, 12, 1 (1988); pp. 195–214.

Blyn, George: 'Green Revolution Revisited', in: *Economic Development and Cultural Change*, 31, 4 (July 1983); pp. 705–725.

Boahen, Adu: 'A New Look of the History of Ghana', in: *African Affairs*, 65, 260 (July 1966); pp. 212–222.

Bodian, Miriam: '"Men of the Nation": The Shaping of Converse Identity in Early Modern Europe', in: *Past and Present*, 143 (May 1994); pp. 48–76.

Boeckh, Andreas: 'Staatliche Gewerkschaftspolitik und abhängige Entwicklung', in: *Verfassung und Recht in Übersee*, 11, 3 (1978); pp. 261–281.

Boeckx, Cécile: 'Reforme agraire et structures sociales en Egypte nassérienne', in: *Civilisations*, 21, 4 (1971); pp. 373–390.

Boehm, Christopher: 'Egalitarian Behavior and Reverse Dominance Hierarchy', in: *Current Anthropology*, 34, 3 (June 1993); pp. 327–351.

Bogart, Dan; Richardson, Gary: 'Making Property Productive. Reorganizing Rights to Real and Equitable Estates in Britain, 1660 to 1830', in: *European Review of Economic History*, 13, 1 (April 2009); pp. 3–30.

Bogason, Peter: 'Postmodernism and American Public Administration in the 1990s.', in: *Administration and Society*, 33, 2 (May 2001); pp. 165–193.

Boggs, Carl: 'The Great Retreat: Decline of the Public Sphere in the Late Twentieth-Century America', in: *Theory and Society*, 26, 6 (December 1997); pp. 741–780.

Boldt, Frank: *Die Rückkehr Ost-Mittel-Europas in seinen historischen Kontext. Johann-Amos-Comenius-Club Band 33* (Bonn, 2004).

Boles, Elson: 'Critiques of World-Systems Analysis and Alternatives: Unequal Exchange and Three Forms of Class and Struggle in the Japan–US Silk Network, 1880–1890', in: *Journal of World-Systems Research*, 8, 2 (Spring 2002); pp. 150–212.

Bolino, August C.: 'British and American Horology: A Comment on Hoke', in: *Journal of Economic History*, 48, 3 (September 1988); pp. 665–667.

Bonhoeffer, Friedrich: 'Investitionen in der Industrie bleiben zurück', in: *Wirtschaftskonjunktur*, 19, 4 (1967); pp. 19–28.

Bonner, Michael: 'Poverty and Economics in the Qur'an', in: *Journal of Interdisciplinary History*, 35, 3 (Winter 2005); pp. 391–406.

Bonoli, Giuliano: 'Two Worlds of Pension Reform in Western Europe', in: *Comparative Politics*, 35, 4 (July 2003); pp. 399–416.

Bootsma, N.A.: 'The Recuperation of Sovereign Rights by Asian Countries, circa 1870–1945. From Capitulations to Equal Relations, the Dutch Experience', in: *Itinerario*, 29, 2 (2005); pp. 53–72.

Borkenau, Franz: *Der Übergang vom feudalen zum bürgerlichen Weltbild: Studien zur Geschichte der Philosophie der Manufakturperiode* (Paris: Félix Alcan, 1934).

Boron, Atilio A.: 'State Decay and Democratic Decadence in Latin America', in: *Socialist Register*, 35 (1999); pp. 208–226.

Bortkiewicz, Ladislaus von: 'Wertrechnung und Preisrechnung im Marxschen System (3)', in: *Archiv für Sozialwissenschaft und Sozialpolitik*, 25, 2 (1907); pp. 445–489.

Bose, Sutapa: 'The Problem of Primitive Accumulation', in: *Economic and Political Weekly*, 23, 23 (4 June 1988); pp. 1169–1174.

Boshof, Egon: *Die Salier* (Stuttgart: Kohlhammer, 1987).
Bosl, Karl: 'Eine Geschichte der deutschen Landgemeinde', in: *Zeitschrift für Agrargeschichte und Agrarsoziologie*, 9, 2 (October 1961); pp. 129–142.
Bosma, Ulbe: 'Citizens of Empire: Some Comparative Observations on the Evolution of Creole Nationalism in Colonial Indonesia', in: *Comparative Studies in Society and History*, 46, 4 (October 2004); pp. 656–681.
Botticelli, Peter: 'The British Engineering Press During the Second Industrial Revolution: Responses to Corporate Capitalism', in: *Business History Review*, 71, 2 (Summer 1997); pp. 260–286.
Boughton, James M.: 'Harry Dexter White and the International Monetary Fund', in: *Finance and Development*, 35, 3 (September 1998); pp. 39–41.
Bouissou, Julien: 'Les ouvriers du textile se révoltent au Bangladesh', in: *Le Monde*, (11 August 2010); p. 10.
Boulard, Gilles: 'L'ordonnance de Villers-Cotterêts: le temps de la clarté et la stratégie du temps (1539–1992)', in: *Revue historique*, 123, 609 (1999); pp. 45–100.
Bourdieu, Pierre: *Sozialer Raum und Klassen. Leçon sur leçon* (Frankfort on the Main: Suhrkamp, 1991).
Bourg, Jean-François: 'Les très hauts revenus des Superstars du sport. Un état des approches théoriques et empiriques', in: *Revue d'économie politique*, 118, 3 (May–June 2008); pp. 375–394.
Bourlès, Jean; Lorenzi, Jean-Hervé: 'L'innovation, moteur de la croissance: application à la période actuelle', in: *Economies et Sociétés*, D 3 (May–June 1998); pp. 201–256.
Bowden, Brett: 'The River of Inter-civilisational Relations: The Ebb and Flow of Peoples, Ideas and Innovations', in: *Third World Quarterly*, 28, 7 (2007); pp. 1359–1374.
Bowen, Merle L.: 'Beyond Reform: Adjustment and Political Power in Contemporary Mozambique', in: *Journal of Modern African Studies*, 30, 2 (1992); pp. 255–279.
Bowles, Paul; Wang, Boatai: '"Flowers and criticism": The Political Economy and the Renminbi Debate', in: *Review of International Political Economy*, 13, 2 (Spring 2006); pp. 233–257.
Bowles, Samuel: 'Technical Change and the Profit Rate: A Simple Proof of the Okishio Theorem', in: *Cambridge Journal of Economics*, 5, 2 (1981); pp. 183–186.
Boyd, Rosalind: 'Labour's Response to the Informalization of Work in the Current Restructuring of Global Capitalism: China, South Korea, and South Africa', in: *Canadian Journal of Development Studies*, 27, 4 (2006); pp. 487–502.
Boyer, Robert: 'Le bout du tunnel ? Stratégies conservatrices et nouveau régime d'accumulation', in: *Economies et Sociétés*, R 5 (December 1990); pp. 5–66.
Bradford, Helen: 'Mass Movements and the Petty Bourgeoisie: The Social Origins of ICU Leadership, 1924–29', in: *Journal of African History*, 25, 3 (1984); pp. 295–310.

Bradley, James E.; Baigent, Elizabeth: 'The Social Sources of Late Eighteenth-Century English Radicalism: Bristol in the 1770s and 1780s', in: *English Historical Review*, 124, 510 (October 2009); pp. 1075–1108.

Bradley, Mark Philip: 'Becoming Van Minh: Civilizational Discourse and Visions of the Self in Twentieth-Century Vietnam.', in: *Journal of World History*, 15, 1 (March 2004); pp. 65–83.

Brady, Dorothy: 'Relative Prices in the Nineteenth Century', in: *Journal of Economic History*, 24, 2 (June 1964); pp. 145–203.

Brailey, Nigel: 'The Scramble for Concessions in 1880s Siam.', in: *Modern Asian Studies*, 33, 3 (July 1999); pp. 513–549.

Bramall, Chris: 'Rural Industrialisation and Spatial Inequality in China, 1978–2006', in: *Economic and Political Weekly*, 43, 52 (27 December 2008); pp. 43–50.

Brandewie, Ernest: 'The Place of the Big Man in Traditional Hagen Society in the Central Highlands of New Guinea', in: *Ethnology*, 10, 2 (April 1971); pp. 194–210.

Brara, Rita: 'Kinship and the Political Order: The Afghani Sherwani Chiefs of Malerkotha (1454–1947)', in: *Contributions to Indian Sociology*, 28, 2 (July 1994); pp. 203–242.

Brasseul, Jacques: 'Les grandes interprétations de la révolution industrielle', in: *Economies et Sociétés*, AF 31 (June 2004); pp. 929–994.

Bratton, Michael: 'The Politics of Government-NGO Relations in Africa', in: *World Development*, 17, 4 (April 1989); pp. 569–587.

Braudel, Fernand: *La Méditerranée et le monde méditerranéen à l'époque de Philippe II (1)* (Paris: Armand Colin, 1966).

———: *Civilisation matérielle et capitalisme* (Paris: Armand Colin, 1967).

Braun, Hans: 'Helmut Schelskys Konzept einer nivellierten Mittelstandsgesellschaft', in: *Archiv für Sozialgeschichte*, 29 (1989); pp. 199–224.

Braun, Oscar; Joy, Leonard: 'A Model of Economic Stagnation: A Case Study of the Argentine Economy', in: *Economic Journal*, 78, 312 (December 1968); pp. 868–887.

Brehme, Gerhard: *Sozialistische Orientierung national befreiter Staaten. Grundprobleme* (Berlin: Staatsverlag der DDR, 1985).

Brenner, Robert: 'The Civil War Politics of London's Merchant Community', in: *Past and Present*, 58 (February 1973); pp. 53–107.

———: 'The Origins of Capitalist Development: A Critique of Neo-Smithian Marxism', in: *New Left Review*, 104 (July–August 1977); pp. 25–92.

———: 'The Low Countries in the Transition to Capitalism', in: *Journal of Agrarian Change*, 1, 2 (April 2001); pp. 169–241.

Brentjes, Burchard: 'Zur Einheit der vorkapitalistischen Klassengesellschaft', in: *Ethnographisch-Archäologische Zeitschrift*, 14, 2 (1973); pp. 277–284.

Brett, Michael: 'Modernization in 19th Century North Africa', in: *Maghreb Review*, 7, 1/2 (January–April 1982); pp. 16–22.

Breuer, Stefan: *Imperien der Alten Welt* (Stuttgart: Kohlhammer GmbH, 1987).
Brewer, John: *The Sinews of Power War, Money and the English State, 1688–1783* (London et al.: Kuwin Hyman, 1989).
Breysig, Kurt: *Die Anfänge der Menschheit* (Berlin: Waltrer de Gruyter, 1955).
Bridbury, A.R.: 'The Black Death', in: *Economic History Review*, 26, 4 (1973); pp. 577–592.
———: 'Sixteenth Century Farming', in: *Economic History Review*, 27, 4 (1974); pp. 538–556.
Bridge, Carl: 'Conservatism and Indian Reform, 1929–1939: Towards a Prerequisites Model in Imperial Constitution Making', in: *Journal of Imperial and Commonwealth History*, 4, 2 (January 1976); pp. 176–193.
Bridier, Manuel: 'La révolution coloniale et le mouvement ouvrier français', in: *Revue internationale du socialisme*, 5, 25 (1968); pp. 82–120.
Brimble, Peter; Doner, Richard F.: 'University-Industry Linkages and Economic Development: The Case of Thailand', in: *World Development*, 35, 6 (June 2007); pp. 1021–1036.
Brito, L.; Williamson, Jeffrey Gale: 'Skilled Labor and Nineteenth Century Anglo-American Managerial Behavior', in: *Explorations in Economic History*, 10, 3 (Spring 1973); pp. 235–252.
Broad, John: 'Housing the Rural Poor in Southern England, 1650–1850', in: *Agricultural History Review*, 48, 2 (Summer 2000); pp. 151–170.
Broadberry, Stephen N.: 'Manufacturing and the Convergence Hypotheses: What the Long- Run Data Show', in: *Journal of Economic History*, 53, 4 (December 1993); pp. 772–795.
———: 'Anglo-German Productivity Differences, 1870–1990: A Sectoral Analysis', in: *European Review of Economic History*, 1, 2 (June 1997); pp. 247–267.
———; Fremdling, Rainer; Solar, Peter: 'European Industry, 1700–1870', in: *Jahrbuch für Wirtschaftsgeschichte*, 2 (2008); pp. 141–171.
———; Gupta, Bishnupriya: 'The Early Modern Great Divergence: Wages, Prices and Economic Development in Europe and Asia, 1500–1800', in: *Economic History Review*, 59, 1 (February 2006); pp. 2–31.
———: 'Lancashire, India, and Shifting Competitive Advantage in Cotton Textiles, 1700–1850: The Neglected Role of Factor Prices', in: *Economic History Review*, 62, 2 (May 2009); pp. 279–305.
Brocheux, Pierre: 'Crise économique et société en Indochine française', in: *Revue française d'histoire d'outre-mer*, 63, 232–233 (July–December 1976); pp. 655–667.
Broda, Christian: 'Exchange Rate Regimes and National Price Levels', in: *Journal of International Economics*, 70, 1 (September 2006); pp. 52–81.
Brodkin, Karen: 'Global Capitalism: What's Race Got to Do with It', in: *American Ethnologist*, 27, 2 (May 2000); pp. 237–256.
Broeze, Frank: 'Underdevelopment and Dependency: Maritime India During the Raj', in: *Modern Asian Studies*, 18, 3 (August 1984); pp. 429–457.

Bromley, Simon: 'Making Sense of Structural Adjustment', in: *Review of African Political Economy*, 23, 65 (1995); pp. 339–348.
Bronfenbrenner, Martin: 'Elements of Stagflation Theory', in: *Zeitschrift für Nationalökonomie*, 36, 1 (1976); pp. 1–8.
Brooks, George: 'Peanuts and Colonialism: Consequences of the Commercialisation of Peanuts in West-Africa, 1830–1870', in: *Journal of African History*, 16, 1 (1975); pp. 29–54.
Brötel, Dieter: *Französischer Imperialismus in Vietnam. Die koloniale Expansion und die Errichtung des Protektorats Annam Tongking 1880–1885* (Zurich; Freiburg: Atlantis Verlag, 1971)
Brown, E. Cary: 'Fiscal Policy in the Thirties: A Reappraisal', in: *American Economic Review*, 46, 5 (December 1956); pp. 857–879.
Brown, Ian: 'British Financial Advisors in Siam in the Reign of King Chulalongkorn', in: *Modern Asian Studies*, 12, 2 (May 1978); pp. 193–215.
———: 'Rural Distress in South Asia during the World Depression in the Early 1930s: A Preliminary, in: *Journal of Asian Studies*, 45 (November 1986); pp. 995–1025.
Brown, John Christopher: 'Imperfect Competition and Anglo-German Trade Rivalry: Markets for Cotton Textiles before 1914', in: *Journal of Economic History*, 55, 3 (September 1995); pp. 494–528.
Brown, Judith; Goodman, Jordan: 'Women and Industry in Florence', in: *Journal of Economic History*, 40, 1 (March 1980); pp. 73–80.
Brown, Nathan J.: 'Who Abolished Corvee Labour in Egypt and Why?', in: *Past and Present*, 144 (August 1994); pp. 116–137.
Brown, Rajeswary Ampalavanar: 'Indonesian Corporations, Cronyism, and Corruption', in: *Modern Asian Studies*, 40, 4 (Winter 2006); pp. 953–992.
Brown, Shannon R.: 'The Partially Opened Door: Limitations on Economic Exchange in China in the 1860s', in: *Modern Asian Studies*, 12, 2 (May 1978); pp. 177–192.
Brown, Stephen: 'Foreign Aid and Democracy Promotion: Lessons from Africa', in: *European Journal of Development Research*, 17, 2 (June 2005); pp. 179–198.
Brubaker, Earl R.: 'Embodied Technology, the Asymptotic Behavior of Capital's Age and Soviet Growth', in: *Review of Economics and Statistics*, 50, 3 (August 1968); pp. 304–311.
Bruno, Sebastiano: 'The Emilian Model: Productive Decentralisation and Social Integration', in: *Cambridge Journal of Economics*, 6, 2 (June 1982); pp. 167–184.
Brunschwig, Henri: 'Politique et économique dans l'Empire français d'Afrique Noire 1870–1914', in: *Journal of African History*, 11, 3 (1970); pp. 401–417.
Bryson, Phillip J.: 'Economy and "New Economy" in the United States and Germany', in: *Intereconomics*, 36, 4 (July/August 2001); pp. 180–190.
Bucharin, Nikolai: *Imperialismus und Weltwirtschaft* (Vienna; Berlin: Verlag für Literatur und Politik, 1929).
Buck, P.W.: *The Politics of Mercantilism* (New York: Octagon, 1964).

Bugra, Ayse: 'Labour, Capital, and Religion: Harmony and Conflict among the Constituency of Political Islam in Turkey', in: *Middle Eastern Studies*, 38, 2 (April 2002); pp. 187–204.

Bulow, Jeremy; Rogoff, Kenneth: 'Cleaning up Third World Debt without Getting Taken to the Cleaners', in: *Journal of Economic Perspectives*, 4, 1 (Winter 1990); pp. 31–42.

Burçak, Berrak: 'Modernization, Science and Engineering in the Early Nineteenth Century Ottoman Empire', in: *Middle Eastern Studies*, 44, 1 (January 2008); pp. 69–83.

Burck, Gilbert; Silberman, Charles: 'What Caused the Great Depression?', in: *Fortune*, 51 (February 1955); pp. 94–99, 204–206, 209–211.

Burke, Edmund: 'Pan–Islam and Moroccan Resistance to French Penetration 1900–1912', in: *Journal of African History*, 13, 4 (1972); pp. 97–118.

Buszello, Horst; Blicke, Peter; Endres, Rudolf: *Der deutsche Bauernkrieg* (Paderborn: Ferdinand Schöningh, 1984).

Büttner, Thea: 'Probleme des Feudalismus in Afrika in der vorkolonialen Periode', in: *Zeitschrift für Geschichtswissenschaft*, 12, 3 (March 1964); pp. 460–471.

———: 'Genesis, Charakter und Ergebnisse der nationalen Befreiungsrevolution des sub-saharischen Afrika bis zur Erringung der politischen Unabhängigkeit', in: *Asien-Afrika-Lateinamerika*, 2, 2 (1975); pp. 295–324.

———: 'Religiös-politische Bewegungen in Afrika', in: *Zeitschrift für Geschichtswissenschaft*, 33, 6 (June 1985); pp. 528–535.

Byres, Terry J.: 'The Dialectic of India's Green Revolution', in: *South Asian Review*, 5, 2 (January 1972); pp. 99–116.

Cadoret, Isabelle; Guéguen, Chantal: 'Le rôle des services dans la croissance française sur la période 1970–1997', in: *Economie appliquée*, 57, 1 (March 2004); pp. 83–105.

Cameron, Rondo E.: 'Economic Growth and Stagnation in France, 1815–1914', in: Supple, Barry Emmanuel (ed.): *The Experience of Economic Growth. Case Studies in Economic History* (New York: Random House, 1963); pp. 328–339.

Campbell, Bonnie K.: 'Eléments pour la révision des théories marxistes de l'impérialisme en fonction du rôle de l'Etat et de l'établissement de rapports néocoloniaux', in: *Etudes internationales*, 8, 3 (September 1977); pp. 429–444.

Campbell, Gwyn: 'The State and Pre-Colonial History: The Case of 19th Century Madagascas', in: *Journal of African History*, 32, 3 (1991); pp. 415–445.

Canessa, Andrew: 'Contesting Hybridity: Evangelistas and Kataristas in Highland Bolivia', in: *Journal of Latin American Studies*, 32, 1 (February 2000); pp. 115–144.

Cantwell, John: 'Technological Look-in of Large Firms since the Interwar Period', in: *European Review of Economic History*, 4, 2 (August 2000); pp. 147–174.

Canu, Jean: 'Le nouveau monde et l'or espagnol', in: Lacour-Gayet, Jacques (ed.): *Histoire du commerce (4): Le commerce du XVe siècle jusqu'au milieu de XIXe siècle* (Paris: SPID, 1951); pp. 9–148.

Caporaso, James A.: 'The European Union and Forms of State: Westphalian, Regulatory or Post-Modern', in: *Journal of Common Market Studies*, 34, 1 (May 1996); pp. 29–51.

Carmoy, Guy de: *Le dossier européen de l'énergie* (Paris, 1971).

Carothers, Thomas: 'The End of the Transition Paradigm', in: *Journal of Democracy*, 13, 1 (January 2002); pp. 5–21.

Carr, Barry: 'The Mexican Communist Party and Agrarian Mobilization in the Laguna, 1920–1940: A Worker-Peasant Alliance?', in: *Hispanic American Historical Review*, 67, 3 (August 1987); pp. 371–404.

———: 'Mill Occupation and Soviets: The Mobilisation of Sugar Workers in Cuba 1917–1933', in: *Journal of Latin American Studies*, 28, 1 (February 1996); pp. 129–158.

Carrère d'Encausse, Hélène: 'Khrouchtchev était-il vraiment nécessaire', in: *Revue française de science politique*, 15, 6 (December 1965); pp. 1050–1078.

———; Schram, Stuart: *Le marxisme et l'Asie 1853–1964* (Paris: Armand Colin, 1964).

Cartier, Michel: 'Commerce du sel et accumulation du capital en Chine', in: *Annales. Economie, Société, Civilisation*, 28, 4 (1973); p. 922.

Casar, José I.; Ros, Jaime: 'Trade and Capital Accumulation in a Process of Import Substitution', in: *Cambridge Journal of Economics*, 7, 3/4 (September–December 1983); pp. 257–267.

Case, William: 'Malaysia: New Reforms, Old Continuities, Tense Ambiguities', in: *Journal of Development Studies*, 41, 2 (February 2005); pp. 184–309.

Caspers, Elisabeth C.L.: 'Sumer, Coastal Arabia, and the Indus Valley in Protoliterate and Early Dynastic Eras', in: *Journal of the Economic and Social History of the Orient*, 21, 2 (1978); pp. 121–135.

Centre National d'Etudes et d'Analyses pour la Planification: *Programmes d'Activités du Ce.N.E.A.P.* (Algiers: République Algérienne Démocratique et Populaire, 1986).

Cervenka, Zdenek: 'Africa and the New International Economic Order', in: *Verfassung und Recht in Übersee*, 9, 2 (1976); pp. 187–199.

Chaganti, Sruti: 'Creation of a Third World in the First. Economics of Labour Migration', in: *Economic and Political Weekly*, 39, 22 (29 May 2004); pp. 2220–2226.

Chakrabarty, Dipesh: 'Class Consciousness and the Indian Working Class: Dilemmas of Marxist Historiography', in: *Journal of Asian and African Studies (Leiden)*, 23, 1/2 (January–April 1988); pp. 21–31.

———: 'Legacies of Bandung: Decolonisation and the Politics of Culture', in: *Economic and Political Weekly*, 40, 46 (12 November 2005); pp. 4812–4818.

Chakravarty, Sukhamoy: 'Aspects of India's Development Strategy for 1980s', in: *Economic and Political Weekly*, 19, 20/21 (19 May 1984); pp. 845–852.

———: 'The State of Development Economics', in: *Manchester School of Economic and Social Studies*, 55, 2 (June 1987); pp. 125–143.

Champlon, D.; Girard, C.; Daubignard, E.: 'Oil and Gas Reserves of the Middle East and North Africa', in: *Natural Resources Forum*, 15, 3 (August 1991); pp. 202–214.

Chan, Adrian: 'Confucianism and Development in East Asia', in: *Journal of Contemporary Asia*, 26, 1 (1996); pp. 28–46.

Chandavarkar, Rajnarayan: 'Customs of Governance: Colonialism and Democracy in Twentieth Century India', in: *Modern Asian Studies*, 41, 3 (May 2007); pp. 441–470.

Chandhoke, Neera: 'The "Civil" and the "Political" in Civil Society', in: *Democratization*, 8, 1 (Summer 2001); pp. 1–24.

Chandler, Alfred D.: 'Managerial Enterprise and Competitive Advantage', in: *Business History*, 34, 1 (January 1992); pp. 14–41.

Chandra, Bipan: 'Elements of Continuity and Change in the Early Nationalist Activity', in: *Studies in History*, 1, 1 (1979); pp. 73–88.

———: *Indian National Movement: The Long-Term Dynamics* (New Delhi: Vikas, 1988).

Chandra, Nirmal Kumar: 'China and India: Convergence in Economic Growth and Social Tensions?', in: *Economic and Political Weekly*, 44, 4 (24 January 2009); pp. 41–53.

Chandra, Satish: 'Some Institutional Factors in Providing Capital Inputs for the Improvement and Expansion of Civilization in India', in: *Indian Historical Review*, 3, 1 (July 1976); pp. 82–98.

———: 'Mughal India', in: Habib, Irfan; Raychaudhuri, Tapan (eds.): *The Cambridge Economic History of India (1): Circa 1200–1750* (Cambridge: Cambridge University Press, 1982); pp. 458–470.

Chang, Ha-Joon: 'The Political Economy of Industrial Policy in Korea', in: *Cambridge Journal of Economics*, 17, 2 (April 1993); pp. 131–157.

———; Park, Hong-Jae; Yoo, Chul Gyue: 'Interpreting the Korean Crisis: Financial Liberalisation, Industrial Policy and Corporate Governance', in: *Cambridge Journal of Economics*, 22, 6 (November 1998); pp. 735–746.

Chapman, Dennis: 'The Establishment of the Jute Industry. A Problem of Location Theory', in: *Review of Economic Studies*, 6, 16 (October 1938); pp. 33–56.

Chapman, Stanley D.: 'Fixed Capital Formation in the British Cotton Industry', in: *Economic History Review*, 23, 2 (1970); pp. 235–266.

Chaponniere, Jean-Raphaël: 'La crise renforcera l'Asie. La croissance asiatque repose de plus en plus sur la demande intérieure', in: *Le Monde* (4 October 2008); pp. 19.

Charlesworth, Neil: 'The "Middle Peasant Thesis" and the Roots of Rural Agitation in India, 1914–1947', in: *Journal of Peasant Studies*, 7, 3 (April 1980); pp. 259–280.

Chase, Kerry A.: 'Moving Hollywood Abroad: Divided Labor Markets and the New Politics of Trade in Services', in: *International Organization*, 62, 4 (Autumn 2008); pp. 653–687.

Chatterjee, Partha: 'The Colonial State and Peasant Resistance in Bengal, 1920–1947', in: *Past and Present*, 110 (February 1986); pp. 169–204.

———: 'Democracy and Economic Transformation in India', in: *Economic and Political Weekly*, 43, 16 (19 April 2008); pp. 53–72.

Chattopadhyaya, Brajadulal: 'Political Processes and the Structure of Polity in Early Medieval India', in: Kulke, Hermann (ed.): *The State in India, 1000– 1700* (Cambridge, Mass. et al.: Oxford University Press, 1997); pp. 195–232.

Chaudhuri, Binay Bhusan: 'The Process of Depeasantization in Bengal and Bihar', in: *Indian Historical Review*, 2, 1 (July 1975); pp. 105–165.

Chaudhuri, K.N.: 'India's International Economy in the 19th Century: An Historical Survey', in: *Modern Asian Studies*, 2, 1 (1968); pp. 31–50.

———: *The Economic Development of India Under the East India Company, 1814-58* (Cambridge et al.: Cambridge University Press, 1971).

Chaunu, Pierre: 'Malthusianisme démographique et malthusianisme économique. Refléxion sur l'échec industriel de la Normandie à l'époque du démarrage', in: *Annales. Economie, Société, Civilisation*, 27, 1 (January–February 1972); pp. 1–19.

Chayanov, Alexander V.: *The Theory of Peasant Economy* (Homewood, Ill.: Richard D. Irwin, 1966).

Chen, Gang: 'China's Diplomacy on Climate Change', in: *Journal of East Asian Affairs*, 22, 1 (2008); pp. 145–174.

Chen, Haichun; Gordon, M.J.; Zhiming, Yan: 'The Real Income and Consumption of an Urban Chinese Family', in: *Journal of Development Studies*, 31, 1 (October 1994); pp. 201–213.

Chen, Martha; Sebstad, Jennefer; O'Connell, Lesley: 'Counting the Invisible Workforce: The Care of Homebased', in: *World Development*, 27, 3 (1999); pp. 603–610.

Chenntouf, Tayeb: 'Remarques sur la naissance des partis politiques en Algérie', in: *Revue algérienne des sciences juridiques, économiques et politiques*, 15, 2 (June 1977); pp. 221–227.

Cheru, Fantu; Obi, Cyril: 'Introduction-Africa in the Twenty-First Century: Strategic and Development Challenges', in: Cheru, Fantu; Obi, Cyril (eds.): *The Rise of China in India and Africa* (London/New York: ZED Books, 2010); pp. 1–9.

Chesneaux, Jean: 'Stages in the Development of the Vietnam National Movement 1862–1940', in: *Past and Present*, 7 (April 1955); pp. 63–75.

———: 'Les hérésies coloniales. Leur rôle dans le développement des mouvements d'Asie et d'Afrique à l'époque contemporaine', in: *Recherches internationales à la lumière du marxisme*, 6 (March–April 1958); pp. 170–188.

———: *Popular Movements and Secret Societies in China, 1840–1950* (Stanford, Cal.: Stanford University Press, 1972).

Chhibber, Pradeep K.: 'State Policy, Rent Seeking, and the Electoral Success of a Religious Party in Algeria', in: *Journal of Politics*, 58, 1 (1996); S. 126–148.

Chichilnisky, Graciela: 'Terms of Trade and Domestic Distribution. Export-Led Growth with Abundant Labour', in: *Journal of Development Economics*, 8, 2 (April 1981); pp. 141–161.

Chikh, Bouamrane: 'Ibn Bâdis (1889–1940): Aperçu sur l'homme et l'oeuvre', in: *Etudes islamiques*, 3 (2003); pp. 87–100.

Chirot, Daniel: 'Herder's Multicultural Theory of Nationalism and its Consequences', in: *East European Politics and Societies*, 10, 1 (Winter 1996); pp. 1–15.

———: 'The Growth of the Market and Service Labor Systems in Agriculture', in: *Journal of Social History*, 8, 2 (Winter 1974); pp. 66–78.

Choe, Jae-Heyon: 'Strategic Groups of Nationalism in Nineteenth Century Korea', in: *Journal of Contemporary Asia*, 16, 2 (1986); pp. 223–236.

Chorley, Patrick: 'The Cloth Exports of Flanders and Northern France during the Thirteenth Century: A Luxury Trade?', in: *Economic History Review*, 40, 3 (1987); pp. 349–379.

———: 'Rascie and the Florentine Cloth Industry during the Sixteenth Century', in: *Journal of European Economic History*, 32, 3 (Winter 2003); pp. 487–527.

Choudhary, Mohammed Ali; Orszag, J. Michael: 'Costly Customer Relations and Pricing', in: *Oxford Economic Papers*, 59, 4 (October 2007); pp. 641–666.

Chowdhry, N.K.: *Assembly Elections, 1993* (Delhi: Shipra, 1994).

Chowdhuri, Satyabrata Rai: *Leftist Movements in India: 1917–1947* (Calcutta: Minerva Associates, 1976).

Chu, Samuel C.: 'Liu Ming-Chuan and Modernization of Taiwan', in: *Journal of Asian Studies*, 23, 1 (November 1963); pp. 37–53.

Chun, Allen: 'The Lineage-Village Complex: South Eastern China', in: *Current Anthropology*, 37, 3 (June 1996); pp. 429–440.

Chun, Lin: 'Recasting Development in China', in: *Development: Journal of the Society for International Development*, 50, 3 (September 2007); pp. 11–16.

Church, R.A.: 'Nineteenth-Century Clock Technology in Britain, the United States and Switzerland', in: *Economic History Review*, 28, 4 (1975); pp. 616–630.

Çizakça, Murat: 'A Short History of the Bursa Silk Industry (1500–1900)', in: *Journal of the Economic and Social History of the Orient*, 23, 1/2 (April 1980); pp. 142–152.

Claessen, Henri J.M.: 'The Internal Dynamics of the Early State', in: *Current Anthropology*, 25, 4 (August–October 1984); pp. 366–370.

Clapp, Jennifer: 'Africa, NGOs and the International Toxic Waste Trade', in: *Journal of Environment and Development*, 3, 2 (Summer 1994); pp. 16–46.

Clarence-Smith, Gervase: 'The Impact of the Spanish Civil War and the Second World War on Portuguese and Spanish Africa', in: *Journal of African History*, 26, 4 (1985); pp. 309–326.

Clark, Gregory: 'The Long March of History: Farm Wages, Population, and Economic Growth, England 1209–1869', in: *Economic History Review*, 60, 1 (February 2007); pp. 97–135.

Clark, Gregory: 'In Defense of the Malthusian Interpretation of History', in: *European Review of Economic History*, 12, 2 (August 2008); pp. 175–200.

Clark, Janine: 'Social Movement Theory and Patron-Clientelism: Islamic Social Institutions and the Middle Class in Egypt, Jordan, and Yemen', in: *Comparative Political Studies*, 37, 8 (October 2004); pp. 941–968.

Clark, W. Edmund: *Socialist Development and Public Investment in Tanzania, 1964–73* (Toronto; Buffalo; London: University of Toronto Press, 1978).

Clauss, Manfred: 'Mithras und Christus', in: *Historische Zeitschrift*, 243, 3 (October 1986); pp. 265–287.

Clayton, Eric S.: 'Agrarian Reform, Agricultural Planning and Employment in Kenya', in: *International Labour Review*, 102, 5 (November 1970); pp. 431–453.

Clemens, Walter C. Jr.: 'North Korea's Future: What Pyongyang, Seoul, and Washington Could Learn from East Europe, the Former USSR, and China', in: *Journal of East Asian Affairs*, 21, 1 (Spring 2007); pp. 1–48.

Clough, Shepard Bancroft; Marburg, Theodore F.: *The Economic Basis of American Civilization* (New York: Thomas Y. Crowell, 1968).

Clymer, Kenton J.: 'Indian Nationalism and Anglo-American Relations in the Second World War: Another Look at Some Unauthorized Disclosures', in: *International Studies*, 25, 4 (October–December 1988); pp. 343–362.

Coats, A.W.: 'The Relief of Poverty: Attitudes to Labour, and Economic Change in England 1660–1782', in: *International Review of Social History*, 21, 1 (1976); pp. 98–115.

Cocks, Peter: 'Towards a Marxist Theory of European Integration', in: *International Organization*, 34, 1 (Winter 1980); pp. 1–40.

Coelho, Philip R.P.; Shephard, James E.: 'Regional Differences in Real Wages: The United States, 1851– 1880', in: *Explorations in Economic History*, 13, 2 (April 1976); pp. 203–230.

Cohen, Elie: 'Europe between Market and Power: Industrial Policies. Specialization, Technology, Competition and Foreign Trade.', in: Mény, Yves; Muller, Pierre; Quermonne, Jean-Louis (eds.): *Adjusting to Europe. The Impact of the European Union on National Institutions and Policies*. (London; New York: Routledge, 1996); pp. 137–156.

Cohen, Robin: 'The "New" International Division of Labour: A Conceptual, Historical and Empirical Critique', in: *Migration*, 1, 1 (1987); pp. 21–46.

Cohen, Wesley M.; Levinthal, Daniel A.: 'Absorptive Capacity: A New Perspective on Learning and Innovation', in: *Administrative Science Quarterly*, 35, 1 (1990); pp. 128–152.

Cole, Charles Woolsey: *Colbert and a Century of French Mercantilism (1)* (New York: Frank Cass, 1939).

Collectif rémois: 'Une approche globale du travail des femmes mariées à des prolétaires', in: *Critiques de l'économie politique* (January–March 1977); pp. 104–125.

Collins, Kins: 'Marx on the English Agricultural Revolution', in: *History and Theory*, 6, 3 (1967); pp. 351–381.

Collins, Susan M.; Bosworth, Barry P.: 'Economic Growth in East Asia: Accumulation versus Assimilation', in: *Brookings Papers on Economic Activity*, 2 (Summer 1996); pp. 135–203.

Commander, Simon: 'The Jajmani System in North India. An Examination of its Logic and Status across Two Centuries', in: *Modern Asian Studies*, 17, 2 (May 1983); pp. 283–311.

Comte, Auguste: *Discours sur l'esprit positif* (Paris: Union Générale d'Editions, 1963).

Conklin, Alice L.: 'Colonialism and Human Rights, A Contradiction in Terms? The Case of France and West Africa, 1895–1914', in: *American Historical Review*, 103, 2 (April 1998); pp. 419–442.

Contursi, Janet A.: 'Militant Hindus and Buddhist Dalits: Hegemony and Resistance in an Indian Slum', in: *American Ethnologist*, 16, 3 (August 1989); pp. 441–457.

Cooke, Nola: 'Regionalism and the Nature of Nguyen Rule in Seventeenth-Century Dang Trong (Cochinchina)', in: *Journal of Southeast Asian Studies*, 29, 1 (March 1998); pp. 122–161.

Cooper, Andrew Scott: 'Showdown at Doha: The Secret Oil Deal That Helped Sink the Shah of Iran', in: *Middle East Journal*, 62, 4 (Autumn 2008); pp. 567–592.

Coquery-Vidrovitch, Catherine: 'Recherches sur un mode de production africain', in: *La Pensée*, 144 (March–April 1969); pp. 61–78.

———: 'Les structures du pouvoir et la communauté rurale précoloniale', in: *Canadian Journal of African Studies*, 15, 3 (1981); pp. 433–449.

Cortázar, René; Downey, Ramón: 'Efectos redistributivos de la reforma agraria', in: *Trimestre Económico*, 44, 175 (July–September 1977); pp. 685–714.

Corten, André: 'La société civile en question: Pentecôtisme et démocratie', in: *Tiers Monde*, 46, 181 (2005); pp. 167–184.

Cosmo, Nicola di: *Ancient China and its Enemies: The Rise of Nomadic Power in East Asian History*. (Cambridge et al.: Cambridge University Press, 2002).

Costa, Ionara; Robles Reis de Queiroz, Sérgio: 'Foreign Direct Investment and Technological Capabilities in Brazilian Industry', in: *Research Policy*, 31 (2002); pp. 1431–1443.

Couland, Jacques: *L'éveil du monde arabe* (Paris: Editions Sociales, 1964).

Court, W.H.B.: *British Economic History 1870–1914. Commentary and Documents* (Cambridge: Cambridge University Press, 1965).

Cowling, Keith; Sugden, Roger: 'Strategic Trade Policy Reconsidered: National Rivalry versus Free Trade versus International Cooperation', in: *Kyklos*, 51, 3 (1998); pp. 339–357.

Cox, Gary W.; Ingram, James W.: 'Suffrage Expansion and Legislative Behaviour in Nineteenth-Century Britain', in: *Social Science History*, 16, 4 (Winter 1992); pp. 539–560.

Craeybeckx, J.: 'The Brabant Revolution: A Conservative Revolt in a Backward Country?', in: *Acta Historiae Neerlandica*, 4 (1970); pp. 49–82.
Crafts, Nicholas F.R.; Ireland, N.J.: 'Family Limitation and the English Demographic Revolution: A Simulation Approach', in: *Journal of Economic History*, 36, 3 (1976); pp. 598–623.
Craig, Albert M.; Fairbank, John K.; Reischauer, Edwin O.: *East Asia. The Modern Transformation* (Boston, Mass.: Houghton Mifflin, 1965).
Crawley, W. F.: 'Kisan Sabhas and Agrarian Revolt in the United Provinces, 1920 to 1921', in: *Modern Asian Studies*, 5, 2 (April 1971); pp. 95–109.
Crockett, Andrew: 'Exchange Rate Regimes in Theory and Practice', in: Mizen, Paul (ed.): *Monetary History, Exchange Rates and Financial Markets. Essays in Honour of Charles Goodhart. Volume Two* (Cheltenham: Elgar, 2003); pp. 96–125.
Croft, Pauline: 'Free Trade and the House of Commons 1605–06', in: *Economic History Review*, 28, 1 (1975); pp. 13–27.
Croll, Elizabeth J.; Ping, Huang: 'Migration for and against Agriculture in Eight Chinese Villages', in: *China Quarterly*, 38, 149 (May 1997); pp. 128–146.
Cronin, Stephanie: 'Importing Modernity: European Military Missions to Qajar Iran', in: *Comparative Studies in Society and History*, 50, 1 (January 2008); pp. 197–226.
Cross, Harry E.; Brading, D.A.: 'Colonial Silver Mining: Mexico and Peru', in: *Hispanic American Historical Review*, 52, 4 (November 1972); pp. 545–579.
Crotty, James: 'Structural Causes of the Global Financial Crisis: A Critical Assessment of the "New Financial Architecture"', in: *Cambridge Journal of Economics*, 33, 4 (July 2009); pp. 563–580.
Crowder, Michael: 'Indirect Rule: French and British Style', in: *Africa: Journal of the International African Institute*, 34, 3 (July 1964); pp. 197–204.
Cubertafond, Bernard: 'Le rôle des pays arabes dans les groupements de producteurs de pétrole', in: *Maghreb-Machrek/Monde Arabe*, 74 (October–December 1976); pp. 30–41.
Cunningham, Hugh: 'The Employment and Unemployment of Children in England. 1680–1851', in: *Past and Present* (1990); pp. 105–150.
Curran, Louise: 'The Impact of the Financial and Economic Crisis on World Trade and Trade Policy', in: *Intereconomics*, 44, 5 (September–October 2009); pp. 264–268.
Dahlman, Carl J.; Sercovitch, Francisco: *Local Development and Exports of Technology. The Comparative Advantage of Argentina, Brazil, India, the Republic of Korea, and Mexico. World Bank Staff Working Paper 667* (Washington: World Bank, 1984).
Dahrendorf, Ralf: 'Recent Changes in the Class Structure of European Societies', in: *Daedalus*, 93, 1 (Winter 1964); pp. 225–269.
Dale, Richard S.: 'Financial Markets Can Go Mad: Evidence of Irrational Behaviour During the South Sea Bubble', in: *Economic History Review*, 58, 2 (May 2005); pp. 233–271.

Dale, Stephen F.: '"Silk Road, Cotton Road or" Indo-Chinese Trade in Pre-European Times', in: *Modern Asian Studies*, 43, 1 (January 2009); pp. 79–88.

Dalton, George: 'Traditional Producers in Primitive African Economies', in: Dalton, George (ed.): *Tribal and Peasant Economies. Readings in Economic Anthropology* (Garden City, N.Y.: Natural History Press, 1967); pp. 61–80.

Danielewski, Angelika: 'Die Salzstraßen des aztekischen Staates: Vernetzung des Handels und Tribut', in: *Ethnographisch-Archäologische Zeitschrift*, 34, 1 (1993); pp. 69–87.

Dann, Otto: *Nation und Nationalismus in Deutschland, 1770–1990* (Munich: Beck, 1994).

Dardess, John: 'The Transformation of Messianic Revolt and the Founding of the Ming Dynasty', in: *Journal of Asian Studies*, 29, 3 (May 1970); pp. 539–558.

Das Gupta, Ranajit: 'Peasants, Works and Freedom Struggle, Jalpaiguri', in: Gupta, Amit Kumar (ed.): *Myth and Reality: The Struggle for Freedom in India, 1945–47* (New Delhi: Prints India, 1987); pp. 415–459.

Dasgupta, Partha; Ray, Debraj: 'Inequality as a Determinant of Malnutrition and Unemployment', in: *Economic Journal*, 97, 385 (March 1987); pp. 176–188.

Dasgupta, Sabyasachi: 'The Rebel Army in 1857: At the Vanguard of the War of Independence or a Tyranny of Arms?', in: *Economic and Political Weekly*, 42, 19 (12 May 2007); pp. 1729–1733.

Datta, Anindya: 'Understanding East Asian Economic Development', in: *Economic and Political Weekly*, 22, 14 (4 April 1987); pp. 602–605.

Dauderstädt, Michael: *Standortkonkurrenz, Arbeitsplatzexport und Beschäftigung* (Bonn: Friedrich-Ebert-Stiftung, September 2004).

David, Faure: 'La société lignagère: La révolution rituelle du XVIe siècle et l'Etat impérial chinois', in: *Annales. Histoire, Sciences Sociales*, 61, 6 (November–December 2006); pp. 1291–1316.

Davies, James Chowning: *When and Why Men Revolt. A Reader in Political Violence and Revolution* (New York; London: Free Press; Collier Macmillan, 1971).

Davies, Thomas M.: 'The Indigenismo of the Peruvian Aprista Party: A Reinterpretation', in: *Hispanic American Historical Review*, 51, 4 (November 1971); pp. 626–645.

Davis, John: 'An Anthropologist's View of Exchange', in: *Oxford Development Studies*, 24, 1 (1996); pp. 47–60.

Davis, Nancy J.; Robinson, Robert V.: 'Their Brothers' Keepers? Orthodox Religionists, Modernists, and Economic Justice in Europe', in: *American Journal of Sociology*, 104, 6 (March 1999); pp. 1631–1665.

Dawson, Andrew: 'The Paradox of Dynamic Technological Change and the Labor Aristocracy in the United States, 1880–1914', in: *Labor History*, 20, 3 (Summer 1979); pp. 325–351.

Day, John: '"Crise du féodalisme" et conjoncture des prix à la fin du moyen âge', in: *Annales. Economie, Société, Civilisation*, 34, 2 (February–March 1979); pp. 305–313.

D'Costa, Anthony P.: 'Uneven and Combined Development: Understanding India's Software Exports', in: *World Development*, 31, 1 (January 2003); pp. 211–226.

de Carvalho, José Murilo: 'Armed Forces and Politics in Brazil, 1930–1945', in: *Hispanic American Historical Review*, 62, 2 (May 1982); pp. 193–223.

Deeb, Marius: 'Labour and Politics in Egypt 1919–1939', in: *International Journal of Middle East Studies*, 11, 2 (May 1979); pp. 187–203.

Deere, Carmen Diana: 'Rural Women's Subsistence Production in the Capitalist Periphery', in: *Review of Radical Political Economics*, 8, 1 (Spring 1976); pp. 9–16.

Dekker, C.: 'The Representation of the Freeholders in the Drainage Districts of Zeeland West of the Scheldt during the Middle Ages', in: *Acta Historiae Neerlandicae*, 8 (1975); pp. 1–30.

Dekmejian, Hrair R.: 'The Anatomy of Islamic Revival: Legitimacy Crisis, Ethnic Conflict and the Search for Islamic Alternatives', in: *Middle East Journal*, 34, 1 (Winter 1980); pp. 1–12.

Delacroix, Jacques; Ragin, Charles C.: 'Structural Blockage: A Cross-National Study of Economic Dependency, State Efficiency and Underdevelopment', in: *American Journal of Sociology*, 86, 6 (May 1981); pp. 1311–1347.

Délégation Générale du Gouvenement en Algérie: *Plan de Constantine, 1959–1963. Rapport Général* (Algiers: Direction du Plan et des Etudes Economiques, 1960).

Dème, Kalidou: 'Les classes sociales dans le Sénégal précolonial', in: *La Pensée*, 130 (November–December 1966); pp. 11–35.

Demel, Walter: 'The Images of the Japanese and the Chinese in Early Modern Europe: Physical Characteristics, Customs and Skills: A Comparison of Different Approaches to the Cultures of the Far East', in: *Itinerario*, 25, 3/4 (2001); pp. 34–53.

Denison, Edward F.: 'The Unimportance of the Embodied Question', in: *American Economic Review*, 54, 2 (March 1964); pp. 90–94.

———: 'Sources of Postwar Growth in Nine Western Countries', in: *American Economic Review*, 57, 2 (May 1967a); pp. 325–332.

———: *Why Growth Rates Differ: Postwar Experience in Nine Western Countries*. (Washington D.C.: Brookings Institution, 1967b).

———: 'The Contribution of Capital to Economic Growth', in: *American Economic Review*, 70, 2 (May 1980); pp. 221–224.

Deppe, Frank; Lange, Hellmuth: 'Zur Soziologie des Arbeiter- und Klassenkampfbewusstseins. Ein kritischer Literaturbericht (2)', in: *Argument*, 12, 62 (1970); pp. 803–821.

Deron, Francis: 'Angkor, mégalopole médiévale', in: *Le Monde* (16 August 2007); p. 17.

Derry, Thomas K.; Williams, Trevor I.: *A Short History of Technology. From the Earliest Times to A. D. 1900* (Oxford: Clarendon Press, 1960).

Desai, Ashok V.: 'Technology and Market Structure under Government Regulation. A Case Study of Indian Textile Industry', in: *Economic and Political Weekly*, 18, 5 (25 January 1983); pp. 150–160.

———: 'The Slow Rate of Industrialisation: A Second Look', in: *Economic and Political Weekly*, 19, 31/33 (August 1984); pp. 1267–1272.

Desai, Radhika: 'Conclusion: From Developmental to Cultural Nationalisms', in: *Third World Quarterly*, 29, 3 (2008); pp. 647–670.

Deshpande, Satish: 'Declining Simplistic Narratives', in: *Economic and Political Weekly*, 43, 5 (2 February 2008); pp. 25–28.

Deshpande, V.D.: 'Code of Conduct for Rural Voluntary Agencies', in: *Economic and Political Weekly*, 21, 30 (26 July 1986); pp. 1304–1306.

Destanne de Bernis, Gérard: 'Le rôle du secteur public dans l'industrialisation', in: *Economie appliquée*, 15, 1/2 (January–June 1962); pp. 135–174.

Deutschmann, Christoph: 'Marx, Schumpeter und Mythen ökonomischer Rationalität', in: *Leviathan*, 24, 3 (September 1996); pp. 323–338.

Devèze, Michel: *L'Europe et le monde à la fin du XVIIe siècle* (Paris: Albin Michel, 1970).

Devine, Thomas M.: 'L'évolution agraire et sociale des lowlands d'Ecosse de 1680 à 1815', in: *Histoire, économie et société*, 18, 1 (1999); pp. 159–185.

DeWit, Andrew: *'Change' Comes to Japan?* (Berlin: Friedrich-Ebert-Stiftung, October 2009).

Diallo, Youssouf: 'Barani: une chefferie satellite des grands Etats du XIXe siècle', in: *Cahiers d'études africaines*, 34, 133–135 (1994); pp. 359–384.

Diehl, Markus: 'Wechselkurspolitik in ostasiatischen Schwellenländern', in: *Weltwirtschaft*, 47, 4 (1996); pp. 444–467.

Diener, Paul; Robkin, Eugene E.: 'Ecology, Evolution, and the Search for Cultural Origins: The Question of Islamic Pig Prohibition', in: *Current Anthropology*, 19, 3 (September 1978); pp. 493–509.

Dieterich, Heinz: 'Some Theoretical and Methodological Observations about the Inca Empire and the Asiatic Mode of Production', in: *Latin American Perspectives*, 9, 4 (Autumn 1982); pp. 110–132.

Digby, William: *'Prosperous' British India. A Revelation from Official Records* (London: T. Fisher Unwin, 1901).

Diggins, John P.: 'Reification and the Cultural Hegemony of Capitalism: The Perspectives of Marx and Veblen', in: *Social Research*, 44, 2 (Summer 1977); pp. 354–383.

Dimier, Véronique: 'Three Universities and the British Elite: A Science of Colonial Administration in the UK', in: *Public Administration*, 84, 2 (2006); pp. 337–366.

Dimitrov, A.: 'La Renaissance bulgare et les problèmes de la continuité historique des époques moderne et contemporaine', in: *Bulgarian Historical Review*, 36, 1–2 (2008); pp. 26–46.

Dingwerth, Klaus: 'Globale Politiknetzwerke und ihre demokratische Legitimation: Eine Analyse der Weltstaudammkommission', in: *Zeitschrift für Internationale Beziehungen*, 10, 1 (2003); pp. 69–109.

Diop, Thierno: 'Cheikh Anta Diop et le matérialisme historique', in: *Africa Development*, 23, 1 (1998); pp. 87–113.

Dirlik, Arif: *After the Revolution: Waking to Global Capitalism* (Hanover, NH: Wesleyan University Press, 1994).

——: 'Narrativizing Revolution: The Guangzhou Uprising (11–13 December 1927) in Workers' Perspective', in: *Modern China*, 23, 4 (1997); pp. 363–397.

Dittmer, Kunz: 'Zur Geschichte Afrikas (4): Die ältere Geschichte Westafrikas und des Sudans', in: *Saeculum*, 18, 4 (1967); pp. 322–329.

Dobado González, Rafael; Gómez Galvarriato, Aurora; Williamson, Jeffrey G.: 'Mexican Exceptionalism: Globalization and De-Industrialization, 1750–1877', in: *Journal of Economic History*, 68, 3 (September 2008); pp. 758–811.

Dobb, Maurice Herbert: 'Prelude to the Industrial Revolution', in: *Science and Society*, 28, 1 (Winter 1964); pp. 31–47.

Dobbin, Christine: 'Islamic Revivalism in Minang Kaban at the Turn of the Nineteenth-Century', in: *Modern Asian Studies*, 8, 3 (July 1974); pp. 318–356.

Dobson, Richard B.: *The Peasants' Revolt of 1381* (London et al.: Macmillan, 1970).

Dodge, Dorothy: *African Politics in Perspective* (New York: Van Nostrand, 1966).

Dodgen, Randall: 'Hydraulic Religion: "Great King" Cults in the Ming and Qing', in: *Modern Asian Studies*, 33, 4 (October 1999); pp. 815–833.

Dollar, David: 'Outward-oriented Developing Economies Really Do Grow More Rapidly: Evidence from 95 LDCs, 1976–1985', in: *Economic Development and Cultural Change*, 40, 3 (April 1992); pp. 524–543.

Domar, Evsey D.: 'The Capital-Output Ratio in the United States: Its Variation and Stability', in: Lutz, F.A.; Hague, D.C. (eds): *The Theory of Capital. Proceedings of a Conference Held by the International Economic Association* (New York; London: Macmillan; St. Martins Press, 1961); pp. 95–117.

Donges, Jürgen B.: 'A Comparative Survey of Industrialization Policies in Fifteen Semi-Industrial Countries', in: *Weltwirtschaftliches Archiv*, 112, 4 (1976); pp. 626–659.

Donnachie, Ian: 'Sources of Capital and Capitalization in the Scottish Brewing Industry, c. 1750–1830', in: *Economic History Review*, 30, 3 (1977); pp. 269–283.

Döring, Herbert E.: 'Wählen Industriearbeiter zunehmend konservativ? Die Bundesrepublik Deutschland im westeuropäischen Vergleich', in: *Archiv für Sozialgeschichte*, 29 (1989); pp. 225–272.

Dormois, Jean-Pierre; Bardini, Carlo: 'La productivité du travail dans l'industrie de divers pays d'Europe avant 1914', in: *Economies et Sociétés*, AF 21 (December 1995); pp. 77–103.

Dornbusch, Rüdiger: 'El problema mundial de la deuda', in: *Trimestre Económico*, 54, 216 (December 1987); pp. 805–824.

Dorner, Peter; Felstehausen, Herman: 'Agrarian Reform and Employment: The Columbian Case', in: *International Labour Review*, 102, 3 (September 1970); pp. 221–239.

Dorraj, Manochehr; Dodgson, Michael: 'Neo-populism in Comparative Perspective: Iran and Venezuela', in: *Comparative Studies of South Asia, Africa and the Middle East*, 29, 1 (2009); pp. 137–151.

Dossogne, Caroline: 'Anxiété et choix, les prémisses d'un processus identitaire?', in: *Cahiers d'études africaines*, 48, 185 (2007); pp. 145–173.

Dovring, Folke: 'Unemployment in Traditional Agriculture', in: *Economic Development and Cultural Change*, 15, 2 (January 1967); pp. 163–173.

Drelichman, Mauricio: 'American Silver and the Decline of Spain', in: *Journal of Economic History*, 65, 2 (June 2005a); pp. 532–535.

———: 'The Curse of Moctezuma: American Silver and the Dutch Disease', in: *Explorations in Economic History*, 42, 3 (October 2005b); pp. 349–380.

Dresdner Bank: *Die wirtschaftlichen Kräfte der Welt* (Berlin: Dresdner Bank AG, 1930).

Drezner, Daniel W.: *U.S. Trade Strategy. Free Versus Fair* (Council of Foreign Relations, 2006).

Dronne, Raymond: 'Entretien', in: Ouaissa, Rachid (ed.): *Les carnets d'Hartmut Elsenhans: La guerre d'Algérie vue par ses acteurs français* (Algiers: Casbah, 2009); pp. 251–258.

Dua, R.P.: *The Impact of the Russo-Japanese (1905) War on Indian Politics* (Delhi et al.: S. Chand, 1966).

Duara, Prasenjit: 'The Discourse of Civilization and Pan-Asianism', in: *Journal of World History*, 12, 1 (Spring 2001); pp. 99–130.

DuBoff, Richard B.: 'Electrification and Capital Productivity: A Suggested Approach', in: *Review of Economics and Statistics*, 48, 4 (November 1966); pp. 426–431.

Dudenhöffer, Ferdinand: 'Wie viel Deutschland steckt im Porsche?', in: *IFO-Schnelldienst*, 58, 24 (December 2005); pp. 3–5.

Duffield, Ian: 'John Eldred Taylor and West African Opposition to Indirect Rule in Nigeria', in: *African Affairs*, 70, 280 (July 1981); pp. 252–268.

Dugast, Stéphan: 'Classes d'âge, chefferie et organisation dualiste: les Abouré de la Basse Côte d'Ivoire', in: *Cahiers d'études africaines*, 35, 138–139 (1995); pp. 403–445.

Duiker, William J.: 'The Red Soviets of the Nghe-Tinh: An Early Communist Rebellion in Vietnam', in: *Journal of Southeast Asian Studies*, 4, 2 (September 1973); pp. 186–196.

Dumont, Louis: 'World Renunciation in Indian Religions', in: *Contributions to Indian Sociology*, 4 (April 1960); pp. 33–62.

Dunkerley, Harold B.: 'Exchange Rate Systems in Conditions of Continuing Inflation. Lessons from Colombian Experience', in: Papanek, Gustav F. (ed.): *Development Policy. Theory and Practice* (Cambridge, Mass.: Harvard University Press, 1968); pp. 117–176.

Dunn, Kevin C.: '"Sons of the Soil" and Contemporary State Making: Autochthony, Uncertainty and Political Violence in Africa', in: *Third World Quarterly*, 30, 1 (February 2009); pp. 113–127.

Dunning, Thad: 'Conditioning the Effects of Aid: Cold War Politics, Donor Credibility, and Democracy in Africa', in: *International Organization*, 58, 2 (Spring 2004); pp. 409–423.

Dupâquier, J.; Lachivier, M.: 'Sur les débuts de la contraception en France: Les deux malthusianismes', in: *Annales. Economie, Société, Civilisation*, 24, 5 (September–October 1969); pp. 1391–1402.

Duran, Burhanettin; Yildirim, Engin: 'Islamism, Trade Unionism and Civil Society: The Case of Hak-Is Labour Confederation in Turkey', in: *Middle Eastern Studies*, 41, 2 (March 2005); pp. 227–247.

Durau, Joachim: *Arbeitskooperation in der chinesischen Landwirtschaft. Die Veränderung bäuerlicher Produktionsbeziehungen zwischen Agrarrevolution und Kollektivierung, 1927–1957* (Bochum: Brockmeyer, 1983).

Dutt, Amitava Krishna: 'The Origins of Uneven Development: The Indian Sub-continent', in: *American Economic Review*, 82, 2 (May 1992); pp. 146–150.

Dutt, Palme Rajani: *India Today* (Calcutta: Manisha, 1970).

Duvall, Raymond D.; Freeman, John R.: 'The Techno-Bureaucratic Elite and the Entrepreneurial State in Dependent Industrialization', in: *American Political Science Review*, 77, 3 (September 1983); pp. 569–587.

Dyer, Christoph: 'The Consumer and the Market in the Later Middle Ages', in: *Economic History Review*, 42, 3 (1989); pp. 305–327.

Eastman, Lloyd E.: 'Political Reformism in China Before the Sino-Japanese War', in: *Journal of Asian Studies*, 27, 4 (August 1968); pp. 695–710.

Eaton, Richard M.: *The Rise of Islam and the Bengal Frontier, 1204–1760* (Berkeley, Cal., et al.: University of California Press, 1993).

Ebenroth, Carsten Thomas; Bühler, Stephan: 'Die Implementierung der Brady-Initiative in Mexiko und den Philippinen', in: *Recht der Internationalen Wirtschaft*, 36 (January 1990); pp. 23–28.

Ebrey, Patricia: 'Conceptions of the Family in the Sung Dynasty', in: *Journal of Asian Studies*, 43, 1 (February 1984); pp. 219–245.

Eckert, Andreas: 'Exportschlager Wohlfahrtsstaat. Europäische Staatlichkeit und Kolonialismus in Afrika nach dem Zweiten Weltkrieg', in: *Geschichte und Gesellschaft*, 32, 4 (October–December 2006); pp. 467–488.

Edelman, Marc: 'A Central American Genocide: Rubber, Slavery, Nationalism, and the Destruction of the Guatusos-Malekus', in: *Comparative Studies in Society and History*, 40 (1998); pp. 356–390.

Edes, Bart W.: 'Asia after the Crisis: Social protection and Inclusive Growth', in: *OECD Observer*, 276–277 (January 2010); pp. 19–20.

Egret, Jean: *La pré-révolution française (1787 –1788)* (Paris: Presses Universitaires de France, 1962).

Eichengreen, Barry; Mitchener, Kris J.: 'The Great Depression as a Credit Boom Gone Wrong', in: *Research in Economic History*, 22 (2004); pp. 183–237.

Eickelman, Dale F.: 'Is There an Islamic City? The Making of a Quarter in a Moroccan Town', in: *International Journal of Middle East Studies*, 5, 3 (August 1974); pp. 274–294.

Eley, Geoff: 'Defining Social Imperialism: Use and Abuse of an Idea', in: *Social History*, 1, 3 (October 1976); pp. 265–290.

Elliot, J. H.: 'A Europe of Composite Monarchies', in: *Past and Present*, 137 (November 1992); pp. 47–71.

Ellis, Gene: 'The Backward-Bending Supply Curve of Labour in Africa: Models, Evidence and Interpretations and Why It Makes a Difference', in: *Journal of Developing Areas*, 15, 2 (January 1981); pp. 251–274.

Elman, Benjamin A.: 'Naval Warfare and the Refraction of China's Self-Strengthening Reforms into Scientific and Technological Failure 1865–1895', in: *Modern Asian Studies*, 38, 2 (May 2004); pp. 283–326.

Elsenhans, Hartmut: 'Entwicklungstendenzen der Welterdölindustrie', in: Elsenhans, Hartmut (ed.): *Erdöl für Europa* (Hamburg: Hoffmann & Campe, 1974a); pp. 7–47.

———: 'Erdöl und Politik. Die Entwicklungstendenzen des Weltmarkts und die internationale Erdölindustrie', in: *Internationale Entwicklung*, 2 (1974b); pp. 14–24.

———: 'Lohnerhöhungen: Wachstumschance für den Kapitalismus. Eine Kritik am Gesetz vom tendenziellen Fall der Profitrate', in: *Forum DS. Zeitschrift für Theorie und Praxis des demokratischen Sozialismus*, 1, 2 (1976); pp. 78–133.

———: *Algerien. Koloniale und postkoloniale Reformpolitik* (Hamburg: Institut für Afrikakunde im Verbund der Stiftung Deutsches Übersee-Institut, 1977a).

———: 'Konflikt in der OPEC. Die Festigung der Achse Riad-Washington', in: *Dritte-Welt-Magazin*, 1 (January 1977b); pp. 11–13.

———: 'Die Staatsklasse/Staatsbourgeoisie in den unterentwickelten Ländern zwischen Privilegierung und Legitimationszwang', in: *Verfassung und Recht in Übersee*, 10, 1 (1977c); pp. 29–42.

———: 'Agrarverfassung, Akkumulationsprozeß, Demokratisierung', in: Elsenhans, Hartmut (ed.): *Agrarreform in der Dritten Welt* (Frankfurt on the Main; New York: Campus, 1979a); pp. 505–652.

———: 'Gesellschaftsreform und Wirtschaftswachstum. Akkumulationsprobleme in der Bundesrepublik', in: *Forum DS. Zeitschrift für Theorie und Praxis des demokratischen Sozialismus*, 4, 8 (1979b); pp. 135–170.

———: 'Englisches Poor Law und egalitäre Agrarreform in der Dritten Welt. Einige Aspekte der Theorie, daß Wachstum historisch die Erweiterung des Massenmarktes erforderte und heute die Erweiterung des Massenmarktes erfordert', in: *Verfassung und Recht in Übersee*, 13, 4 (1980); pp. 283–318. English translation Elsenhans, Hartmut: 'English Poor Law and Egalitarian Agrarian Reform in the Third World', in: Elsenhans, Hartmut: *Equality and Development* (Dhaka: Center for Social Studies, 1992); pp. 130–162.

Elsenhans, Hartmut: *Abhängiger Kapitalismus oder bürokratische Entwicklungsgesellschaft. Versuch über den Staat in der Dritten Welt* (Frankfort on the Main; New York: Campus, 1981a).

———: 'Social Consequences of the NIEO. No Change for Continued Reformist Strategies in the Centre without Structural Change in the Periphery', in: Jahn, Egbert; Sakamoto, Yoshikazu (eds): *Elements of World Instability: Armaments, Communication, Food, International Division of Labour. Proceedings of the Eighth International Peace Research Association Conference* (Frankfort on the Main; New York: Campus, 1981b); pp. 86–95.

———: *Price Rises for Coffee through Cartellization: Estimation to the Response of West German Consumers. Joint Session of Workshops. Workshop: International Political Economy* (Aarhus: ECPR, 1982).

———: 'Égalité et développement. L'expérience européenne et le monde sous-développé d'aujourd'hui', in: *Cultures et développement*, 15, 2 (1983a); pp. 187–216.

———: 'Rising Mass Incomes as a Condition of Capitalist Growth: Implications for the World Economy', in: *International Organization*, 37, 1 (Winter 1983b); pp. 1–38.

———: 'Endettement: Echec d'une industrialisation du Tiers Monde', in: *Tiers Monde*, 25, 99 (July–September 1984); pp. 551–564.

———: 'Dependencia, Underdevelopment and the Third World State', in: *Law and State*, 36 (1987); pp. 65–94.

———: 'Appropriate Technology and the Entry into Most Modern Technology', in: Cyranek, Günter; Büsselmann, Hans-Hermann; Rojas, René González (eds.): *Computers against Poverty—Poverty through Computers? Perspectives of a Basic Needs Oriented Approach to Informatics Devloping Countries Needs* (Paris: UNESCO, 1990); pp. 1–23.

———: 'Capitalism: Subtle Appeal (A Report)', in: *Jawaharlal Nehru University News*, 13, 2 (February 1991a); pp. 22–24.

———: 'Political Obstacles to Private Sector Development', in: Bennett, James G. (ed.): *Private Sector Development in Bangladesh* (Cologne: Oase, 1991b); pp. 205–245.

———: 'Problems Central to Economic Policy Deregulation in Bangladesh', in: *Internationales Asienforum*, 22, 3/4 (November 1991c); pp. 259–286.

———: 'Fundamentalismus in der Dritten Welt als Herausforderung an das internationale System des 21. Jahrhunderts: Kultursoziologie oder Politökonomie als Therapie', in: *Comparativ. Leipziger Beiträge zur Universalgeschichte und vergleichenden Gesellschaftsforschung*, 4, 6 (1994a); pp. 9–20.

———: 'Rent, State and the Market: The Political Economy of the Transition to Self-sustained Capitalism', in: *Pakistan Development Review*, 33, 4 (December 1994b); pp. 393–428.

———: 'Marginality, Rent and Non-Governmental Organizations', in: *Indian Journal of Public Administration*, 41, 2 (April–June 1995); pp. 139–159.

Elsenhans, Hartmut: 'A Welfare Capitalist World System or the Feudalisation of the Global System', in: Babu, B. Ramesh (ed.): *Changing Global Political/Ideological Context and Afro-Asia Strategies for Development* (New Delhi: South Asian Books, 1996a); pp. 57–130.

———: 'Non-Governmental Organisations, Marginality and Underdevelopment, and the Political Economy of Civil Society', in: Gopal, K.S.; Bumke, Peter J. (eds.): *Foreign Funding in Andhra Pradesh* (Hyderabad: Centre for Environmental Concerns, 1996b); pp. 129–148.

———: *State, Class and Development* (New Delhi; London; Columbia, Mo.: Radiant; Sangam; South Asia Books, 1996c).

———: 'Individualistische Strategien der Haushalte zur Zukunftssicherung: Grundlage für den Niedergang des wohlfahrtstaatlichen Kapitalismus', in: *Comparativ. Leipziger Beiträge zur Universalgeschichte und vergleichenden Gesellschaftsforschung*, 9, 3 (1999); pp. 114–142.

———: 'Globalisation in a Labourist Keynesian Approach', in: *Journal of Social Studies*, 89 (July–September 2000a); pp. 1–66.

———: *La guerre d'Algérie, 1954–1962. La transition d'une France à une autre. Le passage de la IV à la Ve République* (Paris: Publisud, 2000b).

———: 'The Rise and Fall of Really Existing Socialism', in: *Journal of Social Studies*, 87 (January–March 2000c); pp. 1–16.

———: 'Die Globalisierung der Finanzmärkte und die Entstehung einer neuen Rentenklasse', in: Menzel, Ulrich (Hrsg.) (ed.): *Vom Ewigen Frieden und vom Wohlstand der Nationen. Dieter Senghaas zum 60. Geburtstag* (Frankfort on the Main: Suhrkamp, 2000d); pp. 518–542.

———: *Das Internationale System zwischen Zivilgesellschaft und Rente* (Münster: Lit, 2001a).

———: 'Renten in der exportorientierten Industrialisierung: Zur notwendigen und widerspruchsvollen Rolle des Staats', in: Gärtner, Peter (ed.): *Staatlichkeit im Epochenbruch? Antworten aus der Perspektive des Südens und Ostens* (Hamburg: Hamburgisches Welt-Wirtschafts-Archiv, 2001b); pp. 251–296.

———: 'Macroeconomics in Globalization: Productivity, Wages, Profits, and Exchange Rates in an Era of Globalization', in: *Brazilian Journal of Political Economy*, 22, 85 (January–March 2002); pp. 53–78.

———: 'Les contribuables ont payé, les banques sont sauvées et le tiers monde s'engouffre dans la dette. Comment on gère une crise en gestation', in: Catalano, Pierangelo; Sid Ahmed, Abdelkader (eds.): *La dette contre le développement: Quelle stratégie pour les peuples méditerranées* (Paris: Publisud, 2003); pp. 323–343.

———: 'Globalisation, Devaluation and Development', in: *Rajasthan Economic Journal*, 27, 1 (October 2004); pp. 1–14.

———: 'A Benign Globalization vs. a Doomsday Scenario: How to Make Globalization in a Capital and Welfare Perspective', in: *Review of Global Politics*, 10 (April 2005); pp. 1–66.

Elsenhans, Hartmut: *Geschichte und Ökonomie der europäischen Welteroberung. Vom Zeitalter der Entdeckungen zum 1. Weltkrieg. Herausgegeben mit einem Vorwort von Matthias Middell* (Leipzig: Leipziger Universitätsverlag, 2007a).

———: 'Politische Ökonomie der Sklaverei vom 16.-18. Jh.', in: Reichardt, Tobias; Erdem, M. (eds): *Unfreie Arbeit. Ökonomische und kulturgeschichtliche Perspektiven* (Zürich/NewYork/Hildesheim: Georg Olms, 2007b); pp. 242–259.

———: *Kapitalismus kontrovers. Zerklüftung im nicht so sehr kapitalistischen Weltsystem. WeltTrends Papiere 9* (Potsdam: Universitätsverlag Potsdam, 2009).

———: 'Les manifestations de décembre 1960 et la reconnaissance de la révolution algérienne', in: Djerbal, Daho (ed.): *Décembre 1960. Le Dien Bien Phu politique de la guerre d'Algérie* (Algiers: NAQD, July 2010); pp. 27–62.

———: 'External and Internal Factors of the Crisis in Africa', in: *African Development Perspectives Yearbook*, 15 (2011); pp. 59–88.

———: 'The Rise of New Cultural Identitarian Movements in Africa and Asia in the Emerging Multipolar System', in: *Comparative Studies of South Asia, Africa and the Middle East* (2012); pp. 642–661.

———; Junne, Gerd: 'Zu den Hintergründen der gegenwärtigen Ölkrise', in: *Blätter für deutsche und internationale Politik*, 18, 12 (December 1973); pp. 1305–1317.

———; Kleiner, Elmar; Dreves, Reinhart Joachim: *Développement, équité et extension du marché des masses. Une autre alternative. Le cas algérien. L'enjeu des PME industrielles* (Paris: Publisud, 2000).

———; Kleiner, Elmar; Dreves, Reinhart Joachim: *Gleichheit, Markt, Profit, Wachstum. Kleinindustrie und Expansion des Massenmarkts mit einer Untersuchung aus Algerien* (Hamburg: Deutsches Übersee-Institut, 2001).

———; Olschewski, Margit: 'Der Fall Kaffee. Rohstoffpreissteigerung oder Fortsetzung der Armut durch UNCTAD', in: *Dritte-Welt-Magazin*, 14, 1 (January–February 1976); pp. 8–17.

———; Werde-Bräuniger, Claudia: 'Die Auseinandersetzungen zwischen den Förderländern und den Ölkonzernen', in: Elsenhans, Hartmut (ed.): *Erdöl für Europa* (Hamburg: Hoffmann & Campe, 1974); pp. 84–131.

Eltis, David; Jennings, Lawrence C.: 'Trade between Western Africa and the Atlantic World in the Pre-Colonial Era', in: *American Historical Review*, 93, 4 (October 1988); pp. 936–959.

Eltis, Walter: 'The Contasting Theories of Industrialization of François Quesnay and Adam Smith', in: *Oxford Economic Papers*, 40, 3 (June 1988); pp. 269–288.

Emigh, Rebecca Jean: 'Economic Interests and Sectoral Relations: The Undevelopment of Capitalism in Fifteenth-Century Tuscany', in: *American Journal of Sociology*, 108, 5 (March 2003); pp. 1075–1113.

Emmanuel, Arghiri: *L'échange inégal. Essai sur les antagonismes dans les rapports économiques internationaux* (Paris: Maspéro, 1969).

Emmanuel, Arghiri: *Technologie appropriée ou technologie sous-développée? Suivi d'une discussion avec Celso Furtado et Hartmut Elsenhans* (Paris: Presses Universitaires de France, 1981).

Emmer, Pieter C.: 'Engeland, Nederland, Afrika en de Sklavenhandel en de Negentiende Eeuw', in: *Economisch en sociaal-historisch Jaarboek*, 36 (1973); pp. 146–215.

———: 'Surinam and the Decline of the Dutch Slave Trade', in: *Revue française d'histoire d'outre-mer*, 62, 226–227 (January–June 1975); pp. 245–251.

Engels, Friedrich: 'Über den Verfall des Feudalismus und das Aufkommen der Bourgeoisie [1884]', in: Marx, Karl; Engels, Friedrich: *Marx Engels Werke. Band 21* (Berlin: Dietz, 1972); pp. 392–401.

Engelsing, Rolf: 'Probleme der Lebenshaltung in Deutschland im 18. und 19. Jahrhundert', in: *Zeitschrift für die gesamte Staatswissenschaft/Journal of Institutional and Theoretical Economics*, 126, 2 (1970); pp. 290–308.

Engerman, Stanley L.; Sokoloff, Kenneth L.: 'The Evolution of Suffrage Institutions in the New World', in: *Journal of Economic History*, 65, 4 (December 2005); pp. 891–921.

Epperlein, Siegfried: 'Bündnisses zwischen Bauern und Bürgern in Nordwestdeutschland im 13. Jahrhundert', in: *Jahrbuch für Wirtschaftsgeschichte*, 3, 1 (1962); pp. 69–91.

Erbe, René: *Die nationalsozialistische Wirtschaftspolitik, 1933–1939 im Lichte der modernen Theorie* (Zurich: Polygraphischer, 1958).

Erber, Georg; Sayed-Ahmed, Amid: 'Offshore Outsourcing. A Global Shift in the Present IT Industry', in: *Intereconomics*, 40, 2 (March/April 2005); pp. 100–112.

Erdmann, Gero: 'Hoffnung für die Demokratisierung in Afrika?: Stand und Perspektiven', in: *Journal für Entwicklungspolitik*, 16, 2 (2000); pp. 111–127.

Erdmann, Karl Dietrich: 'Die geschichtliche Lage des Kommunismus in Indien', in: *Vierteljahrshefte für Zeitgeschichte*, 12, 2 (April 1964); pp. 170–200.

Ertl, Thomas: 'Mediävistik und Chinahistorie', in: *Zeitschrift für Weltgeschichte*, 7, 2 (2006); pp. 9–34.

Esping-Andersen, Gøsta: 'Towards a Postindustrial Welfare State', in: *Internationale Politik und Gesellschaft*, 3 (1997); pp. 236–245.

Esteban, Javier Cuenca: 'The Rising Share of British Industrial Exports in Industrial Output, 1700–1851', in: *Journal of Economic History*, 57, 4 (December 1997); pp. 879–906.

Esthus, Raymond A.: 'The Changing Concept of Open Door, 1899–1910', in: *Mississippi Valley Historical Review*, 46, 3 (December 1959); pp. 435–454.

Estudillo, Jonna P.; Otsuka, Keijiro: 'Lessons from Three Decades of Green Revolution in the Philippines', in: *Developing Economies*, 44, 2 (June 2006); pp. 123–148.

Etienne, Bruno: *L'islamisme radical* (Paris: Hachette, 1987).

Ettl, Harald: 'Der Welttextilmarkt. Entwicklung—Struktur—multinationale Macht', in: *Informationen über Multinationale Konzerne*, 82, 3 (1982); pp. 4–8.

Evaluation of Performance of Industrial Public Enterprises: Criteria and Policies. UNIDO/IS. 382. 27 April 1983 (Vienna: United Nations Industrial Development Organization, April 1983).

Evans, Peter B.: 'Multinationals, State-Owned Corporations and the Transformation of Imperialism: A Brazilian Case Study', in: *Economic Development and Cultural Change*, 26, 1 (October 1977); pp. 43–64.

Evers, Hans-Dieter: 'Trade and State Formation: Siam in the Early Bangkok Period', in: *Modern Asian Studies*, 21, 4 (November 1987); pp. 751–771.

Fabricant, Solomon: *The Output of Manufacturing Industries, 1899–1937* (New York: NBER, 1940).

———: *Basic Facts on Productivity Changes. Occasional Paper 63* (New York: National Bureau of Economic Research, 1959).

Facchini, François: 'L'invention des institutions de la liberté en Europe: la fragmentation politique et territoriale et la religion', in: *Economie appliquée*, 61, 1 (March 2008); pp. 71–106.

Fagerberg, Jan: 'Technological Progress, Structural Change and Productivity Growth: A Comparative Study', in: *Structural Change and Economic Dynamics*, 11, 4 (December 2000); pp. 393–411.

Fairbank, John K.: 'China's Response to the West: Problems and Suggestions', in: *Cahiers d'histoire mondiale* (1956); pp. 381–406

Faksh, Mahmud A.: 'The Alawi Community of Syria: A New Dominant Political Force', in: *Middle Eastern Studies*, 20, 1 (January 1984); pp. 133–153.

Fall, Babacar: 'Le travail forcé en Afrique Occidentale Française', in: *Civilisations*, 41, 1–2 (1993); pp. 329–336.

Fanon, Frantz: *The Wretched of the Earth* (New York: Grove Press, 1965).

Fareed, A.E.: 'Formal Schooling and the Human-Capital Intensity of American Foreign Trade: A Cost Approach', in: *Economic Journal*, 82, 326 (Juni 1972); S. 629–640.

Fasseur, C.: 'A Cheque Drawn on a Failing Bank: The Adress Delivered by Queen Wilhelmina on 6th/7th December 1942', in: *Acta Historiae Neerlandicae*, 15 (1982); pp. 102–116.

Fasseur, C.; Koeff, D.H.A.: 'Some Remarks on the Development of Colonial Bureaucracies in India and Indonesia', in: *Itinerario*, 18, 1 (1996); pp. 31–56.

Fassin, Didier: 'Les économies morales revisitées', in: *Annales. Histoire, Sciences Sociales*, 64, 6 (November–December 2009); pp. 1237–1267.

Fatton, Robert: 'Africa in the Age of Democratization: The Civic Limitations of Civil Society', in: *African Studies Review*, 38, 2 (September 1995); pp. 67–99.

Faujas, Alain: 'Que ferions-nous sans la Chine?', in: *Le Monde* (4 January 2008); p. 2.

Faust, Konrad: 'Ifo-Patentstatistik: Deutsche Unternehmen bleiben hinter ihren Konkurrenten aus den USA und Japan zurück', in: *IFO-Schnelldienst*, 46, 31 (November 1993); pp. 14–21.

Fay, Chin Kok; Nordhaug, Kristen: 'Why are There Differences in the Resilience of Malaysia and Taiwan to Financial Crisis?', in: *European Journal of Development Research*, 14, 1 (June 2002); pp. 77-100.

Fayard, Janinies; Gerbert, Marie-Claude: 'Fermeture de la noblesse et pureté de sang en Castille à travers les procès de hidalguía au XVIe siècle', in: *Histoire, économie et société*, 1, 2 (1982); pp. 51-76.

Feenstra, Robert C.: 'Integration of Trade and Disintegration of Production in the Global Economy', in: *Journal of Economic Perspectives*, 12, 4 (Autumn 1998); pp. 31-50.

Fei, John C.H.; Ranis, Gustav: *Development of a Labor Surplus Economy. Theory and Policy* (Homewood, Ill.: Irwin, 1964).

Felix, David: 'Monetarists, Structuralists and Import Substituting Industrialization. A Critical Appraisal', in: *Studies in Comparative International Development*, 1, 10 (October 1965); pp. 137-153.

Ferguson, Niall: *Empire: The Rise and Demise of the British World Order and the Lessons for Global Power*. (New York: Basic Books, 2002).

Fernandes, Leela: *India's New Middle Class. Democratic Politics in an Era of Economic Reform* (Minneapolis/London: University of Minnesota Press, 2006).

Fernandez, Aloysius P.: 'NGO's in South Asia: People's Participation and Partnership', in: *World Development*, 15 (1987); pp. 39-49.

Fernando, M.R.: 'Famine in a Land of Plenty: Plight of a Rice-growing Community in Java, 1883-1884', in: *Journal of Southeast Asian Studies*, 41, 2 (June 2010); pp. 291-320.

Feuerwerker, Albert: *China's Early Industrialisation* (Cambridge, Mass.: Harvard University Press, 1958).

————: 'Handicraft and Manufactured Cotton Textiles in China, 1871-1910', in: *Journal of Economic History*, 30, 2 (June 1970); pp. 338-378.

Field, Alexander James: 'Land Abundance, Interest/Profit Rates, and Nineteenth-Century American and British Technology', in: *Journal of Economic History*, 43, 2 (June 1983); pp. 405-431.

Fieldhouse, David K.: *Merchant Capital and Economic Decolonization. The United Africa Company, 1929-1987* (Oxford: Clarendon, 1994).

Fine, Ben; Waeyenberge, Elisa van: 'Correcting Stiglitz: from Information to Power in the World of Development', in: *Socialist Register*, 42 (2006); pp. 146-168.

Fine, Robert: 'Civil Society Theory and the Politics of Transition in South Africa', in: *Review of African Political Economy*, 20, 55 (November 1992); pp. 71-84.

Fischer, Claude S.; Carroll, Glenn R.: 'Telephone and Automobile Diffusion in the United States, 1902-1937', in: *American Journal of Sociology*, 93, 5 (March 1988); pp. 1153-1178.

Fisher, Humphrey J.: '"He Swalloweth the Ground with Fierceness and Rage": The Horse in the Central Sudan(1): Its Introduction', in: *Journal of African History*, 13, 3 (1972); pp. 369-388.

Fitzgerald, John: 'The Misconceived Revolution, State and Society in China's Nationalist Revolution, 1923-1926', in: *Journal of Asian Studies*, 49, 2 (May 1990); pp. 323-343.

———: 'Warlords, Bullies, and State Building in Nationalist China: The Guangdong Cooperative Movement, 1932-1936', in: *Modern China*, 23, 4 (October 1997); pp. 420-458.

Forsyth, Peter J.; Nicholas, Stephen J.: 'The Decline of Spanish Industry and the Price Revolution: A Neoclassical Analysis', in: *Journal of European Economic History*, 12, 3 (Winter 1983); pp. 601-610.

Foster, Andrew D.; Rosenzweig, Mark R.: 'Learning by Doing and Learning from Others: Human Capital and Technical Change in Agriculture', in: *Journal of Political Economy*, 110, 6 (1995); pp. 1176-1209.

Foster, John Bellamy: 'A Failed System', in: *Monthly Review*, 60, 10 (March 2009); pp. 1-29.

Fowler, Alan: 'NGDOs as a Moment in History: Beyond Aid to Social Entrepreneurship or Civic Innovation', in: *Third World Quarterly*, 21, 4 (August 2000); pp. 637-654.

Fox, Richard G.: 'Urban Class and Communal Consciousness in Colonial Punjab: The Genesis of India's Intermediate Regime', in: *Modern Asian Studies*, 18, 3 (August 1984); pp. 459-489.

Frank, André Gunder (published under Frank, Andrew Gunder): 'Mexico: The Janus Faces of 20th Century Bourgeois Revolution', in: *Monthly Review*, 14, 7 (November 1962); pp. 370-389.

———: 'Development and Underdevelopment in the New World: Smith and Marx Versus the Weberians', in: *Theory and Society*, 6, 4 (Winter 1975); pp. 431-466.

———: 'American Roulette in the Globonomic Casino: Retrospect and Prospect on the World Economic Crisis Today', in: Singer, Hans Wolfgang; Hatti, Neelamber; Tandon, Rameshwar (eds.): *Adjustment and Liberalization in the Third World* (New Delhi: Indus Publishing Company, 1991); pp. 191-242.

———: *ReOrient. Global Economy in the Asian Age* (Berkeley, Cal. et al.: University of California Press, 1998).

———; Gills, Barry K.: *The World System* (London: Routledge, 1993).

Frantzen, Dirk: 'Innovation, International Technological Diffusion and the Changing Influence of R&D on Productivity', in: *Cambridge Journal of Economics*, 24, 2 (March 2000); pp. 193-210.

Freeman, Richard; Schettkat, Ronald: 'Skill Compression, Wage Differentials, and Employment: Germany Vs the US', in: *Oxford Economic Papers*, 53, 3 (July 2001); pp. 582-603.

Fremdling, Rainer: 'Railroads and German Economic Growth: A Leading Sector Analysis with Comparison to the United States and Great Britain', in: *Journal of Economic History*, 36, 3 (September 1977); pp. 583-604.

Fremdling, Rainer; and Jong, Herman de; Timmer, Marcel P.: 'British and German Manufacturing Productivity Compared: A New Benchmark for 1935/36 Based on Double Deflated Value Added', in: *Journal of Economic History*, 67, 2 (June 2007); pp. 350–378.

Fritz, Rüdiger: 'Personality Types and the Application of Modern Technology: An Empirical Study of Attitudes to the Application of Modern Technology among a Future Elite in a West-African State', in: *Vierteljahresberichte der FES - Probleme der Entwicklungsländer*, 53 (September 1973); pp. 253–262.

Fuhr, Harald: *Bauern und Parteifunktionäre: eine Untersuchung zur politischen Dynamik des peruanischen Agrarsektors, 1969–1981* (Saarbrücken, Fort Lauderdale: Breitenbach, 1987).

Fukuchi, Takao/Satoh, Masayo: 'Technological Distance between Indonesia and Brazil: A Comparative Study of Technical Input Structures', in: *Developing Economies*, 37, 3 (September 1999); pp. 274–283.

Fukuyama, Francis: 'The End of History?', in: *National Interest*, 16 (Summer 1989); pp. 3–18.

Funke, Michael: 'Technikwahl und Profitrate. Ein kritischer Überblick über die augenblickliche Diskussion zum Gesetz des tendenziellen Falls der Profitrate', in: *Zeitschrift für Wirtschafts- und Sozialwissenschaften*, 104, 3 (1984); pp. 307–325.

Furtado, Celso: 'Development and Stagnation in Latin America: A Structuralist Approach', in: *Studies in Comparative International Development*, 1, 11 (November 1965); pp. 159–175.

———: 'Développement et stagnation en Amérique latine', in: *Annales. Economie, Société, Civilisation*, 21, 1 (January–February 1966); pp. 1–31.

Fusé, Toyosama: 'Cultural Values and Social Behaviour of the Japanese: A Comparative Analysis', in: *Civilisations*, 32, 1 (1982); pp. 97–132.

Gadgil, D.R.: *The Industrial Evolution of India in Recent Times 1860–1939* (Bombay: Oxford University Press, 1971).

Gafar, John: 'Devaluation and its Impact on the Demand for Imports in an Open Economy: The Case of Jamaica', in: *Indian Journal of Economics*, 63, 249 (October 1982); pp. 223–237.

Gaiha, Raghav: 'Impoverishment, Technology and Growth in Rural India', in: *Cambridge Journal of Economics*, 11, 1 (March 1987); pp. 23–46.

Gala, Paulo: 'Real Exchange Rate Levels and Economic Development: Theoretical Analysis and Econometric Evidence', in: *Cambridge Journal of Economics*, 32, 2 (March 2008); pp. 273–288.

Galeano, Eduardo: *Die offenen Adern Lateinamerikas. Die Geschichte eines Kontinents von der Entdeckung bis zur Gegenwart* (Wuppertal: Peter Hammer, 1973).

Galenson, David W.: 'The Rise and Fall of Indentured Servitude in the Americas: An Economic Analysis', in: *Journal of Economic History*, 44, 1 (1984); pp. 1–26.

Gallagher, John; Robinson, Ronald: 'The Imperialism of Free Trade', in: *Economic History Review*, 6, 3 (1953); pp. 1–15.

Gallissot, René: 'Lutte de classes et Etat national social', in: *Homme et la société*, 117–118 (July–December 1995); pp. 81–89.

Galtung, Johan: '"A Structural Theory of Imperialism"—Ten Years Later', in: *Millennium: Journal of International Studies*, 9, 3 (Winter 1980); pp. 183–196.

Gambarotto, Francesca; Solari, Stefano: 'Regional Dispersion of Economic Activities and Models of Capitalism in Europe', in: *Economie appliquée*, 62, 1 (March 2009); pp. 5–38.

Gardner, Lloyd C.: *Economic Aspects of New Deal Diplomacy* (Madison, Wis.: The University of Wisconsin Press, 1964).

———: 'The American "Cause" in Vietnam, 1941–1965', in: *Itinerario*, 22, 3 (1998); pp. 59–78.

Gascon, Richard: *Grand Commerce et vie urbaine au XVIe siècle. Lyon et ses marchands (des environs de 1520 aux environs de 1580)* (Paris; The Hague: Mouton, 1971).

Gause, F. Gregory III: 'Urgent: How to Reform Saudi Arabia without Handing It to Extremists', in: *Foreign Policy*, 144 (September/October 2004); pp. 66–70.

Geary, Dick: 'Working-Class Identities in Europe, 1850s–1930s', in: *Australian Journal of Politics and History*, 45, 1 (March 1999); pp. 20–34.

Gehlen, Arnold: *Der Mensch. Seine Natur und seine Stellung in der Welt* (Königstein, Taunus: Athenäum, 1962).

Gehler, Michael; Kaiser, Wolfram: 'Transnationalism and Early European Integration: The Nouvelles Equipes Internationales and the Geneva Circle 1947–1957', in: *Historical Journal*, 44, 3 (2001); pp. 773–796.

Geiss, Heinz: 'Die kretisch-mykenische Kultur: Aufstieg und Untergang', in: *Ethnographisch-Archäologische Zeitschrift*, 21, 4 (1980); pp. 567–581.

Gerbier, Bernard: *L'impérialisme géoéconomique: Stade actuel du capitalisme* (Grenoble: MS, 1999).

Geremek, Bronislaw: *La potence ou la pitié: L'Europe et les pauvres du Moyen Age à nos jours* (Paris: Gallimard, 1987).

Gerfin, Harald: 'Die interindustrielle Lohnstruktur in der Bundesrepublik Deutschland. Neue Tendenzen und ihre möglichen Ursachen', in: *Jahrbücher für Nationalökonomie und Statistik*, 192, 2 (1977); pp. 127–147.

Gericke, Horst: 'Zur Dialektik von Produktivkraft und Produktionsverhältnis im Feudalismus', in: *Zeitschrift für Geschichtswissenschaft*, 14, 5 (1966); pp. 914–932.

Gerstenberger, Wolfgang: 'Wachstum ohne Jobs in Europa: Wo liegen die Ursachen?', in: *IFO-Schnelldienst*, 52, 7 (March 1999); pp. 10–19

Geyer, Dietrich: 'Die russische Revolution als zeitgeschichtliches Problem', in: *Vierteljahrshefte für Zeitgeschichte*, 16, 1 (January 1968); pp. 36–47.

Ghose, Ajit Kumar; Griffin, Keith: 'Rural Poverty and Development Alternatives in South and Southeast Asia', in: *Development and Change*, 11, 4 (October 1980); pp. 545–572.
Ghosh, D.N.: 'FDI and Reform. Significance and Relevance of Chinese Experience', in: *Economic and Political Weekly*, 40, 51 (17 December 2005); pp. 5388–5392.
Ghosh, Peter: 'Some Problems with Talcott Parsons', in: *Archives Européennes de Sociologie*, 35, 1 (1994); pp. 104–126.
Ghosh, Suniti Kumar: 'Indian Bourgeoisie and Imperialism', in: *Economic and Political Weekly*, 23, 45/47 (November 1988); pp. 2445–2458.
Gibson, Charles: 'Colonial Institutions and Contemporary Latin America: Social and Cultural Life', in: *Hispanic American Historical Review*, 43, 3 (August 1963); pp. 380–389.
Giersch, Herbert: 'Probleme stabilitätskonformer Lohnpolitik', in: *Kyklos*, 20, 1 (1967); pp. 146–165.
———: 'Arbeit, Lohn und Produktivität', in: *Weltwirtschaftliches Archiv*, 119, 1 (1983); pp. 1–18.
Gifford, Paul: 'Christian Fundamentalism and Development', in: *Review of African Political Economy*, 19, 52 (November 1991); pp. 9–20.
Gilbert, Dennis L.: *The Oligarchy and the Old Regime in Peru* (Ithaca, N.Y.: Ph.D. Diss., 1977).
Gilboy, Elizabeth Waterman: 'Demand as a Factor in the Industrial Revolution', in: Cole, Arthur H.; Dunham, A.L.; Gras, N.S.B. (eds): *Facts and Factors in Economic History* (New York: Russell & Russell, 1932); pp. 620–639.
———: 'Time Series and the Derivation of Demand and Supply Curves. A Study of Coffee and Tea', in: *Quarterly Journal of Economics*, 48, 3 (August 1934); pp. 667–685.
Gillin, Donald G.: '"Peasant Nationalism" in the History of Chinese Communism', in: *Journal of Asian Studies*, 23, 2 (February 1964); pp. 269–289.
Gilman, Antonio: 'The Development of Social Stratification in Bronze Age Europe', in: *Current Anthropology*, 22, 1 (February 1981); pp. 1–8.
Glotz, Peter: 'Kritik der Entschleunigung', in: *Neue Gesellschaf*(1999); pp. 621–628.
Godelier, Maurice: 'Infrastructures, Societes and History', in: *Current Anthropology*, 19, 4 (December 1978); pp. 763–770.
Godfrey, Martin: 'Trade and Exchange Rate Policy in Subsaharan Africa', in: *IDS Bulletin*, 16, 3 (July 1985); pp. 31–38.
Goguel, Francois: *La politique des partis sous la IIIe République* (Paris: Seuil, 1946).
Goh, Gavin: 'The World Trade Organization, Kyoto and Energy Tax Adjustments at the Border', in: *Journal of World Trade*, 38, 3 (2004); pp. 395–423.
Gohain, Hiren: 'Positions on Assam History', in: *Economic and Political Weekly*, 45, 8 (20th February 2010); pp. 37–42.

Goldberg, Pinelopi Koujianou; Knetter, Michael M.: 'Goods Prices and Exchange Rates: What Have We Learned?', in: *Journal of Economic Literature*, 35, 3 (September 1997); pp. 1243–1272.

Goldenberg, Boris: 'Der Kommunismus in Chile', in: *Vierteljahresberichte der FES: Ostblock und die Entwicklungsländer*, 26 (December 1966); pp. 377–397.

Goldmann, Lucien: *Weltflucht und Politik* (Neuwied: Luchterhand, 1967).

Goldschmidt, Walter: 'The Structure of the Peasant Family', in: *American Anthropologist*, 73, 5 (October 1971); pp. 1058–1076.

Goldstone, Jack A.: 'The Rise of the West—Or Not? A Revision to Socio-economic History', in: *Sociological Theory*, 18, 2 (2000); pp. 175–194.

———: 'Efflorescences and Economic Growth in World History: Rethinking the "Rise of the West" and the Industrial Revolution', in: *Journal of World History*, 13, 2 (Autumn 2002); pp. 323–389.

Goldthwaite, Richard A.: 'The Florentine Wool Industry in the Late Sixteenth Century. A Case Study', in: *Journal of European Economic History*, 32, 3 (Winter 2003); pp. 527–554.

Gommans, Jos: 'The Eurasian Frontier After the First Millennium A.D.: Reflections Along the Fringe of Time and Space', in: *Medieval History Journal*, 1, 1 (Spring 1998); pp. 125–143.

Gompers, Paul; Leiner, Josh: 'The Venture Capital Revolution', in: *Journal of Economic Perspectives*, 15, 2 (Spring 2001); pp. 145–168.

Gongora, Mario: 'Urban Social Stratification in Colonial Chile', in: *Hispanic American Historical Review*, 55, 3 (August 1975); pp. 431–448.

Goode, Richard; Lent, George E.; Ohja, P.D.: 'The Role of Export Taxes in Developing Countries', in: *IMF Staff Papers*, 13, 3 (November 1966); pp. 453–502.

Goodell, Grace E.: 'Paternalism, Patronage, and Potlatch: The Dynamics of Giving and Being Given To', in: *Current Anthropology*, 26, 2 (April 1985); pp. 247–266.

Goody, Jack: 'Feudalism in Africa', in: *Journal of African History*, 4, 1 (1963); pp. 1–18.

Goonatilake, Susantha: *Recolonisation: Foreign Funded NGOs in Sri Lanka* (Beverly Hills, Cal.; London; New Delhi: Sage, 2006).

Gordon, Alec: 'North Vietnam's Collectivization Compaigns: Class Struggle, Production and the Middle Peasant Problem', in: *Journal of Contemporary Asia*, 11, 3 (1981); pp. 19–43.

Gordon, Robert J.: *Has the 'New Economy' Rendered the Productivity Slowdown Obsolete?* (Evanston, Ill.: MS, 1999a).

———: *U.S. Economic Growth since 1870: One Big Wave? Revised Version of Forthcoming Paper in American Economic Review, May 1999* (Evanston, Ill.: MS, 1999b).

Gordon R., Sara: 'La cultura política de las organizaciones no gubernamentales en México', in: *Revista Mexicana de Sociología*, 59, 1 (January–March 1997); pp. 53–67.

Gosovic, Branislav; Ruggie, John Gerard: 'On the Creation of a New International Economic Order: Issue Linkage and the Seventh Special Session of the U.N. General Assembly', in: *International Organization*, 30, 2 (Spring 1976); pp. 309–345.

Gossaert, Vincent: 'Bureaucratie, taxation et justice.Taoisme et construction de l'Etat au Jiangnan (Chine), XVII-XIX siècle', in: *Annales. Histoire, Sciences Sociales*, 65, 4 (July–August 2010); pp. 999–1027.

Goswami, Omkar: 'Agriculture in Slump:The Peasant Economy of East and North Bengal in the 1930s', in: *Indian Economic and Social History Review*, 21, 3 (July–September 1984); pp. 335–364.

Goto, Ken'ichi: 'Impuls und Erbe der japanischen Militärherrschaft in Indonesien', in: *Zeitschrift für Geschichtswissenschaft*, 47, 2 (1999); pp. 109–128.

Gottlieb, Roger S.: 'Feudalism and Historical Materialism: A Critique and Synthesis', in: *Science and Society*, 48, 1 (Spring 1984); pp. 1–37.

Gough, Kathleen: 'The Indian Revolutionary Potential', in: *Monthly Review*, 20, 9 (February 1969); pp. 22–35.

———: 'Colonial Economics in Southeast India', in: *Economic and Political Weekly*, 12, 13 (26 March 1977); pp. 541–552.

Gould, J.D.: 'The Price Revolution Reconsidered', in: *Economic History Review*, 17, 2 (1964); pp. 249–266.

Gould, William: 'Congress Radicals and Hindu Militancy: Sampurnand and Purushottam. Das Tandon in the Politics of the United Provinces 1930–1947', in: *Modern Asian Studies*, 36, 3 (July 2002); pp. 619–655.

———: *Hindu Nationalism and the Language of Politics in Late Colonial India* (Cambridge et al.: Cambridge University Press, 2004).

Gowan, Peter: 'Causing the Credit Crunch: The Rise and Consequences of the New Wall Street System', in: *Journal für Entwicklungspolitik*, 25, 1 (2009); pp. 18–43.

Grabowski, Richard: 'Agriculture, Mechanisation and Land Tenure', in: *Journal of Development Studies*, 27, 1 (October 1990); pp. 43–53.

———: 'East Asian Industrialisation and Agriculture', in: *Journal of Asian Economics*, 4, 1 (Spring 1993); pp. 41–58.

———: 'European and East-Asian Exceptionalism: Agriculture and Economic Growth', in: *Journal of International Development*, 6, 4 (July–August 1994); pp. 437–451.

———: 'Development, Market and Trust', in: *Journal of International Development*, 10, 3 (May/June 1998); pp. 357–371.

Graf, Dieter: *Produktivkräfte und nichtkapitalistischer Weg* (Berlin: Akademie-Verlag, 1973).

Grandguillaume, Gilbert: 'L'enseignement au Maghreb', in: *Maghreb-Machrek/Monde Arabe*, 78 (October–December 1977); pp. 34–43.

Gray, Kevin: 'Challenges to the Theory and Practice of Polyarchy: The Rise of the Political Left in Korea', in: *Third World Quarterly*, 29, 1 (2008); pp. 107–124.
Green, Fletcher M.: 'Cycles of American Democracy', in: *Mississippi Valley Historical Review*, 48, 1 (June 1961); pp. 1–23.
Green, Maia: 'Confronting Categorical Assumptions About the Power of Religion in Africa', in: *Review of African Political Economy*, 33, 110 (December 2006); pp. 635–650.
Green, Reginald Herbold: 'The Role of the State as an Agent of Economic and Social Development in the Least Developed Countries', in: *Journal of Development Planning*, 6 (1974); pp. 1–39.
Greenfield, Gerard: 'Bandung Redux: Imperialism and Anti-Globalization Nationalism in Southern Asian', in: *Socialist Register*, 41 (2005); pp. 166–196.
Gregory, James R.: 'Image of Limited Good or Expectation of Reciprocity', in: *Current Anthropology*, 16, 1 (March 1975); pp. 73–83.
Gregory, Mary; Zissimos, Ben; Greenhalgh, Christine: 'Jobs for the Skilled: How Technology, Trade, and Domestic Demand Changed the Structure of UK Employment, 1979–90', in: *Oxford Economic Papers*, 53, 1 (January 2001); pp. 20–46.
Griliches, Zvi: 'The Discovery of the Residual. A Historical Note', in: *Journal of Economic Literature*, 34, 3 (September 1996); pp. 1324–1330.
Grischow, Jeff D.; McKnight, Glenn H.: 'The Power of Social Capital: Historical Studies from Colonial Uganda and the Gold Coast', in: *Canadian Journal of African Studies*, 42, 1 (2008); pp. 98–128.
Grobart, Fabio: 'The Cuban Working Class Movement from 1925 to 1933', in: *Science and Society*, 39, 1 (Spring 1975); pp. 73–103.
Groff, Ruth: 'Class Politics by any Other Name: Organizing the Unemployed', in: *Studies in Political Economy*, 54 (Autumn 1997); pp. 91–118.
Grossman, Gene M.; Helpman, Elhanan: 'Product Development and International Trade', in: *Journal of Political Economy*, 97, 6 (December 1989); pp. 1261–1283.
———: 'Endogenous Innovation in the Theory of Growth', in: *Journal of Economic Perspectives*, 8, 1 (Winter 1994); pp. 23–44.
Grübler, Arnulf: *Technology and Global Change* (Cambridge et al.: Cambridge University Press, 2003).
Gu, Wei: 'A court terme, une réévaluation massive du yuan est impossible', in: *Le Monde*, 16 April 2010); p. 17.
Guha, Sumit: 'Theatre State or Box Office State? A Note on the Political Economy of Eiteenth-Century India', in: *Indian Economic and Social History Review*, 31, 4 (1994); pp. 519–528.
———: 'Civilisations, Markets and Services: Village Servants in India from the Seventeenth to the Twentieth Centuries', in: *Indian Economic and Social History Review*, 41, 1 (January–March 2004); pp. 79–101.

Guillaumont-Jeanneney, Sylviane; Hua, Ping: 'Politique du change et développement des exportations manufacturées en Chine', in: *Revue économique*, 47, 3 (May 1996); pp. 851–860.

Gujral, Surinder S.: 'New Evidence in Indian Nineteenth Century Family Budgetary Structures', in: *Indian Economic Journal*, 27, 4 (April–June 1980); pp. 1–11.

Gunasekaran, S.: 'Cattle Raiding and Heroic Tradition: Sedentary Pastoralism in Upland Tamil Nadu (Sixth to Tenth Century CE)', in: *Indian Historical Review*, 34, 1 (January 2007); pp. 91–124.

Gupta, M.L.: 'Outflow of High-Level Manpower from the Philippines, with Special Reference to the Period 1965–1971', in: *International Labour Review*, 107, 2 (February 1973); pp. 167–191.

Gurukkat, Rajan: 'Shift of Trust from Words to Deeds: Implications of the Proliferation of Epigraphs in the Tamil South', in: *Indian Historical Review*, 34, 2 (July 2007); pp. 16–35.

Gustafsson, Björn; Zhong, Wei: 'How and Why has Poverty in China Changed? A Study Based on Microdata for 1988 and 1995.', in: *China Quarterly*, 164 (December 2000); pp. 983–1006.

Guttmann, Robert: 'Die strategische Rolle der Pensionsfonds', in: *Prokla: Zeitschrift für kritische Sozialwissenschaft*, 28, 113 (December 1998); pp. 643–650.

Haarmann, Ulrich: 'Die Sphynx. Synkretische Volksreligiösität im spätmittelalterlichen islamischen Ägypten', in: *Saeculum*, 29, 4 (Winter 1978); pp. 366–384.

Habib, Irfan: 'Changes in Technology in Medieval India', in: *Studies in History*, 2, 1 (1980); pp. 15–39.

———: 'Classifying Pre-Colonial India', in: *Journal of Peasant Studies*, 12, 2/3 (January–April 1985a); pp. 44–53.

———: 'Studying a Colonial Economy—Without Perceiving Colonialism', in: *Modern Asian Studies*, 19, 3 (1985b); pp. 355–381.

———: *Essays in Indian History: Towards a Marxist Perception* (New Delhi: Tulika, 1995).

Haggard, Stephan Mark: *Pathways from the Periphery: The Newly Industrializing Countries in the International System* (Berkeley, Cal.: Ph.D. Diss., 1983).

Haipeter, Thomas; Banyuls, Josep: 'Arbeit in der Defensive? Globalisierung und die Beziehungen zwischen Arbeit und Kapital in der Automobilindustrie', in: *Leviathan*, 35, 3 (September 2007); pp. 373–400.

Håkansson, N. Thomas: 'Rulers and Rainmakers in Precolonial South Pare, Tanzania: Exchange and Ritual Experts in Political Centralization', in: *Ethnology*, 37, 3 (Summer 1998); pp. 263–283.

Halbach, Axel J.: 'Multinationale Unternehmen in der Dritten Welt—Ihr Beitrag zur Entwicklung des industriellen Zulieferwesens', in: *IFO-Schnelldienst*, 38, 1/2 (January 1985); pp. 33–40.

Hall, John A.: 'Religion and the Rise of Capitalism', in: *Archives Européennes de Sociologie*, 26, 1 (1985); pp. 193–223.

Hall, Kenneth R.: 'Peasant, State and Society in Chola Times: A View from the Tiruvidaimaradur Urban Complex', in: *Indian Economic and Social History Review*, 18, 3/4 (July–September 1981); pp. 394–410.

Hallett, Robin: *Africa to 1875. A Modern History* (East Lansing, Mich.: University of Michigan Press, 1970).

Hallgarten, George Wolfgang F.: 'War Bismarck ein Imperialist? Die Außenpolitik des Reichsgründers im Licht der Gegenwart', in: *Geschichte in Wissenschaft und Unterricht*, 22, 5 (1971); pp. 257–265.

Halpern, Manfred: 'Egypt and the New Middle Class: Reaffirmations and New Explorations', in: *Comparative Studies in Society and History*, 11, 1 (January 1969); pp. 97–108.

Hamilton, Earl J.: 'The Decline of Spain', in: *Economic History Review*, 8, 2 (May 1938); pp. 168–179.

———: 'Profit Inflation and the Industrial Revolution 1751–1800', in: *Quarterly Journal of Economics*, 56, 2 (February 1942); pp. 256–273.

Hamilton, Nora Louise: 'Mexico: The Limits of State Autonomy', in: *Latin American Perspectives*, 2, 2 (Summer 1975); pp. 81–108.

Hamm, Frank: 'Buddhismus und Jinismus. Zwei Typen indischer Religiösität und ihr Weg in die Geschichte', in: *Saeculum*, 15, 1 (1964); pp. 41–56.

Hammarström, Ingrid: 'The Price Revolution in the Sixteenth Century: Some Swedish Evidence', in: *Scandinavian Economic History Review*, 5, 2 (1957); pp. 118–154.

Hammouda, N.E.: 'Enquête main d'oeuvre et démographie', in: *Statistique*, 5 (October–December 1984); pp. 61–76.

Hampton, Mark P.; Christensen, John: 'Offshore Pariahs? Small Island Economies, Tax Havens, and the Re-Configuration of Global Finance', in: *World Development*, 30, 9 (September 2002); pp. 1657–1673.

Hanes, Christopher: 'The Development of Nominal Wage Rigidity in the Late 19th Century', in: *American Economic Review*, 83, 4 (September 1993); pp. 732–746.

Hanf, Theodor: 'Erziehung und politischer Wandel in Schwarzafrika', in: *Kölner Zeitschrift für Sozialwissenschaft und Sozialpsychologie*, 21, 13 (1969); pp. 276–327.

Hanisch, Rolf: 'Nichtregierungsorganisationen und Demokratisierung in Südostasien', in: *Aus Politik und Zeitgeschichte*, 21–22 (May 2004); pp. 22–31

Hanson, Philip; Vogel, Heinrich: 'Technology Transfer between East and West: A Review of the Issues', in: *Osteuropa-Wirtschaft*, 23, 2 (June 1978); pp. 97–110.

Harhoff, Dietmar: 'Innovation, Entrepreneurship and Demographie', in: *Perspektiven der Wirtschaftspolitik*, 9, SH (2008); pp. 46–72.

Harms, Bernhard: *Deutschlands Anteil am Welthandel und Weltschiffahrt* (Stuttgart; Berlin; Leipzig: Union Deutsche Verlagsgesellschaft, 1916).

Harnetty, Peter: 'Cotton Exports and Indian Agriculture 1861–1970', in: *Economic History Review*, 24, 3 (1971); pp. 414–429.

———: '"Deindustrialization" Revisited: The Handloom Weavers of the Central Provinces of India c. 1800–1947', in: *Modern Asian Studies*, 25, 3 (August 1991); pp. 455–510.

Harnisch, Hartmut: 'Rechtsqualität des Bauernlandes und Gutsherrschaft. Probleme und Materialien einer vergleichenden und retrospektiven Auswertung von statistischen Massendaten aus dem 18. Jh und der Zeit der kapitalistischen Agrarreformen für die Agrar und Siedlungsgeschichte', in: *Jahrbuch für Geschichte des Feudalismus*, 3 (1979); pp. 311–363.

Harnischfeger, Johannes: 'Religion und Politik im nachmodernen Afrika', in: *Leviathan*, 33, 3 (September 2005); pp. 284–305.

Harris, G.T.; Bin Abdul Rashid, Zakariah: 'The Employment Performance of Developing Countries', in: *Developing Economies*, 24, 3 (September 1986); pp. 272–287.

Harris, Gerald: 'Political Society and the Growth of Government in Late Medieval England', in: *Past and Present*, 138 (February 1993); pp. 28–57.

Harrison, James P.: 'Communist Interpretations of Chinese Peasant Wars', in: *China Quarterly*, 6, 24 (December 1965); pp. 92–118.

Harrison, Royden: 'British Labour and the Confederacy', in: *International Review of Social History*, 2, 1 (1957); pp. 78–105.

Harriss, John: 'Antinomies of Empowerment: Observations on Civil Society, Politics and Urban Governance in India', in: *Economic and Political Weekly*, 42, 26 (30 June 2007); pp. 2716–2724.

Hartshorn, J.E.: *Oil Companies and Governments. An Account of the International Oil Industry in its Political Environment* (London: Faber & Faber, 1969).

Harvey, Charles; Press, Jon: 'The City and International Mining, 1870–1914', in: *Business History*, 32, 3 (July 1990); pp. 98–119.

Harvey, David: 'The "New" Imperialism: Accumulation by Dispossession', in: *Socialist Register*, 40 (2004); pp. 63–87.

Harvey, Ross: *Comparison of Household Saving Ratios: Euro Area, United States, Japan. OECD Statistics Briefs 4* (Paris: OECD, June 2004).

Hashemi, Syed M.: *NGOs in Bangladesh: Development Alternative or Alternative Rhetoric* (Manchester: University of Manchester, 1990).

Hashim, S.R.: 'Forty Years of Indian Economy: Structure and Dimensions of Growth', in: *Indian Economic Journal*, 38, 3 (January–March 1991); pp. 1–18.

Hatejar, Neeraj: 'Farmers and Markets in Pre-Colonial Deccan: The Plausibility of Economic Growth in Traditional Society', in: *Past and Present*, 178 (February 2003); pp. 116–147.

Haude, Rüdiger: 'Alphabet und Demokratie', in: *Saeculum*, 50, 1 (1999); pp. 1–28.

Hauser-Schäublin, Brigitta: 'The Precolonial Balinese State Reconsidered: A Critical Evaluation of Theory Construction on the Relation between Irrigation, the State and Ritual', in: *Current Anthropology*, 44, 2 (April 2003); pp. 155–169.

Havrylyshyn, Oli: 'Capital Intensity Biasis in Developing Country Technical Choice', in: *Journal of Development Economics*, 5, 3 (September 1978); pp. 215–231.

Hawthorn, Geoffrey: *Thinking about Third World Politics*. Paper presented at the International Conference on 'Political Institutions in the the Third World in the Process of Adjustment and Modernization' organized by DSE, Berlin, 4–7 July 1989 (Berlin; Bonn: Deutsche Stiftung für Internationale Entwicklung, 1989).

Hawtrey, Ralph George: *Trade Depression and the Way Out* (London; New York: Longman & Green, 1933)

Hayami, Yujiro: 'Rice Policy in Japan's Economic Development', in: *American Journal of Agricultural Economics*, 54, 1 (February 1972); pp. 19–31.

Hayek, Friedrich A. von: *The Pure Theory of Capital* (Chicago, Ill.: University of Chicago Press, 1941).

———: *Geldtheorie und Konjunkturtheorie* (Salzburg: Wolfgang Neugebauer, 1976).

Hayes, Carlton J.H.: 'Contributions of Herder to the Doctrine of Nationalism', in: *American Historical Review*, 32 (1927); pp. 719–736.

Headrick, Daniel R.: 'Botany, Chemistry, and Tropical Development', in: *Journal of World History*, 7, 1 (Autumn 1996); pp. 1–20.

Hearn, Julie: 'The "NGO-isation" of Kenyan Society: US AID and the Restructuring of Health Care', in: *Review of African Political Economy*, 25, 75 (January 1998); pp. 89–100.

———: 'The "Uses and Abuses" of Civil Society in Africa', in: *Review of African Political Economy*, 28, 87 (March 2001); pp. 43–53.

Heaton, Herbert: 'Financing the Industrial Revolution', in: *Bulletin of the Business Historical Society*, 11, 1 (February 1937); pp. 1–10.

Hechter, Michael: 'From Class to Culture', in: *American Journal of Sociology*, 110, 2 (September 2004); pp. 400–445.

Heesterman, J.C.: 'The "Hindu Frontier"', in: *Itinerario*, 13, 1 (1989); pp. 1–15.

Heipel, Gerd: *Nichtkapitalistische Produktionsverhältnisse und Konkurrenz-Die Entwicklung des Kapitalismus im Kaffeeesektor von São Paolo 1822–1967* (Pfaffenweiler: Centaurus, 1986).

Helmstädter, Ernst: *Der Kapitalkoeffizient. Eine kapitaltheoretische Untersuchung* (Stuttgart: Gustav Fischer, 1969).

Helpman, Elhanan: 'Increasing Returns, Imperfect Markets and Trade Theory', in: Jones, Ronald W.; Kenen, Peter B. (eds.): *Handbook of International Economics* (Amsterdam: Elsevier Science Publ., 1984); pp. 325–365.

———: 'Imperfect Competition and International Trade : Opening Remarks', in: *European Economic Review*, 31, 1–2 (February–March 1987); pp. 77–81.

———: 'The Structure of Foreign Trade', in: *Journal of Economic Perspectives*, 13, 2 (Spring 1999); pp. 121–144.

Henderson, Ian: 'The Origins of Nationalism in East and Central Africa: The Zambian Case', in: *Journal of African History*, 11, 4 (1970); pp. 591–603.

Henderson, William O.: 'Die Manufaktur in Deutschland im 18. Jahrhundert', in: *Jahrbücher für Nationalökonomie und Statistik*, 199, 6 (1984); pp. 586–602.

Hengsbach SJ., Friedhelm: *Gerechtigkeit und Solidarität im Schatten der Globalisierung. Handlungsoptionen reifer Volkswirtschaften. Policy Paper 26* (Bonn; Duisburg: Stiftung Entwicklung und Frieden, 2007).

Henley, David: 'Conflict, Justice, and the Stranger-King. Indigenous Roots of Colonial Rule in Indonesia and Elsewhere', in: *Modern Asian Studies*, 38, 1 (February 2004); pp. 85–144.

Hentsch, Thierry: 'L'orient méditerranéen du moyen âge chrétien: La rencontre de l'Islam', in: *Etudes internationales*, 17, 3 (September 1986); pp. 509–534.

Herbst, Jeffrey: 'Political Liberalization in Africa after Ten Years.', in: *Comparative Politics*, 33, 3 (April 2001); pp. 357–375.

Hess, Gary: 'Franklin Roosevelt and Indochina', in: *Journal of American History*, 59, 2 (September 1972); pp. 353–368.

Hesse, Helmut; Gahlen, Bernhard: 'Das Wachstum des Nettoinlandsprodukts in Deutschland, 1850–1913. Berechnung von makroökonomischen Produktionsfunktionen', in: *Zeitschrift für die gesamte Staatswissenschaft / Journal of Institutional and Theoretical Economics*, 121, 3 (1965); pp. 452–497.

Heßler, Martina: "Elektrische Helfer" für Hausfrau, Volk und Vaterland. Ein technisches Konsumgut während des Nationalsozialismus', in: *Technikgeschichte*, 68, 3 (2001); pp. 203–230.

Heuzé, Gérard: 'Les nationalistes hindous aux prises avec le développement: De l'homme nouveau au consommateur frustré', in: *Tiers Monde*, 40, 160 (1999); pp. 729–750.

———: (Published under Heuzé, Djallal Gérard): 'L'hindouisme nationalisé et internationalisé: Croyances. Avatars du religieux en Asie et en Amérique, in: *Tiers Monde*, 44, 173 (2003); pp. 99–126.

Hewett, Edward A.: 'The Economics of East European Technology Imports from the West', in: *American Economic Review*, 65, 2 (May 1975); pp. 377–382.

Heylen, Freddy; Goubert, Lucia; Omey, Eddy: 'Unemployment in Europe: A Problem of Relative or Aggregate Demand of Labour', in: *International Labour Review*, 135, 1 (1996); pp. 17–37.

Hild, Reinhard: 'Automobilindustrie: Stark reduzierte Wertschöpfungsrate und getrennte Produktionsentwicklung', in: *IFO-Schnelldienst*, 58, 20 (November 2005); pp. 39–46.

Hill, Christopher: *Reformation to Industrial Revolution. The Making of Modern English Society, 1530–1780* (New York: Pantheon Books, 1967).

Hill, Jonathan D.: 'Social Equality and Ritual Hierarchy: the Arawakan Wakuénai of Venezuela', in: *American Ethnologist*, 11, 3 (August 1984); pp. 528–544.

Hillman, John: 'The Emergence of the Tin Industry in Bolivia', in: *Journal of Latin American Studies*, 16, 2 (November 1984); pp. 403–437.

Hilton, Rodney H.: 'Peasant Movements in England Before 1381', in: *Economic History Review*, 2, 2 (1949); pp. 117–136.

———: 'A Crisis of Feudalism', in: *Past and Present*, 80 (August 1978); pp. 3–19.

Hindess, Barry; Hirst, Paul Q.: *Pre-Capitalist Modes of Production* (London; Boston, Mass.: Routledge & Kegan Paul, 1975).

Hintze, Otto: *Staat und Verfassung. Gesammelte Abhandlungen zur allgemeinen Verfassungsgeschichte* (Göttingen: Vandenhoeck & Ruprecht, 1962).

Hirschman, Albert O.: *The Strategy of Economic Development* (New Haven, Conn.: Yale University Press, 1958).

Ho, Tsung-Wo: 'Income Thresholds and Growth Convergence: A Panel Data Approach', in: *Manchester School of Economic and Social Studies*, 74, 2 (March 2006); pp. 170–189.

Hobsbawm, Eric John: *Sozialrebellen. Archaische Sozialbewegungen im 19. und 20. Jahrhundert* (Neuwied: Luchterhand, 1962).

———: *Industry and Empire* (Harmondsworth: Penguin, 1968).

Hobson, John Atkinson: *Imperialism. A Study* (London: Allen & Unwin, 1938).

Hocquet, J.C.: 'Capitalisme marchand et classe marchande à Venise au temps de la Renaissance', in: *Annales. Economie, Société, Civilisation*, 34, 2 (March–April 1979); pp. 279–304.

Hodgkin, Thomas: 'Islam and National Movements in West Africa', in: *Journal of African History*, 3, 2 (1962); pp. 323–327.

Hoffmann, Stanley: *Gulliver's Troubles oder die Zukunft des internationalen Systems* (Gütersloh: Bertelsmann, 1970).

Hoffmann, Walter G.: 'Die Entwicklung von Kapitalkoeffizient und Lohnquote im wirtschaftlichen Wachstum', in: *Jahrbücher für Nationalökonomie und Statistik*, 180, 2/3 (March–April 1967); pp. 179–210.

———: 'Der tertiäre Sektor im Wachstumsprozeß', in: *Jahrbücher für Nationalökonomie und Statistik*, 183, 1 (1969); pp. 1–29.

Hojman, David E.: 'Why the Latin American Debtor Countries will Never Form a Debtor's Cartel', in: *Kyklos*, 40, 2 (1987); pp. 198–218.

Hoksbergen, Roland; Madrid, Noemí Espinoza: 'The Evangelical Church and the Development of Neoliberal Society: A Study of the Role of the Evangelical Church and Its NGOs in Guatemala and Honduras', in: *Journal of Developing Areas*, 32, 1 (Autumn 1997); pp. 37–52.

Holderness, B.A.: 'The English Land Market in the Eighteenth Century: The Case of Lincolnshire', in: *Economic History Review*, 27, 4 (1974); pp. 557–576.

Holding, Grayson: 'Respectable Militants: The Lancashire Textile Machinery Makers, c. 1800–1939 (Salford University PhD., 1987)', in: *Labour History Review/Bulletin of the Society for the Study of Labour History*, 52, 3 (November 1987); pp. 41–42.

Holland, Robert: 'The British Experience of Decolonization', in: *Itinerario*, 20, 2 (1996); pp. 51–63.

Holler, Manfred J.: 'Why the Latin American Countries Do Not Form a Debtors' Cartel', in: *Kyklos*, 42, 1 (1989); S. 89–102.

Holtgrave, Wilfried: *Industrialisierung in Singapur. Chancen und Risiken industrieorientierter Spezialisierung* (Frankfort on the Main; New York: Campus, 1987).

Holthus, Manfred: 'Transnationals and New Economic Order', in: *Intereconomics*, 10, 12 (December 1975); p. 362.
Homan, Gerlof D.: 'The Netherlands, the United States and the Indonesian Question, 1948', in: *Journal of Contemporary History*, 25, 1 (January 1990); pp. 123–141.
Honour, Hugh: *Chinoisieries. The Vision of Cathay* (London: John Murray, 1961).
Hopcroft, Rosemary L.; Emigh, Rebecca Jean: 'Divergent Paths of Agrarian Change. Eastern England and Tuscany Compared', in: *Journal of European Economic History*, 29, 1 (Spring 2000); pp. 9–52.
Hopwood, Derek: *Egypt: Politics and Sciety, 1945–1981* (London: Allen & Unwin, 1982).
Hornung-Draus, Renate: 'Das Vermögen der privaten Haushalte in der Bundesrepublik Deutschland', in: *Jahrbücher für Nationalökonomie und Statistik*, 206, 1 (1989); pp. 18–47.
Horowitz, Richard S.: 'International Law and State Transformation in China, Siam, and the Ottoman Empire during the Nineteenth Century', in: *Journal of World History*, 15, 4 (December 2004); pp. 445–486.
Hostetler, Laura: 'Qing Connections to the Early Modern World: Ethnography and Cartography in Eighteenth-Century China.', in: *Modern Asian Studies*, 34, 3 (July 2000); pp. 623–662.
Hou, Chi-Ming: 'External Trade, Foreign Investment, and Domestic Development: The Chinese Experience 1840–1937', in: *Economic Development and Cultural Change*, 10, 1 (October 1961); pp. 21–41.
Hounshell, David A.: *From the American System to Mass Production 1800–1932. The Development of Manufacturing Technology in the United States* (Baltimore, Md.; London: Johns Hopkins University Press, 1984).
Houtard, François: 'Mouvements religieux du Tiers monde, formes de protestation contre l'introduction des rapports sociaux capitalistes', in: *Civilisations*, 37, 2 (1977); pp. 245–258.
Howard, Earl Dean: *The Cause and Extent of the Recent Industrial Progress of Germany* (Cambridge, Mass.: Houghton Mifflin, 1907).
Howell, Cicely: 'Stability and Change 1300–1700. The Socio-Economic Context of the Self-Perpetuating Family Farm in England', in: *Journal of Peasant Studies*, 2, 4 (July 1975); pp. 468–492.
Hroch, Miroslav: 'Can Nation-Forming Processes be Used as a Criterion of Uneven Development', in: Hroch, Miroslav; Klusáková, Luda (eds.): *Criteria and Indicators of Backwardness. Essays on Uneven Development in European History* (Prague: Charles University, 1996); pp. 129–142.
Hsieh, Chang-Tai: 'Measuring the Effects of Trade Expansion on Employment. A Review of Some Research', in: *International Labour Review*, 107, 1 (January 1973); pp. 1–29.
Hsing, Yu; Chen, Yvonne: 'Impacts of Macroeconomic Policies and Financial Market Performance on Output in Singapore: A VAR Approach', in: *Journal of Developing Areas*, 37, 2 (Spring 2004); pp. 119–135.

Hsu, Cho-yun: 'The Changing Relationship Between Local Society and the Central Political Power in Former Han', in: *Comparative Studies in Society and History*, 7, 4 (July 1965); pp. 358–370.

Huang, Philip C. C.: 'Centralized Minimalism: Semiformal Governance by Quasi Officials and Dispute Resolution in China', in: *Modern China*, 34, 1 (January 2008); pp. 9–35.

Huber Stephens, Evelyn: 'Minerals Strategies and Development: International Political Economy, State Class, and the Role of the Bauxite/Aluminium and Copper Industries Jamaica and Peru', in: *Studies in Comparative International Development*, 22, 3 (Autumn 1987); pp. 60–102.

Huberman, Michael; Meissner, Christopher: 'Riding the Wave of Trade: The Rise of Labor Regulations in the Golden Age of Globalisation', in: *Journal of Economic History*, 70, 3 (September 2010); pp. 657–685.

Hudson, Ken: 'The Disposable Worker', in: *Monthly Review*, 52, 11 (April 2001); pp. 43–55.

Huffmann, T.N.: 'The Rise and the Fall of Zimbabwe', in: *Journal of African History*, 13, 3 (1972); pp. 353–366.

Hufton, Olwen Hazel: *The Poor of 18th Century France 1750–1789* (Oxford: Clarendon, 1974).

Hugon, Philippe: 'Les blocages socio-culturele du développement en Afrique noire', in: *Tiers Monde*, 8, 31 (July–September 1967); pp. 699–709.

———: 'Les petites activités marchandes dans les espaces urbains africains', in: *Tiers Monde*, 21, 82 (April–June 1980); pp. 405–424.

Hummel, Marlies, et al.: 'Stärken und Schwächen Deutschlands im internationalen Wettbewerb um Einkommen und Arbeitsplätze', in: *IFO-Schnelldienst*, 49, 3 (January 1996); pp. 3–18.

Hunt, Ian: 'An Obituary or a New Life for the Tendency of the Rate of Profit to Fall', in: *Review of Radical Political Economics*, 15, 1 (Spring 1983); pp. 131–148.

Hunter, Guy: 'The Transfer of Institutions from Developed to Developing Countries', in: *African Affairs*, 67, 266 (January 1968); pp. 8–10.

Huntington, Samuel P.: 'The Clash of Civilizations?', in: *Foreign Affairs*, 72, 3 (Summer 1993); pp. 22–49.

Huot, Jean-Louis: 'Vers l'apparition de l'Etat en Mésopotamie. Bilan des recherches récentes', in: *Annales. Histoire, Sciences Sociales*, 60, 5 (September–October 2005); pp. 953–973.

Husain, Afzal: 'Elements of Continuity and Stability in the Mughal Nobility under Akbar and Jahangir', in: *Studies in History*, 2, 2 (July–December 1980); pp. 21–32.

Husson, Michel: 'L'inadéquation des besoins à l'offre comme obstacle à l'expansion', in: *Economies et Sociétés*, AF28 (July/August 2001); pp. 1291–1313.

Huzel, James P.: 'Malthus, The Poor Law, and Population in Early Nineteenth-Century England', in: *Economic History Review*, 22, 3 (1969); pp. 430–452.

Ibn Khaldûn, Abd-al-Rahman: *Discours sur l'Histoire universelle. Al-Muqaddima. Traduction nouvelle, préface et notes par Vincent Monteil* (Paris: Sindbad, 1967).

Ibrahim, Ferhad: 'Rente und Zivilgesellschaft in Ägypten', in: *Orient. Deutsche Zeitschrift für Politik und Wirtschaft des Orients*, 35, 3 (1994); pp. 425–440.

Igbafe, Philip A.: 'Slavery and Emancipation in Benin, 1897–1945', in: *Journal of African History*, 16, 3 (1975); pp. 409–429.

Ihonvbere, Julius O.: 'Beyond Governance: The State and Democratization in Sub-Saharan Africa', in: *Journal of Asian and African Studies (Tokyo)*, 50 (1995); pp. 141–158.

Iida, Masafumi: 'China's Cooperative Strategy toward East Asia - Aiming to Seize Regional Leadership', in: Tsunekawa, Jun; Iida, Masafumi (eds.): *East Asian Strategic Review 2007. The National Institute for Defense Studies Japan* (Tokyo: National Institute for Defense Studies, 2007); pp. 9–35.

'The I.I.P.O. Directory of the Hundred Largest Companies in India 1977–78. Public and Private Sectores', in: *Monthly Commentary on Indian Economic Conditions* (September 1979).

Iliffe, John: 'Poverty in Nineteenth-Century Yorubaland', in: *Journal of African History*, 25, 1 (1984); pp. 43–57.

Illing, Gerhard: *Zentralbanken im Griff der Finanzmärkte. Umfassende Regulierung als Voraussetzung für eine effiziente Geldpolitik*. WISO Diskurs (Bonn-Bad Godesberg: Friedrich Ebert Stiftung, July 2011)

Imam, Zafar: *Colonialism in East-West Relations. A Study of Soviet Policy Towards India and Anglo-Soviet Relations: 1917–1947* (New Delhi: Patriot, 1969).

Inden, Ronald: 'Hierachies of Kings in Early Medieval India', in: *Contributions to Indian Sociology*, 15, 1/2 (1981); pp. 99–125.

Inglehart, Ronald; Baker, Wayne E.: 'Modernization, Cultural Change, and the Persistence of Traditional Values', in: *American Sociological Review*, 65, 1 (February 2000); pp. 19–51.

Ingleson, John: 'Life and Work in Colonial Cities: Harbour Workers in Java in the 1910s and 1920s', in: *Modern Asian Studies*, 17, 3 (August 1983); pp. 455–476.

Ingrao, Charles: 'War and Legitimation in Germany in the Revolutionary Age', in: Duchhardt, Heinz; Kunz, Andreas (eds.): *Reich oder Nation? Mitteleuropa, 1780–1815* (Mayence: Verlag Philipp von Zabern, 1998); pp. 1–20.

Inomata, Takeshi: 'The Power and Ideology of Artistic Creation', in: *Current Anthropology*, 42, 3 (June 2001); pp. 321–335.

Intal, Ponciano S.: 'Real Exchange Rates, Price Competitiveness and Structural Adjustment in Asian and Pacific Economies', in: *Asian Development Review*, 10, 2 (1992); pp. 86–123.

Inukai, Ichiro: 'African Socialism and Agricultural Development Strategy: A Comparative Study of Kenya and Tanzania', in: *Developing Economies*, 12, 1 (March 1974); pp. 3–22.

Ip, Hung-Yok; Hon, Tze-Ki; Lee, Chiu-Chun: 'The Plurality of Chinese Modernity: A Review of Recent Scholarship on the May Fourth Movement', in: *Modern China*, 29, 4 (October 2003); pp. 490–509.

Irsch, Norbert: *Lohnbestimmungsmechanismen bei restringierten Substitutionsbeziehungen. Kritische Analyse grenzproduktivitätstheoretischer Verteilungsaussagen* (Aachen: Rheinisch-Westfälische Hochschule Aachen, 1979).

Isenberg, Dorene: 'The Political Economy of Monetary Policy in the European Union', in: *Review of Radical Political Economics*, 30, 3 (Summer 1998); pp. 46–55.

Isichei, Elizabeth: 'The Quest for Social Reform in the Context of Traditional Religion: A Neglected Theme of West-African History', in: *African Affairs*, 77, 309 (October 1978); pp. 463–478.

Islam, Nazrul: 'Unresolved Questions of Economic and Social History of Bangladesh', in: *Journal of Social Studies*, 129 (January–March 2011); pp. 1–49.

Islam, Nurul: *Development Planning in Bangladesh. A Study in Political Economy* (Dhaka: Dhaka University Press, 1979).

Issawi, Charles: 'Egypt Since 1800. A Study in Lop-Sided Development', in: *Journal of Economic History*, 21, 1 (March 1961); pp. 1–26.

———: *The Economic History of the Middle East, 1800–1914* (Chicago, Ill.; London: University of Chicago Press, 1966).

Isvilanonda, Somporn; Ahmad, Alia; Hossain, Mahabub: 'Recent Changes in Thailand's Rural Economy. Evidence from Six Villages', in: *Economic and Political Weekly*, 35, 52/53 (30 December 2000); pp. 4644–4649.

Iwami, Toru: 'Japan's Experiences under the Bretton Woods System: Capital Controls and the Fixed Exchange Rate', in: *Banca Nazionale del Lavoro Quarterly Review*, 183 (December 1992); pp. 431–462.

IZA: 'Arbeitslosigkeit von Geringqualifizierten - Sonderfall Schweiz?', in: *IZA Compact* (Spring 2003); pp. 6–7.

Jackson, Gregory; Deeg, Richard: 'From Comparing Capitalisms to the Politics of Institutional Change', in: *Review of International Political Economy*, 15, 4 (October 2008); pp. 680–709.

Jacobsson, Staffan J.: 'Technical Change and Industrial Policy: The Case of Computer Numerically Controlled Lathes in Argentina, Korea and Taiwan', in: *World Development*, 13, 3 (March 1985); pp. 353–370.

Jacoby, Henry: *Die Bürokratisierung der Welt* (Frankfort on the Main; New York: Campus, 1984).

Jaffrelot, Christophe: *Les nationalistes hindous. Idéologie, implantation et mobilisation des années 1920 aux années 1990* (Paris: C.E.R.I., Presses de la F.N.S.P., 1993).

———: *The Hindu Nationalist Movement and Indian Politics 1925 to the 1990s. Strategies of Identity-Building, Implantation and Mobilisation (with Special Reference to Central India)* (London: Hurst, 1996).

———: 'The Sangh Parivar between Sanskritization and Social Engineering', in: Hansen, Thomas Blom; Jaffrelot, Christophe (eds.): *The BJP and the Compulsions of Politics in India* (Oxford: Oxford University Press, 1998); pp. 22–71.

Jaisingh, Hari: *India and the Non-Aligned World. Search for a New Order* (New Delhi: Vikas, 1983).

Jalée, Pierre: *Le pillage du tiers monde* (Paris: Maspéro, 1965).

James, Jeffrey: 'The Choice of Technology in Public Enterprise: A Comparative Study of Manufacturing Industry in Kenya and Tanzania', in: Stewart, Frances (ed.): *Macro-Policies for Appropriate Technology in Developing Countries* (Boulder, Colo.: Westview Press, 1987); pp. 219–247.

Janosi, Peter E.; Grayson, Leslie E.: 'Patterns of Energy Consumption and Economic Growth and Structure', in: *Journal of Development Studies*, 8, 2 (January 1972); pp. 241–250.

Jansen, Jan: 'From Guild to Rotary: Hunters' Associations and Mali's Search for a Civil Society', in: *International Review of Social History*, 53, S16 (November 2008); pp. 249–270.

Janvry, Alain de: 'The Role of Land Reform in Economic Development: Policies and Politics', in: *American Journal of Agricultural Economics*, 63, 2 (May 1981); pp. 384–392.

Jaspers, Karl: 'Die Achsenzeit in der Weltgeschichte', in: *Monat*, 1, 6 (June 1948); pp. 3–9.

———: 'Die Achsenzeit', in: Schulin Ernst (ed.): *Universalgeschichte* (Cologne: Kiepenheuer & Witsch, 1974); pp. 96–107.

Jayawardena, Lal: 'Recyling Mechanisms: A Survey of Current Policy Options', in: *IDS Bulletin*, 14, 3 (July 1983); pp. 53–57.

Jeffries, Ian: 'Revisionism in the Economics of Backwardness', in: *Journal of Development Studies*, 5, 1 (October 1968); pp. 44–58.

Jenkins, Rhys: 'Internationalization of Capital and the Semi-Industrialized Countries: The Case of the Motor Industry', in: *Review of Radical Political Economics*, 17, 1/2 (Spring–Summer 1985); pp. 59–81.

Jensen, Richard J.: 'The Causes and Cures of Unemployment in the Great Depression', in: *Journal of Interdisciplinary History*, 19, 4 (Spring 1989); pp. 553–583.

Jessop, Bob: 'Towards a Schumpeterian Workforce State? Remarks on Post-Fordist Political Economy', in: *Studies in Political Economy*, 40 (Spring 1993); pp. 7–40.

Jevons, William Stanley: *The Coal Question. An Inquiry Concerning the Progress of the Nation on the Possible Exhaustion of Our Coal Mines* (London: Macmillan, 1865).

Jewsiecki, B.: 'La contestation sociale et la naissance du prolétariat au Zaire au cours de la première moitié du XXe siècle', in: *Canadian Journal of African Studies*, 10, 1 (1976); pp. 47–71.

Joebges, Heike: *Exporte um jeden Preis? Zur Diskussion um das Wachstumsmodell. WISO direkt Analysen und Konzepte zur Wirtschafts- und Sozialpolitik* (Bonn: Friedrich-Ebert-Stiftung, October 2010).

Johnson, Marion: 'Technology, Competition, and African Crafts', in: Dewey, Clive; Hopkins, A.G. (eds.): *The Imperial Impact: Studies in the Economic History of Africa and India* (London: Athlone, 1978); pp. 259–269.

Jomo, Kwame Sundaram: 'Export-oriented Industrialisation, Female Employment and Gender Wage Equity in East Asia', in: *Economic and Political Weekly*, 44, 1 (3rd January 2009); pp. 41–49.

Jonas, Friedrich: *Soziologische Betrachtungen zur Französischen Revolution* (Stuttgart: Ferdinand Enke, 1982).

Jones, David Martin: 'Democratization, Civil Society, and Illiberal Middle Class Culture in Pacific Asia', in: *Comparative Politics*, 30, 2 (January 1998); pp. 147–169.

Jones, Eric L.: 'Agriculture and Economic Growth in England 1660–1750', in: *Journal of Economic History*, 25, 1 (March 1965); pp. 1–18.

———: 'Agricultural Origins of Industry', in: *Past and Present*, 40 (July 1968); pp. 58–71.

———: *Agriculture and the Industrial Revolution* (Oxford: Basil Blackwell, 1974).

———: *The European Miracle: Environments, Economies and Geopolitics of the History of Europe and Asia* (Cambridge: Cambridge University Press, 1981).

Jones, Ronald W.: 'Trade, Technology, and Income Destribution', in: *Indian Economic Review*, 32, 2 (July-07–12 December 1997); pp. 129–140.

Jones, S.R.H.; Ville, Simon P.: 'Efficient Transactors or Rent-Seeking Monopolists? The Rationale for Early Chartered Companies', in: *Journal of Economic History*, 56, 4 (December 1996); pp. 898–914.

Jones, William I.: *Planning and Economic Policy: Socialist Mali and Her Neighbors* (Washington: Connecticut Press, 1976).

Jordan, Sara R.: 'Situating Administrative Responsibility: A Comparison of Medieval Christian and Islamic Administrative Thought', in: *Public Administration*, 84, 3 (2006); pp. 563–581.

Joseph, Richard A.: 'Class, State and Prebendal Politics in Nigeria', in: *Journal of Commonwealth and Comparative Politics*, 21, 3 (November 1983); pp. 21–38.

Josh, Bhagwan: 'Nationalism, Third International and Indian Communists: Communist Party and the United National Front (1934–39)', in: *Studies in History*, 3, 1/2 (1981); pp. 147–200.

Jreisat, Jamil E.: *Comparative Public Administration and Policy* (Boulder, Colo.: Westview Press, 2002).

Juk, Hugo: 'Die bargeldlose Wirtschaft - Vom Tempeltausch bis zum Barter-Club', in: *Bankhistorisches Archiv-Zeitschrift zur Bankengeschichte*, 10, 1 (July 1984); S. 54–73.

Julien, Charles-André: *L'Afrique du Nord en marche. Nationalismes musulmans et souveraineté française* (Paris: Juillard, 1972).

Jungnickel, Rolf; Schüller, Margot: *Asiens internationale Wettbewerbsfähigkeit auf dem Prüfstand* (Berlin: Friedrich-Ebert-Stiftung, February 2008).

Kaak, Heinrich: 'Vom Erbzinsrecht zur Leibeigenschaft - Entstehung agrarischer Zwangsformen im frühneuzeitlichen Brandenburg', in: *Zeitschrift für Weltgeschichte*, 8, 1 (Spring 2007); pp. 71–104.

Kabo, Vladimir: 'The Origins of the Food-producing Economy', in: *Current Anthropology*, 26, 5 (December 1985); pp. 601–616.

Kadam, V.S.: 'Forced Labour in Mahārāstra in the Seventheenth and Eighteenth Centuries', in: *Journal of the Economic and Social History of the Orient*, 34, 1 (February 1991); pp. 55–87.

Kaelble, Hartmut: 'Le changement structurel de l'emploi en Europe aux XIXe XXe siècles', in: *Histoire, économie et société*, 17, 1 (January–March 1998); pp. 13–37.

Kahin, George Mac Turnan: *Nationalism and Revolution in Indonesia* (Ithaca, N.Y.; London: Cornell University Press, 1952).

Kaiser, Robert: 'High-Tech Policies: Institutionelle Determinanten staatlicher Innovationspolitik im internationalen Vergleich', in: *Zeitschrift für Politikwissenschaft*, 18, 1 (2008); pp. 5–24.

Kalecki, Michal: 'Political Aspects of Full Employment', in: *Political Quarterly*, 14 (1944); pp. 322–331.

Kamen, Henry: 'The Decline of Spain: A Historical Myth', in: *Past and Present*, 81 (November 1978); pp. 24–50.

———: *European Society, 1500–1700* (London: Hutchinson, 1984).

Kamieniecki, Sheldon: 'Political Mobilization, Agenda Building and International Environmental Policy', in: *Journal of International Affairs*, 45, 2 (Winter 1991); pp. 339–358.

Kander, Astrid; Lindmark, Magnus: 'Energy Consumption, Pollutant Emissions and Growth in the Long Run: Sweden through 200 Years', in: *European Review of Economic History*, 8, 3 (December 2004); pp. 297–335.

Kantorowicz, Ernst: *Kaiser Friedrich II* (Düsseldorf; Munich: Helmut Küppers, 1963).

Kantowsky, Detlef: *Max Weber on India and Interpretations of Weber. Seventh European Conference on Modern Asian Studies* (London: School of Oriental and African Studies, 1981).

———: 'Die Fehlrezeption von Max Webers Studie über "Hinduismus und Buddhismus" in Indien: Ursachen und Folgen', in: *Zeitschrift für Soziologie*, 14, 6 (December 1985); pp. 466–474.

Kaplan, Marcos: 'El Leviatán criollo: Estatismo y sociedad en la América Latina contemporánea', in: *Revista Mexicana de Sociología*, 40, 3 (July–September 1978); pp. 795–829.

Kaplan, Stephen B.: 'The Political Obstacles to Greater Exchange Rate Flexibility in China', in: *World Development*, 34, 7 (July 2006); pp. 1182–1200.

Kaplinsky, Raphael: 'Radical Technical Change and Export Oriented Industrialization: The Impact of Micro-Electronics', in: *Vierteljahresberichte der FES - Probleme der Entwicklungsländer*, 83 (March 1981); pp. 81–99.

Kaplow, Susan B.: 'The Mudfish and the Crocodile: Underdevelopment of a West African Bourgeosie', in: *Science and Society*, 41, 3 (Autumn 1978); pp. 316–333.

Kappel, Robert: 'Weltmarkt und endogene Entwicklung. Entwicklungstheoretische Rück- und Vorblicke', in: *Nord-Süd Aktuell*, 3 (1999); pp. 434–446.

Karabel, Jerome: 'The Failure of American Socialism Reconsidered', in: *Socialist Register*, 16 (1979); pp. 204–227.

Karl, Terry Lynn: *The Paradox of Plenty. Oil Booms and Petro-States* (Berkeley, Cal. et al.: University of California Press, 1997).

Karlström, Mikael: 'Modernity and its Aspirants. Moral Community and Developmental Eutopianism', in: *Current Anthropology*, 45, 5 (December 2004); pp. 595–610.

Karpat, Kemal H.: 'The Transformation of the Ottoman State, 1789–1908', in: *International Journal of Middle East Studies*, 3, 3 (August 1972); pp. 243–281.

Karwal, G.D.: 'Kautilyanism', in: *Indian Journal of Economics*, 46, 183 (April 1966); pp. 369–395.

Kaufmann, Chaim D.; Pape, Robert A.: 'Explaining Costly International Moral Action: Britain's Sixty-year Campaign Against the Atlantic Slave Trade', in: *International Organization*, 53, 4 (Autumn 1999); pp. 631–668.

Kaur, Amarjit: 'Indian Labour, Labour Standards, and Workers' Health in Burma and Malaya, 1900–1940', in: *Modern Asian Studies*, 40, 2 (Summer 2006); pp. 425–476.

Kautiliya: *The Arthsastra. Edited, Rearranged, Translated, and Introduced by L.N. RangarajaneN* (Harmondsworth et al.: Penguin, 1987).

Kautsky, Karl: 'Der Imperialismus', in: *Neue Zeit*, 32, 2 (1914); pp. 908–922.

Kaviraj, Sudipta: *On State, Society and Discourse in India. Paper presented at the Conference on 'Political Institutions in the Third World in the Process of Adjustment and Modernization' organized by DSE, Berlin, 4–7 July 1989* (Unpulished manuscript, Berlin: Deutsche Stiftung für Entwicklungspolitik, 1989).

———: 'Modernity and Politics in India', in: *Daedalus*, 129, 1 (Winter 2000); pp. 137–162.

Kawada, Junzo: 'Segmentation et hiérarchie: le cas des systèmes politiques précoloniaux mosi-mamprusi-dagomba', in: *Journal of Asian and African Studies (Tokyo)*, 14 (1977); pp. 144–168.

Kay, Cristóbal: 'Why East Asia Overtook Latin America: Agrarian Reform, Industrialisation and Development', in: *Third World Quarterly*, 23, 6 (2002); pp. 1073–1102

Keddie, Nikki R.: 'Religion and Irreligion in Early Iranian Nationalism', in: *Comparative Studies in Society and History*, 4, 3 (April 1962); pp. 265–295.

Keddie, Nikki R.: 'The Origins of the Religious-Radical Alliance in Iran', in: *Past and Present*, 34 (July 1966); pp. 70–80.

———: 'Iranian Politics 1900–1905: Background to Revolution (III)', in: *Middle Eastern Studies*, 6, 3 (July 1970); pp. 234–250.

Keen, Ian: 'Constraints on the Development of Enduring Inequalities in Late Holocene Australia', in: *Current Anthropology*, 47, 1 (February 2006); pp. 7–38.

Kellenbenz, Hermann: 'Bäuerliche Unternehmertätigkeit im Bereich der Nord- und Ostsee vom Hochmittelalter bis zum Ausgang der neueren Zeit', in: *Vierteljahrschrift für Sozial- und Wirtschaftsgeschichte*, 49, 1 (1962); pp. 1–40.

Kemp, Tom: *Industrialisation in Nineteenth Century Europe* (London: Longmans & Green, 1969).

Kendrick, John W.: *Productivity Trends in the United States: A Study by the National Bureau of Economic Research* (Princeton, N.J.: Princeton University Press, 1961).

———; Sato, Ryuzo: 'Factor Prices, Productivity and Growth', in: *American Economic Review*, 53, 5 (December 1963); pp. 974–1003.

Kennedy, Richard S.: 'The King in Early South India, as Chieftain and Emperor', in: *Indian Historical Review*, 3, 1 (July 1976); pp. 1–15.

Kenney, Martin; Florida, Richard: 'Japanese Maquiladoras: Production Organization and Global Commodity Chains', in: *World Development*, 22, 1 (January 1994); pp. 27–44.

Kent, John: 'United States Reactions to Empire, Colonialism, and Cold War in Black Africa 1949–1957', in: *Journal of Imperial and Commonwealth History*, 33, 2 (May 2005); pp. 195–220.

Kenwood, Albert G.; Lougheed, Alan L.: *The Growth of the International Economy, 1820–1960. An Introductory Text* (London; New York: Routledge, 1972).

Kerr, Malcom: 'The Emergence of a Socialist Ideology in Egypt', in: *Middle East Journal*, 16, 2 (Spring 1962); pp. 127–144.

Keyder, Çaglar: 'The Cycle of Share-Cropping and the Consolidation of Small Peasant Ownership in Turkey', in: *Journal of Peasant Studies*, 10, 2/3 (January–April 1983); pp. 131–145.

Keynes, John Maynard: *A Treatise on Money* (London: Macmillan, 1930).

———: *The General Theory of Employment, Interest, and Money* (London: Macmillan, 1936).

———: 'Relative Movements of Real Wages and Output', in: *Economic Journal*, 49, 193 (March 1939); pp. 34–57.

———: *A Treatise on Money (2): The Applied Theory of Money* (Cambridge et al.: Cambridge University Press, 1971).

Khan, Mohammad Irshad: 'A Note on Consumption Patterns in the Rural Areas of East Pakistan', in: *Pakistan Development Review*, 3, 3 (Autumn 1963); pp. 399–413.

Khosrokhavar, Farhad: 'Le paradox iranien', in: *Le Monde*, 1 July 2005; p. 14.

———: 'Les nouveaux intellectuels en Iran', in: *Cahiers internationaux de sociologie*, 55, 125 (July–December 2008); pp. 347–363.

Kiernan, Victor Gordon: 'The Peasant Revolution', in: *Socialist Register*, 8 (1971); pp. 9–37.

Kikuchi, Masao; Hayami, Yujiro: 'Inducements to Institutional Innovations in an Agrarian Community', in: *Economic Development and Cultural Change*, 29, 1 (October 1980); pp. 21–36.

Kim, Dong-Hi: 'Small Farmer Economy and Development Policy with Special Reference to Korea', in: *Asian Economies*, 5, 19 (December 1976); pp. 5–22.

Kim, Linsu: 'Stages of Development of Industrial Technology in a Developing Country: A Model', in: *Research Policy*, 9, 3 (July 1980); pp. 254–277.

Kim, Sun Joo: 'Taxes, the Local Elite and the Rural Populace in the Chinju Uprising of 1862', in: *Journal of Asian Studies*, 66, 4 (November 2007); pp. 993–1028.

Kim, Yung Myong: 'Patterns of Dependency and Development. A Comparative Analysis of Radical and Conservative State Policies in Peru, Egypt, Brazil, and South Korea', in: *Korea and World Affairs*, 8, 4 (Winter 1984); pp. 812–845.

Kinda, Noraogo: 'Les Etats-Unis et le nationalisme en Afrique Noire à l'épreuve de la décolonisation (Deuxième guerre mondiale - 1960)', in: *Revue française d'histoire d'outre-mer*, 79, 297 (1992); pp. 533–555.

Kindleberger, Charles P.: 'Foreign Trade and Economic Growth. Lessons from Britain and France 1850–1913', in: *Economic History Review*, 14, 3 (December 1961); pp. 289–305.

———: *Economic Growth in France and Britain* (Cambridge, Mass.: Harvard University Press, 1964).

———: 'Germany's Overtaking of England 1806–1914 (2)', in: *Weltwirtschaftliches Archiv*, 111, 3 (1975a); pp. 477–504.

———: 'The Rise of Free Trade in Western Europe 1820–1875', in: *Journal of Economic History*, 35, 1 (March 1975b); pp. 20–55.

Kirby, Dianne: 'Divinely Sanctioned: The Anglo-American Cold War Alliance and the Defence of Western Civilization and Christianity, 1945–48', in: *Journal of Contemporary History*, 35, 3 (September 2000); pp. 385–412.

Kircheisen, Peter: 'Sozialer Wandel und politische Machtverlagerung im vorrevolutionären England', in: *Zeitschrift für Geschichtswissenschaft*, 35, 11 (November 1987); pp. 985–996.

Kisch, Herbert: 'The Textile Industry in Silesia and the Rhineland: A Comparative Study in Industrialization', in: *Journal of Economic History*, 19, 4 (December 1959); pp. 540–565.

Kitching, Gavin: *Class and Economic Change in Kenya. The Making of an African Petty Bourgeoisie 1905–1970* (New Haven, Conn.; London: Yale University Press, 1980).

Ki-Zerbo, Joseph: *Histoire de l'Afrique noire d'hier à demain* (Paris: Hatier, 1978).

Klasen, Stephan: 'Inequality in Emerging Countries: Trends, Interpretations, and Implications for Development and Poverty Reduction', in: *Intereconomics*, 44, 6 (November–December 2009); pp. 360–363.

Klaus, Václav: *Blauer Planet in grünen Fesseln. Was ist bedroht: Klima oder Freiheit?* (Vienna: Carl Gerold's Sohn, 2007).

Klaveren, Jacob van: 'Die historische Erscheinung der Korruption', in: *Vierteljahrschrift für Sozial- und Wirtschaftsgeschichte*, 45, 4 (1958); pp. 433–504.

———: 'Die Manufakturen des Ancien Régime', in: *Vierteljahrschrift für Sozial- und Wirtschaftsgeschichte*, 51, 2 (July 1964); pp. 145–191.

Klengel, Horst: 'Zur Entwicklung des Handels im alten Vorderasien', in: *Ethnographisch-Archäologische Zeitschrift*, 19, 2 (1978); pp. 211–225.

Kliman, Andrew J.: 'The Okishio Theorem: An Obituary', in: *Review of Radical Political Economics*, 29, 3 (Autumn 1997); pp. 42–50.

Kluge, Arnd: *Die Zünfte* (Stuttgart: Franz Steiner, 2007).

Kmuche, Wolfgang: *Wirtschaftswachstum und Energieverbrauch. Vergangenheitsentwicklung und Zukunftsperspektiven am Beispiel der Bundesrepublik Deutschland* (München: Tuduv, 1982); 122 S.

Knetter, Michael M.: 'International Comparisons of Pricing to Market Behaviour', in: *American Economic Review*, 83, 3 (June 1993); p. 473.

Knirsch, Peter: 'The CMEA Attitude to a New Economic Order', in: *Intereconomics* (May–June 1978); pp. 103–107.

Kocka, Jürgen: *Arbeiterverhältnisse und Arbeiterexistenzen: Grundlagen zur Klassenbildung im 19. Jahrhundert* (Bonn: J.H.W. Dietz Nachf., 1990)

Kocoglu, Yusuf: 'La productivité du capital productif fixe sur longue période: une analyse empirique sur la France', in: *Histoire, économie et société*, 20 (January–March 2001); pp. 65–86.

Koenig, Wolfgang: 'Der internationale Währungsfonds und die Politik multipler Wechselkurse in Lateinamerika', in: *Außenwirtschaft*, 22, 4 (1967); pp. 380–399.

Kohl, Philip L.: 'The Balance of Trade in Southwestern Asia in the Mid-Third Millennium B.C.', in: *Current Anthropology*, 19, 3 (September 1978); pp. 462–492.

Kohn, Hans: *Geschichte der nationalen Bewegung im Orient* (Berlin: Vowinckel, 1928).

———; Sokolsky, Wallace: *African Nationalism in the Twentieth Century* (Princeton, N.J.: Van Nostrand, 1965).

Komarow, E.N.; Grasche, W.I.: 'Einige Angaben über die gesellschaftliche Arbeitsteilung und die ökonomische Struktur des Handwerks in Indien an der Wende vom 18. zum 19. Jahrhundert', in: Ruben, Walter (ed.): *Die ökonomische und soziale Entwicklung Indiens. Sowjetische Beiträge zur indischen Geschichte* (Berlin: Akademie-Verlag, 1959); pp. 132–153.

Kopits, George F.: 'Intra-Firm Royalties Crossing Frontiers and Transfer Pricing Behaviour', in: *Economic Journal*, 86, 344 (December 1976); pp. 791–805.

Koppes, Clayton R.: 'The Good Neighbour Policy and the Nationalization of Mexican Oil: A Reinterpretation', in: *Journal of American History*, 69, 1 (June 1982); pp. 62–81.

Koralka, Jiří: 'Peasant Movements in the Czech Lands from the End of the XVIIIth Century to the Second World War', in: *Cahiers Internationaux d'Histoire Economique et Sociale*, 7 (1976); pp. 127–154.

Korn, L.: 'Geschichte der bäuerlichen Rechtsverhältnisse in der Mark Brandenburg von der Zeit der deutschen Colonisation bis zur Regierung des Königs Friedrich I. (1700)', in: *Zeitschrift für Rechtsgeschichte*, 1, 1 (1873); pp. 1–44.

Kornai, János: 'Paying the Bill for Goulash Communism: Hungarian Development and Macro-Stabilization in a Political-Economy Perspective', in: *Social Research*, 63, 4 (Winter 1996); pp. 943–1040.

Körner, Heiko: 'Die Folgen kolonialer Herrschaft', in: *Zeitschrift für die gesamte Staatswissenschaft / Journal of Institutional and Theoretical Economics*, 119, 3 (1963); pp. 458–475.

Korzeniewicz, Roberto: 'Labor Unrest in Argentina, 1930–1943', in: *Latin American Research Review*, 28, 1 (Spring 1993); pp. 7–40.

Kosminsky, E.A.: 'The Evolution of Feudal Rent in England from the XIth to the XVth Centuries', in: *Past and Present*, 7 (April 1955); pp. 12–34.

Kothari, Rajni: 'Non-Party Political Process', in: *Economic and Political Weekly*, 19, 5 (4 February 1984); pp. 216–224.

———: 'NGO's, the State and World Capitalism', in: *Economic and Political Weekly*, 21, 50 (December 1986); pp. 2177–2183.

Krasner, Stephen D.: 'The Great Oil Sheikdown', in: *Foreign Policy*, 13 (Winter 1973); pp. 123–138.

Krause, Wolfgang; Puffert, Douglas J.: 'Chemicals, Strategy and Tariffs: Tariff Policy and the Soda Industry in Imperial Germany', in: *European Review of Economic History*, 4, 3 (December 2000); pp. 285–303.

Kregel, Jan A.: *Price Stability and Full Employment as Complements in a New Europe. A Market-Based Price Stabilisation Policy for the new ECB.* Paper presented at the Fifth Post Keynesian Workshop: Full Employment and the Price Stability in a Global Economy, organised by *Journal of Postkeynesian Economics*, University of Tennessee, Knoxville, 25 June–1 July 1998.

Kreile, Michael: 'West Germany: The Dynamics of Expansion', in: *International Organization*, 31, 4 (Autumn 1977); pp. 775–808.

Kreile, Renate: 'Staat und Geschlechterverhältnisse im Mittleren Osten', in: *Peripherie*, 13, 50 (June 1993); pp. 37–71.

Kreissig, Heinz: 'Zwei Produktionsweisen die der kapitalistischen vorhergehen', in: *Ethnographisch-Archäologische Zeitschrift*, 10, 3 (1969); pp. 361–368.

Kremendahl, Hans: 'Ohne wirtschaftspolitisches Leitbild', in: *Neue Gesellschaft - Frankfurter Hefte*, 42, 11 (November 1995); pp. 970–975.

Kreps, I.J.: 'Dividends, Interest, Profit, Wages 1923–1935', in: *Quarterly Journal of Economics*, 49, 4 (August 1935); pp. 561–599.

Krippendorff, Ekkehart: *Die amerikanische Strategie* (Frankfort on the Main, 1970).

Krishnamurty, J.: 'Deindustrialization in Gangetic Bihar during the 19th Century: Another Look at Evidence', in: *Indian Economic and Social History Review*, 22, 4 (October 1985); pp. 399–416.

Kristiansen, Kristian; Larsson, Thomas B.: 'L'âge du Bronze, un période historique. Les relations entre Europe, Méditerranée et Proche Orient', in: *Annales. Histoire, Sciences Sociales*, 60, 5 (September–October 2005); pp. 975–1007.

Kroll, Ethan: 'Early Modern Sanskrit Thought and the Quest for a Perfect Understanding of Property', in: *IIAS Newsletter*, 43 (Spring 2007); p. 12.

Krugman, Paul R.: 'Increasing Returns, Monopolistic Competition, and International Trade', in: *Journal of International Economics*, 9, 4 (November 1979); pp. 469–479.

———: *Strategic Trade Policy and the New International Economics* (Cambridge, Mass.: MIT, 1986).

———: 'The Myth of Asia's Miracle', in: *Foreign Affairs*, 73, 6 (November–December 1994); pp. 62–78.

———: 'What Should Trade Negotiators Negotiate About?', in: *Journal of Economic Literature*, 35, 1 (March 1997); pp. 113–120.

———: *Die Große Rezession. Was zu tun ist, damit die Weltwirtschaft nicht kippt* (Frankfort on the Main; New York: Campus, 1999a).

———: 'The Return of Depression Economics', in: *Foreign Affairs*, 78, 1 (January/February 1999b); pp. 56–74.

Kudrna, Jaroslav: 'Die historische und kulturelle Bedeutung des italienischen Stadtstaates', in: *Jahrbuch für Geschichte des Feudalismus*, 14 (1990); pp. 97–104.

Kuhn, Berthold: *Participatory Development and Local Self-Government Reform in Rural India* (New Delhi: Radiant, 1998).

———: *Zivilgesellschaft in und aus der Perspektive der Entwicklungsländer* (Unpublished Paper, 2001).

Kühne, Winrich: *Sowjetische Afrikapolitik in der "Ära Gorbatschow". Eine Analyse ihrer grundlegenden Probleme Mitte der 80er Jahre, ausgehend von den Entwicklungen in Moçambique, Angola und Äthiopien* (Ebenhausen: Stiftung Wissenschaft und Politik, 1986).

Kühnlenz, André; Kaelble, Martin: 'Amerika schlägt globalen Währungspakt vor', in: *Financial Times* 22thOctober 2010); p. 11.

Kulke, Hermann: 'The Early and the Imperial Kingdom: A Processural Model of Integrative State Formation in Early Medieval India', in: Kulke, Hermann (ed.): *The State in India 1000– 1700* (Cambridge, Mass. et al.: Oxford University Press, 1997); pp. 233–262.

Kulke, Roland: *The Hindu Nationalists' Attempt to Gain Intellectual Hegemony* (Leipzig: Ph.D. Diss., October 2008).

Kumar, Arun: 'Tackling the Current Global Economic and Financial Crisis: Beyond Demand Management', in: *Economic and Political Weekly*, 44, 13 (28 March 2009); pp. 151–157.

Kuntowidjojo: 'The Indonesian Muslim Middle Class in Search of Identity', in: *Itinerario*, 10, 1 (1986); pp. 177–196.

Kuntz: 'Tata machts möglich', in: *Süddeutsche Zeitung* (17 May 2010), http://www.sueddeutsche.de/auto/autoland-indien-tata-machts-moeglich-1.604867 (03.06.2011).

Kunze, Jürgen: 'Zur sozialen Stellung und Formierung der Bourgeoisie im subsaharischen Afrika', in: *Asien-Afrika-Lateinamerika*, 7, 4 (1979); pp. 653–672.

Künzler, Daniel: *Is There Something New Out of Africa? Paper for the Ad Hoc Session on 'Africa and the Future of World Society' at the XVI International Sociological Association World Congress of Sociology, Durban, 26 July 2006* (Unpublished paper, Dublin: July 2006).
Kupferschmidt, Uri M.: 'Reformist and Militant Islam in Urban and Rural Egypt', in: *Middle Eastern Studies*, 23, 4 (October 1987); pp. 403–418.
Kuran, Timur: 'Now out of Never: The Element of Surprise in the East European Revolution of 1989', in: *World Politics*, 43, 1 (October 1991); pp. 7–48.
Kurth, Wilhelm: *Wandlungen des Rohstoffverbrauchs in der Oberbekleidungsindustrie* (Opladen: Westdeutscher Verlag, 1965).
Küttler, Wolfgang: 'Nochmals zur Klassenposition des Junkertums während und nach der bürgerlichen Umwälzung', in: *Zeitschrift für Geschichtswissenschaft*, 33, 3 (1985); pp. 238–246.
Kwon, Ik-Whan; Cordell, Larry; Kim, Joe H.: 'Public Policy and Economic Development', in: *Indian Journal of Economics*, 65, 258 (January 1985); pp. 259–277.
Laaser, Claus-Friedrich; Schrader, Klaus: 'Offshoring von Arbeitsplätzen: Ein Empirischer Befund Für Deutschland', in: *Außenwirtschaft*, 64, 2 (June 2009); pp. 183–204.
Lachmann, Richard: 'Feudal Elite Conflict and the Origins of English Capitalism', in: *Politics and Society*, 14, 3 (Spring 1985); pp. 349–378.
Lacoste, Yves: *Ibn Khaldoun. Naissance de l'histoire passée du tiers monde* (Paris: Maspéro, 1973).
Lafay, Gérard: 'Spécialisation internationale et croissance nationale. Une approche par la théorie des créneaux', in: *Revue économique*, 26, 3 (July 1975); pp. 395–436.
Laibman, David: 'Modes of Production and Theories of Transition', in: *Science and Society*, 48, 3 (Autumn 1984); pp. 257–294.
Lakha, Salim: 'The New International Division of Labour and of Indian Computer Software Industry', in: *Modern Asian Studies*, 28, 2 (May 1994); pp. 381–408.
Lakshmi, R. Champak: 'Growth of Urban Centres in South India: Kudamukku-Palaiyarai, the Twin-City of the Colas', in: *Studies in History*, 1, 1 (1979); pp. 1–29.
Lamartine Yates, Paul: *Forty Years of Foreign Trade. A Statistical Handbook with Special Reference to Primary Products and Underdeveloped Countries* (London: Allen & Unwin, 1959).
Lamicq, Hélène: 'La mise en valeur du Nord. Manifestation de l'impérialisme dans l'espace chilien', in: *Tiers Monde*, 16, 61 (January–March 1975); pp. 183–217.
Lancaster, C. S.: 'Ethnic Identity, History, and "Tribe" in the Middle Zambezi Valley', in: *American Ethnologist*, 1, 4 (November 1974); pp. 707–730.
Landes, David S.: 'Some Thoughts on the Nature of Economic Imperialism', in: *Journal of Economic History*, 21, 4 (December 1961); pp. 496–512.
———: 'Why Europe and the West? Why Not China?', in: *Journal of Economic Perspectives*, 20, 2 (Spring 2006); pp. 3–22.

Landmann, Oliver: 'Die Globalisierung: Wachstumsmotor oder Job-Killer', in: *Hamburger Jahrbücher für Wirtschafts- und Gesellschaftspolitik*, 44 (1999); pp. 133–152.

———; Jerger, Jürgen: 'Unemployment and the Real Wage Gap', in: *Weltwirtschaftliches Archiv*, 129, 1 (1993); pp. 689–716.

Langer, Erick D.: 'Labor Strikes and Reciprocity on Chuquisace Haciendas', in: *Hispanic American Historical Review*, 65, 2 (May 1985); pp. 255–277.

Langer, Herbert: 'Fragen der Absolutismusforschung', in: *Jahrbuch für Geschichte des Feudalismus*, 3 (1979); pp. 365–391.

Lanning, Greg; Mueller, With Marti: *Africa Undermined. Mining Companies and the Underdevelopment in Africa* (Harmondsworth: Penguin, 1979).

Lapidus, Ira M.: 'Muslim Cities and Islamic Societies', in: Lapidus, Ira M. (ed.): *Middle Eastern Cities: A Symposium on Ancient Islamic and Contemporary Middle Eastern Urbanism* (Berkeley, Cal.: University of California Press, 1969); pp. 47–79.

———: 'Islamic Revival and Modernity: The Contemporary Movements and the Historical Paradigms', in: *Journal of the Economic and Social History of the Orient*, 40, 4 (November 1997); pp. 444–460.

Laroui, Abdallah: *Histoire du Maghreb. Un essai de synthèse* (Paris: Maspero, 1970).

Laue, Theodor H. von: 'The Witte System in Russia', in: *Journal of Economic History*, 13, 4 (Autumn 1953); pp. 425–448.

Law, Robin: 'A West African Cavalry State: The Kingdom of Oyo', in: *Journal of African History*, 16, 1 (1975); pp. 1–15.

Le Guay, François; Royer, Jacques: 'Développement endogène: contraintes internationales', in: *EADI Bulletin*, 2 (1985); pp. 123–152.

Le Naëlou, Anne: 'Pour comprendre la professionalisation dans les ONG: Quelques apports d'une sociologie des professions', in: *Tiers Monde*, 45, 180 (October–December 2004); pp. 773–798.

Leach, E.R.: *Political Systems of Highland Burma. A Study of Kachin Social Structure* (London: G. Bell & Sons, 1954).

———: 'Hydraulic Society in Ceylon', in: *Past and Present*, 15 (April 1959); pp. 2–26.

League of Nations: *La production mondiale et les prix, 1925–1932* (Geneva: League of Nations, 1933).

———: *Industrialisation and Foreign Trade* (Geneva: League of Nations, 1945).

Leclerc, Gérard: 'Le monde arabo-islamique dans la mondialité', in: *NAQD - Revue d'Études et de Critique Sociale*, 13 (Autumn/Winter 2000); pp. 47–74.

Leclerc, Jacques: 'Quelques concepts de la révolution d'octobre et le mouvement de libération nationale in Indonésie, 1920–1942', in: *Revue française de science politique*, 31, 4 (August 1981); S. 790–798.

Lee, Ching Kwan; Selden, Mark: 'Inequality and Its Enemies in Revolutionary and Reform China', in: *Economic and Political Weekly*, 43, 52 (27 December 2008); pp. 27–36.

Lee, Chunli: *Chinas Automobilindustrie in der Globalisierung. Berichte des Arbeitsbereichs Chinaforschung 15* (Bremen: Institut für Weltwirtschaft und Internationales Management der Universität Bremen, April 2001).
Lee, Eddy: 'Egalitarian Peasant Farming and Rural Development: The Case of South Korea', in: *World Development*, 7, 4/5 (April–May 1979); pp. 493–517.
Leff, Nathaniel H.: 'Optimal Investment Choice for Developing Countries. Rational Theory and Rational Decision-Making', in: *Journal of Development Economics*, 18, 2/3 (August 1985); pp. 335–360.
Lehmann, Frederick: 'Great Britain and the Supply of Locomotives to India: A Case Study of Economic Imperialism', in: *Indian Economic and Social History Review*, 2, 4 (October 1965); pp. 297–306.
Lehment, Harmen: 'Zur Bestimmung des beschäftigungsneutralen Lohnerhöhungsspielraums', in: *Weltwirtschaft*, 50, 1 (1999); pp. 79–89.
Leibfritz, Willi: 'Mit expansiver Lohnpolitik die Beschäftigung erhöhen? Anmerkungen zu der "Münchhausen- Theorie"', in: *IFO-Schnelldienst*, 51, 36 (December 1998); pp. 24–32.
Leicher, Renate: 'Historische Grundlagen der landwirtschaftlichen Besitz- und Bodenverhältnisse in Italien. Eine Übersicht über Landschaftstypen', in: *Vierteljahrschrift für Sozial- und Wirtschaftsgeschichte*, 45, 2 (1958); pp. 144–185.
Lembke, Hans H.: 'Die Grundbedürfnisrelevanz ländlicher Elektrifizierungsprogramme in Thailand. Ein Beitrag zur Methodik der Grundbedürfnisorientierten Evaluierung', in: Gsänger, Hans (ed.): *Grundbedürfnisorientierte ländliche Entwicklungspolitik* (Berlin: Deutsches Institut für Entwicklungspolitik, 1980); pp. 155–192.
Lemoine, Françoise; Ünal-Kesenci, Deniz: 'Assembly Trade and Technology Transfer: The Case of China', in: *World Development*, 32, 5 (May 2004); pp. 829–850.
Lenin, Wladimir Iljitsch: 'Die Ereignisse auf dem Balkan und in Persien', in: Lenin, Wladimir Iljitsch: *Werke Band 16* (Berlin: Dietz, 1962); S. 216–226.
———: *Die Entwicklung des Kapitalismus in Rußland. Der Prozeß der Bildung des inneren Marktes für die Großindustrie [1899]. Lenin Werke 3* (Berlin: Dietz, 1972).
———: 'Imperialismus als höchstes Stadium des Kapitalismus [1916]', in: *Lenin Werke*, vol. 22 (Berlin, Bonn: Dietz, 1977); pp. 189–309.
Lentz, Carola: *Die Konstruktion von Ethnizität. Eine politische Geschichte Nord-West-Ghanas 1870–1990* (Cologne: Rüdiger Köppe, 1998).
———: 'Chieftaincy has come to stay: La chefferie dans les sociétés acéphales du Nord-Ouest Ghana', in: *Cahiers d'études africaines*, 40, 159 (2000); pp. 593–613.
Lepsius, M. Rainer: 'The Nation and Nationalism in Germany', in: *Social Research*, 52, 1 (Spring 1985); pp. 43–64.
Lerner, Abba P.: 'Economic Theory and Socialist Economy', in: *Review of Economic Studies*, 2, 4 (October 1935); pp. 51–61.

Lescure, Jean: 'Prix, monnaie et crédit', in: *Economic Essays in Honour of Gustav Cassel* (London: Allen & Unwin, 1933); pp. 387–398.

LeTourneau, Roger: *Evolution politique de l'Afrique du Nord musulmane 1920–1961* (Paris: Armand Colin, 1962).

Levadoux, B.: 'Marxisme et crises: Quelques enseignements d'un vieux débat', in: *Economies et Sociétés*, P 32 (1980); pp. 946–970.

Levene, Mark: 'Why Is the Twentieth Century the Century of Genocide?', in: *Journal of World History*, 11, 2 (Autumn 2000); pp. 305–336.

Levenson, Joseph R.: 'Confucian and Taiping Heaven: The Political Implications of Clashing Religious Concepts', in: *Comparative Studies in Society and History*, 4, 4 (July 1962); pp. 436–454.

Levi, Mario: 'Colloque franco-allemand sur l'énergie, Rouen', in: *Politique étrangère*, 38, 3 (Autumn 1973); pp. 343–364.

Levine, Arnold S.: 'The Structure of Scientific and Technical Education in Britain 1859–1899', in: *Economisch en sociaal-historisch Jaarboek*, 38 (1975); pp. 300–334.

Levitsky, Steven; Way, Lucan A.: 'The Rise of Competitive Authoritarianism', in: *Journal of Democracy*, 13, 2 (April 2002); pp. 51–65.

Levy, Daniel C.: 'Latin America's Think Tanks: The Roots of Nonprofit Privatization', in: *Studies in Comparative International Development*, 30, 2 (Summer 1995); pp. 3–25.

Lewin, Günter: 'Die staatliche Leitung und Kontrolle von Manufakturen und handwerklicher Produktion im China der frühen Song Zeit', in: *Jahrbuch für Wirtschaftsgeschichte*, 3 (1974); pp. 179–199.

Lewis, Diane K.: 'Rules for Agrarian Change: Negri Sembilan Malays and Agricultural Innovation', in: *Journal of Southeast Asian Studies*, 7, 1 (March 1976); pp. 74–91.

Lewis, I.M.: 'Culture and Conflict in Africa', in: *Millennium: Journal of International Studies*, 6, 2 (Autumn 1977); pp. 175–188.

Lewis, Todd T.: 'Newars and Tibetans in the Kathmandu Valley. Ethnic Boundaries and Religious History', in: *Journal of Asian and African Studies (Tokyo)*, 38 (1989); pp. 31–57.

Lewis, William Arthur: 'Economic Development with Unlimited Supply of Labour', in: *Manchester School of Economic and Social Studies*, 22, 4 (May 1954); pp. 139–191.

Lewkowski, A.I.: 'Über die niederen Formen kapitalistischen Unternehmertums in der indischen Industrie (gezeigt am Beispiel der Handweberei)', in: Ruben, Walter (ed.): *Die ökonomische und soziale Entwicklung Indiens. Sowjetische Beiträge zur indischen Geschichte* (Berlin: Akademie-Verlag, 1959); pp. 236–256.

Lieberman, Victor: 'Transcending East-West Dichotomies: State and Culture Formation in Six Ostensibly Disparate Areas', in: *Modern Asian Studies*, 31, 3 (1997); pp. 463–546.

Liedholm, Carl; MacPherson, Michael; Chuta, Enyinna: 'Small Enterprise Employment Growth in Rural Africa', in: *American Journal of Agricultural Economics*, 76, 5 (December 1994); pp. 1175–1181.

Lieten, G. K.: 'Hindu Communalism: Between Caste and Class', in: *Journal of Contemporary Asia*, 26, 2 (1996); pp. 236–252.

Lin, Justin Yifu: 'The Needham Puzzle: Why the Industrial Revolution Did Not Originate in China', in: *Economic Development and Cultural Change*, 43, 2 (January 1995); pp. 269–292.

Lind, Michael: 'The End of Atlanticism: America and Europe beyond the US Election', in: *Internationale Politik und Gesellschaft*, 1 (2005); pp. 25–42.

Lindberg, Anna: 'Class, Caste and Gender among Cashew Workers in the South Indian State of Kerala 1930–2000', in: *International Review of Social History*, 46, 2 (August 2001); pp. 155–188.

Linde, Hans: 'Proto-Industrialisierung: Zur Justierung eines Leitbegriffs der sozialgeschichtlichen Forschung', in: *Geschichte und Gesellschaft*, 6, 1 (1980); pp. 103–124.

Linder, Staffan Burenstam: *An Essay on Trade and Transformation* (Stockholm; New York: Almqvist & Wicksell; John Wiley, 1961).

Lindsay, C.M.: 'Measuring Human Capital Returns', in: *Journal of Political Economy*, 79, 6 (November–December 1971); pp. 1195–1215.

Little, Jane S.: 'Communist China's Use of Nationalism in Its Policies Toward the Third World', in: *Public Policy*, 14 (1967); pp. 76–111.

Liu, Alan P.L.: *Communications and National Integration in Communist China* (Berkeley, Cal.; Los Angeles; London: University of California Press, 1971).

Liu, Xinru: *Ancient India and Ancient China: Trade and Religious Exchanges* (New Delhi: Oxford University Press, 1988).

Lockard, Craig A.: 'The Unexplained Miracle. Reflections on Vietnamese National Identity and Survival', in: *Journal of Asian and African Studies (Leiden)*, 29, 1/2 (January–April 1994); pp. 10–25.

Lofchie, Michael F.: 'Agrarian Crisis and Economic Liberalisation in Tanzania', in: *Journal of Modern African Studies*, 16, 3 (1978); pp. 451–475.

Logan, Bernard I.: 'The Reverse Transfer of Technology from Sub-Saharan Africa to the United States', in: *Journal of Modern African Studies*, 25, 4 (October 1987); pp. 597–612.

———: 'An Assessment of the Environmental and Economic Implications of Toxic-Waste Disposal in Subsaharan Africa', in: *Journal of World Trade*, 25, 1 (February 1991); pp. 61–76.

Lohda, Sanjay: 'Rajasthan: India Shines as BJP Trounces Congress', in: *Economic and Political Weekly*, 39, 51 (Winter 2004); pp. 5456–5462.

Lokanathan, P.S.: *Industrial Organization in India* (London: Allen & Unwin, 1935).

Lombard, J.: 'The Kingdom of Dahomey', in: Forde, Daryll; Kaberry, P.M.: *West African Kingdoms in the Nineteenth Century* (London: Oxford University Press, 1967); pp. 70–93.

Long, Clarence D.: 'The Illusion of Wage Rigidity Long and Short Cycles in Wages and Labor', in: *Review of Economics and Statistics*, 48, 2 (May 1966); pp. 140–151.

Longman, Timothy P.: 'Empowering the Weak and Protecting the Powerful: The Contradictory Nature of Churches in Central Africa', in: *African Studies Review*, 41, 1 (April 1998); pp. 49–72.

Louis, Wim Rogers; Robinson, Ronald: 'The Imperialism of Decolonization', in: *Journal of Imperial and Commonwealth History*, 22, 3 (September 1994); pp. 462–511.

Lovejoy, Paul E.: *Transformations in Slavery. A History of Slavery in Africa.* (Cambridge et al.: Cambridge University Press, 1983).

——: *Salt of the Desert Sun: A History of Salt Production in the Central Sudan* (Cambridge: Cambridge University Press, 1986).

Low, D.A.: 'Sequence, Crux and Means: Some Asian Nationalisms Compared', in: Jeffrey, Robin (ed.): *Asia - The Winning of Independence. The Philippines, India, Indonesia, Vietnam, Malaya* (London: Macmillan, 1981); pp. 258–321.

Lowe, Donald Ming-dah: *The Idea of China in Marx, Lenin and Mao: A Study in Marxist Ideological Persistence and Transformation* (Berkeley, Cal.: Ph.D. Diss., 1963).

Lowe, Nichola; Kenney, Martin: 'Foreign Investment and the Global Geography of Production: Why the Mexican Consumer Electronics Industry Failed', in: *World Development*, 27, 8 (August 1999); pp. 1427–1442.

Löwy, Michael: 'The Socio-Religious Origins of Brazil's Landless Rural Workers Movement', in: *Monthly Review*, 53, 2 (June 2001); pp. 32–40.

Lubell, Harold; Zarour, Cherbel: 'Resilience Amidst Crisis: The Informal Sector of Dakar', in: *International Labour Review*, 129, 3 (May–June 1990); pp. 387–396.

Lublinskaya, A.D.: 'The Contemporary Bourgeois Conception of Absolute Monarchy', in: *Economy and Society*, 1, 1 (February 1972); pp. 64–92.

Lucas, Robert E. Jr.: 'Making a Miracle', in: *Econometrica*, 61, 2 (1993); pp. 251–272.

Ludden, David: 'Patronage and Irrigation in Tamil Nadu: A Long-Term View', in: *Indian Economic and Social History Review*, 16, 2 (1979); pp. 347–365.

Lugard, Frederick D.: *The Dual Mandate in British Tropical Africa* (London, 1922).

Lukacz, Georg: *Histoire et conscience de classe. Essai de dialectique marxiste* (Paris: Minuit, 1960).

Lukauskas, Arvid: 'Financial Restriction and the Developmental State in East Asia. Toward a More Complex Political Economy', in: *Comparative Political Studies*, 35, 4 (May 2002); pp. 379–412.

Lumer, Robert: 'Flexible Konterrevolution: Die Suche Präsident Kennedys nach einer Verteidigungsstrategie', in: *Zeitschrift für Geschichtswissenschaft*, 35, 3 (1987); pp. 298–307.

Lund-Thomsen, Peter: 'The Global Sourcing and Codes of Conduct Debate: Five Myths and Five Recommendations', in: *Development and Change*, 39, 6 (November 2008); pp. 1005–1019.

Luong, Hy Van: 'Agrarian Unrest from an Anthropological Aspect', in: *Comparative Politics*, 17, 2 (January 1985); pp. 153–174.

Lustig, Nora: 'Characteristics of Mexican Economic Growth. Empirical Testing of Some Latin American Structuralist Hypothesis', in: *Journal of Development Economics*, 10, 3 (June 1982); pp. 355–376.

Lusztig, Michael: 'Solving Peel's Puzzle. Repeal of the Corn Laws and Institutional Preservation', in: *Comparative Politics*, 27, 4 (July 1995); pp. 393–408.

Lutchman, Harold Alexander: *From Colonialism to Co-operative Republic. Aspects to Political Development in Guyana* (Rio Pedras: Caribbean Studies, 1974).

Lütkenhorst, Wilfried; Minte, Horst: 'The Petrodollars in the World Economy', in: *Intereconomics*, 14, 3/4 (March–April 1979); pp. 84–89.

Lütt, Jürgen: "Indien in seiner weltgeschichtlichen Bedeutung'—124 Jahre nach Max Müller', in: *Saeculum*, 57, 2 (2006); pp. 269–288.

Lutz, Hans: *Das Kupfer als Welthandelsware* (Würzburg-Aumühle: Konrad Triltsch, 1939).

Luxemburg, Rosa: *Die Akkumulation des Kapitals. Ein Beitrag zur ökonomischen Erklärung des Imperialismus [1912]* (Berlin: Vereinigung internationaler Verlagsanstalten, 1923).

Mabbett, I.W.: 'The "Indianization" of Southeast Asia: Reflections on the Historical Sources', in: *Journal of Southeast Asian Studies*, 8, 2 (September 1977); pp. 143–161.

MacCloskey, Donald N.: 'Magnanimous Albion: Free Trade and British National Income, 1841–1881', in: *Explorations in Economic History*, 17, 3 (July 1980); pp. 303–320.

———; Sandberg, Lars: 'From Damnation to Redemption: Judgments on the Late Victorian Entrepreneur', in: *Explorations in Economic History*, 9, 1 (Autumn 1971); pp. 89–108.

MacFarlane, Alan: *The Origins of English Individualism. The Family, Property and Social Transition* (Oxford: Basil Blackwell, 1978a).

———: 'The Origins of English Individualism: Some Surprises', in: *Theory and Society*, 6, 2 (September 1978b); pp. 255–277.

MacGaffee, Wyatt: *Religion and Society in Central Africa: The Bakongo of Lower Zaire* (Chicago, Ill.: University of Chicago Press, 1986).

MacKintosh, Maureen: 'Agricultural Marketing and Socialist Accumulation: A Case Study of Maize Marketing in Mozambique', in: *Journal of Peasant Studies*, 14, 2 (January 1987); pp. 243–268.

Madjarian, Grégoire: *La question coloniale et la politique du Parti Communiste Français. 1944–1948. Crise de l'impérialisme colonial et mouvement ouvrier* (Paris: Maspéro, 1977).

Madrid, Raúl: 'The Rise of Ethnopopulism in Latin America', in: *World Politics*, 60, 3 (April 2008); pp. 475–508.
Magdoff, Harry: *The Age of Imperialism. The Economics of U.S. Foreign Policy* (New York; London: Monthly Review Press, 1969).
Mager, Wolfgang: 'Protoindustrialisierung und Protoindustrie. Vom Nutzen und Nachteil zweier Konzepte', in: *Geschichte und Gesellschaft*, 14, 3 (1988); pp. 275–303.
Mahalanobis, P.C.: 'Some Observations on the Process of Growth of National Income', in: *Sankhya*, 12, 4 (1953); pp. 307–312.
Mährdel, Christian: 'Die Rolle der Armee in der nationalen Befreiungsrevolution afrikanischer Völker', in: *Zeitschrift für Geschichtswissenschaft*, 15, 8 (August 1967); pp. 1406–1421.
Mair, Lucy: *Primitive Government. A Study of Traditional Political Systems in Eastern Africa* (Bloomington, Ind.; London: Indiana University Press, 1977).
Majumdar, R. C.; Raychaudhuri, H. C.; Datta, Kalikinkar: *An Advanced History of India. Fourth Edition* (Delhi et al.: Macmillan India, 1978).
Malik, Salahuddin: 'Nineteenth Century Approaches to the Indian Mutiny', in: *Journal of Asian History*, 7, 2 (1973); pp. 95–127.
Malinvaud, Edmond: 'The Legacy of European Stagflation', in: *European Economic Review*, 31, 1–2 (February–March 1987); pp. 53–65.
Mallaby, Sebastian: 'NGOs: Fighting Poverty, Hurting the Poor', in: *Foreign Policy*, 144 (September/October 2004); pp. 50–58.
Mallet, Serge: *La nouvelle classe ouvrière* (Paris: Seuil, 1969).
Malowist, Marian: 'The Problem of Inequality of Economic Development in Europe in the Later Middle Ages', in: *Economic History Review*, 19, 1 (April 1966); pp. 15–28.
Malthus, Thomas Robert *An Essay on the Principle of Population or a View of its Past and Present Effects on Human Happiness, with an Inquiry into our Prospects Respecting the Future Removal or Mitigation of the Evils which it Occasions* (London; New York: J.M. Dent & Sons, 1958).
Mamalakis, Markos: 'La teoría mineral del crecimiento', in: *Trimestre Económico*, 45, 180 (October–December 1978); pp. 841–878.
Mandelbaum, David G.: 'Alcohol and Culture', in: *Current Anthropology*, 6, 3 (Juni 1965); S. 281–288.
Manes, René Pierre: 'The Quality and Pricing of Crude Oil: The American Experience', in: *Journal of Industrial Economics*, 12, 2 (March 1964); pp. 151–163.
Manning, Chris: 'Approaching the Turning Point? Labor Market Change under Indonesia's New Order', in: *Developing Economies*, 33, 1 (March 1995); pp. 52–81.
Mansouri-Acherar, Leila: 'La scolarisation des filles en Algérie', in: *Recherches Internationales*, 43–44 (Winter–Spring 1996); pp. 179–190.
Mantoux, Paul: *La Révolution industrielle au XVIIIe siècle. Essai sur les commencements de la grande industrie moderne en Angleterre* (Paris, 1905).

Mardin, Serif A.: 'Power, Civil Society and Culture in the Ottoman Empire', in: *Comparative Studies in Society and History*, 11, 3 (July 1969); pp. 258–281.

Markoff, John: 'Governmental Bureaucratization: General Processes and an Anomalous Case', in: *Comparative Studies in Society and History*, 17, 4 (October 1975); pp. 479–503.

Markov, Walter: 'Wege und Formen der Staatsbildung in Asien und Afrika seit dem Zweiten Weltkrieg', in: *Zeitschrift für Geschichtswissenschaft*, 18 (1970); pp. 725–749.

Markovitch, Tihomir J.: 'L'industrie lainière française au début du XVIIIe siècle', in: *Revue d'histoire économique et sociale* (1968); pp. 550–579.

Markovitz, Irving Louis: *Power and Class in Africa. An Introduction to Change and Conflict in African Politics* (Englewood Cliffs, N.J.: Prentice Hall, 1977).

Marquez, Jaime; MacNeilly, Caryl: 'Income and Price Elasticities for Exports of Developing Countries', in: *Review of Economics and Statistics*, 70, 2 (May 1988); pp. 322–330.

Marsden, Keith: 'Progressive Technologies for Developing Countries', in: *International Labour Review*, 101, 5 (May 1970); pp. 475–501.

Marx, Karl: 'Zur Judenfrage [1843]', in: Marx, Karl; Engels, Friedrich: *Marx Engels Werke. Band 1* (Berlin: Dietz, 1972); pp. 347–377.

———: 'Das revolutionäre Spanien [1854]', in: Marx, Karl; Engels, Friedrich: *Marx Engels Werke 10* (Berlin: Dietz, 1970); pp. 430–486.

———: *Grundrisse der politischen Ökonomie [1857–1858]* (Frankfort on the Main: Europäische Verlagsanstalt, 1974).

———: *Zur Kritik der politischen Ökonomie [1858]. Erstes Heft* (Berlin: Dietz, 1963).

———: *Das Kapital: Kritik der politischen Ökonomie (1): Der Produktionsprozeß des Kapitals [1867]. MEW 23* (Berlin: Dietz, 1972).

———: *Das Kapital (3): Der Gesamtprozeß der kapitalistischen Akkumulation [1894]. MEW 25* (Berlin: Dietz, 1972).

———; Engels, Friedrich: 'Manifest der Kommunistischen Partei' [1848], in: Marx, Karl; Engels, Friedrich: *Marx Engels Werke. Band 4* (Berlin: Dietz, 1948); pp. 459–493.

———: 'Die deutsche Ideologie: Kritik der neuesten deutschen Philosophie in ihren Repräsentanten Feuerbach, B. Bauer und Stirner, und des deutschen Sozialismus in seinen verschiedenen Propheten', in: Marx, Karl; Engels, Friedrich: *Marx Engels Werke. Band 3* (Berlin: Dietz, 1969); pp. 9–530.

Maschke, Erich: 'Die Wirtschaftspolitik Kaiser Friedrichs II im Königreich Sizilien', in: *Vierteljahrschrift für Sozial- und Wirtschaftsgeschichte*, 53, 3 (1966); pp. 289–328.

Masselman, George: 'Dutch Colonial Policy in the Seventeenth Century', in: *Journal of Economic History*, 21, 4 (December 1961); pp. 455–468.

Masters, William A.: 'Paying for Prosperity: How and Why to Invest in Agricultural Research and Development in Africa', in: *Journal of International Affairs*, 58, 2 (Spring 2005); pp. 35–64.

Masubuchi, Katsuhiko: *Japan's Household Savings Ratio* (Tokyo: Economic and Social Research Institute (ESRI), September 2006).

Mathew, W.M.: 'Foreign Contractors and the Peruvian Government at the Outset of the Guano Trade', in: *Hispanic American Historical Review*, 52, 4 (November 1972); pp. 598–620.

Mathur, P.N.; Ezekiel, Hannan: 'Marketable Surplus of Food and Price Fluctuations in a Developing Country', in: *Kyklos*, 14, 4 (1961); pp. 396–408.

Mathy, Sandrine: 'Comment intégrer les pays en développement dans des politiques climatiques fondées sur un système de quotas d'émissions?', in: *Tiers Monde*, 45, 177 (January–March 2004); pp. 85–105.

Matsumura, Masayoshi: 'Japan's Public Diplomacy in the Russo-Japanese War, 1904–5', in: *Teikyo Journal of Comparative Cultures*, 10 (1997); pp. 309–315.

Matthews, Derek: 'Serendipity or Economics? Tin and the Theory of Mineral Discovery and Development', in: *Business History*, 32, 3 (July 1990); pp. 15–48.

Mattick, Paul: *Marx und Keynes. Die Grenzen des "gemischten" Wirtschaftssystems* (Frankfort on the Main: Europäische Verlagsanstalt, 1969).

Mauro, Frédéric: 'La bourgeoisie portugaise au XVIIe siècle', in: *Dix-Septième-Siècle*, 10, 40 (July–September 1958); pp. 235–252.

Mauss, Marcel: *Manuel d'ethnographie* (Paris: Payot, 1947).

Mayor, Thomas: 'The Decline of the United States Capital-Output Ratio', in: *Economic Development and Cultural Change*, 16, 4 (July 1968); pp. 495–516.

Mazaheri, Nimah: 'An "Informal" Revolution: State-Business Conflict and Institutional Change in Iran', in: *Middle Eastern Studies*, 44, 4 (July 2008); pp. 585–602.

Meier, Charles S.: 'The Foundations of Productivity: Foundations of American International Economic Policy after World War II', in: *International Organization*, 31, 4 (Autumn 1977); pp. 607–633.

Meikins Wood, Ellen: 'The Uses and Abuses of Civil Society', in: *Socialist Register*, 26 (1990); pp. 60–84.

Meillassoux, Claude: *Anthropologie économique des Gouro de Côte d'Ivoire. De l' économie de subsistance à l'agriculture commerciale* (The Hague; Paris: Mouton, 1964).

———: 'Kinship Relations and Relations of Production', in: Seddon, David (ed.): *Relations of Production: Marxist Approaches to Economic Anthropology* (London: Frank Cass, 1978); pp. 289–330.

Meinecke, Friedrich: *Die Idee der Staatsräson in der neueren Geschichte* (Munich: Oldenbourg, 1963).

Meister, Albert: 'Développement communautaire et animation rurale en Afrique (1)', in: *Homme et la société*, 19 (January–March 1971); pp. 121–138.

Menck, Karl Wolfgang: 'Problems of a Code of Conduct', in: *Intereconomics*, 10, 10 (October 1975); pp. 313–316.

Mendels, Franklin F.: 'Protoindustrialization: The First Phase of the Industrialization Process', in: *Journal of Economic History*, 32, 1 (March 1972); pp. 240–261.

Mendels, Franklin F.: 'Social Mobility and Phases of Industrialization', in: *Journal of Interdisciplinary History*, 7, 2 (Autumn 1976); pp. 193–216.

Menon, Visalakshi: 'The Indian National Congress and Mass Mobilisation: A Study of the U.P. 1937–39', in: *Studies in History*, 2, 2 (July–December 1980); pp. 111–140.

Menon, Visalakshi: 'The U.P. Congress Socialist Party, 1937–1939', in: *Studies in History*, 6, 1 (August 1990); pp. 205–228.

Menzel, Ulrich: 'Das Ende der Dritten Welt und das Scheitern der großen Theorie. Zur Soziologie einer Disziplin auch in selbstkritischer Absicht', in: *Politische Vierteljahresschrift*, 32, 1 (March 1991); pp. 4–34.

———: *Das Ende der Dritten Welt und das Scheitern der großen Theorie* (Frankfort on the Main: Suhrkamp, 1992).

Mercier, Paul: 'Les classes sociales et les changements politiques récentes en Afrique Noire', in: *Cahiers internationaux de sociologie*, 12, 38 (January–June 1965); pp. 143–154.

Merkel, Wolfgang; Puhle, Hans-Jürgen; Croissant, Aurel; Eicher, Claudia; Thiery, Peter: *Defekte Demokratie. Theorien und Probleme. Defekte Demokratien (1):* (Leverkusen; Opladen: Leske und Budrich, 2001).

———: *Defekte Demokratie* (Opladen: Leske & Budrich, 2003).

Messelken, Karl Heinz: 'Zur Durchsetzung des Christentums in der Spätantike. Strukturell-funktionale Analyse eines historischen Gegenstandes', in: *Kölner Zeitschrift für Sozialwissenschaft und Sozialpsychologie*, 29, 2 (1977); pp. 261–284.

Meyer, Dirk: 'Die Entmachtung der Politik. Zur Frage der Überlebensfähigkeit demokratischer Nationalstaaten in einer globalisierten Weltwirtschaft', in: *Leviathan*, 33, 3 (September 2005); pp. 306–324.

Meyer, Jörg Udo; Seul, Dieter; Klingner, Karl-Heinz: *Die zweite Entwicklungsdekade der Vereinten Nationen* (Düsseldorf: Bertelsmann, 1971).

Meynier, Gilbert: 'Préface', in: Elsenhans, Hartmut: *La guerre d'Algérie 1954–1962. La transition d'une France à une autre. Le passage de la IV à la Ve République* (Paris: Publisud, 2000); pp. 7–60.

———: 'Problématique historique de la nation algérienne', in: *NAQD—Revue d'Études et de Critique Sociale*, 14–15 (Herbst–Winter 2001); S. 25–54.

———: *Histoire intérieure du FLN 1954–1962* (Paris: Fayard, 2002).

Michels, Robert: *Zur Soziologie des Parteiwesens in der modernen Demokratie: Untersuchungen über die oligarchischen Tendenzen des Gruppenlebens* (Leipzig: Kröner, 1925).

Mieck, Ilja: *Europäische Geschichte der Frühen Neuzeit: Eine Einführung.* (Stuttgart et al.: Kohlhammer GmbH, 1994).

Miller, Beatrice D.: 'The Web of Tibetan Monasticism', in: *Journal of Asian Studies*, 21, 2 (February 1961); pp. 97–203.

Millward, Robert: 'An Economic Analysis of the Organisation of Serfdom in Eastern Europe', in: *Journal of Economic History*, 42, 3 (September 1982); pp. 513–548.

Milonakis, Dimitris: 'Commodity Production and Price Formation Before Capitalism: A Value Theoretic Approach', in: *Journal of Peasant Studies*, 23, 2 (January 1995); pp. 327–365.

Milward, Alan S.: *The European Rescue of the Nation-State* (London; New York: Routledge, 1992).

———; Saul, Samuel B.: *The Economic Development of Continental Europe 1780–1870* (London: Allen & Unwin, 1973).

Minhas, Bagicha Singh: 'Rural Poverty, Land Redistribution and Development Strategy: Facts and Policy', in: *Indian Economic Review*, 5, 1 (April 1970); pp. 92–128.

Mishkin, Frederic S.: 'The Household Balance Sheet and the Great Depression', in: *Journal of Economic History*, 38, 4 (December 1978); pp. 918–937.

Mittenzwei, Ingrid: 'Aufgeklärter Absolutismus und Klassenverhältnisse in Brandenburg - Preußen', in: *Jahrbuch für Geschichte des Feudalismus*, 4 (1980); pp. 315–341.

Mizrahi, Yemile: 'Rebels Without a Cause? The Politics of Entrepreneurs in Chihuahua', in: *Journal of Latin American Studies*, 26, 1 (February 1994); pp. 137–158.

Mizuno, Koichi: 'Thai Pattern of Social Organization: Notes on a Contemporative Study', in: Ichimura, Shinichi (Ed.) (ed.): *South East Asia: Nature, Society and Development* (Honolulu, Hawaii: University Press of Hawaii, 1976); pp. 13–23.

Mo, Pak Hung: 'Effective Competition and Economic Development of Imperial China', in: *Kyklos*, 48, 1 (1995); pp. 87–103.

Moaddel, Manzoor: 'Class Struggle in Post-Revolutionary Iran', in: *International Journal of Middle East Studies*, 23, 3 (August 1991); pp. 317–343.

Moene, Karl Ove: 'Poverty and Landownership', in: *American Economic Review*, 82, 1 (March 1992); pp. 52–64.

Mohan, C. Raja: *Crossing the Rubicon: the Shaping of India's New Foreign Policy.* (New Delhi: Viking, 2003).

———: 'Re-making of Indian Foreign Policy: Ending the Marginalisation of International Relations Community', in: *International Studies*, 46, 1–2 (April–July 2009); pp. 147–163.

Moll-Murata, Christine: 'Chinese Guilds from the Seventeenth to the Twentieth Centuries: An Overview', in: *International Review of Social History*, 53, S16 (November 2008); pp. 213–247.

Mommsen, Ernst-Wolf: 'Strukturwandlungen in der Rohstoffversorgung der europäischen Eisen- und Stahlindustrie', in: *Kyklos*, 15, 4 (1962); pp. 758–776.

Monkiewicz, Jan: *International Technology Flows and the Technology Gap. The Experience of Eastern European Socialist Countries in International Perspective* (Frankfort on the Main; New York: Campus, 1989).

Moore, Barrington: *Social Origins of Dictatorship and Democracy: Lord and Peasant in the Making of the Modern World* (London: Allen Lane, 1966).

Moore, David: '"Sail on, O Ship of State": Neo-Liberalism, Globalisation and the Governance of Africa', in: *Journal of Peasant Studies*, 27, 1 (October 1999); pp. 61–96.
Moore, Karl James; Lewis, David Charles: 'Multinational Enterprise in Ancient Phoenicia', in: *Business History*, 42, 2 (April 2000); pp. 17–42.
Moorehouse, H. F.: 'The Marxist Theory of Labour Aristocracy', in: *Social History*, 3, 1 (1978); pp. 61–82.
Moreland, William Harrison: 'The Revenue System of the Mughal Empire', in: Haig, Wolsley; Burn, Richard (eds.): *The Mughal Period.The Cambridge History of India (4)* (New Delhi: S. Chand, 1987); pp. 449–474.
Morenz, Ludwig de: 'Die Phonetisierung des Bildes und ihre Folgen. Ein Modell für die Entstehung der ägyptischen Schrift', in: *Saeculum*, 53, 2 (2002); pp. 175–193.
Morillo, Stephen: 'A "Feudal Mutation"? Conceptual Tools and Historical Patterns in World History', in: *Journal of World History*, 14, 2 (December 2003); pp. 531–550.
Morineau, Michel: 'Or brésilien et gazettes hollandaises', in: *Revue d'histoire moderne et contemporaine* (January–March 1978); pp. 3–58.
Mörke, Olaf: 'Die Fugger im 16. Jahrhundert. Städtische Elite oder Sonderstruktur?', in: *Archiv für Reformationsgeschichte*, 74, 2 (1983); pp. 141–161.
Morlang, Thomas: '"Prestige der Rasse" contra "Prestige des Staates". Diskussion über die Befugnisse farbiger Polizeisoldaten gegenüber Europäern in den deutschen Kolonien', in: *Zeitschrift für Geschichtswissenschaft*, 49, 6 (2001); pp. 498–509.
Morony, Michael G.: 'Economic Boundaries? Late Antiquity and Early Islam', in: *Journal of the Economic and Social History of the Orient*, 47, 2 (2004); pp. 166–194.
Morris, David Morris: 'Towards a Reinterpretation of Nineteenth Century Indian Economic History', in: *Indian Economic and Social History Review*, 5, 1 (March 1968); pp. 1–15.
Morris, Ian: 'Economic Growth in Ancient Greece', in: *Journal of Institutional and Theoretical Economics*, 160, 4 (December 2004); pp. 709–742.
Mosler, Warren: *Soft Currency Economics* (West Palm Beach, Florida, September 1995).
———: *A General Analytical Framework for the Analysis of Currencies and Other Commodities*. Paper presented at the Fifth Post Keynesian Workshop: Full Employment and the Price Stability in a Global Economy, organised by *Journal of Postkeynesian Economics*, University of Tennessee, Knoxville, 25 June–1 July 1998.
Mottek, Hans: *Wirtschaftsgeschichte Deutschlands (1): Von den Anfängen bis zur Zeit der Französischen Revolution* (Berlin: VEB Verlag der Wissenschaften, 1964).
Mousnier, Roland: *Peasant Uprisings in Seventeenth-Century France, Russia and China* (New York: Harper & Row, 1967).

Moutoukian, Zacharias: 'Réseaux personnels et autorité coloniale: Les négociants de Buenos Aires au XVIIIe siècle', in: *Annales. Economie, Société, Civilisation*, 47, 4/5 (July/October 1992); pp. 899–915.

Mukherjee, Aditya: 'The Workers' and Peasants' Parties, 1926–30: An Aspect of Communism in India', in: *Studies in History*, 3, 1/2 (1981); pp. 1–44.

Mukherjee, Mridula: 'Peasant Movement in Patiala State, 1937–48', in: *Studies in History*, 1, 2 (1979); pp. 215–283.

Mukherjee, Sanjeeb: 'Civil Society in the East, and the Prospects of Political Society', in: *Economic and Political Weekly*, 45, 5 (30th January 2010); pp. 57–63.

Mukherji, Partha Nath: 'Do Challenges to Nation Building Ever End', in: *Kerala Sociologist*, 37, 2 (December 2009); pp. 5–14.

Mukhia, Harbans: 'Was There Feudalism in Indian History?', in: Kulke, Hermann (ed.): *The State in India 1000– 1700* (Cambridge, Mass. et al.: Oxford University Press, 1997); pp. 86–133.

Müller, Hans-Heinrich: 'Der agrarische Fortschritt und die Bauern in Brandenburg vor den Reformen von 1807', in: *Zeitschrift für Geschichtswissenschaft*, 12, 4 (1964); pp. 623–641.

Müller, Herta: *Marktwirtschaft und Islam: Ökonomische Entwicklungskonzepte in der islamischen Welt unter besonderer Berücksichtigung Algeriens und Ägyptens* (Baden-Baden: Nomos, 2002).

Müller, Johannes: *Die Industrialisierung der deutschen Mittelgebirge. Eine wirtschaftliche Frage der Vergangenheit—ein wirtschaftspolitisches Problem der Gegenwart* (Jena: Gustav Fischer, 1938).

Müller, Katharina: 'Pension Privatization in Latin America', in: *Journal of International Development*, 12, 4 (2000); pp. 507–518.

Müller, Kurt: 'Das "revolutionär-demokratische" Vorfeld des pluralistischen Kommunismus im Entwicklungsraum', in: *Vierteljahresberichte der FES - Probleme der Entwicklungsländer*, 27 (March 1967); pp. 1–14.

Mumenthaler, Rudolf: 'Spätmittelalterliche Städte West- und Osteuropas im Vergleich: Versuch einer verfassungsgeschichtlichen Typologie', in: *Jahrbuch für die Geschichte Osteuropas*, 46, 1 (1998); pp. 39–68.

Munro, John H.: 'Industrial Transformations in the North-West European Textile Trades, 1290–1340: Economic Progress or Economic Crisis?', in: Campbell, Bruce M. (ed) (ed.): *Before the Black Death. Studies in the Crisis of the Early Fourteenth Century* (1991); pp. 140–149.

Murphey, Rhoads: 'City and Countryside as Ideological Issues: India and China', in: *Comparative Studies in Society and History*, 14, 2 (1972); pp. 221–267.

Musson, Albert E.: *The Growth of British Industry* (London: Batsford, 1978).

Mytelka, Lynn Krieger: 'The Transfer of Technology: Myth or Reality?', in: Cosgrove, Carol; Jamar, J. (eds.): *The European Community's Development Policy: The Strategies Ahead. Conference organised at the College of Europe, Bruges, 4–6 July 1985* (Brugge: De Tempel, 1986); pp. 243–281.

Nadkarni, M.V.: 'Is Caste System Intrinsic to Hinduism? Demolishing a Myth', in: *Economic and Political Weekly*, 38, 45 (8th November 2003); pp. 4783–4793.

Nasir, Sadia: *Rise of Extremism in South Asia. Paper 7* (Islamabad: Islamabad Policy Research Institute, 2004).

Nath, Vijay: 'Puranic Tirthas: A Study of their Indigenous Origins and Transformation (Based Mainly on the Skanda Purana)', in: *Indian Historical Review*, 34, 1 (January 2007); pp. 1–46.

Nathan, Otto: *The Nazi Economic System. Germany's Mobilization for War* (Durham, N.C.: Duke University Press, 1944).

Nayar, Baldev Raj: 'Nationalist Planning for Autarky and State Hegemony: Development Strategy Under Nehru', in: *Indian Economic Review*, 32, 1 (1997); pp. 13–38.

Ndongko, Wilfried A.: 'The Political Economy of Development in Cameroon: Relations Between the State, Indigenous Businessmen and Foreign Investors', in: *Vierteljahresberichte der FES—Probleme der internationalen Zusammenarbeit*, 101 (September 1985); pp. 231–248.

Nef, John Ulric: *Industry and Government in France and England 1540–1640* (Philadelphia, Penn.: The American Philosophical Society, 1940).

———: *Cultural Foundations of Industrial Civilization* (Cambridge: Cambridge University Press, 1958).

Neil-Tomlinson, Barry: 'The Nyassa Chartered Company 1891–1929', in: *Journal of African History*, 18, 1 (1977); pp. 109–128.

Nelson, Richard R.: 'The Agenda for Growth Theory: A Different Point of View', in: *Cambridge Journal of Economics*, 22, 2 (July 1998); pp. 497–520.

Neumann, Hans: 'Frühe Hochkulturen: Mesopotamien', in: Jockenhövel, Albrecht (ed.): *WBG Weltgeschichte. Eine globalae Geschichte von den Anfängen bis ins 21.Jahrhundert(1): Grundlagen der globalen Welt vom Beginn bis 1200 v.Chr.* (Darmstadt: Wissenschaftliche Buchgesellschaft, 2009); pp. 484–215.

Newfarmer, Richard S.: *The International Market Power of Transnational Corporations: A Case Study of the Electrical Industry. UNCTAD/ST/MD/13* (Geneva: UNCTAD, April 1978).

Nickel, Herbert J.: 'Zur Immobilität und Schuldknechtschaft mexikanischer Landarbeiter. Universitätsschwerpunkt Lateinamerikaforschung Arbeitspapiere 5,' (January 1976); pp. 1–51.

Nicolas, Guy: *Dynamique de l'Islam au Sud du Sahara* (Paris: Publications Orientalistes de France, 1981).

Nigam, Aditya: *The Insurrection of Little Selves: The Crisis of Secular-Nationalism in India* (Cambridge, Mass. et al.: Oxford University Press, 2006).

Nissimi, Hilda: 'Illusions of World Power in Kenya: Strategy, Decolonization, and the British Base, 1946–1961', in: *International History Review*, 23, 4 (December 2001); pp. 757–1008.

Nitsch, Manfred; Diebel, Frank: *Guanxi Economics: Confucius Meets Lenin, Keynes, and Schumpeter in Contemporary China* (Berlin: Ms., 2006).

Njammasch, Marlene: 'Einige Aspekte der sozialen Gliederung in den altindischen Staaten in der zweiten Hälfte des 1. Jahrtausends', in: *Jahrbuch für Wirtschaftsgeschichte*, 4 (1978); pp. 107–123.

Nohlen, Dieter; Sturm, Roland: 'Über das Konzept der strukturellen Heterogenität', in: Nohlen, Dieter; Nuscheler, Franz (eds): *Handbuch der Dritten Welt (1): Unterentwicklung und Entwicklung-Theorien, Strategien, Indikatoren* (Hamburg: Hoffmann & Campe, 1982); pp. 92–116.

Nolan, Peter; Zhang, Jin: *The Challenge of Globalization for Large Chinese Firms. Discussion Paper 162* (Geneva: UNCTAD, July 2002).

Nolte, Hans Heinrich: 'Technologietransfer in Rußland vor 1914: Möglichkeiten und Grenzen nachholender Entwicklung', in: *Technikgeschichte*, 51, 4 (1984); pp. 319–330.

———: 'Pleading for a Set Indicators and Nonlinear Research: The European System in the Middle Ages', in: Hroch, Miroslav; Klusáková, Luda (eds): *Criteria and Indicators of Backwardness. Essays on Uneven Development in European History* (Prague: Charles University, 1996); pp. 29–46.

Noun, Christoph: 'Zwischenfall in Konitz. Antisemitismus und Nationalismus im preußischen Osten um 1900', in: *Historische Zeitschrift*, 266, 2 (April 1998); pp. 387–413.

Nouschi, André: *Les armes retournées. Colonisation et décolonisation françaises* (Paris: Éditions Belin, 2005).

Nurkse, Ragnar: *Problems of Capital Formation in Underdeveloped Countries* (New York: Oxford University Press, 1953).

Nuti, Domenico Mario: 'Capitalism, Socialism and Steady Growth', in: *Economic Journal*, 80, 317 (March 1970); pp. 32–57.

Nworah, Kenneth D.: 'The Integrative Stand in British West-Africa 1868–1940', in: *Genève-Afrique*, 13, 1 (1974); pp. 5–22.

O'Brien, Patrick Karl: 'Agriculture and the Home Market for English Industry', in: *English Historical Review*, 100, 397 (October 1985); pp. 773–800.

———: 'Imperialism and the Rise and Decline of the British Economy, 1688–1989', in: *New Left Review*, 238 (November–December 1999); pp. 48–80.

O'Brien, Richard: 'Oil Markets and the Developing Countries', in: *Third World Quarterly*, 8, 4 (October 1986); pp. 1309–1324.

Ochel, Wolfgang: 'Die asiatischen Schwellenländer—eine Gefahr für die deutsche Investitionsgüterindustrie?', in: *IFO-Schnelldienst*, 37, 28 (October 1984); pp. 3–14.

O'Donnell, Guillermo A.: 'Reflections on the Patterns of Change in the Bureaucratic-Authoritarian State', in: *Latin American Research Review*, 13, 1 (Spring 1978); pp. 3–38.

Ogilvie, Sheilagh: 'Consumption, Social Capital, and the "Industrious Revolution" in Early Modern Germany', in: *Journal of Economic History*, 70, 2 (June 2010); pp. 287–325.

O'Hear, Ann: 'Craft Industries in Ilorin: Dependency or Independence', in: *African Affairs*, 86, 345 (October 1987); pp. 505–521.

Ohnuki-Tierney, Emiko: 'The Emperor of Japan as Deity (Kami)', in: *Ethnology*, 30, 3 (July 1991); pp. 199–215.

Oki, Akira: 'The Dynamics of Subsistance Economy in West Sumatra', in: Turton, Andrew; Tanabe, Shigeharu (eds.): *History and Peasent Consciousness in South East Asia*. SENRI Ethnological Studies, No. 13 (Osaka: National Museum of Ethnology, 1984); pp. 267–291.

Okishio, Nobuo: 'Technical Change and the Rate of Profit', in: *Kobe University Economic Review*, 7 (1961); pp. 85–99.

Oksenberg, Michel C.: 'Political Changes and Their Causes in China, 1949–1972', in: *Political Quarterly*, 45, 1 (January–March 1974); pp. 95–114.

Olds, Kelly B.; Liu, Ruey-Hua: 'Economic Cooperation in 19th Century Taiwan: Religion and Informal Enforcement', in: *Journal of Institutional and Theoretical Economics*, 156, 2 (June 2000); pp. 404–430.

Olivier, Roland: 'The Problem of Bantu Expansion', in: *Journal of African History*, 7, 3 (1966); pp. 361–376.

Olney, Martha L.: 'Consumer Durables in the Interwar Years: New Estimates, New Pattern', in: *Research in Economic History*, 12 (1989); pp. 119–150.

Oman, Charles: *Policy Competition for Foreign Direct Investment: A Study of Competition among Governments to Attract FDI. Development Centre Studies* (Paris: OECD, 2000).

Omvedt, Gail: *Buddhism in India: Challenging Brahmanism and Caste* (Beverly Hills, Cal.; London; New Delhi: Sage, 2003).

Oommen, Tharaileth Koshy: 'Sources of Deprivation and Styles of Protest: The Case of the Dalits in India', in: *Contributions to Indian Sociology*, 18, 2 (May 1984); pp. 45–61.

———: 'Citizenship and National Identity in India: Towards a Feasible Linkage', in: Oommen, Tharaileth Koshy (ed.): *Citizenship and National Identity. From Colonialism to Globalism* (London: Sage, 1997); pp. 143–172.

Osborne, Evan: 'Labor Surplus in Korea: A Reassessment', in: *International Economic Journal*, 14, 4 (Winter 2000); pp. 125–141, http://gsis.ewha.ac.kr/kiea/ (24.05.2001)

Oshima, Harry T.: 'Employment Generation: The Long-Term Solution to Poverty', in: *Asian Development Review*, 8, 1 (1990); pp. 44–70.

Osiander, Andreas: 'Sovereignty, International Relations, and the Westphalian Myth', in: *International Organization*, 55, 2 (Spring 2001); pp. 251–287.

———: *Before the State: Systemic Political Change in the West from the Greeks to the French Revolution* (Cambridge, Mass. et al.: Oxford University Press, 2007).

Osterhammel, Jürgen: *China und die Weltgesellschaft. Vom 18. Jahrhundert bis in unsere Zeit* (Munich: Beck, 1989).

Otayek, René: 'Démocratie, culture politique, sociétés plurales: Une approche comparative à partir de situations africaines', in: *Revue française de science politique*, 47, 6 (December 1997); pp. 798–821.

Otsuka, Keijiro; Chuma, Hiroyuki; Hayami, Yujiro: 'Land and Labor Contracts in Agrarian Economies: Theories and Facts', in: *Journal of Economic Literature*, 30, 4 (December 1992); pp. 1965–2018.

Ouaissa, Rachid: *Staatsklasse als Entscheidungsakteur in den Ländern der Dritten Welt: Struktur, Entwicklung und Aufbau der Staatsklasse am Beispiel Algeriens* (Münster: LIT Verlag, 2004).

———: *Les carnets d'Hartmut Elsenhans: La guerre d'Algérie vue par ses acteurs français* (Algiers: Casbah, 2009).

———: 'Revolution ohne Revolutionäre. Bemühungen um eine islamische Demokratie', in: Hofbauer, Martin; Loch, Thorsten (eds.): *Wegweiser zur Geschichte Nordafrikas* (Paderborn: Ferdinand Schöningh, 2011); pp. 297–307.

Overton, Mark: 'English Agriculture History 1500–1850', in: *NEHA-Jaarboek*, 61 (1995); pp. 46–65.

Oxfeld, Ellen: '"When You Drink Water, Think of Its Source": Morality, Status, and Reinvention in Rural Chinese Funerals', in: *Journal of Asian Studies*, 63, 4 (November 2004); pp. 961–990.

Oxley, Geoffrey W.: *Poor Relief in England and Wales 1601–1834* (North Pomfret; Vancouver: David & Charles; Newton Abbott, 1974).

Pach, Zsoltan P.: 'Die Getreideversorgung der ungarischen Städte vom XV. bis zum XVIII. Jahrhundert', in: *Jahrbücher für Nationalökonomie und Statistik*, 179, 2 (1966); pp. 140–159.

———: 'Tendenze della produzione per il mercato nell'agricultura ungherese dei secoli XV–XVIII', in: *Studi Storici*, 9, 3/4 (July–December 1968); pp. 641–654.

Page, John et al.: *The East Asian Miracle. Economic Growth and Public Policy* (Washington: World Bank, 1993).

Page, Sheila: 'The Role of Trade in the New NICs', in: *Journal of Development Studies*, 27, 3 (April 1991); pp. 39–60.

Pagenstecher, Ulrich: 'Einflüsse der Tariflohnpolitik auf das Preisniveau', in: *Zeitschrift für die gesamte Staatswissenschaft / Journal of Institutional and Theoretical Economics*, 120, 4 (1964); pp. 713–736.

Pamuk, Sevket: 'The Ottoman Empire in the Eighteenth Century', in: *Itinerario*, 20, 3/4 (2000); pp. 104–116.

Pant, Fandita N.: 'What Sort of Incentives for Export?', in: *Economic and Political Weekly*, 7, 8 (19 February 1972); pp. 465–468.

Panuescu, Mihai: 'Wettbewerbsfähigkeit und Dynamik institutioneller Standortbedingungen: Ein empirischer Test des 'Varieties of Capitalism'—Ansatzes', in: *Schmollers Jahrbuch. Journal of Applied Social Science Studies*, 124, 1 (2004); pp. 31–59.

Papadakis, Maria: 'Did (or Does) the United States Have a Competivity Crisis', in: *Journal of Policy Analysis and Management*, 13, 1 (Winter 1994); pp. 1–20.

Paranjape, H.K.: 'Jawaharlal Nehru and the Planning Commission', in: *Indian Journal of Public Administration*, 10, 2 (April–June 1964).

Pares, Richard: 'The Economic Factors in the History of the Empire', in: *Economic History Review*, 7, 2 (May 1937); pp. 119–144.

Parijs, Philippe van: 'The Falling-Rate-of-Profit Theory of Crisis: A Rational Reconstruction by Way of Obituary', in: *Review of Radical Political Economics*, 12, 1 (Spring 1980); pp. 1–16.

Parker, David: 'French Absolutism, the English State and the Utility of the Base Superstructure Model', in: *Social History*, 15, 3 (November 1990); pp. 287–301.

Parry, John Horace: *The Discovery of the Sea* (London: Weidenfeld & Nicolson, 1975).

Parsons, Frederick V.: *The Origins of the Morocco Question, 1880–1900* (London: Duckworth, 1976).

Parthasarathi, Prasannan: 'Rethinking Wages and Competitiveness in the Eighteenth Century: Britan and South India', in: *Past and Present*, 158 (February 1998); pp. 79–109.

Pasara, Luis; Santistevan, Jorge: '"Industrial Communities" and Trade Unions in Peru: A Preliminary Analysis', in: *International Labour Review*, 108, 2/3 (August–September 1973); pp. 127–142.

Pasinetti, Luigi L.: *Growth and Income Distribution* (Cambridge: Cambridge University Press, 1974).

Paskaleva, Virginia: 'Über die Selbstverwaltung der Gemeinden in den europäischen Provinzen des osmanischen Reiches', in: *Bulgarian Historical Review*, 10, 1 (1982); pp. 50–56.

Pataki, George E.; Vilsack, Thomas J.; Levi, Michael A.: *Confronting Climate Change: A Strategy for U.S. Foreign Policy. Report of an Independent Task Force* (New York: Council of Foreign Relations, 2008).

Patel, Surendra J.: 'Main Features of Economic Growth Over the Century', in: *Indian Economic Journal*, 11, 3 (January–March 1963); pp. 286–303.

Patnaik, Prabhat: 'Speculation and Growth under Contemporary Capitalism', in: *Artha Vijnana*, 51, 1 (March 2009); pp. 1–11.

Paula, Luiz F.R.; Alves, Antonio J.: *Speculative Attack and Financial Instability: A Post Keynesian Crtique Appraisal of Conventional Currency Crises Models*. Paper presented at the Fifth Post Keynesian Workshop: Full Employment and the Price Stability in a Global Economy, organised by *Journal of Postkeynesian Economics*, University of Tennessee, Knoxville, 25 June–1 July 1998.

Pavier, Barry: 'The Telengana Armed Struggle', in: *Economic and Political Weekly*, 9, 32/34 (9 August 1974); pp. 1416–1420.

Payne, P.L.: 'The Emergence of Large-Scale Company in Great Britain, 1870–1914', in: *Economic History Review*, 20, 3 (1967); pp. 519–542.

Pearson, M.N.: 'Decline of the Mughal Empire', in: *Journal of Asian Studies*, 35, 2 (February 1976); pp. 221–236.

Pedroletti, Brice: 'Le combat des salariés d'Honda "pour toute la Chine"', in: *Le Monde*, (7 June 2010); p. 12

Peet, Richard: 'Industrial Devolution, Underconsumption and Third World Debt Crisis', in: *World Development*, 15, 6 (June 1987); pp. 777–788.

Pellicani, Luciano: 'On the Genesis of Capitalism', in: *Telos*, 20, 74 (Winter 1987); pp. 43–62.
Penrose, Edith: 'Origins and Development of the International Oil Crisis', in: *Millennium: Journal of International Studies*, 3, 1 (Spring 1974); pp. 37–44.
Penzkofer, Horst; Schmalholz, H.; Scholz, L.: 'Innovation, Wachstum und Beschäftigung', in: *IFO-Schnelldienst*, 42, 1/2 (January 1989); pp. 14–23.
Perdue, Peter C.: 'Insiders and Outsiders. The Xiangtau Riot of 1819 and Collective Action in Hunan', in: *Modern China*, 12, 2 (April 1986); pp. 166–201.
Pereira, Anthony W.: 'Economic Underdevelopment, Democracy and Civil Society: The North-East Brazilian Case', in: *Third World Quarterly*, 14, 2 (1993); pp. 365–380.
Perlmutter, Amos: 'Egypt and the Myth of the New Middle Class: A Comparative Analysis', in: *Comparative Studies in Society and History*, 9, 1 (1967); pp. 47–65.
Perroux, François: 'Le multiplicateur d'investissement dans les pays sous-développés', in: *Tiers Monde*, 7, 27 (July–September 1966); pp. 511–532.
Persson, Karl Gunnar: 'The Malthus Delusion', in: *European Review of Economic History*, 12, 2 (August 2008); pp. 165–176.
Pertev, Rashid: 'A New Model of Share Cropping and Peasant Holdings', in: *Journal of Peasant Studies*, 14, 1 (October 1986); pp. 27–49.
Peter, Chris Maina: 'Imperialism and Export of Capital', in: *Journal of Asian and African Studies (Leiden)*, 25, 3/4 (July–October 1990); pp. 197–212.
Petras, James F.: 'New Perspectives on Imperialism and Social Classes in the Periphery', in: *Journal of Contemporary Asia*, 5, 3 (1975); pp. 291–308.
———: 'The "Peripheral State": Continuity and Change in the International Division of Labour', in: *Journal of Contemporary Asia*, 12, 4 (October–December 1982); pp. 415–431.
———: 'Imperialism and the NGOs in Latin America', in: *Monthly Review*, 49, 7 (December 1997); pp. 10–27.
———; Veltmeyer, Henry: 'The "Development State" in Latin America: Whose Development, Whose State?', in: *Journal of Peasant Studies*, 34, 3 (July–October 2007); pp. 371–407.
Petzina, Dieter: *Autarkie im Dritten Reich. Der nationalsozialistische Vierjahresplan* (Stuttgart: Deutsche Verlagsans talt, 1968).
Pfaller, Alfred; Witte, Lothar: 'Wie sichern wir unsere Renten? Plädoyer für eine globale Strategie', in: *Internationale Politik und Gesellschaft*, 1/2002 (2002); pp. 121–136.
Phelps, Edmund S.: 'Second Essay on the Golden Rule of Accumulation', in: *American Economic Review*, 55, 4 (September 1965); pp. 793–814.
Phillips, C.A.; Mc Manus, T.F.; Nelson, R.W.: *Banking and the Business Cycle. A Study of the Great Depression in the United States* (New York: Macmillan, 1938).

Phillips, John A.; Wetherell, Charles: 'The Great Reform Act of 1832 and the Political Modernization of England', in: *American Historical Review*, 100, 2 (April 1995); pp. 410–436.

Phillips, Richard; Henderson, Jeffrey: 'Global Production Networks and Industrial Upgrading: Negative Lessons from Malaysian Electronics', in: *Journal für Entwicklungspolitik*, 25, 2 (Summer 2009); pp. 38–61.

Phimister, Ian: 'Corners and Company-Mongering: Nigerian Tin and the City of London', in: *Journal of Imperial and Commonwealth History*, 28 (May 2000); pp. 23–41.

Phlix, Dianne Furaha: *Förderung und gesellschaftspolitische Einbeziehung der Frauen in die Demokratisierungsprozesse Afrikas: Der Fall Ruanda* (Leipzig: Ph.D. Diss., 2009).

Pierenkemper, Toni: '"Dienstbotenfrage" und Dienstmädchenarbeitsmarkt am Ende des 19. Jahrhunderts', in: *Archiv für Sozialgeschichte*, 28 (1988); pp. 173–202.

Pieterse, Jan Nederveen: *Development Theory. Deconstructions/Reconstructions* (Beverly Hills, Cal.; London; New Delhi: Sage, 2001).

Pike, Ruth: 'The Genoese in Seville and the Opening of the New World', in: *Journal of Economic History*, 22, 3 (September 1962); pp. 348–378.

Pinto-Duschinsky, Michael: 'The Bad Government of "Good Government": Some Problems of "Civil Society" Organisations', in: Jain, Randhir Bahadur (ed.): *Governing Development: Challenges and Dilemmas of an Emerging Sub-Discipline in Political Science* (Opladen; Farmington Hills: Barbara Budrich, 2007); pp. 147–164.

Piore, Michael J.; Sabel, Charles F.: *The Second Industrial Divide, Possibilities for Prosperity* (New York; London: Basic Books, 1984).

Pirenne, Henri: *Histoire économique de l'Occident médiéval* (Brugge: Desclme De Brouwer, 1951).

Pitelis, Christos: 'The Transnational Corporation: A Synthesis', in: *Review of Radical Political Economics*, 21, 4 (Winter 1989); pp. 1–11.

Platt, Desmond Christopher M.: 'The Role of the British Consular Service in Overseas Trade 1825–1914', in: *Economic History Review*, 15, 3 (1963); pp. 495–512.

———: *Latin America and British Trade 1808–1914* (London: Adam & Charles Black, 1972).

———: 'Further Objections to an "Imperialism of Free Trade", 1830–1860', in: *Economic History Review*, 26, 1 (February 1973); pp. 77–91.

Plessner, Hellmuth: *Die verspätete Nation. Über die politische Verführbarkeit des bürgerlichen Geistes* (Stuttgart: Kohlhammer GmbH, 1959).

Pohl, Hans: 'Economic Powers and Political Powers in Early Modern Europe', in: *Journal of European Economic History*, 28, 1 (Spring 1999); pp. 139–168.

Polanyi, Karl: *The Great Transformation* (New York; Toronto: Farrar & Rinehart, 1944).

Pollard, Sidney: 'The Factory Village in the Industrial Revolution', in: *English Historical Review*, 79, 312 (July 1964); pp. 513–531.
Pomeranz, Kenneth: *The Great Divergence. Europe, China, and the Making of the Modern World Economy* (Princeton, N.J.: Princeton University Press, 2000).
———: 'Orthopraxy, Orthodoxy, and the Goddess(es) of Taishan', in: *Modern China*, 33, 1 (January 2007); pp. 22–46.
Poncet, Jean: 'D'Ibn Khaldoun au sous-développement', in: *La Pensée*, 131 (February 1967); pp. 22–39.
Popkin, Samuel: 'Colonialism and the Ideological Origins of the Vietnamese Revolution. A Review Article', in: *Journal of Asian Studies*, 44, 2 (February 1985); pp. 349–358.
Posnansky, Merrick: 'Bantu Genesis - Archeological Reflections', in: *Journal of African History*, 9, 1 (1968); pp. 1–11.
Posner, M.V.: 'International Trade and Technical Change', in: *Oxford Economic Papers*, 13, 3 (October 1961); pp. 323–341.
Potter, David C.: 'Manpower Shortage and the End of Colonialism. The Case of the Indian Civil Service', in: *Modern Asian Studies*, 7, 1 (January 1973); pp. 47–73.
Powell, Mike; Seddon, David: 'NGOs and the Development Industry', in: *Review of African Political Economy*, 24, 71 (March 1997); pp. 3–10.
Powis, Jonathan: 'Gallican Liberties and the Politics of Later Sixteenth Century France', in: *Historical Journal*, 26, 3 (September 1983); pp. 513–530.
Prasad, M. Madhava: 'Fan Bhakti and Subaltern Sovereignty: Enthusiasm as a Political Factor', in: *Economic and Political Weekly*, 44, 29 (18 July 2009); pp. 68–76.
Prasad, P.H.: 'Poverty in Rural India', in: *Journal of Social and Economic Studies*, 3, 1 (January–March 1986); pp. 69–87.
Prebisch, Raúl: 'The Economic Development of Latin America and its Principal Problems', in: *Economic Bulletin for Latin America*, 7, 1 (February 1962); pp. 1–22.
Price, Barbara J.: 'Prehispanic Irrigation Agriculture in Nuclear America', in: *Latin American Research Review*, 6, 3 (Autumn 1971); pp. 3–60.
Psacharopoulos, George; Layard, Richard: 'Human Capital and Earnings: British Evidence and a Critique', in: *Review of Economic Studies*, 46, 144 (July 1979); pp. 485–503.
Puhani, Patrick A.: 'What Happened to Wage and Non-employment Structures during the Dutch Employment Miracle?', in: *Applied Economics Quarterly*, 50, 2 (2004); pp. 209–215.
Pulsfort, Ernst: 'Die religiösen Wurzeln des politischen Hinduismus', in: *Asien-Afrika-Lateinamerika*, 24, 5 (1996); pp. 523–536.
Pye, Lucian W.: *Asian Power and Politics. The Cultural Dimensions of Authority* (Cambridge, Mass. et al.: Belknap, 1985).
Qin, Yaqing: 'Development of International Relations Theory in China', in: *International Studies*, 46, 1–2 (April–July 2009); pp. 185–201.

Qu, Geping: 'China's Dual-Thrust Energy Strategy', in: *Natural Resources Forum*, 16, 1 (February 1992); pp. 27–31.
Quilliot, Roger: *La SFIO et l'exercise du pouvoir 1944–1958* (Paris: Fayard, 1972).
Rader, Trout: *The Economics of Feudalism* (New York; London; Paris: Gordon & Breach, 1971).
Ram, Mohan: 'The Telengana Peasant Armed Struggle', in: *Economic and Political Weekly*, 8, 23 (9 April 1973); pp. 1025–1032.
Ramaswamy, Vijaya: 'Artisans in Vijayanagar Society', in: *Indian Economic and Social History Review*, 22, 4 (October 1985); pp. 417–444.
Rancière, Jacques: 'The Myth of the Artisan. Critical Reflections on a Category of Social History', in: *International Labor and Working Class History*, 24 (Autumn 1983); pp. 1–16.
Rankin, Mary Backus: *Early Chinese Revolutionaries. Radical Intellectuals in Shanghai and Chekiang, 1902–1911* (Cambridge, Mass.: Harvard University Press, 1971).
Rao, C. H. Hanumantha: 'Growing Regional Disparities in Development in india', in: *Indian Economic Journal*, 54, 1 (April–June 2006); pp. 52–61.
Raouf, Abbas Hamed: 'The Egyptian Labour Movement between the World Wars', in: *Journal of Asian and African Studies (Tokyo)*, 40 (1990); pp. 13–27.
Rapley, John: *Understanding Development. Theory and Practice in the Third World* (Boulder, Colo. et al.: Lynne Rienner, 1996).
Räth, Norbert; Braakman, Albert et al: 'Bruttoinlandsprodukt 2009', in: *Volkswirtschaftliche Gesamtrechnung* (2010); pp. 13–28.
Rathmann, Lothar: 'Die nationaldemokratische Entwicklung im arabischen Raum', in: *Zeitschrift für Geschichtswissenschaft*, 15, 8 (August 1967); pp. 1357–1387.
Ratnagar, Shereen: 'Le citadin et les liens tribaux à Mohenjo-daro. Habitat, parenté, voisinage', in: *Annales. Histoire, Sciences Sociales*, 59, 1 (January–February 2004); pp. 39–71.
Rauch, James E.: 'Networks versus Markets in International Trade', in: *Journal of International Economics*, 48, 1 (June 1999); pp. 7–35.
Raup, Philip M.: 'Land Reform and Agricultural Development', in: Southworth, Herman M.; Johnston, Bruce F. (eds.): *Agricultural Development and Economic Growth* (Ithaca, N.Y.: Cornell University Press, 1967a); pp. 267–314.
———: 'Some Interrelationships Between Public Administration and Agricultural Development', in: *Public Policy*, 14 (1967b); pp. 29–58.
Ray, Hemen: 'Changing Soviet Views on Mahatma Gandhi', in: *Journal of Asian Studies*, 29, 1 (November 1969); pp. 85–106.
Ray, Himanshu Prabha: 'Early Trade in the Bay of Bengal', in: *Indian Historical Review*, 14, 1/2 (July–January 1987); pp. 79–89.
———: 'The Archaeology of Bengal: Trading Networks, Cultural Identities', in: *Journal of the Economic and Social History of the Orient*, 49, 1 (2006); pp. 68–96.
Ray, Rajat Kanta: 'Chinese Financiers and Chetti Bankers in Southern Waters: Asian Mobile Credit during the Anglo-Dutch Competition for the Trade

of the Eastern Archipelago in the Nineteenth Century', in: *Itinerario*, 11, 1 (1987); pp. 209–234.

Reda Mezoui, Mohamed: 'La phénomène de la "rumeur" publique: Un aspect du fonctionnement de la communication sociale', in: *Revue algérienne des sciences juridiques, économiques et politiques*, 24, 2 (June 1986); pp. 272–290.

Reddy, K. Venugopal: 'Against the Colonial State: Working Class in India's Struggle for Freedom', in: *Indian Historical Review*, 33, 2 (July 2006); pp. 112–133.

———: 'Congress Ministry and the Labour Policy, 1937–1939: Madras Presidency', in: *Indian Historical Review*, 34, 2 (July 2007); pp. 122–147.

Regul, Rudolf August: *Energiequellen der Welt; Betrachtungen und Statistiken zur Energiewirtschaft* (Hamburg: Hanseatische Verlagsanstalt, 1937).

Reid, Donald M.: 'The Syrian Christians and Early Socialism in the Arab World', in: *International Journal of Middle East Studies*, 5, 2 (May 1974); pp. 177–193.

Reinecke, Christiane: 'Governing Aliens in Times of Upheaval: Immigration Control and Modern State Practice in Early Twentieth-Century Britain, Compared with Prussia', in: *International Review of Social History*, 54, 1 (April 2009); pp. 39–65.

Reischauer, Edwin O.; Fairbank, John K.: *East Asia. The Great Tradition* (Boston, Mass.: Houghton Mifflin, 1960).

Remmelinck, W.: 'Expansion without Design: The Snare of Javanese Politics', in: *Itinerario*, 12, 1 (1988); pp. 111–128.

Renan, Ernest: 'Qu'est-ce qu'une Nation?', in: Renan, Ernest: *Qu'est-ce qu'une Nation? Et autres écrits politiques.* (Paris: Imprimerie Nationale, 1996); pp. 223–243.

Renten, Geert: 'Accumulation of Capital and the Foundation of the Tendency of the Rate of Profit to Fall', in: *Cambridge Journal of Economics*, 15, 1 (March 1991); pp. 79–93.

Reza, Sadrel; Mahbubul Alam, A.H.M.; Ali Rashid, M.: *Private Foreign Investment in Bangladesh* (Dhaka: University Press, 1987).

Rezneck, Samuel: 'The Rise and Early Development of Industrial Consciousness in the United States 1760–1830', in: *Journal of Economic and Business History*, 4, 4 (1931); pp. 784–811.

Ricardo, David: *On the Principles of Political Economy and Taxation [1817]. The Works and Correspondence of David Ricardo (1)* (Cambridge et al.: Cambridge University Press, 1951).

Richards, John F.: 'Warriors and the State in Early Modern India', in: *Journal of the Economic and Social History of the Orient*, 47, 3 (2004); pp. 390–400.

Richardson, Henry: 'Real Wage Movements', in: *Economic Journal*, 49, 195 (September 1939); pp. 425–441.

Rieger, Brigitte: *Rentiers, Patrone und Gemeinschaft:Soziale Sicherung im Libanon* (Frankfurt am Main et al.: Lang, 2003).

Riley, Dylan: 'Privilege and Property: The Political Foundations of Failed Class Formation in Eighteenth-Century Austrian Lombardy', in: *Comparative Studies in Society and History*, 45, 1 (January 2003); pp. 190–213.

Rinalsi, Alberto: 'The Emilian Model Revisited: Twenty Years After', in: *Business History*, 47, 2 (April 2005); pp. 244–266.
Risse, Thomas; Ropp, Stephen C.: 'International Human Rights Norms and Domestic Change: Conclusions', in: Risse-Kappen, Thomas; Ropp, Stephen; Sikkink, Kathryn (eds.): *The Power of Human Rights. International Norms and Domestic Change.* (Cambridge et al.: Cambridge University Press, 2001); pp. 234–278.
Ritter, Gerhard A.: 'Staat und Arbeiterschaft in Deutschland von der Revolution 1848/49 bis zur nationalsozialistischen Machtergreifung', in: *Historische Zeitschrift*, 231, 2 (October 1980); pp. 325–368.
Robb, Peter: 'Town and Country: Economic Linkages and Political Mobilization in Bihar in the Late Nineteenth and Early Twentieth Centuries', in: Hill, John L. (ed.): *The Congress and Indian Nationalism: Historical Perspectives* (London: Curzon Press, 1991); pp. 192–221.
Roberts, Kenneth M.: 'Neoliberalism and the Transformation of Populism in Latin America: the Peruvian Case', in: *World Politics*, 48, 1 (October 1995); pp. 82–116.
Robinson, Joan Violet: 'What Are the Questions?', in: *Journal of Economic Literature*, 15, 4 (December 1977); pp. 1318–1373.
———: *Aspects of Development and Underdevelopment* (Cambridge: Cambridge University Press, 1979).
Roeder, Philip G.: 'Modernization and Participation in the Leninist Development Strategy', in: *American Political Science Review*, 83, 3 (September 1989); pp. 859–884.
Roehl, Richard: 'French Industrialization: A Reconsideration', in: *Explorations in Economic History*, 13, 3 (July 1976); pp. 233–281.
Roemer, John E.: 'Continuing Controversy on the Falling Rate of Profit: Fixed Capital and Other Issues', in: *Cambridge Journal of Economics*, 3, 4 (December 1979); pp. 379–398.
Rogerson, William P.: 'Quality vs. Quantity in Military Procurement', in: *American Economic Review*, 80, 5 (May 1990); pp. 83–92.
Root, Hilton R.: 'Privilege and the Regulation of the Eighteenth-Century French Trades', in: *Journal of European Economic History*, 11, 2 (Autumn 1982); pp. 301–348.
Rosenberg, Nathan: *Perspectives on Technology* (Cambridge: Cambridge University Press, 1976).
Rosenplänter, Johannes: 'Entre agriculture et industrie textile. Trois paroisses au sud du Pays d'Auge de 1600 à 1800 (La Chapelle-Yvon, La Cressonnière, La Croupte)', in: *Annales de Normandie*, 50, 2 (May 2000); pp. 321–368.
Rosenstein-Rodan, P.N.: 'Problems of Industrialization of Eastern and South Eastern Europe', in: *Economic Journal*, 53, 210 (June–September 1943); pp. 202–211.

Rosés, Joan R.: 'Measuring the Contribution of Human Capital to the Development of the Catalan Factory System (1830–1861)', in: *European Review of Economic History*, 1, 1 (April 1997); pp. 25–48.

Ross, Robert; Trachte, Kent: 'Global Cities and Global Classes: The Peripheralization of Labor in New York City', in: *Review (Fernand Braudel Center)*, 6, 3 (Winter 1983); pp. 393–431.

Rostovtzeff, Michail Ivanovic: 'Roman Exploitation of Egypt in the First Century A.D.', in: *Journal of Economic and Business History*, 1 (1929); pp. 337–364.

Rotberg, Robert I.: 'African Nationalism: Concept or Confusion', in: *Journal of Modern African Studies*, 4, 1 (1966); pp. 33–46.

Rothstein, Robert L.: 'Regime-Creation by a Coalition of the Weak: Lessons from the NIEO and the Integrated Program for Commodities', in: *International Studies Quarterly*, 28, 3 (September 1984); pp. 307–328.

Rott, Renate: *Industrialisierung und Arbeitsmarkt. Aspekte der sozioökonomischen Entwicklung der Arbeits- und Gewerkschaftspolitik in Kolumbien und Mexiko* (Meisenheim am Glan: Anton Hain, 1979).

Rounds, J.: 'Lineage, Class, and Power in the Aztec State', in: *American Ethnologist*, 6, 1 (February 1979); pp. 73–86.

Roussel, Louis: 'Employment Problems and Policies in the Ivory Coast', in: *International Labour Review*, 104, 6 (December 1971); pp. 505–525.

Rowthorn, Robert; Ramaswamy, Ramana: 'Growth, Trade and Deindustrialization', in: *IMF Staff Papers*, 46, 1 (März 1999); pp. 18–41.

Roy, Kaushik: 'The Beginning of "People's War" in India', in: *Economic and Political Weekly*, 42, 19 (12 May 2007); pp. 1720–1728.

Roy, Tirthankar: 'The Guild in Modern South Asia', in: *International Review of Social History*, 53, S16 (November 2008); pp. 95–120.

Rubin, Jared: 'Bills of Exchange, Interest Bans, and Impersonal Exchange in Islam and Christianity', in: *Explorations in Economic History*, 47, 2 (April 2010); pp. 213–227.

Rublack, Susanne: 'Fighting Transboundary Waste Streams: Will the Basel Convention Help', in: *Verfassung und Recht in Übersee*, 22, 4 (April 1989); pp. 364–391.

Rudolph, Lloyd I.; Hoeber-Rudolph, Susanne: 'Cultural Policy, the Textbook Controversy and Indian Identity', in: Wilson, A. Jayarah; Dennis Dalton (eds.): *The State of South Asia. Problems of National Integration* (London; Rome: Hamish Hamilton, 1982); pp. 131–154.

Rueda, David; Pontusson, Jonas: 'Wage Inequality and Varieties of Capitalism', in: *World Politics*, 52, 3 (April 2000); pp. 350–383.

Rutherford, Bruce K.: 'What Do Egypt's Islamists Want? Moderate Islam and the Rise of Islamic Constitutionalism', in: *Middle East Journal*, 60, 4 (Autumn 2006); pp. 707–731.

Rutten, Mario: *Rural Capitalists in Asia. A Comparative Analysis on India, Indonesia and Malaysia* (London; New York: Routledge Curzon, 2003).

Saberwal, Satish: 'On the Rise of Institutions, Or: The Church and Kingship in Medieval Europe', in: *Studies in History*, 7, 1 (1991); pp. 108–134.

Sadria, Mody-Ta-Ba: 'L'Indonesie: Interaction et conflits idéologiques avant la deuxième guerre mondiale', in: *Etudes internationales*, 17, 1 (March 1986); pp. 49–62.

Safari, Joseph F.: *Grundlagen und Auswirkungen des Maji-Maji-Aufstandes von 1905. Kulturgeschichtliche Betrachtungen zu einer Heilserwartungsbewegung in Tansania* (Cologne: Ph.D. Diss., 1972).

Sahota, Gian Singh: 'Theories of Personal Income Distribution: A Survey', in: *Journal of Economic Literature*, 16, 1 (March 1978); pp. 1–55.

Sakbani, Michael: *A Re-examination of the Architecture of the International Economic System in a Global Setting: Issues and Proposals*. UNCTAD Discussion Papers, No. 181 (October 2005).

Sala-I-Martin, Xavier: 'I Just Ran Two Million Regressions', in: *American Economic Review*, 87, 2 (May 1997); pp. 179–183.

Salter, Wilfried E. G.: *Productivity and Technical Change* (Cambridge et al.: Cambridge University Press, 1960).

Salvadori, Neri: 'Falling Rate of Profit With a Constant Real Wage - An Example', in: *Cambridge Journal of Economics*, 5, 1 (May 1981); pp. 57–66.

Samarin, William J.: 'La politique indigène in the History of Bangui', in: *Revue française d'histoire d'outre-mer*, 79, 294 (1992); pp. 53–85.

Sampson, Anthony: *The Seven Sisters. The Great Oil Companies and the World They Shaped* (New York: Viking, 1975).

Samuel, Geoffrey: 'Tibet as a Stateless Society and Some Islamic Parallels', in: *Journal of Asian Studies*, 41, 2 (February 1982); pp. 215–229.

Samuelson, Paul A.: 'International Trade and the Equalization of Factor Prices', in: *Economic Journal*, 58, 230 (June 1948); pp. 163–184.

——: 'The Economics of Marx: An Ecumenical Reply', in: *Journal of Economic Literature*, 10, 1 (March 1972); pp. 51–57.

Sandbrook, Richard: 'Is Socialism Possible in Africa', in: *Journal of Commonwealth and Comparative Politics*, 19, 1 (July 1981); pp. 197–207.

Sanders, William T.; Webster, David: 'The Mesoamerican Urban Tradition', in: *American Anthropologist*, 90, 3 (September 1988); pp. 521–546.

Sapir, André: 'Trade in Investment-Related Technologaical Services', in: *World Development*, 14, 5 (May 1986); pp. 605–622.

Sarkar, Gautam K.: *The World Tea Economy* (Delhi; Calcutta; Madras: Oxford University Press, 1972).

Sarkar, Jayabrata: 'Power, Hegemony and Politics: Leadership Struggle in Congress in the 1930s', in: *Modern Asian Studies*, 40, 2 (Summer 2006); pp. 333–370.

Sarkar, Sumit: *Modern India, 1885–1947* (Chennai: Macmillan, 1983).

Sarkis, Nicolas: *Le pétrole à l'heure arabe* (Paris: Stock, 1975).

Sarris, Peter: 'Continuity and Discontinuity in the Post-Roman Economy', in: *Journal of Agrarian Change*, 6, 3 (July 2006); pp. 400–413.

Sau, Ranjit: 'A Theory of Rent and Agrarian Relations', in: *Economic and Political Weekly*, 14, 26 (30 June 1979); pp. A42–A46.

Savonnet, Guy: 'Paysans des savanes africaines et paysans du Nordeste brésilien', in: Coquery-Vidrovitch, Catherine (ed.): *Sociétés paysannes du Tiers-Monde. Publication du Laboratoire Connaissance du Tiers-Monde de l'Université de Paris VII* (Lille: Presses Universitaires de Lille, 1980); pp. 41–56.

Sawyer, John E.: 'The Social Basis of the American System of Manufacturing', in: *Journal of Economic History*, 14, 4 (Autumn 1954); pp. 361–379.

Say, Jean-Baptiste: *Traité d'économie politique* (Paris: Calmann-Lévy, 1972).

Sayer, Derek: 'A Notable Administration: English State Formation and the Rise of Capitalism', in: *American Journal of Sociology*, 97, 5 (March 1992); pp. 1382–1415.

———: 'The Language of Nationality and the Nationality of Language: Prague 1780–1920', in: *Past and Present*, 153 (November 1996); pp. 164–210.

Sayers, R.S.: *A History of Economic Change in England, 1880–1939* (London: Oxford University Press, 1967).

Schade, Burkhard: 'Altern in Entwicklungsländern', in: *Zeitschrift für Gerontologie*, 19, 2 (1986); pp. 77–81.

Schaller, Erhard: 'Die Anfänge der Planung in Indien und der Bombay-Plan der indischen Großbourgeoisie aus dem Jahre 1944', in: *Asien-Afrika-Lateinamerika*, 14, 3 (1986); pp. 429–440.

Schaller, Sven: *Marginalität und Agrarreform in Peru. Eine Kritik der Size-Yield-Inverse und der politischen Implikationen* (Leipzig: Ph.D. Diss., Summer 2006).

Schanetzky, Tim: 'Aporien der Verwissenschaftlichung: Sachverständigenrat und wirtschaftlicher Strukturwandel in der Bundesrepublik 1974–1988', in: *Archiv für Sozialgeschichte*, 50 (2010); pp. 153–168.

Scharpf, Fritz W.: *Sozialdemokratische Krisenpolitik in Europa* (Frankfort on the Main; New York: Campus, 1987).

———: *European Governance: Common Concerns vs. the Challenge of Diversity. Jean Monnet Paper 6/01, Symposium: The Commission White Paper on Governance* (New York: New York School of Law, 2001).

Schatz, Klaus-Werner: 'Zum sektoralen und regionalen Strukturwandel in der Bundesrepublik Deutschland', in: *WSI-Mitteilungen*, 29, 11 (November 1976); pp. 653–660.

———: *Die neue weltwirtschaftliche Arbeitsteilung: ihr Beitrag zu einer Strategie der Grundbedürfnisse und zur Lösung des Nord-Süd-Konfliktes* (Kiel: MS, January 1983).

Scheffler, Thomas: 'Politische und gesellschaftliche Stellung von Minderheiten', in: Steinbach, Udo; Robert, Rüdiger; Schmidt-Dumont, Marianne (eds.): *Der Nahe und Mittlere Osten. Politik—Gesellschaft—Wirtschaft—Geschichte—Kultur. Bd.1: Grundlagen, Strukturen, Problemfelder* (Opladen: Leske und Budrich, 1988); pp. 510–510.

Schelsky, Helmut: *Wandlungen der deutschen Familie in der Gegenwart. Darstellung und Deutung einer empirisch-soziologischen Bestandsaufnahme* (Stuttgart: Enke, 1955).
Schiel, Tilman: 'Der Imperialismus als höchstes Stadium des Feudalismus. Fragezeichen zu: "500 Jahre Weltmarkt"' *Peripherie*, 12, 46 (May 1992); pp. 71–93.
———; Stauth, Georg: 'Unterentwicklung und Subsistenzproduktion', in: *Peripherie*, 1, 5/6 (1981); pp. 122–143.
Schlauch, Margaret: 'The Revolt of 1381 in England', in: *Science and Society*, 4, 4 (Autumn 1940); pp. 414–432.
Schlenther, Ursula: 'Über die Auflösung der Theokratien im präkolumbischen Amerika', in: *Ethnographisch-Archäologische Zeitschrift*, 2, 1 (1961); pp. 33–44.
Schmid, Günther: 'Beschäftigungswunder Niederlande? Ein Vergleich der Beschäftigungssysteme in den Niederlanden und in Deutschland', in: *Leviathan*, 25, 3 (September 1997); pp. 302–337.
Schmidt, Hellmut: 'Mir scheint, daß das Deutsche Volk–zugespitzt–5% Preisanstieg eher vertragen kann', in: *Süddeutsche Zeitung* (28 July 1972); p. 8.
Schmidt-Glintzer, Helwig: 'Reich und Gesellschaft in China. Die Geschlossenheit einer offenen Welt', in: *Saeculum*, 55, 2 (2004); pp. 157–174.
Schmitz, Christopher J.: 'The World Copper Industry: Geology, Mining Techniques and Corporate Growth 1870–1939', in: *Journal of European Economic History*, 29, 1 (Spring 2000); pp. 77–108.
Schoenbrun, David L.: 'We Are What We Eat. Ancient Agriculture Between the Great Lakes', in: *Journal of African History*, 34, 1 (1993); pp. 1–31.
Schöffer, I.: 'The Second Serfdom in Eastern Europe as a Problem of Historical Explanation', in: *Historical Studies, Australia and New Zealand*, 9, 33 (November 1959); pp. 46–61.
Schröder, Klaus: *Die Kredit- und Verschuldungspolitik der Sowjetunion gegenüber dem Westen* (Baden-Baden: Nomos, 1987).
Schultz, Helga: 'Bäuerliche Klassenkämpfe zwischen frühbürgerlicher Revolution und Dreißigjährigem Krieg', in: *Zeitschrift für Geschichtswissenschaft*, 20, 2 (February 1972); pp. 156–172.
Schultz, Petra: *Die 'Instance Equité et Réconciliation'. Vergangenheitsaufarbeitung in Marokko* (Leipzig: MA Thesis, 2006).
Schultz, Theodore W.: 'Investment in Human Capital', in: *American Economic Review*, 51, 1 (March 1961); pp. 1–17.
Schumacher, Dieter: 'Trade Developing Countries and Employment in the European Community 1980', in: *Intereconomics*, 16, 3 (July–August 1981); pp. 183–188.
Schumpeter, Joseph Alois: *Kapitalismus, Sozialismus und Demokratie* (Bern: A. Francke, 1950).
Schutz, Erich: 'Non-Produced Inputs, Differential Profit Rates and the Okishio Theorem', in: *Review of Radical Political Economics*, 19, 2 (Summer 1987); pp. 43–60.

Schwecke, Sebastian: *New Cultural Identitarian Political Movements: The Bharatiya Janata Party between Cultural Identity and Middle Class Interests* (London; New York: Routledge, 2011)

Scott, C.V.: 'International Capital and the Oil-Producing States in Africa. An Analysis of Angola, Nigeria and Algeria', in: *Journal of Developing Societies*, 8, 2 (1992); pp. 179–193.

Scott, James C.: 'Protest and Profanation: Agrarian Revolt and the Little Tradition', in: *Theory and Society*, 8, 3 (Autumn 1977); pp. 211–246.

———: 'Revolution in the Revolution', in: *Theory and Society*, 10, 1/2 (January–March 1979); pp. 97–134.

Scrivenor, Harry: *History of the Iron Trade. From the Earliest Records to the Present Period* (London: Longman, Brown, Green & Longmans, 1854).

Sédov, L.: 'La société angkorienne et le problème du mode de production asiatique', in: *La Pensée*, 138 (April 1968); pp. 71–84.

Seefried, Elke: 'Experten für die Planung? 'Zukunftsforscher' als Berater der Bundesregierung 1966–1972/73', in: *Archiv für Sozialgeschichte*, 50 (2010); pp. 109–152.

Seifzadeh, Hossein S.: 'The Landscape of Factional Politics and Its Future in Iran', in: *Middle East Journal*, 57, 1 (Winter 2003); pp. 57–75.

Selden, Mark: 'Yan'an Communism Reconsidered', in: *Modern China*, 21, 1 (January 1995); pp. 8–44.

Semmler, Willi: 'Arbeitsmarkt und Zukunftsperspektiven: USA und Deutschland', in: *Leviathan*, 26, 4 (Dezember 1998); pp. 557–566.

Sen, Siddhartha: 'Some Aspects of State-NGO Relationships in India in the Post-Independence Era', in: *Development and Change*, 30, 2 (1999); pp. 327–355.

Senghaas, Dieter: *Weltwirtschaftsordnung und Entwicklungspolitik. Plädoyer für Dissoziation* (Frankfort on the Main: Suhrkamp, 1977).

———: 'The Development Problematic: A Macro-Micro Perspective', in: *Journal of Peace Research*, 26, 1 (February 1989); pp. 57–67.

———: *Zivilisierung wider Willen: Der Kampf der Kulturen mit sich selbst* (Frankfort on the Main: Suhrkamp, 1998).

Sethi, Rajiv; Somanathan, E.: 'Understanding Reciprocity', in: *Journal of Economic Behaviour and Organization*, 50, 1 (2003); pp. 1–27.

Shafaeddin, S. M.: 'Towards an Alternative Perspective on Trade and Industrial Policies', in: *Development and Change*, 36, 6 (November 2005); pp. 1143–1162.

Shaffer, Edward H.: *The Oil Import Programme of the US* (New York: Praeger, 1968).

Shahin, Emad Eldin: *Political Ascent. Contemporary Islamic Movements in North Africa* (Boulder, Colo.: Westview Press, 1997).

Shaloff, Stanley: 'The Income Tax, Indirect Rule, and the Depression: The Gold Coast Riots of 1931', in: *Cahiers d'études africaines*, 14, 54 (June 1974); pp. 359–376.

Shammas, Carole: 'Food Expenditures and Economic Well-Being in Early Modern England', in: *Journal of Economic History*, 43, 1 (March 1983); pp. 89–100.
Sharma, Mahesh: 'State Formation and Cultural Complex in Western Himalayas', in: *Indian Economic and Social History Review*, 41, 4 (October–December 2004); pp. 387–431.
Sharma, R.S.: 'Problem of Transition from Ancient to Medieval in Indian History', in: *Indian Historical Review*, 1, 1 (July 1974); pp. 1–9.
Sharma, Rajvir: 'The Bharatiya Janata Party: Identitarianism and Governance Agenda', in: Elsenhans, Hartmut; Ouaissa, Rachid; Schwecke, Sebastian; Tetreault, Mary Ann (eds.): *The Transformation of Politised Religion: Zealots Turned into Leaders* (Aldershot: Ashgate, 2014); forthcoming.
Sharma, Shalendra D.: *Development and Democracy in India* (Boulder, Colo. et al.: Lynne Rienner, 1999).
Shaw, Timothy M.: 'The Actors in African International Politics', in: Shaw, Timothy M.; Heard, Kenneth A. (eds.): *The Politics of Africa: Dependence and Development* (New York: Africa Publishing House, 1979); pp. 357–396.
Shaw-Taylor, Leigh: 'Labourers, Cows, Common Rights and Parliamentary Enclosure: The Evidence of Contemporary Comment c.1760–1810', in: *Past and Present*, 171 (May 2001).
Shechter, Relli: 'The Cultural Economy of Development in Egypt: Economic Nationalism, Hidden Economy and the Emergence of Mass Consumer Society during Sadat's Infitah', in: *Middle Eastern Studies*, 44, 4 (July 2008); pp. 571–583.
Shendge, Malati J.: 'Myth and Governance in Early India', in: *Indian Journal of Public Administration*, 28, 4 (October–December 1982); pp. 863–892.
Sheridan, Richard B.: '"Sweet Malefactor": The Social Costs of Slavery and Sugar in Jamaica and Cuba, 1807–1854', in: *Economic History Review*, 29, 2 (May 1976); pp. 237–257.
Sherwood, Marika: 'India at the Founding of the United Nations', in: *International Studies*, 33, 4 (October–December 1996); pp. 405–428.
Sheshinski, Eytan: 'Tests of the "Learning by Doing" Hypothesis', in: *Review of Economics and Statistics*, 49, 4 (November 1967); pp. 568–578.
Shih, Chien-Sheng: 'Economic Development in Taiwan After the Second World War', in: *Weltwirtschaftliches Archiv*, 100, 1 (1968); pp. 112–134.
Shinohara, Miyohei: 'Relative Production Levels of Industrial Countries and Their Growth Potential', in: *Weltwirtschaftliches Archiv*, 86, 1 (1961); pp. 131–145.
Shivji, Issa G.: 'The Silences in the NGO Discourse: The Role and Future of NGOs in Africa', in: *Africa Development*, 31, 4 (2006); pp. 22–51.
Shonfield, Andrew: *Modern Capitalism. The Changing Balance of Public and Private Power* (London: Oxford University Press, 1965).
Sid Ahmed, Abdelkader: *Économie de l'industrialisation à partir de ressources naturelles (I.B.R.). (2) Le cas des hydrocarbures* (Paris: Publisud, 1989).
———: *Un projet pour l'Algérie: Eléments pour un réel partenariat Euro-Méditerranéen* (Paris: Publisud, 1995).

Siebert, Horst: 'The Japanese Bubble: Some Lessons for International Macroeconomic Policy Coordination', in: *Außenwirtschaft*, 55, 2 (June 2000); pp. 233–250.

Siemens, Werner: 'Die Modernisierung bei Siemens & Halske 1972: Der "amerikanische" Saal', in: Ritter, Gerhard Albert; Kocka, Jürgen (eds): *Deutsche Sozialgeschichte 1870–1914: Dokumente und Skizzen* (Munich: C.H. Beck, 1972); pp. 151–152.

Silverman, Julian: 'Shamans and Acute Schizophrenia', in: *American Anthropologist*, 69, 1 (February 1967); pp. 21–31.

Simmons, Colin: '"De-Industrialisation", Industrialization and the Indian Economy, c. 1850–1947', in: *Modern Asian Studies*, 19, 3 (1985); pp. 593–622.

Singer, Hans Wolfgang: 'U.S. Foreign Investment in Underdeveloped Areas. The Distribution of Gains between Investing and Borrowing Countries', in: *American Economic Review*, 40, 2 (May 1950); pp. 473–485.

Singer, Paul I.: 'Reproduction de la force de travail et développement', in: *Tiers Monde*, 17, 68 (October–December 1976); pp. 961–986.

Sinha, P.B.: *Indian National Liberation Movement and Russia (1905–1917)* (New Delhi: Sterling, 1975).

Sinha, Surajit: 'State Formation and Rajput Myth in Tribal Central India', in: Kulke, Hermann (ed.): *The State in India 1000–1700* (Cambridge, Mass. et al.: Oxford University Press, 1997); pp. 304–342.

Sinn, Hans-Werner: *Basar-Ökonomie Deutschland - Exportweltmeister oder Schlusslicht? ifo Schnelldienst Sonderausgabe* (Munich: Ifo-Institut für Wirtschaftsforschung, March 2005a).

———: 'Basar-Ökonomie Deutschland. Exportweltmeister oder Schlusslicht?', in: *IFO-Schnelldienst*, 58, 6 (March 2005b); pp. 3–42.

———: 'Internationaler Vergleich der Arbeitskosten. Warum Deutschland keine starken Lohnerhöhungen veträgt', in: *IFO-Schnelldienst*, 60, 4 (February 2007); pp. 54–58.

Sirc, Ljubo: 'Vergessene Nachfrageelastizitäten', in: *Ordo*, 29 (1978); pp. 320–326.

Skidelsky, Robert: *Keynes' 'New Order': The Genesis of the Clearing Union. Fifth Post Keynesian Workshop: Full Employment and the Price Stability in a Global Economy* (Knoxville: MS, 1998)

Sklar, Richard L.: 'Political Science and National Integration - A Radical Approach', in: *Journal of Modern African Studies*, 5, 1 (1967); pp. 1–11.

Slicher van Bath, B.H.: *The Agrarian History of Western Europe. A. D. 500–1850* (London: Edward Arnold, 1963).

Smith, R.B.: 'Bui Quang Chiêu and the Constitutionalist Party in French Indochina', in: *Modern Asian Studies*, 3, 2 (1969); pp. 131–150.

———: 'The Development of Opposition to French Rule in Southern Vietnam', in: *Past and Present*, 54 (February 1972); pp. 94–133.

Solar, Peter M.: 'Poor Relief and English Economic Development before the Industrial Revolution', in: *Economic History Review*, 58, 1 (1995); pp. 1–22.

Sombart, Werner: *Warum gibt es in den Vereinigten Staaten keinen Sozialismus?* (Tübingen: Mohr, 1906).
———: *Der moderne Kapitalismus: Die vorkapitalistische Wirtschaft. Vol. 1* (Munich: Duncker und Humblot, 1921a).
———: *Der moderne Kapitalismus: Das europäische Wirtschaftsleben im Frühkapitalismus. Vol. 2* (Munich: Duncker und Humblot, 1921b).
Sonn, Hochul: 'The "Late Blooming" of the South Korean Labor Movement', in: *Monthly Review*, 49, 3 (July/August 1997); pp. 117–1130.
Soret, M.: 'Problèmes fonciers chez les Kongo Nord-Ouest. Problèmes de terres ou problèmes démographiques?', in: *Economies et Sociétés*, V 9 (1965); pp. 141–167.
Soskice, David: 'Globalisierung und institutionelle Divergenz: Die U.S.A. und Deutschland im Vergleich', in: *Geschichte und Gesellschaft*, 25, 2 (April–June 1999); pp. 201–225.
Southall, Aidan W: 'The Segmentary State in Africa and Asia', in: *Comparative Studies in Society and History*, 30, 1 (January 1988); pp. 52–82.
SPD: *Godesberger Programm. Grundsatzprogramm der Sozialdemokratischen Partei Deutschlands von 1959* (Bonn: Haus der Geschichte, November 1959).
Spairs, Mike: 'Agrarian Change and the Revolution in Burkina Faso', in: *African Affairs*, 90, 358 (January 1991); pp. 89–110.
Spengler, Joseph J.: 'Demographic Factors and Early Modern Economic Development', in: *Daedalus*, 97, 2 (Spring 1968); pp. 433–446.
Spoerer, Mark: 'Die Deformation des NS-Wachstums in der volkswirtschaftlichen Gesamtrechnung', in: *Jahrbuch für Wirtschaftsgeschichte*, 2 (2004); pp. 233–239.
Sreenivasan, Govind P.: 'The Social Origins of the Peasants' War of 1525 in Upper Swabia', in: *Past and Present*, 171 (May 2001); pp. 30–65.
Srinivas, M. N.: 'An Obituary on Caste as a System', in: *Economic and Political Weekly*, 38, 5 (1 February 2003); pp. 455–459.
Srinivasan, Krishnan: 'Nobody's Commonwealth? The Commonwealth in Britain's Post-Imperial Adjustment', in: *Commonwealth and Comparative Politics*, 44, 2 (July 2006); pp. 257–269.
Stallings, Barbara: 'Peru and the U.S. Banks: Privatization of Financial Relations', in: Fagen, Richard R. (ed.): *Capitalism and the State in U.S.-Latin American Relations* (Stanford, Cal.: Stanford University Press, 1979); pp. 217–254.
Stannard, David E.: *American Holocaust: The Conquest of the New World* (New York; Oxford: Oxford University Press, 1992).
Starr, Amory; Adams, Jason: 'Anti-Globalization: The Global Fight for Local Autonomy', in: *New Political Science*, 25, 1 (March 2003); pp. 19–42.
Statistisches Bundesamt: *Statistisches Jahrbuch für die Bundesrepublik Deutschland* (Stuttgart: Metzler und Poeschel, 1960).
———: *Statistisches Jahrbuch für die Bundesrepublik Deutschland 1990* (Stuttgart: Metzler & Poeschel, 1990).

Statistisches Bundesamt: *Statistisches Jahrbuch für die Bundesrepublik Deutschland 2009* (Reutlingen: SFG-Servicecenter Fachverlage, 2009).

Stearns, Peter N.: 'Nationalisms: An Invitation to Comparative Analysis', in: *Journal of World History*, 8, 1 (Spring 1997); pp. 57–74.

Steel, Omar: 'La conversion au marché en Egypte et en Algérie: un ajustement par l'informel?', in: *Les Cahiers de l'Orient*, 45 (1997); pp. 45–64.

Stein, Burton: 'State Formation and Economy Reconsidered', in: *Modern Asian Studies*, 19, 3 (1985); pp. 387–413.

Stein, Howard: 'The World Bank and the Application of Asian Policy to Africa. Theoretical Considerations', in: *Journal of International Development*, 6, 3 (1994); pp. 287–305.

Steininger, Hans: 'Der Buddhismus in der chinesischen Geschichte', in: *Saeculum*, 13, 2 (1962); pp. 132–165.

Stiles, Kendall: 'International Support for NGOs in Bangladesh: Some Unintended Consequences', in: *World Development*, 30, 5 (May 2002); pp. 835–846.

Stobart, John: 'The Economic and Social Worlds of Rural Craftsmen – Retailers in Eighteenth-Century Cheshire', in: *Agricultural History Review*, 52, 2 (Summer 2004); pp. 141–160.

Stöber, Horst: 'Die Sakralisierung der Häuptlinge und die Entwicklung des Götterpantheons in Zentralafrika', in: *Ethnographisch-Archäologische Zeitschrift*, 6, 2 (1965); pp. 129–139.

Stocking, George W.: *Middle East Oil. A Study in Political and Economic Controversy* (Nashville, Tenn.: Vanderbilt University Press, 1970).

Stolz, Stéphanie Marie; Wedow, Michael: 'Extraordinary Measures in Extraordinary Times - Public Measures in Support of the Financial Sector in the EU and the United States', in: *Deutsche Bundesbank Discussion Papers Series 1: Economic Studies*, 13 (2010); p. 74.

Strange, Susan: *Casino Capitalism* (Manchester: Manchester Univesity Press, 1986).

Streb, Jochen; Wallusch, Jacek; Yin, Shuxi: 'Knowledge Spill-over from Old to New Industries: The Case of German Synthetic Dyes and Textiles (1878–1913)', in: *Explorations in Economic History*, 44, 2 (July 2007); pp. 203–223.

Strickland, D.A.: 'Kingship and Slavery in African Thought: A Conceptual Analysis', in: *Comparative Studies in Society and History*, 18, 3 (1976); pp. 371–394.

Ströbele-Gregor, Juliana: 'Ein schmaler Pfad zum besseren Leben? - Zu Ursachen und Folgen des Missionierungserfolges fundamentalistischer und evangelikaler Religionsgemeinschaften in Bolivien', in: *Peripherie*, 9, 35 (1989); pp. 57–79.

Stürmer, Michael: 'An Economy of Delight: Court Artisans of the Eighteenth Century', in: *Business History Review*, 53, 4 (Winter 1979); pp. 496–524.

Stürmer, Wilhelmine: 'Die Entwicklungskomponenten des Kapitalkoeffizienten. Dargestellt am Beispiel des Maschinenbaus und der chemischen Industrie der Bundesrepublik', in: *Mitteilungen des Rheinisch-Westfälischen Instituts für Wirtschaftsforschung*, 19, 1 (1968); pp. 13–28.

Subramahnjam, Sanjay: 'Writing History "Backwards": Southeast Asian History (and the Annals' at the Crossroads', in: *Studies in History*, 10, 1 (January 1984); pp. 131–145.
Subramanian, Vidya: 'Rise of English: Conjuncture of Hegemonic Agendas', in: *Economic and Political Weekly*, 44, 32 (8 August 2009); pp. 30–32.
Sugar, Peter F.: 'External and Domestic Roots of Eastern European Nationalism', in: Sugar, Peter; Lederer, Ivo (eds.): *Nationalism in Eastern Europe* (Seattle, Wash.; London: University of Washington Press, 1969); pp. 3–54.
Sunderland, David: 'Principals and Agents: The Activities of the Crown Agents for the Colonies, 1880–1914', in: *Economic History Review*, 73, 2 (May 1999); pp. 284–306.
Sundhausen, Holm: 'Zur Wechselbeziehung zwischen frühneuzeitlichem Außenhandel und ökonomischer Rückständigkeit in Osteuropa', in: *Geschichte und Gesellschaft*, 9, 4 (1983); pp. 544–563.
Sunoo, Harold Hakwon: 'Economic Development and Foreign Control in South Korea', in: *Journal of Contemporary Asia*, 3 (1978); pp. 322–339.
Suntum, Ulrich van: 'Internationale Wettbewerbsfähigkeit einer Volkswirtschaft. Ein sinnvolles wirtschaftspolitisches Ziel', in: *Zeitschrift für Wirtschafts- und Sozialwissenschaften*, 106, 4 (1986); pp. 495–507.
Suret-Canale, Jean: 'Les sociétés traditionnelles en Afrique et le concept de mode de production asiatique', in: *La Pensée*, 117 (October 1964); pp. 21–42.
Sutton, Donald S.: 'Ritual, Cultural Standardization, and Orthopraxy in China: Reconsidering James L. Watson's Ideas', in: *Modern China*, 33, 1 (January 2007); pp. 3–21.
Svennilson, Ingvar: *Growth and Stagnation in the European Economy* (Geneva: United Nations Economic Commission for Europe, 1954).
Swanson, Heather: *Medieval Artisans. An Urban Class in Late Medieval England* (Oxford: Basil Blackwell, 1989).
Sweezy, Paul M.: 'A Critique', in: Hilton, Rodney (ed.): *The Transition from Feudalism to Capitalism* (New York: Science & Society, 1953); pp. 1–20.
———: *Theorie der kapitalistischen Entwicklung* (Cologne: Bund-Verlag, 1959).
———: 'A Critique', in: Hilton, Rodney (ed.): *The Transition from Feudalism to Capitalism* (London: NLB, 1976); pp. 33–56.
Sylvia, Ronald D.; Danopoulos, Constantine P.: 'The Chávez Phenomenon: Political Change in Venezuela', in: *Third World Quarterly*, 24, 1 (2003); pp. 63–76.
Szonyi, Michael: 'Making Claims about Standardization and Orthopraxy in Late Imperial China: Rituals and Cults in the Fuzhou Region in Light of Watson's Theories', in: *Modern China*, 33, 1 (January 2007); pp. 47–71.
Tai, Hue Tam Ho: *Millenarism and Peasant Politics in Vietnam* (Cambridge, Mass. et al.: Harvard University Press, 1983).
Takeyh, Ray: 'Iran at a Crossroads', in: *Middle East Journal*, 57, 1 (Winter 2003); pp. 42–56.

Talbot, Cynthia: 'Temples, Donors and Gifts: Patterns of Patronage in Thirteenth-Century South India', in: *Journal of Asian Studies*, 52, 2 (May 1991); pp. 308–340.

Tammen, Ronald L.: 'The Impact of Asia on World Politics: China and India Options for the United States', in: *International Studies Review*, 8, 4 (Winter 2006); pp. 563–580.

Tawney, Richard Henry: *The Agrarian Problem in the Sixteenth Century* (London: Longmans & Green, 1912).

TAZ 2007 'Even in Bangladesh': *TAZ* 13 December 2010, (download 4-6-2011).

Tazmini, Ghoncheh: 'The Islamic Revival in Central Asia: A Potent Force or a Misconception', in: *Central Asian Survey*, 20, 1 (March 2001); pp. 63–83.

Tchechkov, M.A.: 'La classe dirigeante du Vietnam précolonial', in: *La Pensée*, 144 (March–April 1969); pp. 28–40.

Tejapira, Kasian: 'Toppling Thaksin', in: *New Left Review*, 39 (May/June 2006); pp. 5–37.

Temin, Peter: 'Steam and Waterpower in Early Nineteenth-Century', in: *Journal of Economic History*, 26, 2 (June 1966); pp. 186–205.

Teschke, Benno: 'Bürgerliche Revolution, Staatsbildung und die Abwesenheit des Internationalen', in: *Probleme des Klassenkampfs*, 35, 141 (December 2005); pp. 575–600.

Tétreault, Mary Ann: *Globalization and Islamic Radicalism in the Arab Gulf Region. Leipzig Conference 14thMay 2007* (2011).

Thapar, Romila: 'Dissent and Protest in the Early Indian Tradition', in: *Studies in History*, 1, 2 (1979); pp. 177–195.

Thaxton, Ralph: 'On Peasant Revolution and National Resistance: Towards a Theory of Peasant Mobilization and Revolutionary War With Special Reference to Modern China', in: *World Politics*, 30, 1 (October 1977); pp. 24–56.

Ther, Philipp: 'Deutsche Geschichte als transnationale Geschichte. Überlegungen zu einer Histoire Croisée Deutschlands und Ostmitteleuropas', in: *Comparativ. Leipziger Beiträge zur Universalgeschichte und vergleichenden Gesellschaftsforschung*, 13, 4 (2003); pp. 155–180.

Thibon, Christian: 'L'expansion du peuplement dans la région des grands lacs au XIX siècle', in: *Canadian Journal of African Studies*, 23, 1 (1989); pp. 54–72.

Thiemer-Sachse, Ursula: 'Salzgewinnung und Salzhandel bei Zapokca Südmexikos in vorspanischer Zeit', in: *Ethnographisch-Archäologische Zeitschrift*, 28, 4 (1987); pp. 565–579.

Thiesenhusen, William C.: 'Agrarian Reform and Economic Development in Chile', in: *Land Economics*, 42, 3 (August 1966); pp. 282–294.

———: 'What Changing Technology Implies for Agrarian Reform', in: *Land Economics*, 50, 1 (February 1974); pp. 35–50.

Thion, Serge: 'La question agraire en Indochine', in: *Cahiers internationaux de sociologie*, 20, 56 (January–June 1973); pp. 31–60.

Thirsk, Joan: *Economic Policy and Projects. The Development of a Consumer Society in Early Modern England* (Oxford: Clarendon Press, 1978).
Thirumali, I.: 'Peasant Class Assertions in Nalgondo and Warangal Districts of Telangara, 1930–1946', in: *Indian Economic and Social History Review*, 31, 2 (April–June 1994); pp. 217–237.
Thobie, Jacques: *Interêts et impérialisme français dans l'empire othomane (1895–1914)* (Paris: Publications de la Sorbonne, 1977).
Tholfson, Trygve R.: 'The Transition to Democracy in Victorian England', in: *International Review of Social History*, 6, 2 (1961); pp. 226–248.
Thompson, John A.F.: *The Early Tudor Church and Society, 1485– 1529* (London; New York: Longman, 1993).
Thomson, Ross: 'The Eco-Technic Process and the Development of the Sewing Machine', in: *Research in Economic History*, SH 3 (1984); pp. 243–269.
Thoran, Peter: 'Der Krieg und das Feld. Ritter und Söldner in den Heeren Kaiser Friedrichs II', in: *Historische Zeitschrift*, 268, 3 (June 1999); pp. 599–634.
Tignor, Robert L.: 'The Massai Warriors: Pattern Maintenance and Violence in Colonial Kenya', in: *Journal of African History*, 13, 2 (1972); pp. 271–290.
Tillotson, J. H.: 'Peasant Unrest in the England of Richard II. Some Evidence from Royal Records', in: *Historical Studies, Australia and New Zealand*, 16, 62 (April 1974); pp. 1–16.
Timmer, Peter C.: 'The Turnip, the New Husbandry and the English Agricultural Revolution', in: *Quarterly Journal of Economics*, 83, 2 (August 1969); pp. 375–396.
Timoshenko, Vladimir P.: 'World Agriculture and the Depression', in: *Michigan Business Review*, 25, 5 (1933); pp. 541–646.
Tinker, Hugh: 'Continuity and Changes in Asian Societies', in: *Modern Asian Studies*, 3, 2 (1969); pp. 97–116.
———: *A New System of Slavery. The Export of Indian Labour Overseas, 1830–1920* (London: Oxford University Press, 1974).
Todaro, Michael P.: 'The Urban Employment Problem in Less Developed Countries', in: *Yale Economic Essays*, 8, 2 (1968); pp. 331–402.
Toh, Swee Hin: 'Canada's Gain from Third World Brain Drain, 1962–1974', in: *Studies in Comparative International Development*, 12, 3 (Autumn 1977); pp. 25–45.
Tolliday, Steven; Zeitlin, Jonathan: 'Between Fordism and Flexibility. The Automobile Industry and its Workers. Past, Present and Future', in: *Archiv für Sozialgeschichte*, 28 (1988); pp. 153–172.
Tönnies, Ferdinand: *Gemeinschaft und Gesellschaft: Grundbegriffe der reinen Soziologie* (Berlin: Curtius, 1935).
Töpfer, Bernhard: 'Tendenzen zur Entsäkularisierung der Herrscherwürde in der Zeit des Investiturstreits', in: *Jahrbuch für Geschichte des Feudalismus*, 6 (1982); pp. 169–174.

Töpper, Barbara: 'Automobilindustrie - Paradigma für peripheren Postfordismus', in: *Peripherie*, 13, 51/52 (December 1993); pp. 171-189.
Toye, John: 'From New Era to Neo-liberalism: US Strategy on Trade, Finance and Development in the United Nations, 1964-82', in: *Forum for Development Studies*, 32, 1 (January 2005); pp. 151-180.
Toynbee, Arnold J.: *Toynbee's Industrial Revolution. A Reprint of Lectures of the Industrial Revolution on England. Popular Adresses, Notes and Other Fragments* (Newton Abbot: David & Charles Reprints, 1969).
Tran, Thi Anh-Dao: 'Libéralisation commerciale et industrialisation en Asie du Sud-Est: Implications pour le Vietnam', in: *Tiers Monde*, 40, 158 (April-June 1999); pp. 397-420.
Tran, Thi Ut; Kajisa, Kei: 'The Impact of Green Revolution on Rice Production in Vietnam', in: *Developing Economies*, 44, 2 (June 2006); pp. 167-189.
Tribe, Keith: *Genealogies of Capitalism* (Atlantic Highlands, N.J.: Humanities Press, 1981).
Trompetter, C.: 'On Entrepreneurship and Capitalism. Joseph Schumpeter and Max Weber on the Role of the Entrepreneur in Capitalist Development', in: *Economisch en sociaal-historisch Jaarboek*, 45 (1982); pp. 270-287.
Tuchscherer, Konrad: 'The Lost Script of the Bagam', in: *African Affairs*, 98, 390 (January 1999); pp. 55-79.
Tucker, Rufus S.: 'Real Wages of Artisans in London, 1729-1935', in: *Journal of the American Statistical Association*, 31, 1 (1936); pp. 73-84.
Tugendhat, Christopher: *Erdöl: Treibstoff der Weltwirtschaft - Sprengstoff der Weltpolitik* (Reinbeck b. Hamburg: Rowohlt, 1972).
Turowski, Jan: *Sozialdemokratische Reformdiskurse* (Wiesbaden: VS Verlag für Sozialwissenschaften, 2010).
Turton, E.R.: 'Bantu, Galla and Somali Migrations in the Horn of Africa: A Reassessment of the Juba/Tana Area', in: *Journal of African History*, 16, 4 (1975); pp. 519-537.
Tyagi, Ruchi: 'Administration in Ancient India: An Introductory Outline', in: *Indian Journal of Public Administration*, 56, 1 (January-March 2010); pp. 148-179.
Ufen, Andreas: 'Islam und Politik in Indonesien', in: *Internationale Politik und Gesellschaft*, 2 (2001); pp. 181-192.
Ukers, William H.: *All About Tea (2)* (New York: The Tea and Coffee Trade Journal Company, 1935).
Unwin, George: 'The Merchant Adventurers' Company in the Reign of Elizabeth', in: *Economic History Review*, 1, 1 (January 1927); pp. 35-64.
Upadhyaya, Ashok K.: 'Class Struggle in Rural Maharashtra (India): Towards a New Perspective', in: *Journal of Peasant Studies*, 7, 2 (January 1980); pp. 213-234.
Vadi, José M.: 'Economic Globalization, Class Struggle and the Mexican State', in: *Latin American Perspectives*, 28, 3 (Summer 2001); pp. 129-147.

Vahdat, Farzin: 'Religious Modernity in Iran: Dilemmas of Islamic Democracy in the Discourse of Mohammad Khatami', in: *Comparative Studies of South Asia, Africa and the Middle East*, 25, 3 (2005); pp. 650–664.
Vakil, C.N.; Brahmananda, P.R.: *Planning for an Expanding Economy: Accumulation, Employment and Technical Progress in Underdeveloped Countries* (Bombay: Vera, 1956).
Vakulabharanam, Vamsi: 'The Recent Crisis in Global Capitalism: Towards a Marxian Understanding', in: *Economic and Political Weekly*, 44, 13 (28 March 2009); pp. 144–150.
Varon, Bension; Takeuchi, Kenji: 'Developing Countries and Non-Fuel Minerals', in: Hoh, Makoto (ed.): *The World Economic Crisis* (New York: W.W. Norton, 1975); pp. 165–178.
Varshney, Ashutosh: *Ethnic Conflict and Civic Life: Hindus and Muslims in India*. (New Haven, Conn. et al.: Yale University Press, 2002).
Vaubel, Roland: 'Das Papsttum und der politische Wettbewerb in Europa', in: *Ordo*, 56 (2005); pp. 187–192.
Vaughan, Olufemi: 'Assessing Grassroot-Politics and Community Development in Nigeria', in: *African Affairs*, 94, 377 (October 1995); pp. 501–518.
Veerathappa, K.: 'Britain and the Indian Problem September 1939–May 1940', in: *International Studies*, 7, 4 (October–December 1965); pp. 537–567.
Venkataramani, M.S.; Shrivastava, B.K.: 'America and the Indian Political Crisis, July–August 1942', in: *International Studies*, 6, 1 (January–March 1964); pp. 1–48.
Vernon, Raymond: 'International Investment and International Trade in the Product Cycle', in: *Quarterly Journal of Economics*, 80, 2 (May 1966); pp. 190–207.
Vicens Vives, Jaime: *An Economic History of Spain* (Princeton, N.J.: Princeton University Press, 1969).
Vickrey, William: 'Chock-Fall Employment Without Increased Inflation', in: *American Economic Review*, 85, 2 (May 1995); pp. 341–345.
Vieweg, Hans-Günther: 'Der Maschinenbau im Zeitalter der Globalisierung und der "New Economy"', in: *IFO-Schnelldienst*, 55, 21 (November 2002); pp. 18–27.
Viguera, Aníbal: '"Populismo" y "neopopulismo" en América Latina', in: *Revista Mexicana de Sociología*, 55, 2 (July–September 1993); pp. 49–68.
Vilar, Pierre: *A History of Gold and Money 1450–1920* (London; Atlantic Highlands, N.J.: NLB Humanities Press, 1969).
Viola, Eduardo; Mainwaring, Scott: 'Transition to Democracy: Brazil and Argentina in the 1980s', in: *Journal of International Affairs*, 39, 2 (Winter 1985); pp. 193–219.
Virmani, Arvind: 'World Economy, Geopolitics and Global Strategy: Indo-US Relations in the 21st Century', in: *Economic and Political Weekly*, 41, 43–44 (11 November 2006); pp. 4601–4612.
Voth, Hans-Joachim: 'Clark's Intellectual Sudoku', in: *European Review of Economic History*, 12, 2 (August 2008); pp. 149–155.

Vries, Jan de; Woude, Ad van der: *The First Modern Economy. Success, Failure, and Perseverance of the Dutch Economy, 1500–1815* (Cambridge: Cambridge Univerity Press, 1997).

Vries, Peer: 'The California School and beyond: How to Study the Great Divergence?', in: *Journal für Entwicklungspolitik*, 24, 4 (2008); pp. 6–49.

Wagman, Bernet: 'Occupation, Power and the Origins of Labor Segmentation in the US', in: *Review of Radical Political Economics*, 27, 1 (March 1995); pp. 1–24.

Wagner, Helmut; Berger, Wolfram: *Financial Globalization and Monetary Policy. DNB Staff Reports No. 95* (Mumbai: De Nederlandsche Bank, 2003).

Wagner, Norbert: 'Die internationale Finanzkrise und die Vereinigten Staaten von Amerika.', in: *KAS Auslandsinformationen*, 24, 12 (December 2008); pp. 24–33.

Wakeman, Frederic: 'The Price of Autonomy: Intellectuals in Ming and Ching Politics', in: *Daedalus*, 101, 2 (Spring 1972); pp. 35–70.

———: 'Rebellion and Revolution: The Study of Popular Movements in Chinese History', in: *Journal of Asian Studies*, 36, 2 (February 1977); pp. 201–237.

Waldner, David: *Civic Exclusion and its Discontents: The Political Economy of Contemporary Islamist Movements* . Paper presented at the annual meeting of the American Political Science Association, New York, September 1994.

Walker, John T.: 'Socialism in Dayton, Ohio, 1912 to 1925: Its Membership, Organization, and Demise', in: *Labor History*, 26, 3 (Summer 1985); pp. 384–404.

Wallerstein, Immanuel Maurice: *The Modern World-System. Capitalist Agriculture and the Origins of the European World-Economy in the Sixteenth Century* (New York et al.: Academic Press, 1974).

———: 'The Great Expansion: The Incorporation of Vast New Zones into the Capitalist World Economy (c. 1750–1850)', in: *Studies in History*, 4, 1/2 (January 1988a); pp. 85–156.

———: 'Typology of Crises in the World System', in: *Review (Fernand Braudel Center)*, 11, 4 (Autumn 1988b); pp. 561–598.

———: 'Marx, der Marxismus-Leninismus und sozialistische Erfahrungen im modernen Weltsystem', in: *Probleme des Klassenkampfs*, 20, 78 (March 1990); pp. 126–148.

———: 'Citizens All? Citizens Some! The Making of the Citizen', in: *Comparative Studies in Society and History*, 45, 4 (October 2003); pp. 650–679.

Walz, Rainer: 'Der vormoderne Antisemitismus: Religiöser Fanatismus oder Rassenwahn', in: *Historische Zeitschrift*, 260, 3 (June 1995); pp. 719–748.

Wang, Leonard F.S.: 'Monetary Effect of Devaluation, the Positively Sloped I.S. Curve and the "Cooper Paradox"', in: *Indian Journal of Economics*, 67, 265 (October 1986); pp. 241–247.

Wang, Q. Edward: 'Encountering the World: China and Its Other(s) in HistoricalNarratives, 1949–89.', in: *Journal of World History*, 14, 2 (September 2003); pp. 327–358.

Wankhede, Harish S.: 'The Political and the Social in the Dalit Movement Today', in: *Economic and Political Weekly*, 43, 6 (February 2008); pp. 50–57.

Wanyama, Fredrick O.: 'Interfacing the State and the Voluntary Sector for African Development: Lessons from Kenya', in: *Africa Development*, 31, 4 (2006); pp. 73–103.

Ward, William A.: 'Relations Between Egypt and Mesopotamia from Prehistoric Times to the End of the Middle Kingdom', in: *Journal of the Economic and Social History of the Orient*, 7, 2 (July 1964); pp. 121–135.

Warde, Paul: 'Subsistence and Sales: The Peasant Economy of Württemberg in the Early Seventeenth Cenury', in: *Economic History Review*, 59, 2 (May 2006); pp. 289–319.

Warren, Bill: 'Imperialism and Capitalist Industrialisation', in: *New Left Review*, 81 (September–October 1973); pp. 3–44.

———: *Imperialism: Pioneer of Capitalism* (London: NLB, 1980).

Washbrook, David A.: 'Progress and Problems: South Asian Economic and Social History c. 1720–1860', in: *Modern Asian Studies*, 22, 1 (February 1988); pp. 57–96.

Watanabe, Susumu: 'Quo vadis Africa? La stratégie de développement de la banque mondiale vu par le Japon', in: *Tiers Monde*, 38, 159 (April–June 1997); pp. 311–330.

Webb, Walter Prescott: *The Great Frontier* (Boston, Mass.: Houghton Mifflin, 1952).

Weber, Max: *Die protestantische Ethik und der Geist des Kapitalismus* (Tübingen: J.C.B. Mohr, 1934).

'Wechselkurs und Außenhandel', in: *Monatsberichte der Deutschen Bundesbank*, 49, 1 (January 1997); pp. 43–62.

Wee, Herman van der: 'Structural Change and Specialization in the Industry of the Southern Netherlands', in: *Economic History Review*, 28, 2 (1975); pp. 203–222.

Wegner, Rodger: 'The Role of NGOs in Development Cooperation. Some Notes on Empirical Research Findings', in: *Intereconomics*, 28, 6 (November–December 1993); pp. 285–292.

Weiher, Sigfried von: '100 Jahre "Made in Germany": Absicht und Auswirkung eines britischen Gesetzes', in: *Technikgeschichte*, 53, 3 (1987); pp. 175–182.

Weiss, Linda: 'Global Governance, National Strategies: How Industrialized States Make Room to Move under the WTO', in: *Review of International Political Economy*, 12, 5 (December 2005); pp. 723–749.

Weizsäcker, Carl Christian von: 'A New Technical Progress Function', in: *German Economic Review*, 11, 3 (August 2010); pp. 248–265.

Wellenreuther, Hermann: 'Korruption und das Wesen der englischen Verfassung im 18. Jahrhundert', in: *Historische Zeitschrift*, 234, 1 (February 1982); pp. 32–62.

Welzk, Stefan: 'Die große Entstaatlichung', in: *Kursbuch*, 168 (Autumn 2007); pp. 52–65.

Werker, Eric; Ahmed, Faisal Z.: 'What Do Nongovernmental Organizations Do?', in: *Journal of Economic Perspectives*, 22, 2 (Spring 2008); pp. 73–92.

Werner, Ernst: 'Ständebildung und hussitische Reformation in Böhmen bis 1419', in: *Zeitschrift für Geschichtswissenschaft*, 35, 7 (1987); pp. 601–618.

Westphal, Larry E.; Kim, Linsu; Dahlman, Carl J.: 'Reflections on the Republic of Korea's Acquistion of Technological Capability', in: Rosenberg, Nathan (ed.): *International Technology Transfer. Concepts, Measures and Comparisons* (New York: Praeger, 1985); pp. 167–221.

White, David Gordon: 'Digging Wells while Houses Burn? Writing Histories of Hinduism in a Time of Identity Politics', in: *History and Theory*, 45, 4 (December 2006); pp. 104–131.

White, Sarah C.: 'NGOs, Civil Society, and the State in Bangladesh: The Politics of Representing the Poor', in: *Development and Change*, 30, 2 (1999); pp. 307–326.

Whitley, J.D.; Wilson, R.A.: 'The Macroeconomic Merits of a Marginal Employment Subsidy', in: *Economic Journal*, 93, 372 (December 1983); pp. 862–880.

Wickham, Chris: *Framing the Early Middle Ages: Europe and the Mediterranean, 400–800* (Oxford: Oxford University Press, 2005).

Willame, Jean Claude: 'Patriarchical Structures and Functional Politics. Towards an Understanding of Dualist Society', in: *Cahiers d'études africaines*, 13, 50 (June 1973); pp. 326–355.

Williams, Eric: *Capitalism and Slavery* (London: André Deutsch, 1964).

Williamson, James A.: *A Short History of British Expansion (1): The Old Colonial Empire* (London: Macmillan, 1965).

Willing, Georg Franz: 'Das Vorspiel der chinesischen Revolution. Der Taiping Aufstand 1850–1864', in: *Saeculum*, 22, 2/3 (Summer 1971); pp. 227–273.

Wils, Oliver: 'Private Sector Monopolies and Economic Reform in (Post) Rentier States: The Case of Jordan', in: *Asien-Afrika-Lateinamerika*, 28, 4 (April 2000); pp. 365–397.

Wilson, Anne: 'Long Distance Trade and the Luba Lonami Empire', in: *Journal of African History*, 13, 4 (1972); pp. 575–589.

Wilson, Charles Henry: *The History of Unilever. A Study in Economic Growth and Social Change* (London: Cassell, 1954).

———: 'The Entrepreneur in the Industrial Revolution in Britain', in: Supple, Barry Emmanuel (ed.): *The Experience of Economic Growth. Case Studies in Economic History* (New York: Random House, 1963); pp. 171–181.

Wink, André: 'Al-Hind: India and Indonesia in the Islamic World Economy', in: *Itinerario*, 12, 1 (1988); pp. 33–72.

Winston, Gordon C.: 'Overinvoicing, Underutilization and Distorted Industrial Growth', in: *Pakistan Development Review*, 10, 4 (Winter 1970); pp. 406–421.

Wirth, John D.: 'Tenentismo in the Brazilian Revolution of 1930', in: *Hispanic American Historical Review*, 44, 2 (May 1964); pp. 161–179.

Wittfogel, Karl August: *Wirtschaft und Gesellschaft Chinas. Versuch der wissenschaftlichen Analyse einer großen asiatischen Agrargesellschaft* (Leipzig: C.L. Hirschfeld, 1931).
———: 'Die natürlichen Ursachen der Wirtschaftsgeschichte (2)', in: *Archiv für Sozialwissenschaft und Sozialpolitik*, 67, 5 (1932); pp. 579–609.
———: *Oriental Despotism. A Comparative Study of Total Power* (New Haven, Conn. et al.: Yale University Press, 1957).
Wolf, Eric R.: *Peasant Wars in Twentieth Century* (New York: Harper & Row, 1968).
———: *Europe and the People Without History* (Berkeley, Cal.: University of California Press, 1982).
Wolfstetter, E.: 'Surplus Labour, Synchronised Labour Costs and Marx's Theory of Value', in: *Economic Journal*, 83, 331 (September 1973); pp. 787–809.
Woolf, Leonard: *Empire and Commerce in Africa. A Study in Economic Imperialism* (London: Allen & Unwin, 1920).
World Trade Organisation: *International Trade Statistics* (Geneva: World Trade Organization, 2010), <<http://wto.org/english/res_e/statis_e/its2010_e/its10_merch_trade_product_e.htm> (27.07.2011).
Woude, Ad van der: 'Sources of Energy in the Dutch Golden Age. The Case of Holland', in: *NEHA-Jaarboek*, 66 (2003); pp. 64–84.
Wright, Mary C.: 'The Chinese Peasant and Communism', in: *Pacific Affairs*, 24, 3 (September 1951); pp. 256–265.
Wright, Neil R.: 'Product Differentiation, Concentration and Changes in Concentration', in: *Review of Economics and Statistics*, 60, 4 (November 1978); pp. 628–631.
Wrigley, E.A.: 'Family Limitation in Pre-Industrial England', in: *Economic History Review*, 19, 1 (1966); pp. 82–109.
Wuyts, Marc: 'Foreign Aid, Structural Adjustment and Public Management: The Mozambican Experience', in: *Development and Change*, 27, 4 (December 1996); pp. 717–749.
Xue, Yong: 'A "Fertilizer Revolution"?: A Critical Response to Pomeranz's Theory of "Geographic Luck"', in: *Modern China*, 33, 2 (April 2007); pp. 195–229.
Yamada, Hideo: 'The Origins of British Colonization of Malaya with Special References to its Tin', in: *Developing Economies*, 9, 3 (September 1971); pp. 225–245.
Yamamura, Kozo: 'More System, Please!', in: *New Left Review*, 54 (November/December 2008); pp. 75–85.
Yanagisawa, Haruka: 'The Handloom Industry and Its Market Structure: The Case of the Madras Presidency in the First Half of the Twentieth Century', in: *Indian Economic and Social History Review*, 30, 1 (January–March 1993); pp. 1–28.
Yang, Dvaid D.: 'Classing Ethnicity: Class. Ethnicity, and Mass Politics of Taiwan's Democratic Transition', in: *World Politics*, 59, 4 (July 2007); pp. 503–538.
Yates, Michael: 'The "New" Economy and the Labour Movement', in: *Monthly Review*, 53, 11 (Spring 2001); pp. 28–43.

Yen, Chung-Ping: 'Zur Geschichte der Baumwollindustrie in China bis zum Ende des ersten Weltkrieges', in: *Jahrbuch für Wirtschaftsgeschichte*, 2, 2 (1961); pp. 199–230.

Yuchao, Zhu: 'Workers, Unions and the State: Migrant Workers in China's Labour-intensive Foreign Enterprises', in: *Development and Change*, 35, 5 (November 2004); pp. 1011–1036.

Zaidi, S. Akbar: 'NGO Failure and the Need to Bring Back the State', in: *Journal of International Development*, 11, 2 (March/April 1999); pp. 259–271.

Zambrano, Eduardo: 'On the Emergence of a Market Pattern', in: *Zeitschrift für die gesamte Staatswissenschaft /Journal of Institutional and Theoretical Economics*, 154, 3 (September 1998); pp. 481–498.

Zanden, Jan Luiten van: 'The Great Divergence from a West European Perspective', in: *Itinerario*, 24, 3 (2000); pp. 9–28.

Zawodny, J.K.: 'Soviet Partisans', in: *Soviet Studies*, 17, 3 (January 1966); pp. 368–377.

Zhou, Kate Xiao; White, Lynn T.: 'Quiet Politic's and Rural Enterprise in Reform China', in: *Journal of Developing Areas*, 29, 4 (July 1995); pp. 461–490.

Zinecker, Heidrun: *Kolumbien und El Salvador im longitudinalen Vergleich. Ein kritischer Beitrag zur Transitionsdebatte aus historisch-struktureller und handlungstheoretischer Perspektive* (Leipzig: Habilitation Dissertation, 2002).

———: 'Regime-Hybridität in Entwicklungsländern: Leistungen und Grenzen der neueren Transitionsforschung', in: *Zeitschrift für Internationale Beziehungen*, 11, 2 (December 2004); pp. 239–272.

———: 'Regime-Hybridity in Developing Countries: Achievements and Limitations of New Research on Transitions', in: *International Studies Review*, 11, 2 (June 2009); pp. 302–331.

Zubaida, Sami: 'Economic and Political Activism in Islam', in: *Economy and Society*, 1, 3 (August 1972); pp. 308–329.

Zucarelli, François: 'De la chefferie traditionelle au canton. Evolution du canton colonial au Sénégal 1855–1960', in: *Cahiers d'études africaines*, 13, 50 (June 1973); pp. 213–238.

Zuñiga, Jean Paul: 'La voix du sang. Du métis à l'idée de métissage en Amérique espagnole', in: *Annales. Histoire, Sciences Sociales*, 54, 2 (March–April 1999); pp. 425–452.

Zurndorfer, Harriett T.: 'Violence and Political Protest in Ming and Qing China: Review and Commentary on Recent Research', in: *International Review of Social History*, 18, 4 (1983); pp. 304–319.

———: 'Beyond Sinology: New Developments in the Study of Chinese Economic and Social History', in: *Journal of the Economic and Social History of the Orient*, 44, 3 (August 2003); pp. 355–371.

Index

absolutism, 50
accumulation, ix–xi, 13, 16, 25, 27, 48, 76, 101, 103, 106, 115, 138, 141, 144, 148, 152
    unlimited, ix
age of discovery
    capitalist character of, 76
    inflow of bullion, 76
agrarian reform, 115, 119
alienation, xiv, 177
ancient empires, 3
anti-colonial movements, 89–90, 94
    coalitions, 178
    communists, 93–94, 177
    cultural nationalists, 91
    demonstration effect of Japan, 92
    Indian Congress, 94
    modernisation vs. tradition, 90
    new middle class, 91–94
        Latin America, 94
    October Revolutions, 92
    orientations, 93
    secular nationalism, 91, 178
    social bases, 90
        educated, 91
Arab, 5, 46, 55, 89, 119, 177, 184, 191–192, 195
Arab, African socialism, 177
average wages, 18

bank, 9–10, 23–24, 41, 100, 141, 145–151, 168, 200

Barone, 105, 171
beggar thy neighbour policies, 195
bicycle, 16, 78
Bortkiewicz, 11–12
bourgeois culture of equal participation, xiii
bourgeois revolution, 50, 91, 180
Britain, 38, 51, 54, 61, 76–81, 84, 94, 100, 109–110, 124, 128, 158, 195, 197
Buddhism, 35, 52, 66, 70, 75

California school, 38
capital, ix–x, 13, 167
capitalism
    an accident in history, 24, 26
    a-cultural, xiii, 6, 60, 65, 70, 153
        protects freedom, 165
    a-cultural, utopias, 174
    average wages, 18, 120
    capital saving, 11, 13
    capitalists
        globalised norms, 183
        and dependency, 171
    economic insecurity, xiv
    empowerment of labour, 160
    and equality, xiii
    expansion, 74
    expansionary, x, 73
    flexibility, 19
    formation of a working class, 18
    high wages imposed, 18

homogeneity, 19
impact on non-economic spheres, xiv
importance of a periphery, 74
limited transformative capacity, 73
limited transition to, xi, 5, 17
monetary policies, 24
not committed to capitalism, xiii, 2, 18
not contagious, 3
patterns of, 60
perfect markets, 2
and postcolonialism, 171
poverty, xiv
propelled by rent-based state intervention, 105
raw material saving, 86
reciprocal empowerment of labour and capital, 23
and rent appropriation, 104
rent permanent, 161
role of technical progress, 25
unchallenged by redistribution, 105
capitalism in future
capital saving, 137, 167
collective goods, 139, 162
declining industrial employment, 197
and democratic socialism, 167
end of progressive character, 198
environment, 164
failure of monetary policy, 142
future needs, 166
heterogenisation of labour, 139
household savings, 162
importance of ideology, 160
increased household savings, 139, 141
increasing imperfection of markets, 168
new importance of ideology, 143, 163
post-materialistic needs, 139
process of disembedding, 140, 143
rent, 167, 169
savings
lack of demand, 163
socialisation of saving, 163
capitalist penetration, 20, 73, 82, 153
deformation, 20, 81
deindustrialization, 83
dependency, 87
differential rents, 84
marginality, 86
rent, 84
surplus labour, 82
terms of trade deterioration, 84
underdevelopment, 73, 82
capital-output ratio, 12, 99, 103, 113, 122, 138, 155
car, 14, 16, 78–79, 128, 138
China
anticolonial resistance, 93, 177–178
emerging power, 197
export orientation, 114–122, 127–128, 155, 185, 195
devaluation, 117, 195
poverty, 115
shoddy products, 122, 128, 131
pre-capitalist structures, 65
colonial partition, 89
deindustrialisation, 78
European admiration for ancient China, 46
luxury production, 39–42
migration, 42
opening through informal colonialism, 78
paper money, 145
peasant resistance, 44
pre-capitalist 'capitalism', 5–6, 200–201
religion, 65
trade routes, 75
primary resistance, 90
Christian Democrats, 185–186
isolated in the South, 185

Index **317**

similarities with cultural nationalists, 185
Christianity, 35, 52
civil society, really existing, 189
class
   as a category of social structuring, 19, 70, 143, 157, 164, 174–177, 185
   liberating dimension of, 70
coal, 76, 80, 85, 110
colonialism, 83–84, 87, 107, 114, 175–178, 188
   bridgeheads, 177
   crimes, 106
   demographic growth, 83
   great power rivalries, 89
   indirect rule, 89
   semicolonies, 89
   threat to freedom, 76
   tributary mode of production, 88
   useless exploitation, 107
community, 29–35, 61–63, 70, 145, 172, 185, 194, 200
   culture, 63
   demographic growth, 31
   differentiation, 30–31
      hardening, 32
      marginality, 32
      religion, 32
      reversibility, 32
   domination/coordination, 62
   migration, 31
   shift to tributary mode of production
      culture, 63
      long-distance trade role of, 75
comparative advantage, 116, 123–124
   shift in, 79
competitiveness, 72, 87, 116–118, 124, 126, 131–137, 169, 196
   and being overtaken, 123–124, 126
   failure of wage restraint, 135
   and industrial policy, 127
   and shift to luxuries, 128
   stable hierarchies, 132
   and strategic trade, 127
   tighten belt, 134
Comte, 25
consumption, 184, 196–199
   class-specific structure, 19–25
   condition for profit, ix–xii, 1–4, 7–16, 49
   and exchange rate, 116
   and exploitation, 76–81
   and free trade, 78
   history-specific structure, 38, 48–51, 59, 89
   luxury, x, 21, 37–42, 57, 68, 72, 199
   mass, xi–xv, 23–25, 28–29, 49, 76–81
   raw materials, 84–89, 160–161
   rising, x–xiv, 49
   and saving, 166, 197
   and state-led development, 97–106
copper, 80, 85
cost of reproduction, 2–4
cultural nationalism, 176–180
   modernisation, 176
   social bases, 179
cultural turn, 59, 66, 70–71, 192
   critique of, 67
culture, xiii, 6, 24–25, 50, 53, 59–71, 153, 160, 169, 176, 179–180, 183
   domination, 64, 68, 71
   domination/coordination, 61
   exploitation, 64
   identity, 69
   instrumentalisation, 68
   reciprocity, 67
   reduced role, 67
cycle, business, xiv

debt crisis 1980s, 100
debt peonage, 2
decolonisation, 178
   Asia, 94
   post-World War II, 178
   start, 88

struggle for rent, 92
deindustrialisation, 92
democratic socialism, xv, 167, 171
    as completion of capitalism, 171
democratisation, 16, 134, 163–164, 189
    limited, 189, 200
    limited for rent-seeking, 134
dependency, 87, 92, 94, 122, 162, 171
devaluation, 87, 116–121, 124, 126, 129, 133–136, 161, 169–173, 185, 196–197
    limits, 121
development, 99–107, 131–133, 142, 170–182, 196–198
    agrarian reform, 96
    capital-output ratio, 99, 138
    and correction of markets, 172
    devaluation, 172
    dissociation, 173
    and dissociation form the world market, 173
    equals transition to capitalism, 171–172
    and exports, 172, 198
    and globalisation, 115
    informal sector, 172
    to internal market, 82, 197
    lop-sided, 101
    market, 101
    mass consumption, 172
    moving up the chain of production, 131
    and NGOs, 185–190
    protectionism, 92
    rent, 73, 92, 100
    state planning, 93
    technology promotion, 173
    technology, 98
    through rent, 172
    uneven, 85, 161
development theory, 94
    crisis of, 181
dialectics between man and nature, 4
Dien Bien Phu, 94

differential rents, 84
disembodied technical progress, 13
drain of India, 176
Dutch disease, 87
dyestuff, 78
dynastic cycle, 37, 41, 47, 90–91

economies of scale, 14–16, 29–30, 127
    and equality of distribution and consumption, 14–15
    and sewing machine, bicycle and car, 16
    and technical progress, 14
effendiyya, 180
efflorescence, 38–39, 42, 50, 199
emerging powers, 195
employment
    as a condition for profit x–xii, 18–24
    and globalisation, 114, 121, 124–131, 169–173, 196–198
    as an instrument of regulation, xi–xv, 2–24, 53, 59, 140
    and Keynesian economics, 162–164
    and neoclassical economics, 136–137
empowerment of labour, 28, 121, 160
    origins, 51
    scarcity of labour, 107
enlightenment, disinterest for the South, 183
environment, xv, 31, 89, 131, 139, 161–164, 172
    rent of sovereignty, 164
    rent-seeking, 164
equality, ix, xii–xiv, 15, 25, 30, 34–35, 52, 63, 69, 92, 142, 165, 167, 198–199
equality of distribution, 14
Europe and Asia, 42
    city autonomy, 45
    constitutionalism, 44–45, 51
    frugal privileged class, 48–49
    marriage pattern, 52
    multiple accidental reasons, 51

property rights, 52
rational bureaucracy, 47
social rebels, 44
exit and voice, 30
property rights, 30
export-led growth, 172
and agrarian reform, 115, 119
agricultural surplus, 118
China, 114
and devaluation, 116–117, 119
case of post 1948 Germany, 121
empowerment of labour, 121
and internal empowerment of labour, 115
and internal mass consumption, 115
propelled by equality of distribution, 121
real wage, 117
and rent, 116, 129–133
turning point, 121
export-oriented manufacturing production, 3

Fanon, 176
female household production, 2
feudalism, 44, 49, 52–53, 64
peasantry, 41, 43
poverty of ruling class, 40
serfdom, 43
shift to tributary mode of production and 'oriental' despotism, 46
weak state, 44, 51
pope vs. emperor, 45–46
financial assets, x, xiii, 17, 48, 84, 107, 142, 146, 149–152, 199
financial crisis 21st century, 107, 151
taxpayer pays, 151
financialisation, 145
and asset inflation, 146
and price stability, 146
productivity growth, 150
renovating capitalism, 152
social basis, 148, 151

food
delocalisation, 80
France, 38, 42, 69–70, 94, 123, 175, 183
free proletarian, 2

German historical school, 25
Germany
capital structure, 13, 138–141
economic depression, 24–25, 152
economic history, 39–46, 51, 61, 68, 77, 122, 124
financial crisis, 157, 196
immigration, 72
and labour, 141
locomotive function, 135–138
post World War II catching up, 121
unfavourable trade specialisation, 128–131
globalisation, ix, 114, 137, 152, 189
benign case, 124
and concentration, 144, 198
disempowerment of labour, 137
and employment, 136
intensify, 197
and overtaking, 115
of rent, 100, 114, 116, 125, 170, 199
and under-consumption, 116, 119–120, 124, 135, 161, 182
upgrading, 122
wage race to the bottom, 122
weakness of political globalisation, 195
weakness of transnational political alliances, 182
Green Revolution, 118–121, 126

Hammurabi, 5
Hayek, 148, 158
historical materialism, 25
homo oeconomicus, 29
household expenditure, 118

human capital, 13–14, 138
hunting and gathering, 29, 31

identity, 59–60, 65, 69–70, 171, 174–178, 195
imperialism, 71, 87, 104, 122, 171, 178
    bridgehead, 88–89
    of free trade, 78
import substituting industrialisation, 169
India, 2, 5, 13, 35, 47, 69–72, 75–78, 89–91, 94, 109–110, 117, 131, 175–179, 197, 200
    18th century industrial exports, 77
industrial policy, 116, 127
industrial revolution, 12, 39, 76, 124, 128, 153
    cheap products, 39, 78
        downgrading, 79
    high wage region, 77
inflation, 23, 54, 100, 107, 117, 121, 138, 142, 146–147, 163
    employment trade-off, 142
international system in future
    intergovernmental, 196
    multipolar, 194
intra-Asiatic trade, 77
investment
    and amortisation, 138
    depends on demand, 10
    and development planning, 95–106
    and empowerment, x, xiii
    financed by credit, 9
    financial 'investment', 151
    foreign direct investment and exploitation, 173
    foreign direct investment and rent, 130
    and mass incomes, 53, 60, 95
    and profit, 7–13, 16–17, 23–25
    and the real economy, 40
    rationalisation or enlargement, 132, 141
    and saving, 141, 173
    self-financing, 28, 48, 150
iron, xiv, 76, 80, 110, 188, 202
Islam, 26, 35, 52, 75, 112, 177, 181

Jainism, 35
Japan, 34, 54, 60, 92, 94, 121, 127, 131, 141, 154, 155, 182

Kautiliya, 68
Kautsky, 114
Keynes, xiv–xv, 17, 23–24, 93, 98, 135–136, 148, 157, 158, 162
    labour oriented Keynesianism, 24
    military Keynesianism, 152
    monetary Keynesianism, xiv, 148
    real economy Keynesianism, xv
    worldwide Keynesianism, 136

labour
    culturally determined norms, 183
    empowerment, x–xv, 160–162
        role for economic regulation and orientation of the social process, 3, 19–24, 53, 69–71, 83, 86, 105–106, 165, 198, 201–202
        and globalisation, 114–115, 121, 137, 169–170, 174
    free vs. unfree, 1–2, 33, 84–89
    globalisation of labour as a requirement, 169
    heterogenisation, 162
    history, 51, 81
    labour aristocracy, 88, 140
    labour movement, 175, 182–186
    (labour) surplus, 19–21, 81–86, 96, 171
    migration 19th century, 89
    nation-building, 69
    North-South estrangement, 185
    reduction to abstract labour, 30
    repetitive/tedious versus innovative, 14–16

scarcity, x, xi, 19–20, 43, 54, 60, 83, 106, 116, 121, 125, 142–143, 166, 170
skilled, 13, 132
strength, xiii
struggle over labour contract, 51, 178
suffrage, 51
theory of value, 149
wage labour, 1, 3
labour in future
  limited power, 23
  loss of ideological autonomy, 143
late colonialism
  reform, 85, 89
  rent sharing, 85, 89
Latin America, 2, 73, 76, 78, 82, 84, 94, 117–118, 126, 155, 175, 180
Lenin, 11, 26, 87, 91, 104–105, 111, 190
letter of exchange, 9, 145–146
liquidity preference, 17, 148
long-distance trade, 3, 50, 65, 73–78
  unfavourable specialisation, 77
lord, 21, 30, 34
Luxemburg, 11, 104

Machiavelli, 68
Malthus, 5, 109
marginal product of labour, 2, 4, 19, 28, 97, 171
marginality, 2, 5, 19–21, 28, 32, 81–82, 86, 172
  of labour in agriculture, 4
  of labour when environmental problems increase, 4
market
  to be defended, xiv
Marx, xiv, 2, 5, 11, 27, 44–45, 51, 65, 70, 74, 92, 102, 122, 142, 165, 200
mass consumption, 14, 115
  new products, 79
meaningless history, 107

means of production, x, 2, 24, 30, 53, 70–71
microelectronics, 14, 124, 138, 140
  capital saving, 138
migration, xi, 89, 169
modes of production, 5, 43–44, 199–201
  pre-capitalist, 6, 10, 56, 70, 81, 172
monetarism, 100
money illusion, 148–149, 160
money multiplier, 10, 145
moral economy, 6, 63, 67, 186
multi-ethnic empires, 176
multinational enterprises, 105, 130, 170, 176
  and host countries
    conflict over rents, 130

nationalism, 68, 176, 178, 180, 186, 195
  India, 69
  patterns of, 68, 70
needs, post-materialist and collective, xi–xii, 70, 139, 159–162, 165–172
  collective, xii
  non-material, xii
neolithical revolution, 29, 73
new cultural identitarian political movements, 174, 176, 180–181, 185–188
  geography of, 180
  in the South and fascism, 185
  in the South social bases drain of India, 186
  trend to moderation, 186
NGO, 71, 187–189
  isolated from new cultural identitarian political movements, 188
  neoimperialism, 71
  oligarchy, 188
  rent, 187
  rivalry with labour, 188
  sell title to moral well being, 187

social basis
    middle class, 189
non-capitalist land owner, ix
non-economic realm, xii

October Revolution, xv
oil, 80, 85, 87, 99, 108–109, 129, 131, 184, 192, 195
old age pension, 150
oligarchy
    iron law of, xiv, 188, 202
OPEC, 85, 99, 184
organic composition of capital, 11

paper (fiat) money, xiv, 9, 145
peasant, peasantry
    anticolonial peasant wars, 92–93, 97, 177–178
    economic strategies, 41–44, 77, 97
    history, 10, 33, 40–45, 52–53
    as a market, 41

perfect markets, 6
pole of popular industry, 40–42, 48–53, 59, 73, 76–79, 83, 86
political struggles, xi–xii
populism, 93
Portugal, 76–77
post-materialist needs, xi
pre-capitalist, x–xi, 4–6, 10, 20, 38, 41, 48, 56, 59, 70–71, 75, 81–84, 171–172, 175–176
pre-capitalist market relations, 2, 5
primary accumulation, 48, 76
    role of the colonies, 76
product cycle, 86, 122–123, 127
profit
    depends on investment spending, 7, 9
    depends on mass mass, xiv–xv, 1–12, 16–18, 23, 26
    limited in the real economy by investment spending, 137–139, 141–144, 148–151, 176, 198
    under market imperfections, modification of profit, 50, 64, 66, 74–76, 102
    negative in crisis, 9
    as non-capitalist rent, 6
    and perfect markets, 6
    tendential fall of the rate of profit, 11
    threatened by private household saving, 142, 159–161
protectionism, 92
proto-industrialisation, 22, 39, 42
public debts, xi

racism, 68, 91
raw materials, 86
    consumer rent, 85
    delocalisation, 80, 84
    demand from emerging countries, 161
    European endowment with, 80
real socialism, xv, 102–106
    competition with capitalism, 104
reciprocity, 61–63, 67
    domination/coordination, 61
reduction of concrete and abstract labour, 30
religion, 32, 52, 93, 176–177, 180, 185
    axial revolution, 34, 52
rent, 1, 10, 28, 33–34, 98–102, 168–174, 177–189, 196, 199–201
    and demise of capitalist structures, 128, 135, 159–164, 168–171, 199–201
    development, 73, 96, 98–102, 177–187
    export-oriented manufacturing, 129–130
    capitalists favour rent, xii, 18, 89, 105–106
    distorts communication, 67
    dutch disease, 131–135
    managing rent, 170–174, 196
    and NGOs, 187–189

from raw materials, 83–89
as a source of finance for development, 172

rent-based structures dominating markets, 134
reverse technical assistance, 13
rising mass consumption, 22, 49, 53
rural by-employment, 119

savings, x–xi, xiv, 10, 15, 23, 107, 132, 141–142, 145, 150, 156–157, 162–163, 167, 199
    threat to profit, 142, 166
scolarisation, 179
script, origin of, 5
secular nationalism, 93, 176–180, 183, 185, 188
    failure, 185
    social bases, 177
    variants of, 176
Sepoy, 90
sewing machine, 16, 78
slavery, 1–2, 22, 33, 68, 71, 76–77, 89, 106, 176, 183
social democracy, 202
    decline in the South, 185
socialism, xv, 102–106, 165–167, 171
    and capitalist rationality, 105
    democratic governance, xv
socio-economic system, ix
Soviet Marxism
    decline in the South, 184
Soviet Union, 89, 93, 99
    raw materials, 99
Spain, 76–77
specialization
    unequal, 98
state
    development, 54, 85, 89–106, 112, 116, 127, 163–170, 173–186
    history, 33, 38, 41–48, 75
    and labour, 140–141
    and money, 145–148, 151–152
    origin, 29–33
    and technology promotion, 159–160
state class, 66, 94, 96, 98, 100, 102, 105, 106, 178–181, 184–185
    capitalist multinational enterprises, 105
    development, 94
    inefficiency, 95
    limited mass consumption, 98
    socialism, 171
    technical dependency, 98
superexploitation, 87
surplus labour, 81–82, 87
surplus production
    origin, 29
Switzerland, 77, 197

technical progress, 7, 13–16, 25, 28, 37, 51, 79–82, 92, 98, 101, 103, 122–123, 137, 161, 199
    disembodied technical progress, 79, 122
    source of growth, 122
    source of stable growth, 16
    two types, 21, 37
terms of trade, 84
    world economic depression, 88, 92
theories of imperialism, 87, 104
tin, 80, 85
trade-based empires, 64
transition to capitalism, 2–4, 10, 19, 28–29, 33–34
    accidental, 53
    agricultural barrier, 19, 22
    appropriation of surplus from non-capitalist sectors, 2
    barrier of marginality, 19, 28
    blockage through wealth, 3, 21, 28
    culture, 25, 49, 59, 66
    and cultural factors, 66, 153, 160
    demography, 42
    and development policy, 121, 171–174

empowerment of labour, 28, 160
ethnic cleavages, 175
European case, 38, 42, 48–49
independent of economic development, 54
and labour, 143, 160, 171–174
limited success, 73, 83
marginal product of labour is positive, 4
multiple patterns, 54
new climbers, 50
not automatical, 105
other successful cases, 54
possible at any level of average productivity, 4
and pre-capitalist long-distance trade, 3
return to pre-capitalist monopoly, 50–51
rising mass consumption, 22, 49, 53
technical progress, 28
tributary mode of production, 39–54, 88
commerce, 33
culture and domination, 65
deindustrialization, 79
dynastic cycle, 37, 41, 47, 90–91
expansion, 75
force and justice, 35
heterogeneity of economic and social basis, 35, 47
labour control, 33
large family, 36
long-distance trade, 65
luxuries, 37
marginality, 36
nation, 65
peasant migration and resistance, 42
protection, 37
religion, 34, 47, 65
social stability, 36
state-building, 47
three tiered crafts, 37, 41
tropical goods, 81
cocoa, 81, 86
coffee, 81, 85, 99
tea, 81, 86
truth
culture-domination, 67

ultra-imperialism, 114
under-consumption, 104, 116, 119, 121, 124, 134–136, 139, 152, 160–161, 167, 182
with import surplus, 120
underdevelopment, xi, 72–73, 82, 87, 92, 94, 96, 100–102, 130, 170–171, 182, 184, 190
absence of conditions for transition to capitalism, 171
deindustrialisation, 92
demographic growth, 82
exploitation, 102, 176
marginality, 82
surplus labour, 82, 87
unequal development in technology production, 131
United States, 68–69, 85, 108, 124, 152, 169, 178, 183–184, 195, 197
19th century growth, 14
racism, 68

Vietnam, 42, 93–94, 177–178, 183, 185, 197

wage, 2–10, 13, 17–19, 23–24, 36, 87, 106, 115–127, 130, 135–137, 169, 174, 197
and average wage formation, 140
and employment, 120, 135, 137
increases, xi, 12–13, 17–18, 119, 125
new neoclassical theory, 120, 136
and productivity, 120
Weber, 44, 47–48, 57
Wittfogel, 44, 56

world capitalism
    polarisation, 86
    rent, 87
    unequal specialisation, 86

world economic depression 1930s, 152
world system, xi–xii, 19, 73, 91, 107, 115, 170
WTO, 133, 155, 196

About the Author

Hartmut Elsenhans is a German political scientist and Emeritus Professor of International Relations at the University of Leipzig. He was also affiliated with the Université de Montréal; Jawaharlal Nehru University, India; Quaid-e-Azam University, Islamabad; Columbia University and University of California, Berkeley.

He studied political science, history and sociology at the University of Tübingen and the Free University of Berlin (FU Berlin). He earned his doctoral degree in 1973 with a study on the decolonisation of Algeria in the Algerian War (1954–1962). In 1976, he gained habilitation at FU Berlin.

His current research includes capitalism and social movements, structure of the international system, rise and demise of the capitalist world system, political economy of European integration and development politics and economics. Throughout his career, Elsenhans expanded his work on the book's topic, publishing a total of five volumes on the subject.

In the late 1970s, he had short stints as a lecturer at the University of Montreal and the University of Frankfurt before settling down for his first professorship (of International Relations) at the University of Marburg, followed shortly by a long-term professorship at Konstanz University. His focus there was on the analysis of underdevelopment, national and social emancipatory movements and public administration in developing countries.

Elsenhans took the opportunity to go to Leipzig after German unification, to help build the department of international relations at the university there. He taught there until 2007, when he retired. He was given honorary membership of the students association of the faculty of political science at the University of Leipzig. Elsenhans currently still resides, lectures and researches in Leipzig.